THE MAKING OF HARCOURT GENERAL

THE MAKING OF HARCOURT GENERAL

A History of Growth through Diversification 1922–1992

BY

BETTYE H. PRUITT

With assistance from

George David Smith

HARVARD BUSINESS SCHOOL PRESS

Boston, Massachusetts

Copyright © 1994 by Harcourt General, Inc.
All rights reserved
Printed in the United States of America
98 97 96 95 94   5 4 3 2 1

Library of Congress Cataloging-in-Publication Data

Pruitt, Bettye Hobbs.
    The making of Harcourt General : a history of growth through
diversification, 1922–1992 / by Bettye H. Pruitt, with assistance
from George David Smith.
        p.   cm.
    Includes bibliographical references and index.
    ISBN 0-87584-509-6
    1. Harcourt General, Inc.—History.   2. General Cinema
Corporation—History.   3. Diversification in industry—United
States—Case studies.   I. Smith, George David.   II. Title.
HD2796.H37P78   1994
338.7'4'0973—dc20   93-50567
                                                                    CIP

The author wishes to thank Bachrach Studios, Boston, for permission to use the photograph of Robert J. Tarr, Jr., and Michael Weymouth of Weymouth Design, Inc. for the 1992 photograph of Richard A. Smith. All other photographs were graciously supplied by Harcourt General, Inc.

The paper used in this publication meets the requirements of the American National Standard for Permanence of Paper for Printed Library Materials Z39.49-1984.

C O N T E N T S

5 PROFESSIONALIZATION OF THE ENTREPRENEURIAL ENTERPRISE 117

6 PATIENT OPPORTUNISM IN AN AGE OF EXCESS 155

7 PATIENCE REWARDED: ACQUISITION OF HBJ 201

8 THE NEW GENERAL CINEMA DEFINED 243

PREFACE

I

When General Cinema Corporation commissioned The Winthrop Group, Inc. to write this history early in 1988, the events described in the final two chapters were unforeseen. Even in the writing of this preface—postponed as long as possible to be as current as possible—the "end" of the story has remained a moving target. Yet today, December 15, 1993, the company, now named Harcourt General, Inc., will complete a spin-off to shareholders of its theater business with the creation of a separate corporate entity, GC Companies, Inc. That act provides a fitting conclusion to these chapters of the company's history, one that dramatizes the extent of the changes of the past six years but also highlights the threads of continuity that link Harcourt General to its origins in Philip Smith Theatrical Enterprises some seventy years ago.

When we arrived on the scene, General Cinema had just completed a record year, with 1987 revenues exceeding $1 billion for the first time. One of the nation's largest independent soft drink bottlers and the fourth largest national theater chain, the company derived 84 percent of its 1987 operating profits from its beverage division and 16 percent from film exhibition. Since 1980, General Cinema had been seeking to acquire a business to balance beverages and theaters. It had played the white knight to department store chain Carter Hawley Hale in 1984 and out of that had gained a 60 percent share of the Neiman Marcus Group, a high-end retail company spun off from Carter Hawley Hale late in 1987. In 1988, the first full year of operations with the new business, General Cinema revenues were $2.3 billion, with 54 percent of operating profits derived from soft drink bottling, 36 percent from retail, and 10 percent from theaters.

Within the year, however, General Cinema announced the sale of its beverage division to PepsiCo in a deal that was consummated early in 1989, bringing nearly $1.8 billion in proceeds. The company then mounted a well-publicized effort to redeploy that cash in the acquisition of a new business, a search that dragged on for almost two years, as General Cinema struggled to identify a suitable target and to avoid paying the prices then prevailing in the overheated market for corporate control. General Cinema finally found its opportunity in the publisher Harcourt Brace Jovanovich (HBJ), a company heavily burdened with high-yield debt and facing the possibility of bankruptcy. The acquisition was completed after another year, spent in protracted negotiations with the many classes of HBJ bondholders and stockholders. Early in 1993 General Cinema changed its name to Harcourt General, acknowledging the transformation wrought by that sequence of events: at the end of 1992, the first full year of publishing operations, the company reported revenues of $3.7 billion, with publishing contributing 52 percent of earnings, retailing 29 percent, HBJ's insurance business 15 percent, and theaters just 4 percent.

For Richard A. Smith, chairman of Harcourt General, finally putting those pieces into place was the capstone to a thirty-year career at the head of the company. Smith joined his father, Philip Smith, in the family business in 1946, when it consisted of nine drive-in theaters located in the Midwest and a few indoor movie houses in the Boston area. His first important contribution—made in his first week on the job—was to suggest selling popcorn in the indoor theaters; his second was to propose diversifying into drive-in restaurants, an idea that was implemented before the year was out. The strategy of diversification was firmly grounded in the financial characteristics of the theater business, which typically generated a cash flow well in excess of what was needed to finance internal growth. Phil and Dick Smith elaborated upon that strategy, working closely together over the next fifteen years. In 1960 they took the theater company public to provide a basis for building a national circuit of shopping-center theaters but also to diversify into bowling.

Phil Smith died in 1961 and so did not see how his dreams for the company fared. For different reasons, neither restaurants nor bowling remained part of the business mix for very long after his death, but diversification remained as a central concern for his son, who succeeded him as chief executive. Dick Smith took the company into soft drink bottling in the late 1960s with a series of acquisitions that more than doubled the company's size in four years and made it a leader in that industry. That move laid the foundation for a much larger corporate edifice, which Smith worked to build for the next twenty-five years and finally completed in 1991.

As an acquisition-minded corporate executive in the 1980s, Dick Smith cut a distinctive figure. A raider of sorts, his objective—to acquire one or two major operating divisions to round out the portfolio of theaters and beverages—was modest by the standards of the era. While he struggled to achieve that goal, his shrewd investments and financial strategy, together with the strong performance of General Cinema's core businesses, steadily increased the company's value and earned him an enviable reputation in the business community. In 1984 the shareholders rewarded him by voting approval of a super stock, which enabled the Smith family to convert its roughly 40 percent stake in the company into an unassailable controlling interest. The protection of the control block freed Dick Smith to continue the acquisition search; and especially in the difficult three years following the sale of the beverage division, it helped to sustain him in his commitment to a long-held vision of the company that he wished to put in place before retirement.

At the beginning of 1992, Smith passed the responsibilities of CEO to Robert J. Tarr, Jr., who had been head of the beverage division from 1978 to 1983 and then chief operating officer. Although Smith has remained an active chairman of the board, it has largely been his successor who has driven recent changes. With the completion of the HBJ acquisition, General Cinema ceased to be a deal company and, under Tarr, became an operating company. First the name change and now the spin-off of GC Companies give outward expression to that shift. While Harcourt General may pursue acquisitions, they will be in industries related to its main lines of business. The company—and Tarr—will be judged on how well it performs in publishing, retailing, and insurance.

GC Companies, on the other hand, will use the strong cash flows of the theater business for investments and acquisitions. It will, in short, return to a strategy of growth through diversification that would be inappropriate for it as a division of Harcourt General. It will be judged only partly on the returns from theater operations and, analysts suggest, as an investment vehicle for its chairman, it will enjoy an advantage in the stock market—the "Dick Smith multiple." Thus, the culminating events in the making of Harcourt General represent the conclusion of one chapter but also the start of the next, both for Smith and for the company he led the way in creating.

These events make fortuitous timing for a book on Harcourt General. Its activity on the mergers and acquisitions scene of the 1980s and early 1990s, and its unusual approach, make the subject significant to anyone who has followed that raucous part of U.S. business history or pondered its implications. Yet the twists and turns of the company's acquisition saga take on greater significance in the context of its seventy-year evolution from a small proprietorship to a multibillion-dollar corporation. In that longer-term perspective, the competitive strategies that provided leadership in the theater industry and soft drink bottling weigh more heavily than the acquisition strategies of the 1980s; the consistency of financial strategy over decades clearly carries greater importance than the intricacies of financing a particular deal; the counterpoint of failures to successes over the years makes evident just how difficult it is to achieve corporate goals in unrelated diversification.

Among highly diversified firms, Harcourt General is unusual for its relatively small size, having had only two major lines of business up to the late 1980s. Because of that, it is possible to examine in depth issues that would be unmanageable in a study of a large conglomerate with many operating divisions. This history chronicles the rise and maturing of two fascinating and culturally significant industries, movie theaters and soft drink bottling, from the perspective of a company that played a central role in each. It examines the relationship between financial strategy and diversification strategy as that evolved over three decades. The history also describes transitions of the sort nearly every growing company must make in the long run—from one generation of leadership to the next; from an entrepreneurial to a professional management culture; from a centralized functional to a more decentralized multidivisional corporate structure. It details the process of assimilating a newly acquired business; considers the tensions inherent in relationships between divisional management and the corporate office in a diversified firm; and contemplates the impact of an embezzlement scandal on the evolution of management structure and policies. Most important, perhaps, in documenting the remarkable continuity of leadership that Harcourt General has enjoyed over the nearly fifty years of Dick Smith's career, the history opens a window through which the changing business environment may be clearly viewed.

For the most part, our perception of critical business issues is shaped by current theory and cases and by analyses that examine many firms in the aggregate. Our understanding would be incomplete, however, without longitudinal studies of single firms, which help us appreciate the complexities of business problems as they arise to confront corporate leaders daily. This is not a typical company—perhaps no company truly is. Yet there is as much learning to be gained from the distinctive details of the Harcourt General story as from the broad themes that run through its core.

II

The author of a commissioned book would be naïve to claim that the work was wholly unbiased, but the bias that creeps into a project of this sort tends to be of a subtle type. The historians of The Winthrop Group strive to adhere closely to the standards of the profession, and the rigor of those standards in research and analysis helps sustain objectivity. Harcourt General exercised no censorship over this work in either the research or the writing phase and provided open access to its records and personnel. The manuscript was read and commented on by the company's executives and corporate counsel, who suggested changes, but none that materially altered the facts presented or the interpretation of events.

For all that, it must be acknowledged that one cannot work with, and for, a company for six years on a project of this scope without taking on the perspective of an insider, at least to some degree. Insiders can be critical and can acknowledge mistakes and shortcomings; but they also tend to tread carefully in certain areas and to place problems in a generally positive context. To the extent that this book falls into that pattern, I must assume responsibility for having succumbed to an occupational hazard. At the same time, I assert, on behalf of those of us who practice history as consultants in the corporate world, that the loss of "total objectivity" (an idealized concept to begin with) is a trade-off well worth making for the opportunity to bring to light a story like *The Making of Harcourt General* at a level of detail and analysis that would not be possible without the active support and participation of the company.

In the course of the research for this book, scores of past and current company managers submitted to lengthy interviews. They spoke openly and often with considerable introspection about their careers and the story of the company as they knew it. Howard Spiess on the theater side, Tom Dennard on the beverage side, and Woody Ives in the corporate office were especially helpful in locating documents. Kay Kilpatrick, assistant to the chairman, provided support without which this project would have bogged down hopelessly on numerous occasions. I hope all these essential contributors will feel that this history rewards them for their efforts.

This book began as a joint project with my Winthrop Group colleague, George D. Smith. George did much of the interviewing and documentary research, especially on the theater side of the business, and he produced an early draft of the history into the mid-1960s. At the beginning of 1990 the project was put on hold for some eighteen months, pending the outcome of General Cinema's acquisition search. By the time it resumed, George's other commitments made it impossible for him to continue as co-author, so the project became mine alone. Since then, he has served as a sounding board for ideas, lent a hand in interviewing as needed, and provided valuable criticism of and commentary on the evolving manuscript.

As in all our efforts, virtually every member of The Winthrop Group made some contribution to this project. Davis Dyer was a helpful reader of a number of draft chapters. Paul Barnhill provided invaluable assistance with the analysis and graphic presentation of financial information, as well as with research in public sources. Dan Jacoby tracked down many useful sources on the early theater industry. Pam Bracken and Susan Surapine oversaw the transcription of interviews and made it possible for me to control the myriad details of project management. Kathleen McDermott gave reliably sound advice on a wide range of issues. Others were simply good and supportive colleagues, kindly tolerant of my six-year preoccupation with this company.

At the Harvard Business School Press, a long-time friend, Pat Denault, served as copy editor for this book and greatly improved it with her intelligent reading. A new friend, Alistair Williamson, has been enthusiastic, supportive, and patient in his role as overall editor of the book. Natalie Greenberg has shepherded the manuscript through publication, and Carol Franco welcomed it in the first place. Three anonymous readers and one known to me, Hugo Uyterhoeven (HBS professor and a Harcourt General director), provided the kind of thoughtful commentary and useful suggestions that one most hopes for in submitting work for publication. The help of all has been much appreciated.

The last word of thanks is reserved for my family, on whose support and forbearance I have drawn heavily in the process of writing this book. Those gifts are gratefully acknowledged.

Cambridge, Massachusetts
December 15, 1993

THE MAKING OF
HARCOURT
GENERAL

C H A P T E R

1

PHILIP SMITH: ENTREPRENEUR

Great entrepreneurs do not simply take risks or merely strike it rich. Rather, they transform economic activity and build for the future. Rarely inventors, they are nonetheless innovators, able to take new ideas, whatever their source, and develop them to commercial feasibility. The most successful are visionaries who seize opportunities, often in unlikely places, and then manage those opportunities into a sustaining stream of profits, in the process creating organizations that outlive them and ultimately outgrow their ambitions.

Philip Smith was just that kind of entrepreneur. A pioneer in movie exhibition, he is hardly a household name like Henry Ford or Steven Jobs. Yet, the American movie industry, though small in total revenues compared to automobiles or computers, has bulked large in cultural significance, and theaters historically were the economic heart of that industry. When Smith set himself up in the theater business in 1922, more established theater entrepreneurs like Marcus Loew and William Fox were already launched into film production and well on the way to building the vertically integrated Hollywood studios that would jointly control the industry through World War II. In the late 1930s and again in the 1950s, however, it was Phil Smith who led the way in adopting innovations that, by anticipating social trends, expanded the market for motion pictures and contributed to the survival of the theater industry through a long period of restructuring and stagnation.[1]

1

Smith was arguably one of the most prescient of his contemporaries in the movie exhibition field. Rather than clinging to established patterns of doing business, he prospected for opportunities at the margin of his industry. Thus in the 1930s, with drive-in theaters, he established a profitable niche as an independent within a mature oligopoly. After World War II, when the Hollywood studios began to divest their theaters under court order, Smith's concept of the family-oriented drive-in formed the basis of the most vital part of the theater industry. In the early 1950s, he foresaw the economic significance of large regional shopping centers and built a theater in one of the first, in Framingham, Massachusetts. In 1960, Smith launched a program to develop a national circuit of shopping-center theaters. That strategy gave his company a first-mover advantage that made it the leader in a restructuring of the industry and, within little more than a decade, the largest national theater circuit.

Just as important, Philip Smith accomplished what many entrepreneurs fail to do—he established an enterprise that survived him. That institutional legacy was achieved in part because his son, Richard, possessed both the entrepreneurial drive and the spirit of opportunism that were the hallmarks of Phil Smith's own approach to business. The company also endured because he passed along a clear strategy for long-term growth and, with his son, built up an organization capable of executing and elaborating on that strategy. As a result, the movie theater business that Philip Smith launched in 1922 would evolve over seventy years into a major diversified firm, Harcourt General, Inc., generating over $3.7 billion in revenues and employing more than 34,000 people.[2]

THE FAMILY TRADE

Philip Smith almost seemed destined to become a movie exhibitor. His father was a bourgeois Lithuanian Jew named Adolph Sandberg who brought his family to Patterson, New Jersey in 1885 and later moved to Syracuse, New York. Philip was born in 1899, the fourth of seven children. On arriving in the United States, Adolph had changed the family name to Smith, a step toward assimilation at a time when the rising tide of Eastern European immigration was stirring public debate and creating a wave of anti-Semitism. In Syracuse, he became the owner of a small hotel and two silent film theaters, which were managed by his second son, George. Young Phil was therefore exposed at an early age to the business of moving pictures.

Movies, Mel Brooks once wrote, are the "collision of art and money."

The Sandberg family understood that relationship well, latching on to the vital new medium of popular culture and building its fortunes on the industry. Adolph's younger brother, Serge, emigrated from Lithuania to Paris in 1900. He taught himself French and, through a friend, secured a job translating letters from Russian into French for the pioneer French film producer Charles Pathé. Pathé taught him the film distribution business, which was then expanding internationally, and in 1906 helped finance the building of a theater circuit in the Loire region; he granted Sandberg a monopoly to show Pathé films in that area. In 1910 Sandberg returned to Paris, where he built four great movie palaces, the first of which was a two thousand–seat theater, Le Tivoli. After World War I, Sandberg entered movie production; he founded one of the three major French movie studios of the era, employing such film luminaries as director Abel Gance and actor Sacha Guitry. He was also an impresario of traditional theater and the founder of a gourmet society and a symphony orchestra, the predecessor to the modern Paris Symphony. All of those activities, in addition to his role in the movie industry, earned Sandberg the Legion d'Honneur in 1966.[3]

Adolph Smith was far more of a dabbler in the movie business. Yet he was part of a large group of late nineteenth century immigrants to the United States who found a place in that "faintly disreputable" industry, which for a short time around the turn of the century had virtually no economic or social barriers to entry. At a time when ethnic prejudice systematically excluded Jews from many of the more established areas of commerce and industry, the marginal status of the early movie industry made it an open field to enterprising immigrants seeking to work themselves into the economic mainstream. The men who built the vertically integrated Hollywood studio system were mostly Jews, mostly of Eastern European descent: Adolph Zukor, the creator of Paramount Pictures; Marcus Loew of Loew's, Inc.; William Fox of Fox Film (Twentieth Century Fox after 1935); Louis B. Mayer, of Metro-Goldwyn-Mayer; the Warner brothers, Harry, Albert, and Jack; Carl Laemmle, founder of Universal Pictures; and many others. In Hollywood, New York, and around the country, the movies became the quintessential ethnic business.[4]

Most of the movie moguls entered the industry through exhibition in the era of nickelodeons, when films were short action subjects— "heavyweight prize fights and French chase comedies"—many of them produced by Pathé and imported from France. This was subject matter that appealed to the urban blue-collar and immigrant populations who inhabited the areas where nickelodeons first flourished. By 1910 this lowbrow form of exhibition had merged with a more traditional entertainment format, vaudeville, creating a hybrid that combined movies with live acts and that began to capture a larger, middle-class audience. Within a few years, seeking to provide their theaters with longer films, more uplifting subject matter, and recognizable stars, both Zukor and Fox began producing movies. Others followed suit, and by the end of the 1920s, the industry was dominated by five integrated production-distribution-exhibition companies—Paramount, Loew's (the parent of Metro-Goldwyn-Mayer), Warner Brothers, Fox, and RKO (formed by the merger of the production subsidiary of Radio Corporation of America and the leading vaudeville theater chain, Keith-Orpheum). Together with three lesser entities—Universal, Columbia, and United Artists—these companies made up the studio system that would hold sway over the industry through the 1930s and 1940s. Within this system the revenues flowed from national circuits of first-run theaters, and key decisions were made in business offices in New York City. But to the outside world, the heart of the industry was Hollywood, where the producers and the stars worked and lived.[5]

The Hollywood studios shaped the substance of the movies to conform to the immigrant producers' image of America as it should be: "An America where fathers were strong, families stable, people attractive, resilient, resourceful, and decent." The history of immigration in this country is full of stories of individuals from various national and ethnic backgrounds who pursued the American dream of fame and fortune and, having captured it, idealized the society that had afforded them such opportunity. Yet no other group has had quite the power of communication that Hollywood producers enjoyed in the studio era. The vision they projected, idealized as it was, captured the public imagination and completed the journey of the cinematic medium from ethnic urban neighborhoods to the cultural mainstream, in the process making the United States a nation of committed moviegoers.[6]

Philip Smith was not destined to be a spinner of celluloid dreams or an empire builder like the Hollywood moguls. Yet over the course of his career, he would demonstrate the same sure feel for public taste in entertainment and the same firm grasp of the dynamics that drove the industry—strengths that would make him one of the most successful entrepreneurs in the theater business. Smith got his start in 1916, at the age of seventeen, shortly after graduating from Drake Business School. The industry then was still in its formative stages. Like his uncle, Serge Sandberg, Smith launched his career with Pathé, working briefly in its American home office in New York City before being drafted into the U.S. Army during World War I. He served in the Army Air Corps as a supply clerk on the nation's first air base at Mineola, Long Island. As soon as he was discharged, Smith returned to Pathé, moving on to the job of film

salesman for upstate New York. By his own account, it was in that job—
"peddling *The Perils of Pauline,* the cliff-hanging adventures of Ruth Ro-
land, and other silent movie serials, as well as regular feature length pictures"—that he developed a lifelong love of movies and theaters.[7]

PHILIP SMITH THEATRICAL ENTERPRISES

Like his uncle in France, Philip Smith learned the ropes and made
essential connections in the film industry through Pathé, but he then
moved on to establish himself as an independent theater operator. In
1918, while still employed by Pathé, he learned that the Novelty Theater
in Syracuse was for sale, and he was able to buy it with the help of his
father. A few years later Smith married Marian Fleischman, the daughter
of a successful Syracuse furniture retailer. The couple then moved to
Boston, where Smith had been hired by the huge vaudeville theater
chain, Keith-Albee-Orpheum, to revive "the Keith chain's big white
elephant"—the National Theater on Tremont Street. His career would
be launched by success in that task.[8]

The National had been erected as a vaudeville house in 1911, its
developers investing $150,000 in furnishings. It was built to seat 3,700,
with standing room for 400 more, and was, they said, "the only large
theater in the world charging 5, 10 and 15 cents for seats." A decade
later, as a movie theater, the National was in chronic financial difficulty,
its large overhead too great a burden on operations, although the price
of tickets was by then at least 25 to 50 cents. Smith revived the patronage
of the National by flooding the screen with fourteen movies per week—
two new films each day—and by reverting to old-time prices, 10 cents
per seat. That high-volume strategy was possible in an era when film
product was abundant, varied, and cheap. It was probably suggested to
him by the contemporary success of New York theaters, which provided
respite from the daily hubbub of downtown shopping and traffic and
prospered by very rapid audience turnover.[9]

Having made the theater profitable, Smith became a lessee-operator
of the National and established himself as Smith Theatrical Enterprises in
1922. From that base, he developed an independent theater circuit in
Boston and around New England, leasing properties and opening movie
theaters in towns such as Weymouth, Reading, and Hudson, Massachusetts and East Greenwich, Rhode Island. In 1925, when his son Richard
was a year old, Smith owned twelve theaters. By the end of the decade,
Smith Theatrical Enterprises had become a circuit of eighteen or twenty

theaters, some of which were held in partnership with other investors. They included a first-run theater in Ipswich, Massachusetts and two theaters in South Boston—the Strand and the Broadway—owned in partnership with a prominent Irish family named Doyle. In that era, Smith also established a film distribution business, named Piedmont Pictures after his office address on Piedmont Street, which handled independent productions that were typically shown as second features.

This was an excellent beginning, but it proved, through unfortunate timing, to be a false start. In the economic debacle that followed the stock market crash of 1929, Smith's business was set back sharply. Not even the advent of "talking pictures," introduced by Warner Brothers, Fox, and RKO in the late 1920s, could save him. In short order, he was forced to close or sell all of his theaters except three, the two in South Boston and the one in Ipswich.

The coming of the depression was disastrous for the movie industry; by the early 1930s all of the major theater chains were struggling for survival and several were in bankruptcy. At the time of the stock market crash, Philip Smith owed roughly $300,000 in short-term notes to a local bank that failed and was taken over by the First National Bank of Boston. He thus began a relationship with First National, but in a way that was rather remarkable for the time. In the general collapse of business, as debtors all around him were cutting deals with anxious bankers and renegotiating their loans at deep discounts, Smith promised to pay off everything he owed as quickly as possible: "He acknowledged his obligations, and he was going to pay them off sooner or later." That act, according to his son, laid the foundation for a long-term relationship between the bank and Smith Theatrical Enterprises and its successor companies that has lasted to the present day. Moreover, Smith repaid the loans sooner rather than later, because he continued to prosper with his three remaining theaters.[10]

Those three theaters, Phil Smith used to tell his children, brought the family through the depression. They also provided the Smith children—Richard and his younger sister, Nancy—many fond memories of those years. Every Sunday the family would spend the afternoon at one of the theaters, where the children watched the matinee and frequently Phil and Marian Smith took over the tasks of management for the day, she being the cashier and he overseeing other matters. On summer weekends Smith took his son to a baseball game whenever possible, but otherwise they would make the rounds of the theaters. Then, Dick Smith got to hang around the box office, trying his hand at selling tickets and sifting the receipts for Indian-head pennies.[11]

Each theater had its own special character, shaped by the local manager. Bill Doyle oversaw the Broadway in South Boston with great good humor. A former all-American football player from Boston College, he presided over an office always filled with "a bunch of guys talking sports." The Strand, on the other hand, was run by a very proper Irishman, Jim Cronin, who dressed "magnificently" and lectured anyone who disturbed the quiet of the theater "about propriety and how to behave in public." He made quite an impression on his boss's young son. "There were no candy wrappers on his floors," Dick Smith remembered, "and no wise kids."[12]

The theater in Ipswich, also called the Strand, had a different character altogether. It was also very clean and "proper," but it was located in a well-to-do area and, just as important, it was a first-run theater. The theater manager, a "strait-laced Yankee" named Picard who knew everyone in town, catered to a clientele who frequently arrived in limousines. The Strand Ipswich was the only theater where northshore residents could see a first-run movie without going into Boston.

A NEW START IN A MATURE INDUSTRY

A healthy cash flow from those three well-located and well-run theaters sustained the Smith family comfortably through the 1930s. However, in order to advance, Phil Smith would need a new angle on the business, because the most valuable theater properties were controlled by a handful of powerful producer-distributors. Although the movie business was originally a highly competitive field, by the 1930s a decade-long consolidation of the industry had run its course, leaving a powerful oligopoly controlled largely by the so-called Big Five companies—Paramount, Warner Brothers, Loew's, Inc., Twentieth Century Fox, and Radio-Keith-Orpheum (RKO)—and to a lesser extent by the Little Three—Universal, Columbia, and United Artists. The studio system that would dominate the industry through the 1940s rested firmly on exhibition, the segment of the business in which most of the capital was invested and from which the revenues flowed. Noted one industry historian, the great studios were in reality "diversified theater chains, producing features, shorts, cartoons, and newsreels to fill their houses." Among them they produced and distributed most of the important movies, and they owned the most advantageously located theaters in which the most lucrative first-run movies were shown. No small-scale exhibitor, especially one who wanted to remain independent, could break into the center of the industry on favorable terms.[13]

Hence, Phil Smith's second life in the theater business was to be lived in unexplored territory. In the summer of 1933, Richard Hollingshead, a wealthy chemicals manufacturer, and his cousin Willis Warren Smith, a service station owner, built an unusual kind of amphitheater for automobiles on a 250,000-square-foot lot in Camden, New Jersey. On the night it opened, some six hundred people paid 25 cents each to see Adolphe Menjou in *Wife Beware,* a three-year-old movie. The new drive-in theater received some notice in New York City papers and in *Business Week,* and Hollingshead and Willis Smith patented the concept. Yet most people at the time passed off their innovation as a short-lived novelty.[14]

Phil Smith, however, was intrigued by the idea, and he observed its progress closely. The original Hollingshead-Smith theater did not fare particularly well, and there were no more than a handful of other drive-ins opened in the mid-1930s, in Massachusetts, California, and Florida. Smith had his eye on the Midwest, and he was encouraged, not deterred, by the problems encountered by the drive-in theater pioneers. "Those drive-ins were put up by people who didn't know the business," he reasoned. "I did, so I built a couple, one in Detroit and one in Cleveland."[15]

Smith financed the new venture with the help of David Stoneman, a prominent Jewish lawyer in Boston and an early venture capitalist already well established in the movie business. Stoneman had participated in the financing of D. W. Griffith's 1915 film classic, *The Birth of a Nation,* and had ongoing connections to MGM. His son, Harold, a contemporary of Phil Smith, owned a theater circuit called Interstate Theaters. Smith had met the Stonemans in the mid-1930s through the Friars' Club, an industry organization then forming in Boston, with the goal of becoming an affiliate of the national organization, the Variety Club. Thus began an alliance of families that would help sustain Smith's business through five decades of growth and diversification.

The Smiths and Stonemans shared a common ethnicity, a love of the theater business and confidence in its economic potential, and a commitment to philanthropy and public service, which found expression initially in their participation in the Variety Club. The association that became known as Variety Clubs International originated in Pittsburgh in 1927 as a social club of theater owners. It became a charitable organization the following year, when it adopted a foundling discovered in the Sheridan Square Theater, owned by one of its members. After that, the Pittsburgh Variety Club adopted an orphan every year, and the concept began to spread to other cities. Early on, Variety adopted circus terminology for its organizational structure, calling its leaders "chief barkers" and its local chapters "tents." The Pittsburgh club was Tent No. 1. Boston would become Tent No. 23 when the Friars' Club changed its name and officially joined Variety International in 1941. In each city the local Variety tent took its own approach to the common goal of helping people, especially children, in need. In its early years the Boston Variety Club specialized in showing movies to shut-ins in hospitals and nursing homes in the area—at least one movie every day and a visit to every hospital and home at least once a month. Both Phil Smith and Harold Stoneman were active in building the Boston Tent, and both would serve as chief barker in the 1950s.[16]

Smith and the Stonemans became close business associates. David Stoneman's firm handled some of Smith's legal affairs, and Stoneman enlisted a number of his entrepreneurially minded legal clients as investors in the drive-in theaters. The Stonemans themselves became major investors. About the same time, Smith became an equal partner with Interstate Theaters in ownership of a group of six theaters on Cape Cod. In 1936, when Harold's younger brother Sidney graduated from law school, he and Phil Smith became fast friends. They kept in daily contact by phone and shared lunch once or twice a week at the Statler Hotel, drawn together by the excitement of their joint business ventures. To Sidney Stoneman, Smith was like a much-admired older brother—a role that Stoneman would play for Smith's son, Dick, in later years.

In 1937 Smith and the Stonemans incorporated a holding company, Mid-West Drive-In Theatres, Inc., to consolidate the ownership of the two open-air theaters then under construction and to prepare for future growth. Mid-West had no employees, but it retained Phil Smith to operate its theaters under a management contract—a common arrangement in the theater industry of that day. Sidney Stoneman was an active member of the board of directors.

The two new theaters opened within ten days of each other, in spring 1938. Touting the world's largest screen and the latest in sound projection, Smith advertised two shows nightly, rain or shine, with a change of program twice a week. Children were admitted free. The opening bill in Detroit was *Big Broadcast of 1938*, followed by *Dead End*. A reporter commenting on the Cleveland opening described "huge shadowy figures prancing around in the big field opposite Thistle Down Race Track," capturing what must have been widespread amazement at the novelty of watching movies outdoors, off a rural road on the outskirts of town.

It may or may not have been the largest screen in the world as boasted but it was sizeable enough to make the heroine's fluttering eyelashes plain as day a half mile away, and the sound apparatus sent the hero's amorous breathing like a gentle wind through the brisk night air into the next township.[17]

The theaters in Detroit and Cleveland were the first commercially successful drive-ins in the country. They inaugurated a long period of profitability and growth in Smith's theater business. By 1940, when they considered the time to be right for expansion, Phil Smith and Sidney Stoneman toured many large cities around the country and chose to build theaters in four new locations—Cincinnati, St. Louis, Indianapolis, and Milwaukee. Mid-West also built second theaters in both Detroit and Cleveland, bringing the total in 1940 to eight. That was a year in which, by the estimate of *Variety* magazine, there were no more than fifteen drive-ins in the entire country. Smith added a ninth theater, in Kansas City in 1941, which completed the expansion of Mid-West Drive-In until after World War II.[18]

THE MARKET LOGIC OF THE DRIVE-IN THEATER

Times were hard when Richard Hollingshead and Willis Smith built the first drive-in, but the idea of establishing a new business in outdoor movies was far from outlandish. Weekly movie attendance had fallen precipitously from a high of ninety million in 1930 to sixty million in 1933. Yet movies remained a popular form of entertainment, a valued escape from depression-era cares. Like daily newspapers, they were an indulgence not easily forgone in hard times. In 1934 movie theater attendance rebounded to seventy million per week, and by 1936 it was almost back to its 1930 high. According to a 1936 *Fortune* magazine survey on national habits, 38 percent of U.S. adults and 56 percent of their children were going to the movies at least once a week. Serious-minded people might object to the content of most movies and fret about their social impact. But, as one writer in *The Economist* pointed out, as a business the movies had become a significant force:

> That the cinema is a great social force is well known to every student. Its . . . "slanguage," the laxness of its morals, the advertisement it gives to violent crime, its rococo aesthetic standards—all these and many more defects perturb the professional viewers with alarm. But even if we forget its more serious aspects and regard the industry, as it would prefer,

merely as entertainment, it is still clear . . . that the moving
picture is one of the economic portents of our time.[19]

In 1930s America, the nation's fascination with the movies was more
than matched by its love for cars. Automobile registrations followed a
pattern similar to movie attendance, bottoming out in 1933 and rising
again after that. However, the drop was not as great, and by 1936 there
were roughly 24 million cars on the road, a million more than the pre-
depression high.[20]

Phil Smith traveled around the country a great deal and was a
thoughtful observer of popular trends. His early commitment to the drive-
in concept demonstrated a firm grasp of the market potential of attaching
his theater business to the social phenomenon of the automobile. He also
considered regional differences in social characteristics and habits that
might affect the success of his new venture. In the years before World
War II, most Americans still viewed rural and small-town occupations as
the norm. They visualized the lives of factory workers as dehumanized by
mechanization and routine, and they imagined industrial cities—Detroit
in particular—to be grim and depressing environments. In choosing Detroit and Cleveland for his first theaters, Smith reasoned that the large
working-class populations in the auto and steel industries would welcome
the escape and entertainment provided by driving to outdoor theaters to
see late-run movies at low prices in the privacy of their own cars. As he
explained to Sidney Stoneman, "there would be fewer diversions and
distractions in those cities than along the eastern seaboard, where you
had beaches and parks and games."[21]

Automobiles represented different things to different people, but to
everyone who owned one, they provided mobility and, at least temporarily, independence and privacy. As a number of contemporary newspapers noted, those freedoms could change the nature of the movie-going
experience in positive ways. Families could see movies together in the
evening, a time when many theaters discouraged children from attending.
The elderly, infirm, and physically handicapped could easily be transported
to and from the drive-in and were likely to be more comfortable there
than in a movie house. In the seclusion of their mobile "box seats," moviegoers would also be freed from dress and behavior codes—such as a ban
on smoking—that were imposed by indoor theaters. For young lovers,
automobiles offered greater comfort and privacy than balcony seats. As
proclaimed by the headline in the *Cleveland Press* following Mid-West
Drive-In's opening night in 1938, not all the romance was on the screen.[22]

Phil Smith was well ahead of the theater industry at large in capitaliz-
ing on the potential appeal of the drive-in. It may have been that his idea

of admitting children free was a creative response to the potential problems posed by the Detroit and Cleveland locations, where, on the western
edge of the eastern time zone, darkness fell very late on summer evenings.
It would be impossible—or far too costly in babysitting fees—for most
parents with young children to attend a double feature that did not begin
until 9:30 P.M. Far more sensible to come a little early, treat the children
to some popcorn or candy, and settle them to sleep in the back seat before
the movies started. That family orientation would become the standard
among drive-ins as they spread to nearly every city and town after World
War II, but in 1938 it was a radically new approach in film exhibition.

Taken together, Smith's siting decisions, his experience in theater
operations, and his innovative policies produced excellent financial results.
By the end of 1941, when new construction was banned for the duration
of World War II, there were many new drive-ins around the country,
most of them located in California and in southern states, where they
could stay open year round. Total industry revenues that year were reported to be $3 million. The nine theaters of Mid-West Drive-In received
a substantial portion of that income—revenues of $500,000, on which
the company earned a pre-tax profit of $98,000—even though they were
closed four months of the year. As the number of drive-ins continued to
grow after the war, Mid-West would lose its predominant position in the
industry. Yet Phil Smith would always be among the most successful film
exhibitors, largely because of his mastery of the basic elements of theater
operation.[23]

FUNDAMENTALS OF THE THEATER BUSINESS

As Smith well understood, properly managed theaters were efficient
money machines. As a lessee-operator, he did not have resources tied up
in large capital investments. In cases where he owned fixtures and furnishings, they were depreciated in financial statements (reducing taxable income) but in fact held their value more or less indefinitely with negligible
expenditures for repair and maintenance. Operations required neither a
large payroll nor substantial working capital—ticket receipts came in before film rentals were due—and were reliably profitable as long as films
were rented at reasonable rates. Those characteristics added up to a dependable stream of cash earnings—money not required to sustain the
profitability of the business and therefore available either for personal
income or for redeployment in expansion of the theater circuit or investment in new businesses.

The critical challenges for the movie exhibitor lay in theater siting (forecasting demand and beating rivals to the best locations), negotiating advantageous terms for leasing or buying theater property, and acquiring good film product at reasonable rates. An established theater that was well located could draw hundreds of patrons in a day. If it was well maintained and showed its fair share of popular movies, those patrons would keep coming back. Such a theater had tremendous potential for generating a dependable cash flow.

Theater operation was relatively straightforward, though it required tight controls and constant attention to detail. Most of the labor was unskilled. The manager of a small-town or neighborhood theater was typically a jack-of-all-trades who booked pictures, sold tickets and candy, and maintained the physical plant. The only other senior employee was a projectionist. A somewhat larger theater might employ more people, part-time, to take over selling and maintenance tasks and perhaps to serve as ushers. The great urban movie palaces, on the other hand, had large payrolls, including an ushering staff, a stage superintendent and janitorial staff, perhaps an engineer, bookkeeping help, and managerial assistants. In such establishments—for example, the National Theater that Smith took over in 1922—controlling operating costs and generating sufficient revenues to cover them could become a serious challenge for management.[24]

The real estate and operational issues for owners of drive-in theaters were essentially the same as those facing indoor theater owners, but with a few new twists. Mid-West Drive-In tried to follow a 20-20-20 formula regarding the land its theaters sat on: 20 acres, leased for 20 years at $1,000 per year, with an option to buy for $20,000. (In the years before World War II, in particular, the company acquired a great deal of valuable suburban property through such arrangements.) Mid-West's first two theaters cost roughly $50,000 each to construct. They followed the layout patented by Richard Hollingshead—a fan-shaped array of parking ramps, with each ramp inclined upward toward the screen to provide unobstructed views. A typical Mid-West screen was 50 × 60 feet. The physical plant also included a projection booth, a tiny concession stand, and toilet facilities.

From 1938 through the 1940s, there was litigation over Hollingshead's patent on the drive-in concept. E. M. Loew opened a drive-in theater in Providence and refused to pay the license fee. Hollingshead won damages at the trial level, but the appeal dragged on until 1949, when the U.S. District Court in Boston ruled that the drive-in theater design was not patentable because nothing in it involved the "faculty of invention." Hollingshead continued to appeal, but the Supreme Court declined to hear the case. Mid-West Drive-In gave up paying the license fee in the early 1940s. Hollingshead sued, but abandoned the case after 1949. After all, noted Sidney Stoneman, "Roman amphitheaters preceded [the drive-in] by a few thousand years."[25]

When they opened, Smith's first drive-in theaters had the latest in sound equipment—directional blast speakers. That technology had been developed by RCA in its Camden, New Jersey research and development laboratory and had been used by Hollingshead in his original theater. Positioned so that a motorist in the last row of a drive-in theater could hear the show with about the same volume and clarity as one in the first row, the large directional blast speakers were powerful enough to be regarded as a public nuisance. Within a month of the opening of the Detroit drive-in in 1938, some 1,200 angry residents persuaded local officials to issue arrest warrants for Philip and Marian Smith, Sidney Stoneman, and their lawyer as well as the local theater managers.[26]

In those early years, most drive-in operators were newcomers to the theater business. In their attempts to draw audiences from established indoor theaters, some of them proved they could be as flamboyant as the flashiest members of the movie fraternity. In 1941 a Chicago burlesque impresario, Nate Barger, invested $165,000 in a huge 1,500-car amphitheater that boasted a giant screen said to display Jimmy Durante's famous nose at a gargantuan six feet. White-uniformed attendants washed windshields, checked oil, and pumped gas, while "comely females in white satin slacks" peddled refreshments and programs. Other drive-ins boasted ushers on bicycles. Such extravagances could be financially disastrous in a seasonal business, although in the long run providing ancillary services proved not to be so far-fetched an idea.[27]

Phil Smith took a comparatively low-key approach. He used tie-in promotions to attract moviegoers and provided parking and windshield service by uniformed ushers. However, the secret to his success in those early years was not the image he projected or the services he provided so much as his ability to rent films at reasonable rates. Far from being an outsider in the theater business, he had the connections and expertise that enabled him to strike the advantageous deals that were essential to profitable operation.

"BUYING" FILM PRODUCT IN A CHANGING INDUSTRY

According to Richard Hollingshead, the problem that contributed the most toward putting his pioneering drive-in theater out of business was his inability to obtain films at reasonable rates. The first film ever shown at the Camden drive-in was three years old and cost $400 for four days. The last time that film had been shown in the area, it had been run at a small South Camden theater that paid $20 a week. Philip Smith fared better than Hollingshead by renting, or "buying," films through an agency that negotiated with distributors on behalf of a group of second-run movie houses in each region. More knowledgeable about the industry, he was able to circumvent what Hollingshead claimed was a concerted effort on the part of movie distributors to protect their established clients against competition from drive-in theaters.[28]

As early as 1938, indoor theater operators began to worry openly, in the pages of *Variety,* about the new threat to their business.[29] The concern was prophetic but greatly exaggerated the immediate problem. In the early years, before World War II, it was far more the novelty of the setting than the quality of the show that attracted people to outdoor theaters. If they kept rental costs low, drive-ins could do very well screening old movies and out-of-date newsreels. The owners of indoor theaters enjoyed an overwhelming advantage over upstart drive-in entrepreneurs that would continue through the war years, when the rationing of gasoline, steel, and rubber diminished drive-in attendance, and an outright ban on new theater construction brought expansion of the industry to a grinding halt.

However, in the postwar era, drive-ins would move into the mainstream and begin in earnest to seek more current and higher quality film product. Then they would become a significant competitive force and a force for structural change in the industry. The context in which change became possible was the antitrust environment of the late 1930s and 1940s.

In 1938 the film industry came under legal attack by the U.S. Department of Justice, as part of a broad-based antitrust movement led by Attorney General Thurman Arnold. At that time the industry had been dominated for many years by the vertically integrated oligopoly of eight producer-distributors. In the mid-1940s, the most powerful of those, the Big Five—Paramount, Warner Brothers, Twentieth Century Fox, Loew's, and RKO—together grossed more than 75 percent of total revenues from film rentals. They also owned and operated more than 2,600 theaters and had interests in 1,800 more, roughly one-fourth of all theaters in the country. More important, perhaps, they controlled some 125 strategically placed first-run movie houses, more than three-fourths of the most important theaters in the nation's twenty-five largest cities. In most cities, distributors derived between 50 and 80 percent of their film revenues from such first-run theaters.[30]

It was at the distributor level that power was exerted over independent theater operators, with the main thrust toward maximizing revenues from first-run theaters. The principal device for accomplishing that was the system of "clearances" that regulated the distribution schedule. For example, a single first-run theater in Boston would be the only theater in the area to play an important new film for two to four weeks. Then there would be a 14- or perhaps 21-day waiting period, or clearance, before the film was made available to second-run theaters in surrounding neighborhoods, where the film would play for a week at most. After that, any theater could play the movie. Distributors regularly set lengthy clearances between first- and second-run theaters, even when they were not truly in competition. As Dick Smith remembered, "The theory was that this is an intangible product and it only had its value as fresh bread has a value. So they made everyone else wait, and if you wanted to see that film on a current basis, you had to go to downtown or to the places playing it."[31]

Another way in which distributors demonstrated their control over the industry was through enforcement of "block booking." Each studio, which might be planning to release as many as fifty movies in a year, would push theaters to contract for an entire year's product in advance, sight unseen. Howard Spiess was a buyer for Cooperative Theaters of Ohio, the booking agency through which Phil Smith obtained some of his films in the 1940s. Spiess recalled that he would typically be forced to book twenty movies for a theater without knowing any more about them than the names of the movies and of their producers, directors, and stars.

When they could, distributors insisted that the cost of film rentals be based on a percentage of ticket sales. However, booking agents like Spiess, representing a big group of theaters, could refuse to pay anything but a flat rate. The movies he bought would be grouped in categories based on anticipated box office appeal. "A" films might cost $200, "B" films $150, "C" films $100, and "D" films $50. The system provided the opportunity to profit from a low-grade film that turned out to be a box-office hit. "Where you bought a year at a time, you got both some good and bad surprises," Spiess noted. "We generally got some real good bargains by that method." The system also provided neighborhood theaters and drive-ins with enough movies in each year to offer moviegoers great variety. A drive-in that showed two different movies during the week and a third on Saturday night, Spiess pointed out, could attract "three different crowds" every week.[32]

The Justice Department's antitrust suit against the major studios moved slowly through the federal courts in the 1940s and concluded in 1948 with a Supreme Court decision that, in order to make the "theaters of the country . . . a free, open, and untrammeled market," the majors would be required to divest their theater holdings. That divestiture would take place over a number of years, under consent decrees filed individually by each of the studios. Other rulings in the case modified the system of film distribution. The court declared that only "reasonable" clearances were to be allowable under the law. It also limited block booking by guaranteeing theaters the right to reject 20 percent of all films offered.[33]

After 1948 it became standard practice for theaters and their booking agents to buy movies in smaller blocks of four or five after viewing them and deciding for themselves which were the most likely to attract audiences. Agents like Howard Spiess then began to spend two or three nights a week screening new films. They had far more control over what they bought. Yet, as Spiess pointed out, that gain was largely offset by the loss of opportunity for profitable "surprises." Said Spiess, "[It] was supposed to be an advantage to the exhibitor and turned out to be of more advantage to the distributor in the end. There were no sleepers, and you began to find out immediately that you had less chance of making a good buy."[34]

Nevertheless, the industry had begun to change in fundamental ways that would open up much greater opportunity in the long run. Most important, the divestiture decision initiated a process that would eventually end the monopoly of the majors over first-run movies and make it cumbersome for the older, large circuits to enter the drive-in business. It set the stage for suburban neighborhood theaters, drive-ins, and future shopping-center theaters to compete with downtown movie houses for top quality film product. In the immediate postwar era, it was the drive-ins that posed the greatest challenge to the status quo.

DRIVE-IN THEATERS ENTER THEIR HEYDAY

The economic conditions that fueled the growth of so many industries after World War II proved to be disastrous for a large segment of the film industry. As the war ended, servicemen returned home and most of the millions of women who had taken their places in offices and factories left their jobs. The Servicemen's Readjustment Act, or G.I. Bill, provided mortgage assistance and college tuition to millions of former soldiers. Those factors combined to create a wave of demographic change—millions of new families created, children born, new homes purchased, and sons, husbands, and fathers off to college. Between caring for homes and babies and trying to make up for lost time in their studies, young adults had relatively little time to devote to entertainment. Atten-

**TABLE 1.1 Average Weekly Theater Attendance
1947–1961**

1947	90	1952	51	1957	45
1948	90	1953	46	1958	40
1949	70	1954	49	1959	42
1950	60	1955	46	1960	40
1951	54	1956	47	1961	42

Source: U.S. Bureau of the Census, *Historical Statistics of the United States, Colonial Times to 1970,* Part I (Washington, D.C., 1975), Series H873, p. 400.

dance dropped off at all types of shows—circuses and carnivals as well as movies.

Disposable income was not the problem, as it had been in the depression era. Pent-up savings drove unprecedented consumer spending. But most of it was devoted to buying and equipping the modern home with appliances, cars, and, after 1947, televisions. Not only was it more difficult to get out for an evening at the movies, but it was also becoming more entertaining to spend the evening at home. Beginning in the late 1940s, weekly theater attendance began a long downward slide that would cut it in half over a period of ten years (see Table 1.1).[35]

In those years, as Richard Smith recalled, drive-ins were "a bright little spark [in an] otherwise terrible industry." Between 1948 and 1951, when the number of indoor theaters contracted from 18,000 to about 15,000, the number of drive-ins increased from just under 1,000 to more than 3,600. That dramatic shift can be explained in part by the fact that, by 1951, 60 percent of American families owned at least one automobile, making drive-ins accessible to more people than ever before. Most significant, however, was that the very changes in national demographics and habits that undermined the popularity of indoor theaters worked in favor of drive-ins. Farsighted owners of outdoor theaters, among whom Phil Smith was still a leader, prospered because they recognized the need to provide inexpensive family entertainment.[36]

The most successful entrepreneurs in the formative years of the movie industry were those who aimed at the widest possible audience—the great American middle class. This was true in production, where the studio builders established their preeminence with films that exuded solid middle-class values. It was equally true in the theater end of the business. There, the standard setter was Balaban & Katz, which in 1925 became the Publix chain, controlled by Paramount. Early on, Balaban & Katz differentiated its Chicago theater circuit with elaborate architecture and technical innovations such as air-conditioning (introduced in 1917). In the years before they had access to first-run films, they offered "presentations" that combined movies with vaudeville. Just as important, they paid careful attention to details that maximized moviegoers' comfort and convenience—spacious foyers decorated with art exhibits; clean, well-appointed restrooms; well-trained, courteous staff; and even free child care. By 1930, the Publix chain was the most profitable in the country, and its guidelines for maintaining "clean, respectable" theaters were scrupulously followed by Loew's, Warner, Fox, and RKO.[37]

Having been in the business of movie exhibition through the 1920s, Phil Smith well understood the forces behind Balaban & Katz's success. By admitting children to his drive-ins for free, he adopted a family-oriented approach that set the standard in his segment of the industry in the postwar years. As the Mid-West Drive-In chain expanded in the late 1940s and 1950s, it would remain in the forefront of developments aimed at attracting middle-class families to the movies—developments that, because of their success, hastened the restructuring of the theater industry.

In the colorful language of *Variety* magazine, drive-ins in the post–World War II era could no longer be dismissed as "passion pits with pix" that attracted patrons solely because of the novelty and the darkness of the outdoor setting. Instead they became "ozoners," a phenomenon of the automobile age that arose with remarkable speed to challenge the "hard-tops," or "four-wall" theaters. This competition was galling to industry veterans because it arose even though drive-ins continued to operate on the fringe of the distribution system and were forced to show old movies most of the time. Drive-in entrepreneurs flourished by making the most of their unconventional setting. By adapting it to changing lifestyles, they appealed to a much broader segment of the population, many of whom had not been regular moviegoers and were happy to see old movies for the first time.[38]

Phil Smith's experience during the war years demonstrated how mass changes in habits could create new markets for unconventional forms of entertainment like drive-ins. At a time when many were forced to close, his outdoor theaters in Detroit and Cleveland did unusually well, because the great automobile and steel plants in those cities, and those of all their suppliers, went to twenty-four–hour shifts to sustain the war effort. "People's lives were disrupted," remembered Dick Smith. "The drive-in theaters provided entertainment all night long for people who worked in the plants."[39]

The patronage of working adults sustained Mid-West Drive-In during the war. Yet, as Phil Smith and others anticipated, the subsequent growth of outdoor theaters would depend on the patronage of parents and their young children. As drive-ins sprang up, seemingly in every cow pasture, they took on new attributes designed to make them more attractive to families and to the communities in which they located. By 1941 RCA had developed small speakers with internal volume controls that could be hung inside the window of each car, and they became standard in postwar drive-in theaters. Blue and amber lights on poles near the back of the amphitheater provided "moonlight flooding" of the parking area, making it possible for people to get to the refreshment stand or bathroom during the show. Better lighting also enabled theaters to provide car-to-car refreshment service. All of those innovations made the "passion pit" a thing of the past. As one commentator noted, with the "doubtful advantages of surrounding cars, artificial moonlight and solicitous wagon boys vending their Good Humors . . . the moral issue has become more of a joke than a threat."[40]

Controlling the behavior of amorous couples was part, but a relatively minor part, of the move toward family-oriented drive-ins in the 1940s. Where most drive-ins had charged admission per car, they now adopted Mid-West's policy of charging per individual, with children under twelve admitted free. Many drive-ins carried the family idea to an extreme, offering free diapers, nurseries, bottle warming, and even laundry service that allowed moviegoers to drop their dirty clothes at the gate and pick them up on the way out washed and damp-dried. Refreshment stands became veritable fast-food restaurants, serving hamburgers and hotdogs as well as the traditional candy, popcorn, and soda. Operators soon realized the economic wisdom of admitting children free, as they discovered the potential for concession sales to hungry kids. One theater reportedly admitted on a single ticket a truckload of twenty children, who then consumed "forty hot dogs, eight packages of popcorn and over fifty soft drinks."[41]

Yet perhaps the most striking aspect of the postwar drive-in was the wide range of entertainment it offered, going well beyond the showing of movies. One commentator who surveyed theater owners noted that the goal of "the new school of exhibitors"—taking a page out of the book that Phil Smith had written in the 1930s—was to "provide an evening out for the entire family." In the process they transformed their drive-in theaters into "community recreation centers."

> Exhibitors built children's play areas, with swings, slides, merry-go-rounds and pony rides. Some installed miniature railroads which hauled kids over several hundred yards of track. Picnic grounds, swimming pools and monkey villages

appeared in the larger theaters. While youngsters disport themselves at these elaborate plants, their parents can have a go at miniature golf courses and driving ranges or they can play shuffleboard, pitch horseshoes and dance before live bands.[42]

Such goings-on were highly distasteful to most owners of indoor theaters. They found it infuriating, for example, that by admitting children free drive-ins could lure unsuspecting—and undiscerning—patrons away from movie houses that were showing much more current, higher quality film product. Groused one "old-time" theater manager: "This carnival stuff cheapens the business."[43]

Of course, the real threat was that drive-ins would begin to show the same quality of films as indoor theaters. That threat was on its way to becoming a reality by 1950. Until then, drive-ins were able to play first-run movies only by accident. In 1946 Mid-West's St. Louis drive-in played *The Jolson Story* as a first-run, thanks to a dispute between Columbia and its usual theater customer in St. Louis. The movie attracted large crowds, and the theater's gross revenues soared, demonstrating just how successful drive-ins could be with good film product.

In fact, as drive-ins became more and more popular, operators began to seek more direct competition with indoor theaters. In the late 1940s, by moving from flat rental rates to paying a percentage of gross ticket sales, they began to obtain higher quality films and shorter clearances. Despite the protests of their long-time customers, distributors reserved the right to opt for the increased revenues that successful drive-ins could provide, though most still balked at releasing first-run movies at a theater other than the leading downtown movie house. Andy Smith, sales vice-president for Twentieth Century Fox, made that position explicit for the readers of *Variety:*

> The proper place for the Drive-In in the distribution system will have to be worked out, but we must always keep in mind our responsibility to the regular theatre, which shows our pictures day in and day out throughout the year. We shall continue to refuse Drive-In theatres first-run showings in any city or town that has adequate conventional first-run outlets.[44]

Some drive-in owners were determined to break down such attitudes, and the legal environment supported them in their efforts. In 1949 Paramount became the first of the majors to negotiate a consent decree with the U.S. Justice Department, under which it began to divest its holdings in movie theaters. By the end of 1950, RKO and Warner Brothers had also fallen into line. Drive-in owners were emboldened to bring suit against distributors in Chicago, Rochester, Buffalo, and Philadelphia, alleging unfair discrimination in film rentals and clearances. "Drive-ins are no longer a novelty," the plaintiffs warned. "They are an established part of the theater business, and the sooner the producers know this the better." The Philadelphia case was won in 1950 with a ruling in which, according to *Variety,* drive-ins "were elevated by judicial order to the same position as conventional houses" in competing for film product.[45]

Phil Smith was not one to sue his distributors. He placed too high a value on relationships built up over decades to be willing to take that approach. Yet he was an aggressive competitor in the markets he entered. Near the end of 1949, he announced a new $450,000 drive-in, to be built on twenty-four acres in Rutherford, New Jersey, including not only the latest in projector, speaker, and screen technology but also a playground, with "extensive landscaping and parkways." He also put money into advertising, making the most of the fact that it was to be the closest drive-in to downtown Manhattan—"only a 12-minute drive from the New York end of the Lincoln Tunnel." When the film distribution system opened up access to first-run movies, Mid-West Drive-In would be ready to bid for them.[46]

EXPANDING THE SCOPE OF THE FAMILY BUSINESS

Phil Smith was as good at recognizing opportunities in the expanding economy of the late 1940s as he had been in the recovering economy of the late 1930s, and he was able to look beyond the bounds of the theater industry. Moreover, in expanding his company Smith successfully negotiated a transition that many entrepreneurs fail to make, creating an organization capable of carrying the enterprise beyond its entrepreneurial beginnings. He began that process by making a partner of his son, Dick.

Since the days when he had weeded out Indian-head pennies from the receipts of the South Boston theaters, Dick Smith had considered working in the family business, although he had never felt compelled to do so. For a brief time he had been intrigued by the idea of pursuing a philosophical life, having fallen under the intellectual influence of the Jewish scholar Joshua Liebman, who probed the connections between psychology and religion in the younger Smith's confirmation class. During World War II, he raced through Harvard in a little over two years, majoring in civil engineering and afterward serving in the Naval Engineers Corps. Because of his education, a wide range of opportunities were open to him at war's end.

After his discharge from the military in 1946, at the age of twenty-one, Dick Smith spent a summer working in the South Boston and Ipswich theaters and considering whether or not to go on to Harvard Business School. On his first day on the job at the Strand Theater in South Boston, he was assigned to watch the fire doors to make sure they were not opened for the neighborhood toughs to sneak in. Within his first week, he scored a coup by persuading his father to construct a concession stand and to sell popcorn as well as the traditional Hershey bars in his indoor theaters. Eventually, he decided to stay with the company, because he had become a believer in the vision his father held for the future of the enterprise. "I came, I think, for the dream, not for what was there," said Dick Smith, ". . . for the idea that the drive-in theater business was going to open up. And there were many more drive-ins to build, and lots of places to see and things to do. That was exciting."[47]

Although many entrepreneurs have the ability to articulate and to inspire others with their dreams of business success, relatively few succeed in bringing successors—family or nonfamily—into the enterprise to ensure that it will outlive them and eventually move beyond the limits of their vision. In particular, many family firms are burdened by the inability of the founder to share authority with rising generations. Phil Smith, on the other hand, made clear from the beginning that he intended his son to become a full partner as quickly as possible. Far from being secretive or overcontrolling, he talked about every aspect and detail of the business and encouraged his son to take responsibility at an early age. Dick Smith lived at home from the time he became active in the business in 1946 until the time of his marriage in 1952 at the age of twenty-eight. That physical proximity, during what would prove to be a critical period of organization building, hastened the flowering of the father-son partnership into a team of equals.[48]

As it turned out, Dick Smith's first travels for the company took him to California, where his uncle, Sidney Smith, was investigating the fast-food business. Phil Smith's younger brother had been employed by Max Factor as a kind of chargé d'affaires in Paris. He had left on the last liner to evacuate Americans before France fell to the Nazis and had ended up in California, where, during World War II, he operated a twenty-four–hour diner located just outside the gates of the Lockheed Aircraft factory in Los Angeles. That enterprise was forced to close after the postwar cutback in aircraft production, and Sidney Smith had begun looking for new opportunities in the same field when his nephew arrived on the scene.

After a month of studying restaurants around California, Dick Smith returned home convinced that the drive-in car-hop restaurant concept would be viable in other parts of the country.

Phil Smith was immediately taken by the idea of drive-in restaurants. He provided the capital to open a prototype, which he named Richard's Drive-In Restaurant, on a corner of the lot occupied by one of Mid-West's drive-in theaters in Detroit. Shortly after the first restaurant opened, in the fall of 1946, Smith organized a Michigan corporation, Richard's Drive-In Enterprises, and mobilized his drive-in theater backers to finance building more restaurants in Detroit, Chicago, and Cleveland. Sidney Smith moved to Chicago to oversee restaurant operations. He was granted stock in and became president of Richard's Drive-In Enterprises, although the entire operation was centrally controlled from Phil Smith's office in Boston.

Amid that rapid expansion of business activities, Phil and Dick Smith officially became partners as fifty-fifty owners of Smith Management Company. Created in 1947, Smith Management took over Phil Smith's management contract with Mid-West Drive-In and subsequently took on a similar contract with Richard's Drive-In. To Dick Smith, looking back on that time, the most striking aspect was the extent of Phil Smith's faith in his son's abilities. In the start-up phase of Richard's Drive-In Enterprises, the youthful namesake took on responsibility for choosing locations, getting the restaurants built, and ultimately for setting the strategy of the business. Concurrently, he began to take on a larger role in the theater business, managing indoor theaters that were wholly or partially owned by his father. In the spring of 1948, he began helping to open and manage the drive-in theaters. It was not a particularly good year, as the first man he hired to manage the concession stand in a newly opened drive-in in Chicago ran off with most of the receipts. Yet, it was characteristic of Phil Smith that, though he played an active mentoring role, he was also willing to let his son learn by making his own mistakes.

By this time it was becoming clear that more people would be needed to handle the affairs of the growing enterprise. The theater circuit required more active oversight, and the whole operation required tighter control from the central office. In short, it was time to move beyond the initial stage of entrepreneurship, to develop the resources to manage the business more actively, and to lay the foundation for further growth. "Business was more complicated," said Dick Smith. "There was a restaurant business, a drive-in business, and an indoor theater business. There were different partners in different pieces of those businesses, and we had lots of recordkeeping and fiduciary responsibilities to people." Father and son would share the responsibility for addressing these issues, and together they took the family business to the next stage of organizational development.[49]

ORGANIZATION BUILDING

Until he took his son in as a partner, Phil Smith had run his theater business largely on his own. Although he had employed Arnold Berger as a general manager for the drive-in theaters, to a great extent he had continued to handle the key aspects of the business himself, striking real estate deals, buying film, and directly supervising the annual spring opening of his far-flung theater circuit. Smith relied on the Stonemans for business advice and on the services of their law partner Emmanuel Kurland. In his Boston office, in the old Metropolitan Theater building, he was supported by a secretary and a bookkeeper, Agnes Whelen. It was a lean staff for a simple business, but one that Mid-West Drive-In had outgrown by the late 1940s.[50]

By then, though Mid-West's revenues were rising, profits were not—a clear sign that it was time to get greater control over operations. Phil Smith took the first step in that direction by hiring Edward E. Lane to develop an internal accounting function. Lane, a 1936 Harvard graduate, had learned accounting at Boston University night school. He served in the Navy during World War II and had worked in the control department of firms in New York and California before and after the war. Lane started work for the Smiths in February 1949, charged with establishing financial controls over the restaurant chain and helping to arrange financing for its expansion. After a few years, he assumed financial oversight of the theater business as well and also became responsible for expanding the office staff as the business grew. Over the next twenty-eight years, Ed Lane would play a central role in the management and growth of the company.

An even more important addition to company ranks in 1949 was Melvin R. Wintman, whom Dick Smith brought in to run the concessions for the drive-in circuit. In setting up his drive-ins in midwestern states, Phil Smith had relied on specialized companies providing services in film booking and concession operation. Through agencies such as Cooperative Theaters of Ohio, he could negotiate for film product as part of a large group of independent theater operators. For concessions, Smith dealt primarily with a New York firm, Drive-In Concession Company, which operated refreshment stands at eight of his theaters. The concessionaire was essentially a tenant, providing his own equipment and personnel, and paying Mid-West Drive-In a rental fee of 20 to 25 percent of receipts. That arrangement had the advantage of limiting Mid-West's capital investment and operating costs. But it also limited its revenues from concessions to about 5 percent of total income at a time when many drive-in operators were reporting that half of their profits were derived from the sale of food and beverages. By the late 1940s, Mid-West was again building new drive-ins, and there was a growing need to internalize such operations.[51]

Wintman was trained as a lawyer but had taken a job with Mid-West Drive-In, managing the concession at its Chicago theater, as a means of supporting himself in the process of relocating his legal practice to Boston. He replaced the concession manager who had absconded with a large portion of the receipts, and he did such a good job that Dick Smith recruited him into the central office to oversee concessions more broadly. Wintman accepted the offer because he rather liked the work, and he was extremely good at it—the percentage of revenues and profits derived from concessions rose steadily after 1949. Like Ed Lane, Mel Wintman would stay to become a key figure in the company's evolution over the next several decades.

Shortly after recruiting Lane and Wintman, the Smiths hired an experienced theater executive, Sam Seletsky, as chief film buyer. By 1950, they had created the core of personnel that would be needed to realize the opportunities they envisioned in drive-in theaters and restaurants. With those three on board, Dick Smith remembered, "We had the beginnings of an organization, with my father and me beginning to act as a team of two, interacting with each other. I had a lot of authority, more than I deserved at that age. But he had a lot of faith in me and somehow I was lucky, some of the first things I did worked."[52]

MID-WEST DRIVE-IN IN A GROWTH MODE

In 1950 Dick Smith stepped up to the biggest challenge of his twenty-six years, when he took complete control of a million-dollar building program to expand the drive-in circuit. By then, the corporate entity, Mid-West Drive-In Theatres, Inc., was both an operating company and a holding company, with ten wholly owned theater subsidiaries, ten partly owned real estate and theater operating affiliates, and nine partly owned Richard's Drive-In affiliates (see Figure 1.1). In the late 1940s the chain of drive-ins had expanded from nine to fourteen, with new theaters in Omaha; Des Moines; Baden, Pennsylvania, on the outskirts of Pittsburgh;

Griffith, Indiana, near Gary; and La Grange, Illinois, a suburb of Chicago. It was then generating annual revenues of more than $1 million on tangible assets of $1.8 million (see Figure 1.2).[53]

The expansion program that the Smiths devised was a bold one that involved moving into the Northeast, where costs, especially land prices, were much higher and competition was greater. (By 1952, Massachusetts would have the most drive-ins per square mile of any state in the nation.) Hedging their bet by joining forces with other theater entrepreneurs, they planned to construct four new drive-ins: one in Natick, Massachusetts, in partnership with Michael Redstone, and three in New Jersey with Julius Rosengard. In addition, they proposed to build two Kiddieland Parks— playgrounds and family amusement parks—attached to drive-ins in Detroit and Saddle River, New Jersey. Altogether it was a $1.2 million building program, including $230,000 for purchasing tracts of land in New Jersey, and requiring a $550,000 loan from First National Bank of Boston. Successfully completed, the project firmly set the course of Dick Smith's career and laid the foundation for further expansion in the 1950s.[54]

Looking back more than forty years later, Smith would marvel at his father's nerve in entrusting such a big project to someone so young. "I don't think I could have delegated as much authority and responsibility to anyone as young as I, had I been in his place," said Smith. "He was absolutely remarkable in that respect." At the same time, Dick Smith identified that project as the turning point in his career, when he demonstrated his capabilities and became a full partner with his father in the family business.[55]

THE GENTLEMAN AS ENTREPRENEUR

If the nerve—and trust—that Phil Smith displayed in developing his successor were remarkable compared to most entrepreneurs, they were nevertheless consistent with his persona as a businessman and a family man. Smith left no personal papers, no record of his private thoughts to provide a glimpse of his character. Yet a composite snapshot of the entrepreneur in his early fifties, based on the recollections of those who knew him, suggests that it would be hard to find a flaw. From oral testimony, he appears to have been both brilliant and charismatic, yet never self-aggrandizing or overbearing. Indeed, if Phil Smith had any failings, no one seems to remember them.[56]

A good part of Smith's stature came from his sheer physical presence.

FIGURE 1.1 Corporate Chart of Mid-West Drive-In Theaters, Inc., Its Subsidiaries, and Affiliates as of March 15, 1950

NOTES: (a) Unless otherwise indicated, a particular corporation has no debentures outstanding.
 (b) In the case of each of the partly owned Richard's Drive-In affiliates, the stock ownership is as follows:
    20% owned by M-W
    25% owned by P. Smith and family
    50% owned by M-W stockholders
 (c) Where stock is indicated to be owned by M-W stockholders, such a statement is generally true but in a particular case there may be a small number of shares owned by persons not stockholders of M-W.
 (d) As set forth in paragraph 10 of the attached Loan Agreement, M-W contemplates distributing 50% of stock of Natick Auto Theatre Corporation to Michael Redstone and his associates.

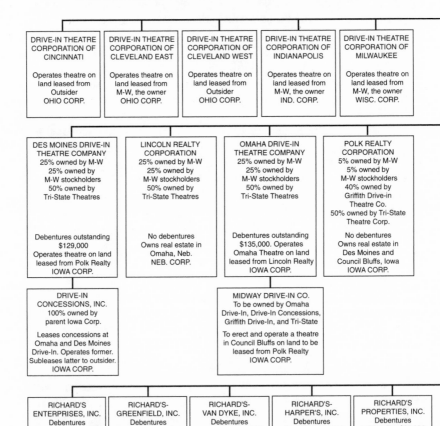

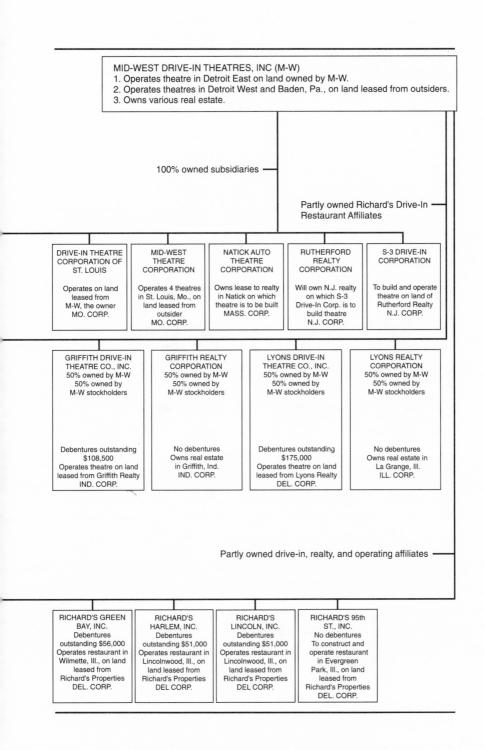

MID-WEST DRIVE-IN THEATRES, INC (M-W)
1. Operates theatre in Detroit East on land owned by M-W.
2. Operates theatres in Detroit West and Baden, Pa., on land leased from outsiders.
3. Owns various real estate.

100% owned subsidiaries

Partly owned Richard's Drive-In Restaurant Affiliates

DRIVE-IN THEATRE CORPORATION OF ST. LOUIS	MID-WEST THEATRE CORPORATION	NATICK AUTO THEATRE CORPORATION	RUTHERFORD REALTY CORPORATION	S-3 DRIVE-IN CORPORATION
Operates on land leased from M-W, the owner MO. CORP.	Operates 4 theatres in St. Louis, Mo., on land leased from outsider MO. CORP.	Owns lease to realty in Natick on which theatre is to be built MASS. CORP.	Will own N.J. realty on which S-3 Drive-In Corp. is to build theatre N.J. CORP.	To build and operate theatre on land of Rutherford Realty N.J. CORP.

GRIFFITH DRIVE-IN THEATRE CO., INC. 50% owned by M-W 50% owned by M-W stockholders	GRIFFITH REALTY CORPORATION 50% owned by M-W 50% owned by M-W stockholders	LYONS DRIVE-IN THEATRE CO., INC. 50% owned by M-W 50% owned by M-W stockholders	LYONS REALTY CORPORATION 50% owned by M-W 50% owned by M-W stockholders
Debentures outstanding $108,500 Operates theatre on land leased from Griffith Realty IND. CORP.	No debentures Owns real estate in Griffith, Ind. IND. CORP.	Debentures outstanding $175,000 Operates theatre on land leased from Lyons Realty DEL. CORP.	No debentures Owns real estate in La Grange, Ill. ILL. CORP.

Partly owned drive-in, realty, and operating affiliates

RICHARD'S GREEN BAY, INC.	RICHARD'S HARLEM, INC.	RICHARD'S LINCOLN, INC.	RICHARD'S 95th ST., INC.
Debentures outstanding $56,000 Operates restaurant in Wilmette, Ill., on land leased from Richard's Properties DEL. CORP.	Debentures outstanding $51,000 Operates restaurant in Lincolnwood, Ill., on land leased from Richard's Properties DEL CORP.	Debentures outstanding $51,000 Operates restaurant in Lincolnwood, Ill., on land leased from Richard's Properties DEL CORP.	No debentures To construct and operate restaurant in Evergreen Park, Ill., on land leased from Richard's Properties DEL. CORP.

FIGURE 1.2 Mid-West Drive-In Operations, 1941–1951

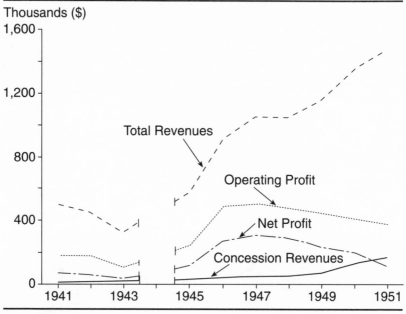

Note: Data unavailable for 1944.

Source: Mid-West Drive-In Theatres, Inc., income statements, in HGI corporate records.

He had piercing eyes that seemed not to miss a thing, and he bore a marked facial resemblance to Thomas E. Dewey, the dashing governor of New York who lost the presidential election to Harry Truman in 1948. Smith's daughter Nancy, however, resented that comparison, which was often made during his lifetime. "He was taller than Thomas Dewey," she explained, "and much more attractive, much more appealing." At five feet-ten he had the refined polish of a 1940s leading man, including a Clark Gable moustache and beautiful clothes that he bought at Louis, a trendy Boston haberdashery. In reminiscences he is described as "immaculate," "fastidious," "elegant." Yet, his secretary said, he was no "show horse." Rather, he "dominated his clothes . . . when you saw that man, he looked like nobody else." (Though in later years another secretary thought he looked like Omar Sharif.) One long-time business associate put it simply: "Phil Smith was the kind of a guy who would walk into a room and people would look."

But, if Smith had charisma, it was a quiet kind—an outward manifestation of an inner self-assurance that had a steadying influence on all his relations, including family, employees, and professional associates. If he was ever racked by turmoil, if he possessed his fair share of conflict and anxiety, it was hard to detect. Though he seemed always in control, ready to take charge, Smith was soft-spoken. No one at the office recalled ever having heard him raise his voice or lose his temper.

Smith was reputed to have a remarkable memory. According to his son, who envied that trait, he had an astonishing capacity for recalling exactly what each picture had grossed at each of his theaters. He also had a reputation as a first-rate "pencil and paper man," meaning that he could analyze the characteristics of any business deal quickly, with mathematical precision and without benefit of adding machine or slide rule.

Smith's employees viewed him as strictly businesslike and correct—holding himself apart, never socializing, keeping his office door closed. Nobody's "pal," he was nonetheless approachable, reasonable, personable, just genial enough to temper his otherwise authoritative presence. On occasion he would show up to work dressed as if for a round of golf—that in a day when proper Boston secretaries, his included, came to work in white gloves. There was, in short, a finely tuned sense of *noblesse oblige*, a benign paternalism that bound him to his employees in a way that they seemed to appreciate as a correct balance between formality and accessibility.

Phil Smith was the "perfect gentleman" in an age when such people lived full, but relaxed and pleasant, lives. In an interview in the mid-1950s, he provided a clear picture of a lifestyle that revolved around his business but was not overwhelmed by it. Questioned about his daily routine, Smith replied:

> Don't get me wrong. I'm no human dynamo. I'm just an ordi-
> nary person. I keep my eye on my business, but I don't work
> hard at it. I never get into my office before 10 in the morning.
> That's a habit I got into when I managed theatres. I'd stay
> around until the place was closed up and then I'd knock off.
> It's the same way now. I usually get home between 1 and
> 2 in the morning, read a little while—business reports and
> such—and then I go to bed. I don't get up until 8 and I take
> my time with breakfast and leaving home.[57]

Successful in business, but not obsessed by it, Phil Smith achieved an admirable balance among work, family, civic responsibility, and recre-ation. With his company growing and a management team in place, Smith had increasing freedom to enjoy the prosperity his success provided. He was a golfer and an excellent bowler and card player. Thoroughbred racing was a popular diversion for men in his industry, and he enjoyed a day at the track as well as one at the ballpark. Yet he understood that the responsibilities of a person in his position extended beyond personal and business life to the larger community. Smith spent a great deal of his time in public service and by the early 1950s was moving into a position of leadership in that area.

In 1948 the Boston tent of the Variety Club joined with the Boston Braves baseball team to create the Children's Cancer Research Foundation, popularly known as the Jimmy Fund. Smith was active in that project and was rising in the ranks of Variety—he would serve a term as chief barker in 1956. He was also to serve as a director or trustee of the American Jewish Council, the Combined Jewish Philanthropies, Brandeis University, the Boston University Development Council, Temple Israel, Beth Israel Hospital, and the Will Rogers Hospital in Saranac Lake, New York.[58]

Although clearly a leader of Boston's Jewish community—and a prominent figure in a strongly ethnic industry—Phil Smith's Jewishness did not sit heavily upon him. He was conscientious but not zealous in religion, and he supported Jewish causes in the same spirit. Smith's wide-ranging business and charitable activities enabled him to travel comfortably in a broad social circle. It was an age when Boston's business and social elites were rife with anti-Semitism. Harvard, where he sent his son for an education, had its unofficial Jewish quota. Yet Smith's role in the Variety Club, particularly in the Jimmy Fund, brought him into contact with the leading sports and political figures of the day. He donated to Catholic charities in the South End and served on the executive committee of the Massachusetts Conference of Catholics, Protestants, and Jews. He belonged to Jewish country clubs in Boston and Palm Beach, but on Florida vacations in the 1930s he socialized at the Breakers Hotel, overcoming the Jewish barrier at one of the more tightly closed institutions in the country. By the mid-1950s, when he began to winter there, Smith was widely known and admired in Palm Beach as the owner of The Colony—"a little jewel of a theater" that screened foreign films and American "art" films for appreciative society audiences, who typically attended openings in formal attire.

The comfortableness and lack of conflict in Phil Smith's business and public life mirrored the situation within his family. At home, remembered his daughter Nancy, he exuded confidence, minimized bad news, and conveyed an upbeat enthusiasm for his life and work. Nancy and her mother, Marian Smith, took no active part in discussions of family business matters, but they were not excluded or kept in the dark. This was a family comfortable with a separation of male and female spheres that kept business and financial matters in the former. Within the sphere of female activities, the focus was largely on the home and beyond that on philanthropy and public service.

In keeping with those distinctions, Smith kept his family and business lives largely separate, and he turned mostly to his adult friends and business associates for golf or racetrack companions. Yet he also spent time with his family and often took his children with him on his summer travels around the drive-in theater circuit. Indeed, Smith was a man who liked to associate with young people, taking a sincere interest in them as individuals. "What I think I remember most as a child," said Nancy, "was that he was very youthful. Young people loved him." That was not just because he was tuned in to sports and entertainment, recalled Dick Smith, but also because he kept track of their careers in school or sports and gave them constant encouragement: "All my friends in school and college would come to him if they had something to discuss or they wanted some advice. I was very proud of him, because it made a kid feel good if one of his peers went to his father to get an insight."[59]

That Phil Smith enjoyed and respected his children and their friends helps to explain the alacrity and smoothness with which he brought his successor into the business. In the years that Phil and Dick worked together—half a dozen of those with Dick unmarried and living at home—there was no aspect of the business that they did not openly discuss. "We might have disagreed," remembered Dick Smith, "but we never fought. There was never any withholding of trust or authority or responsibility." That positive dynamic between father and son laid the groundwork for a virtually seamless transition from the first to the second generation of leadership that would enable Mid-West Drive-In to maintain the upward trajectory on which it was firmly set by 1950.[60]

WIDENING HORIZONS

The building program launched in 1950 would make Mid-West one of the larger drive-in theater companies in the country. Yet the industry was growing at a rate that precluded the kind of leadership position that Philip Smith had been able to establish in 1940. In 1950 there were over 2,000 drive-ins around the country; by 1952 there would be more than 3,600. The great majority of those were individual operations. The cost of building drive-ins had grown tremendously but was still not a severe barrier to people seeking to dabble in the industry. Whereas a "deluxe theater house" was reckoned to cost $250 to $300 per seat in construction, not including provision of parking facilities, a drive-in cost $100 to $150 per paying "seat" with parking provided.[61]

Hence, even as the Smiths aggressively pursued a growth strategy for the drive-in business, they remained open to new opportunities. In 1951, Phil Smith made his first investment in what would prove to be the successor to the drive-in business he had helped to create. The company's first suburban shopping-center theater was built in that year at the new Shopper's World Mall in Framingham, a suburb of Boston. As mundane as that may seem in retrospect, it was an entrepreneurial coup in classic style, a quintessential act of creative destruction. Although the Framingham theater would struggle for several years, in time it flourished. Eventually, the new type of theater would displace the drive-in completely.

CHAPTER

2

FROM FATHER TO SON: THE DRIVE TO LEADERSHIP IN THE THEATER INDUSTRY

Phil Smith entered film exhibition in an era when theater owners were showmen. His faith in the appeal of movies as entertainment enabled him to craft an aggressive strategy amid widespread doubt and timidity in the industry. Within roughly two decades after opening its first suburban shopping-center theater, the enterprise he founded would become the largest, most profitable theater company in the nation. Smith died in 1961 and so did not witness that achievement. Yet he had set the company squarely on a path to preeminence as a national theater chain and beyond that to diversification into new industries.

Dick Smith was part of a generation of theater entrepreneurs who saw themselves primarily as businessmen. His great contribution to Mid-West Drive-In in its formative years was the creation of an organization capable of operating on a national scale. When leadership was thrust upon him prematurely, he devoted himself to realizing his father's dream and ultimately carried it well beyond Phil Smith's vision. Although he shared his father's love of theaters, the defining characteristic of Dick Smith's leadership of the company would be his successful drive to build a major public corporation. Looking back on that achievement, Mel Wintman observed, "Phil Smith was not an aggressive personality in the sense that he wanted to acquire the world. I think had he not had a son named Richard, the company would never have grown as it has grown."[1]

Many U.S. companies prospered in the long period of economic expansion following World War II. Relatively few were able to establish dominance in their industries. Phil Smith's company succeeded, mainly as a result of his firm grasp of the major socio-economic trends of the period and of the opportunities inherent in the restructuring of the theater industry brought about by the 1948 Paramount court decision. The decade of the 1950s was an era of disarray and demoralization among established participants in the theater industry. The majors moved slowly to divest their theater operations, and their control over the film distribution system remained strong. That situation, in the context of steadily falling attendance, kept many experienced theater operators from taking advantage of the opening created by the antitrust action. The number of indoor theaters declined between 1948 and 1958 from nearly 18,000 to about 12,000. The number of drive-ins increased fourfold in the same period to about 4,000, but fell to 3,500 after the recession of 1958 and then stagnated. The result, remembered Dick Smith, was a "marketing vacuum. . . . There was a big market growing up in the suburbs but absolutely no new facilities to serve it."[2]

Like many others in the years immediately after World War II, Smith had seen the future in suburbia. But by 1960 he anticipated that a combination of rising land values, rising incomes, changing age structure, and corresponding changes in the habits of suburban families would eventually limit the potential for growth in the drive-in theater business. Beyond that, he had the creativity to see an alternative in the shopping-center theater. Smith was the first to open a theater in a large regional shopping center and the first to invest seriously in building a theater circuit on the shopping-center idea. His firm would reap the full benefits of its initiative in this field. By 1973, renamed General Cinema Corporation, it would be the largest theater circuit in the country and the leader among a handful of big winners in a restructured industry.

THE IDEA OF THE SHOPPING-CENTER THEATER

Like the drive-in theater, the drive-in restaurant, and the motel, the suburban shopping center appeared with the onset of the automobile age in twentieth-century America. By the mid-1920s retailers realized that there simply was not enough parking space in downtown shopping areas to support the desired level of patronage in their stores. In 1925 Sears,

Roebuck began to open so-called A stores on the outskirts of urban areas, where lower overhead permitted the building of larger stores with big parking lots. Also in 1925, J. Clyde Nichols built the first shopping center, the Country Club Plaza, in Kansas City. The depression and World War II restrained the spread of shopping centers, and by 1946 there were only eight in the country. These were no more than rudimentary versions of the basic form that is now ubiquitous nationwide—strips of small stores, with parking. However, at least one, Highland Park Village in Dallas, included a movie theater among its many other businesses.[3]

By the late 1940s, the concept of the shopping center had evolved to distinguish between neighborhood centers and regional centers that included a wider variety of businesses and sought to attract clientele from a much larger geographical area. In 1950 *Business Week* answered the question, "What's Needed in a Shopping Center?" by specifying at least one major department store and some combination of supporting businesses, carefully selected to meet the needs of the surrounding area, including, "perhaps . . . a theater, bank, restaurant, and other commercial establishments." It was common practice for regional centers to be planned with the help of demographers, sociologists, urban planners, and specialists in retail merchandising and traffic patterns.[4]

Shoppers' World in Framingham, Massachusetts, where the Smiths placed their first shopping-center theater, was one of the most extensively planned regional centers in the country. The developers, National Suburban Centers of Boston, were reported to have spent $500,000 in planning over a period of four years, including a study of traffic flow in the area and "one of the most scientific marketing studies ever made for a shopping center." Considerable planning also went into the architectural design and layout of the shopping center, so that the pedestrian flow within it would foster the greatest possible level of business. In that era the most common pattern was to place the large, "anchor" businesses in separate buildings grouped around a central mall. According to *Architectural Forum,* Shoppers' World was "laid out in the form of a carnival midway, with the main attractions (a theater and a department store) at either end."[5]

It may have been viewed as a main attraction in the final design, but a theater was not by any means part of the developers' original plan. As *Architectural Forum* pointed out, "shopping center financing [was] based almost solely on the validity [that is, creditworthiness] of individual leases." In 1950 a new 1,500-seat theater could hardly have been viewed as a likely prospect for dependable revenues when, according to *Business Week,* theaters were becoming "the new sick industry" because of competition from television. In the end, Phil Smith's most convincing argument, which carried the day with the developers of Shoppers' World, was that his theater would allow them to get use out of their parking lot in the evenings, when it would otherwise be empty.[6]

From Smith's point of view, access to usable parking was one of the principal reasons to locate suburban theaters in shopping centers. His experience with drive-ins made him appreciative of the attraction of easy access by car for moviegoers. Indeed, the shopping-center venue combined some of the best attributes of both downtown theaters and drive-ins. Theaters there were accessible and informal, but they were also comfortable. As the parents of baby boomers became affluent enough to afford sitters, the suburban theaters provided opportunities for an adult evening out that, in ambience, was somewhere between the drive-in and the ornate movie "palace" that was the reigning form in the 1930s and 1940s. Perhaps to stake out that niche in the industry, Smith named the new theater the Cinema, borrowing the European term to lend his convenient suburban theater an air of formality.

The Cinema at Shoppers' World was not a smashing success in its early years. Its clearance from first-run Boston theaters was fourteen days, a period that was a week shorter than neighborhood theaters in the area but still long enough to put a ceiling on attendance. For at least two summers, Smith rented the auditorium to the cartoonists Al Capp (L'il Abner) and Lee Falk (Mandrake the Magician), who ran a summer theater program in the Boston area, bringing in Hollywood actors such as Mae West, Melvyn Douglas, and Marlon Brando to star in their productions. In 1954 the developers of Shoppers' World went bankrupt, and the shopping center was taken over by the principal mortgage holder, Equitable Life. Various reasons were given for the problems, including lack of adequate access roads and the failure to attract a second department store. The developers were also accused of having failed to make allowances "for the conservative shopping habits of proper Bostonians, who tend to frequent the same stores their grandparents did." One of the first large regional centers, Shoppers' World provided a learning experience all around.[7]

The developers' problems notwithstanding, Cinema Framingham, along with most of the individual businesses in Shoppers' World, was beginning to prosper by the 1950s. As they gained confidence in the concept's potential for success, the Smiths began to consider creating a circuit of shopping-center theaters. Indeed, at the time many avenues for growth of the family enterprise looked promising. Independent of Mid-West Drive-In, the Smiths were acquiring indoor theaters, mostly in resort areas; their restaurant business was expanding, and they were looking at other opportunities for diversification as well.

THE SMITH FAMILY BUSINESSES IN THE 1950S

In 1956, a *Boston Sunday Post* interview captured the dynamic character of the family's activities in that era. Clearly, drive-in theaters were the core business. But, Phil Smith pointed out, any business was likely to have up and down cycles. "You have it good in one line and then something happens and you have to change." That, in part, had been his explanation for diversifying into drive-in restaurants in the late 1940s. By 1956 the Smiths had opened twenty Richard's Drive-In restaurants—five in Chicago, five in Detroit, and ten on the East Coast. Richard's was a distinctive chain, every unit of which had the same architecture, menu, and operating procedures for food preparation and car-hop service.

The business also included the Peter Pan Snack Shop chain, bought as seven units in 1953 and expanded to eighteen units by 1956. By 1955—the year that Ray Kroc opened his first McDonald's restaurant in Chicago—Peter Pan Snack Shops had sold more than five million hamburgers. Restaurant revenues in that era were roughly equal to those of Mid-West's theaters (about $6 million in 1956). Though not as profitable as theaters, the restaurant chain kept pace in its growth. When asked how many theaters and restaurants his company owned, Phil Smith liked to answer "I don't know. I haven't been to the office today." He estimated that, altogether, they served thirty thousand customers each week.[8]

This expansion of activity occurred within the framework of ownership and management that had been established in the late 1940s. The restaurant companies were all incorporated as affiliates of Mid-West Drive-In, jointly owned by the company and by a group of individual investors, including the Smith and Stoneman families and a number of other long-term supporters of Mid-West. The Smith family did not hold a majority share in any of these companies. Of the stock of the corporate entities composing Richard's Drive-In Restaurants, for example, Mid-West Drive-In held 20 percent, the Smith family 25 percent, and other individual stockholders of Mid-West 55 percent. At the same time, Phil and Dick Smith had management control of all the companies through long-term contracts with Smith Management.

In the 1930s, when Mid-West Drive-In had been incorporated, it was common practice for theater companies to be managed by outside contractors, who took no salary from the firm but were paid a management fee, usually a percentage of gross revenues. Phil Smith had managed Mid-West under such a contract from the very beginning. That arrangement allowed the Smiths to feel confident in pursuing corporate growth without fear of losing control. The contract provided that the employment of Smith Management was "irrevocable," as long as its duties were performed "conscientiously." With such an agreement in place, they reasoned, the company would not be an attractive target for takeover. They could bring in outside investors to the point where they no longer had a majority position and still, with ten-year renewable management contracts, enjoy some assurance that they would remain in charge. "It was very useful at the time," commented Dick Smith. "I for one was not about to dedicate my business life to something that I could lose control of at an early date. . . . I never felt I had to own all of anything or even the largest or dominant interest in it. But if I was going to work at it, I wanted to be able to control it."[9]

Despite the rather unusual structure, the 1950s was a period when the activities overseen by Smith Management Company most resembled a family business, with active involvement by siblings in two generations. In December 1950 Phil Smith's daughter Nancy married Morris J. Lurie, whom Phil and Dick Smith immediately recruited to help them handle the widening scope of their business affairs. In his early twenties at the time, Lurie had a limited business background, having managed gas stations for an oil company in New Jersey. True to form, Phil Smith gave him a position of responsibility in which to prove himself; and, indeed, he turned out to be an effective manager and aggressive entrepreneur. Lurie worked closely and well with his father- and brother-in-law, albeit as an employee of the restaurant chain, Richard's Drive-In, and not as a partner of Smith Management.

Lurie assumed oversight of operations of the restaurant business in the eastern United States, while Sidney Smith continued to run the midwestern restaurants from Chicago. Shortly thereafter, the family launched a new type of restaurant in New England, named Jeff's Charcoal Broil after Jeff Lurie, Nancy and Morris Lurie's son and Phil Smith's oldest grandchild. In 1952 Dick Smith married Susan Flax, of Newton, Massachusetts. A few years later, when Lurie had the idea of launching a chain of donut shops, they were named after the second grandchild, Dick and Susan's daughter, Amy Joy Smith. By the end of the decade Amy Joy Doughnut and Pancake Houses would compete with Dunkin' Donuts and Mister Donut for preeminence in the New England area.

As the patriarch of this growing family and expanding business enterprise, Phil Smith was able in the 1950s to step back somewhat from day-to-day involvement in the companies he had created. His commitment to the Variety Club and to other charitable and civic activities expanded, and he began to spend several months each winter in Palm Beach. Yet he did not by any means disengage from the strategic issues. An active investor in the stock market with a substantial portfolio, Smith was a voracious reader of the business press. In traveling around the country scouting potential drive-in theater locations, he had acquired a feel for the population movements and consumer trends that were driving the U.S. economy in those years. Perhaps because he could distance himself and thereby gain perspective on his business and its long-term prospects, Smith began in the mid-1950s to reorient his theater strategy away from drive-ins. By the end of the decade, he was prepared to launch the program aimed at building a national circuit of shopping-center theaters.

Between 1950 and 1955, Mid-West Drive-In's outdoor theater circuit grew from fourteen to twenty-six theaters, but after that date the pace of expansion slowed, and additions were made mainly by acquisition rather than by new construction. (The size of the drive-in circuit would peak at fifty in 1965.) Not all of the theaters purchased were drive-ins; for example, in 1959 Mid-West acquired 50 percent ownership of five indoor theaters in Atlantic City, New Jersey. At the same time, the Smiths were building a separate indoor theater circuit with a wholly owned company, the Smith Theatre Group. The Strand in Ipswich, which Philip Smith had owned since the 1920s, was part of this group, as was the Cinema at Shoppers' World. To those, Smith Theatre Group added first-run, suburban, and resort theaters, primarily in New England and Florida, bringing the total to fourteen by the end of the decade.

In 1959 the Smiths began to consolidate these separate theater holdings under the Mid-West Drive-In corporate umbrella in preparation for taking the company public. By that time, the strategic focus was on rapid expansion of the shopping-center theater circuit, but they were also planning to diversify Mid-West's operations into tenpin bowling. Phil Smith recognized in the public corporation a vehicle that could carry him toward both of those goals. Yet the fuel to power that vehicle would come from the core business—drive-in theaters.

DRIVE-INS: THE "BREAD AND BUTTER" BUSINESS

In the late 1950s drive-in theaters approached the height of their popularity, and the well-established, well-managed theaters of Mid-West Drive-In became increasingly profitable. In 1959, when the outdoor and indoor theater circuits were consolidated, drive-ins produced 71 percent of total revenues. Operating profits on the open-air theaters were over 15 percent of revenues, versus only 8 percent for the indoor theater group.

The Smiths were not building new drive-ins, but they were making the kinds of investments in existing theaters that made them increasingly profitable.[10]

Having grown in number to constitute 20 percent of all U.S. theaters by 1954, drive-ins began to gain access to first-run films with regularity, and Mid-West Drive-In was a leader in negotiating that critical change. Howard Spiess joined the company in 1955 as film buyer and division manager for the St. Louis area, where Mid-West expanded in the 1950s to a circuit of five units—the Airway and Manchester drive-ins and the Beverly, the Gem, and the Overland indoor theaters. Spiess was attracted to the Smiths because they were, in his opinion, the most aggressive operators in the field. They were typically out in front in adopting innovations that kept drive-ins competitive with indoor theaters and that enabled them to build up attendance levels to the point that distributors would give them first-run movies.[11]

In 1953 Twentieth Century Fox introduced wide-screen Cinema-Scope and stereophonic sound with the release of *The Robe*. People who viewed film as an art form hated the new technology and the changes it required in cinematic techniques. George Stevens, director of *Gunga Din* (1939), *Talk of the Town* (1942), and *Shane* (1953), offered a typical complaint: CinemaScope was "fine" if you wanted "a system that shows a boa constrictor to better advantage than a man." Yet most people viewed it as the savior of the film industry, because the attraction of its novelty helped to slow the long decline in movie attendance in the 1950s. Indoor theaters adopted it quickly—the installation of the huge new screen at the Cinema at Shoppers' World in 1955 brought an end to the diversion of summer stock productions.[12]

Among drive-in owners, Mid-West was one of the first to make the investment in CinemaScope, building the requisite large screens and installing mixer boxes to channel the stereo sound track into the existing speaker systems at all its drive-ins in the mid-1950s. Another Mid-West innovation of the same period was the introduction of in-car heaters, which allowed its outdoor theaters to operate year-round. Through such tactics the company succeeded in building its box office revenues high enough for Howard Spiess to win first-run bookings in all his theaters. Said Spiess:

> We became competitive because, in the end, we could generate more business than the downtown theater could. Our drive-in theaters were 1,000-car drive-ins—1,200 cars—and could generate in those days a lot of money. The film distributor is

still interested in revenues in the end. We proved to them that
we were capable of this type of business.[13]

One of the first production studios to release first-runs to drive-ins
on a regular basis was Walt Disney. A string of Disney classics came out
in the 1950s: *Peter Pan* (1953), *Lady and the Tramp* (1956), and *Sleeping
Beauty* (1959). At a typical 1,200-car outdoor theater like the one in
Natick, Massachusetts, summer Saturday nights would bring as many as
3,500 adults and children to spend the evening. Mid-West's 2,000-car
Meadows Family Drive-In in Hartford, Connecticut was among the first
to show all first-run movies and was a very profitable operation in the
1950s.[14]

Showing films was only part of the business in those days. During
the 1950s, the proportion of Mid-West's revenues contributed by concessions rose steadily, reaching one-third by the end of the decade. Between
1955 and 1960, the company installed new equipment in all of its drive-
in concession operations, including some of its own design, made specifically for that application and subsequently adopted as standard in the
industry.[15]

The concession stand of that era was a full-scale fast-food operation.
It was set up cafeteria-style and served pizza and hamburgers along with
the usual theater fare of popcorn and candy. During the half-hour break
between features, as many as a thousand people would come to the cafe-
teria for food, and every employee on the lot would be drawn in to help
make the operation run smoothly. On more than one busy summer night,
Mid-West's head of concessions Mel Wintman, on a date at the Natick
drive-in, was known to have left his fiancée in the car while he pitched in
with the theater manager to handle the cash registers so that the cashiers
could help keep the food coming out of the kitchen. That kind of dedication enabled the Mid-West Drive-In management team to feel confident
that, in the words of Howard Spiess, "the company led the field in operation."[16]

Dick Smith was the primary architect of that management team. With
the help of Mel Wintman, Ed Lane, and Sam Seletsky, he developed the
organization necessary to coordinate and control geographically dispersed
operations profitably—capabilities that would contribute greatly to the
company's long-term success. The structure was simple for a relatively
simple business, with regional divisions for oversight of theater management and a functional division of labor in the small home office on Boylston Street in Boston (see Figure 2.1). In fact, "management" was a much
smaller group than it appears in the chart in Figure 2.1. Aside from the
Smiths, Lane and Wintman were the only individuals with substantial

authority—Lane as a quasi–chief financial officer, and Wintman as de facto head of theater operations.

Nevertheless, by the mid-1950s, operating procedures and principles were firmly in place. Ed Lane and his assistant, Philomena Sarno, maintained a well-developed system of financial reporting and control and produced regular profit-and-loss statements—necessarily by hand in those pre-computer days. The company began bringing district managers into Boston for annual meetings. In the field, they could rely on "the bible"—a comprehensive manual, written by Mel Wintman in 1952, that laid out the key elements of "The Smith Management Way."

The operations "bible" makes it clear that the individual theaters in the circuit were bound together by regular reporting and detailed accounting to the home office. Also, at least in theory, they were unified in taking an aggressive approach to advertising and promotion, efficient operation, and maintenance of high standards of cleanliness and service. Those standards were prescribed by the manual, but they were also encouraged by annual contests, with cash prizes, for

> best all around reopening campaign, resulting in biggest increase of business over previous reopening days ($100) . . . best all around management ($250) . . . best all around care and upkeep of theatre property and grounds ($100) . . . best single promotion ($100) . . . best running stunt—any idea or gag that continues over a period of several weeks ($150) . . . safety—least total insurance claims ($100).[17]

Both Phil and Dick Smith involved themselves personally in picking the winners. Indeed, though he had relinquished operating control, Phil Smith remained a highly visible and important figurehead in the business. During the summer months, he made the rounds of the drive-in theater circuit. When he was not traveling, he regularly attended the Natick drive-in, where the manager, James Collins, was careful to save a few parking spots for visitors from the home office, even on the busiest nights. Sometimes Smith would enter on the darkened exit road to test whether the ushers were keeping their eyes open. Once all the operational details were checked to Smith's satisfaction, Collins remembered, he would end up standing in front of the concession building, talking business.

> And those were, as I recall, interesting talks with Philip Smith. He loved to predict grosses. He would, for instance, ask me, "What do you think this picture that you have coming next week will gross? What's your estimate?" And we would kick

FIGURE 2.1 Mid-West Drive-In Management in the 1950s

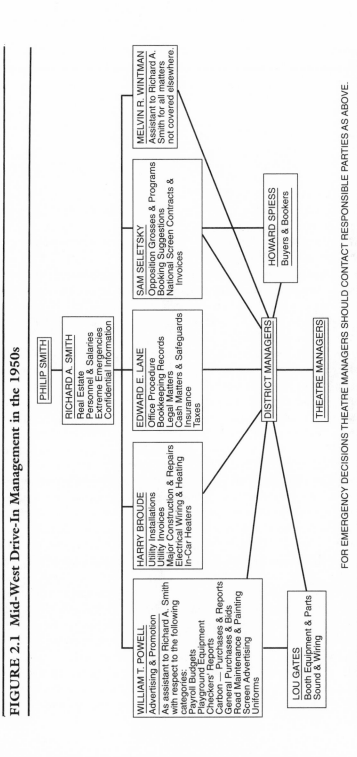

FOR EMERGENCY DECISIONS THEATRE MANAGERS SHOULD CONTACT RESPONSIBLE PARTIES AS ABOVE.

Source: Files of Howard Spiess.

those things about. . . . He would give me an estimate, and
he was very close—very. He had a good sense of film, he
enjoyed film, and he loved to talk film.[18]

GROWTH, DIVERSIFICATION, AND GOING PUBLIC

Phil Smith loved movies and theaters, and he understood both the
potential and the limitations of the business. By the late 1950s his strategy
for the theater company he had created had two main elements. The first
was to build a national circuit of shopping-center theaters. The second
was to enter a new leisure industry, tenpin bowling. In each instance,
Smith saw an opportunity for an aggressive mover to establish a position
of dominance in a field that was wide open, either because of restructuring
within a mature industry, in the case of film exhibition, or because of
rapid growth and expansion into a new area of the country, in the case
of bowling.

Driving that two-pronged competitive strategy was an economic impetus for diversification rooted in the fundamentals of the theater business. The performance of the Smiths' expanding indoor and drive-in circuits had clearly demonstrated that well-managed theaters would throw
off more cash than would be required to sustain growth. The more successful the shopping-center theater strategy, they reasoned, the greater
would be the need to redeploy that free cash flow into building a strong
position in an emerging industry, thereby securing their prospects for
further growth and profitability over the long term. Underpinning it all
was a financial strategy in which taking the company public was the essential first step.

By going public, the Smiths were able to leverage their consistent
and expanding theater cash flow, gaining access to the capital needed to
implement their strategic plans without risking loss of control over what
they had built. In 1959, in preparation for the initial public offering of
stock, they consolidated their theater operations, exchanging ownership
of the Smith Theatre Group for shares of Mid-West stock. At the same
time, Mid-West sold its interests in non-theater businesses, including
Richard's Drive-In Restaurants. What emerged was a theater company
with both open-air and indoor theaters and operations that ranged across
the Midwest, Northeast, and mid-Atlantic regions and Florida. In recognition of its new character, and perhaps even more of its plans for the
future, the company was renamed General Drive-In Corporation.

In June 1960 General Drive-In offered 180,000 shares of common stock for public sale. Its principal underwriter was Paine, Webber, Jackson, and Curtis, and a Paine Webber partner, Maurice M. Wheeler, was one of two outside directors designated to join the board of the new public company. To Paine Webber, one of the more attractive aspects of the company was the underlying value of its drive-in theater real estate. The net worth of General Drive-In was over $5 million, but there was in addition roughly half that amount in appreciated land values not reflected on the books. That fact was comforting to the underwriters though insignificant to the Smiths, who were staking their future on the cash-generating potential of the drive-ins, not on their real estate value.

The consolidated financials presented in the prospectus for the initial public offering clearly indicated the cash flow characteristics of the business (see Figure 2.2). From 1956 through 1959, the theaters achieved an average rate of growth in operating income and cash flow (calculated from financial statements as net profits with depreciation and other non-cash charges added back in) of 16 percent and 10 percent, respectively, on revenue growth of only 9 percent.[19]

The public offering was essential to the Smiths' plan for unleashing the full power of that steady cash flow. By the late 1950s, they had determined that the rising cost of suburban real estate made building more drive-ins impractical. The shopping-center location, which could be leased, provided a theater with ample parking without requiring an investment in real estate. The cash flow from the established theater circuit would make it possible to take advantage of that situation, allowing the firm to sustain a constant high level of leverage, both in the form of long-term leases on theater properties and in direct borrowing to finance further expansion. To obtain such leases, however, the theater company had to establish its creditworthiness with the institutions financing the shopping-center developers.

By early 1960, Phil and Dick Smith had negotiated seven long-term leases for shopping-center theaters. Working as a team, they had succeeded in convincing developers and their mortgage lenders of the potential value of including a theater in a new shopping center—but not without difficulty. Their ability to participate in the continuing expansion of shopping centers would be severely limited if they could not more easily win acceptance by the large insurance companies that provided most of the financing for shopping centers in that era. "I visited a number of these organizations," remembered Dick Smith.

> They were all very curious about the shopping-center theater idea but had no experience and were not necessarily going to

FIGURE 2.2 General Drive-In and Subsidiaries
     Revenues, Operating Income, and Cash Flow, 1955–1959

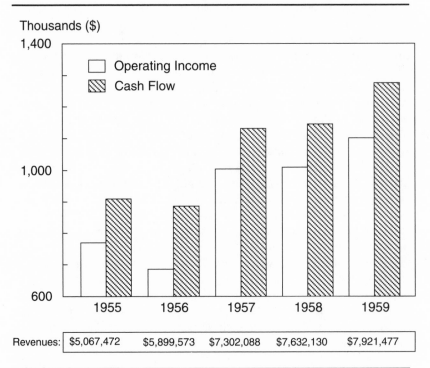

Source: HGI corporate records.

give much credit to the developers for the rentals, the minimum rentals, that these theaters might contribute to a prospec-
tive shopping center. That could be overcome if we could
build up the net worth of the company. We decided that we
could not only build up the net worth, but also gain much
more visibility and recognition by establishing ourselves as a
public company.[20]

Going public would make it possible for the Smiths to use their
leasing strategy as the basis for an aggressive theater expansion program.
At the same time, they made plans to diversify because, as noted, movie
theaters generated more cash than could sensibly be reinvested in the
business. "We went public with our drive-in company in 1960," Dick
Smith recalled, "knowing it would have to diversify."[21]

The limits to overall growth in the movie exhibition industry were in sight by the late 1950s. Although the amount of money Americans spent each year on recreation nearly tripled between 1948 and 1960, spending on movie attendance fell by nearly half. As a result, the theater industry's share of leisure-time expenditures, as Phil Smith would have called them, dwindled from over 15 percent to 5 percent. In addition, film supply was a major constraint on the business, one over which exhibitors had no control. In the decade after the Paramount decision in 1948, the number of films released annually by national distributors declined from 448 to 352. Then, after a disastrous year in 1958, when the industry as a whole lost $19 million, the number fell sharply to 254 and trended steadily downward for the next four years. The Smiths might take heart from the mediocrity of television fare in the late 1950s, but if there was a dearth of popular films to show in their theaters, they could not hope to compete for a larger share of people's leisure time.[22]

Thus, although the shopping-center theater strategy might make General Drive-In the leader in film exhibition, beyond a certain point continued investment in a maturing industry would bring diminishing returns. Distributing free cash flow in the form of higher dividends, which were taxed twice (once as corporate profits and once as personal income), would also limit the ultimate return to the company's shareholders. Over the long term, the greatest returns would come from a steady increase in dividends and a steady appreciation of the value of the company's stock. To accomplish that, the Smiths sought to redeploy the cash flow from the theater circuit into a new business in a growth industry, which they hoped would, through timely investment, capture a major share of its market and, in turn, become a cash generator as its industry matured. By the late 1970s, this strategy of pairing high-cash-flow businesses with developing companies in high-growth industries would be a staple of portfolio management principles, advanced by business consultants to help diversified firms create long-term value for their shareholders and rewarded in the stock market by sophisticated investors. To the Smiths, some twenty years earlier, it was the basic economic imperative of their business, which laid the foundation of a strategy of growth through diversification that would guide the company from 1960 forward.[23]

Phil Smith provided the rationale linking theaters and bowling in General Drive-In's first annual report, in a statement of corporate "philosophy":

General Drive-In plays to the family—where the family lives—
in the suburbs. Its drive-in and indoor theatres, and more
recently shopping center theatres, follow this pattern of opera-

tion. The same philosophy is guiding our new move into the
bowling center field; we will now provide facilities for active
as well as passive family recreation in convenient, wholesome
surroundings.[24]

Smith was an excellent bowler, and in his travels around the country
he had determined that there was a unique opportunity for growth of the
bowling industry in the New England region. Beginning in the mid-
1950s with the introduction of automatic pinsetting machinery, tenpin
bowling had become a popular sport in most areas of the country. "Surprisingly enough," noted the annual report, "it has over one million more
devotees than fishing, which was long considered America's most popular
pastime." However, tenpin bowling had not spread as rapidly in New
England, where the smaller duckpins and candlepins were popular forms.
That seemed to leave an opening that an aggressive entrepreneur could
exploit. As Ed Lane put it: "We were going to come in and milk it right
away." Said Mel Wintman,

> It was a multi-unit kind of a business, in which we had some
> proficiency. It involved a limited amount of simple food prepa-
> ration, at which we had a capability. We could easily build
> these kind of buildings. We were doing it all the time for
> indoor theaters, so that wasn't any problem. So, we thought
> we had all the answers from a management point of view.[25]

The original plan was for fifteen bowling centers with a total of five
hundred lanes, mostly in New England, which would have made General
Drive-In the largest operator in the region. In the first year the company
opened centers in Massachusetts, Rhode Island, and New York, and it
began construction on three more in Massachusetts. All fifteen would be
completed by 1963.[26]

Taking the company public was the enabling step in the Smiths' plan
to mobilize their cash resources for rapid expansion in two industries at
once. It had the advantage of allowing them to finance their ambitious
program through debt and without further dilution of ownership. At the
time of the public offering, General Drive-In had already embarked on a
$1.2 million building program aimed at adding seven new shopping-
center theaters and three bowling centers to its business assets. The proceeds from the initial public offering would cover less than half of that.
However, as the prospectus made clear, raising capital was not the primary
purpose for taking General Drive-In public:

Any necessary funds for its proposed expansion program over
and above the proceeds of the sale of the shares offered hereby
are expected to come from treasury cash, deferred purchase or
other form of long-term debt; or the Company may obtain
necessary equipment and properties through leasing arrangements. The Company does not expect to do any further equity
financing in the near future.[27]

The structure for ensuring the Smiths' control of the business
through a long-term contract with Smith Management remained in place
when General Drive-In went public. In return for the security of a contract, plus 4 percent of gross revenues as a management fee, the agreement
provided that the Smiths could not be compensated in stock options. It
was therefore of critical importance to them that there be avenues for
financing future growth that did not require them to sell stock and dilute
their ownership position. When the assets of the Smith Theatre Group
were brought into the company and the non-theater assets were separated
out, the Smiths owned roughly half of General Drive-In. Once the sale
was complete, they owned just 35 percent. The Stoneman family owned
another 20 percent, and the continuing closeness of the families (and
active involvement of Sidney Stoneman on the board of directors) provided another measure of security against loss of control. However, over
the years, Dick Smith made it a policy never to sell his family's stock in
the company, with the result that its stake in the firm remained virtually
unchanged through more than thirty years of growth and diversification.

DEATH OF THE FOUNDER

In July 1961 Phil Smith died suddenly at the age of sixty-two, just
over a year after taking his theater company public. Tragically, his son-in-
law, Morris Lurie, died at about the same time, following a year-long
battle with cancer. His father's death left Dick Smith the sole proprietor
of Smith Management Company, with executive responsibility for two
family enterprises—General Drive-In and the restaurant chains that Lurie
had helped to run. Over the next few years, with two key executives gone,
Smith would be forced to sell the restaurants. He would also have to
confront the fact that the bowling business was not going to be the success
that his father and he had planned. Yet, if the unexpected death of the
founder left his successor with some hard decisions and unpleasant tasks
to handle on his own, it did not, as in so many cases, precipitate a crisis
of leadership.

For more than twelve years, Phil Smith had been preparing his son to succeed him. By the time of his death, the two were virtually interchangeable in the eyes of company stakeholders, suppliers, and creditors. "My father and I were alter egos for each other," remembered Dick Smith. "We worked that way together. There was never any withholding of trust or authority or responsibility, and people who worked for the theaters all knew that—they knew that talking to me was like talking to Phil or vice versa."[28]

Since the mid-1950s, when he began spending three to four months each winter in Florida, Phil Smith had left the running of the business entirely to his son in his absence. Over the three years preceding his death, they had worked more closely than ever together in the process of creating General Drive-In and taking it public. Every aspect—financial, legal, strategic—had been discussed, decided, and negotiated jointly. "We had the same state of knowledge," said Dick Smith. "If there was a meeting with the investment bankers . . . or something on the law side, I could go or he could go or we both could go. It didn't matter." On a personal level, that closeness undoubtedly made the loss of a parent all the more painful. From a business perspective, it was an unqualified blessing, paving the way for a smooth transition under circumstances that commonly create chaos in family businesses. Said Dick Smith, "I moved into my father's chair, so to speak, the day he couldn't come to work."[29]

Once in that chair, however, Smith had to face the implications of the terrible double loss his family had suffered. "I had to decide what business I was going to be in," he recalled. "I was thirty-six years old and not about to run two important businesses." Had Morris Lurie lived, he might have stepped up to the next level of responsibility on the restaurant side. With only himself and his uncle Sidney, whose role had remained limited to regional restaurant operations, Smith felt compelled to let go of that business. "Making a choice was tough," he said. "My appetite was such that, whatever it took, I would do it. I think I could have, in retrospect, but I didn't know then." The restaurant business was still roughly equal to theaters in revenues, though not in profits; and it was structured as a network of private companies, linked by common ownership and management. In each of those, the Smith family was a minority owner, and Dick Smith felt responsible for protecting the interests of the individual investors collectively holding the majority share, most of whom had been supporters of his family's endeavors since the earliest days of Mid-West Drive-In. With that concern in mind, he decided against the risk of taking on more than he might be able to handle.[30]

Having concluded, unhappily, that he must choose between the two businesses—restaurants and theaters—Smith had little difficulty going with the one he knew best. His closest adviser at that time was Sidney Stoneman, who served on the board of General Drive-In and had assisted the Smiths in taking the company public. Another valuable resource was Charles Moore at the Bank of Boston. At the time, the bank was General Drive-In's sole source of debt financing. As the officer in charge of its account, Moore was, in Dick Smith's words, "essentially the financier of the company." In the 1960s he would join the board of directors. Finally, Smith relied on his inside financial manager, Ed Lane, for assistance in making the critical decisions that faced him.[31]

The advice those men gave was to stick with the theater business and divest the restaurants. Both were profitable, growing businesses. By the early 1960s, however, there was a great deal of competition in the restaurant field. Richard's Drive-In Restaurants, Peter Pan Snack Shops, and Amy Joy Doughnut and Pancake Houses were competitive with McDonald's, Denny's, and Dunkin' Donuts but could hardly hope to gain the kind of edge that General Drive-In was aiming to establish in the theater industry.

So, between 1961 and 1963, Smith sold the restaurant chains, allowing the shareholders to cash out. Sidney Smith took the proceeds from his holdings, moved to Florida, and set himself up in the stock trading business. For Dick Smith, the break would not be quite as clean. Shortly after the completion of the sale, the buying company, having allowed the business to deteriorate through mismanagement, defaulted on its payments. Smith Management Company was forced to repossess the restaurants. Not willing to see the businesses he had helped to build collapse, Smith continued to run them for another five years, until they could be sold to a new party.

In the same period, it became clear that the opportunity the Smiths had envisioned in bowling was not going to materialize. Bowling never became a family sport, as they had predicted it would, but was instead dominated by adult leagues—men in the evening, women during the day. The sport flourished in urban areas with large blue-collar populations. New England communities were characteristically "less blue-collar heavy industry than in the Midwest," reflected Dick Smith, and were "a lot more difficult to organize" into bowling leagues. Thus the market for the business was not quite what they had imagined and not one which they had experience in serving.[32]

Moreover, the aggressiveness with which the Smiths acted to introduce tenpin bowling to New England proved not to confer the competitive advantage they had anticipated. The economic barriers to entering the industry broke down rapidly, as the leading manufacturers of pinsetting equipment, AMF and Brunswick, began to provide financing and marketing support for entrepreneurs who used their equipment. Wherever a new bowling alley went into operation, Dick Smith found, there was likely to be a competitor opening soon nearby. In addition, General Drive-In had difficulty obtaining liquor licenses for its New England centers, where "blue laws" restricted the sale of alcohol to lounges and restaurants, and access to licenses was closely controlled and very competitive. The theater organization was fully capable of managing bowling operations, but the ability to negotiate the highly politicized process of obtaining liquor licenses was not among its organizational strengths. Refreshments, including beer, were a popular aspect of industrial league bowling. Bowling alleys without a liquor license found it difficult to compete for customers and impossible to generate substantial profits.

The biggest problem, however, was that tenpin bowling was never able to displace duckpins and candlepins in New England. The established competitors in the industry, the operators of candlepin lanes in particular, responded to the threat posed by new entrants by quickly adopting automatic pinsetting equipment. Since many of them already had liquor licenses, they had little difficulty maintaining their leading place in the industry.

By the time construction of General Drive-In's fifteen-unit bowling division was completed in 1963, it was already apparent that the venture would be a disappointment. The bowling centers located outside New England (on Long Island and in New Orleans and Cleveland) and holding liquor licenses were relatively profitable, but the business as a whole never quite broke even. The economic impact on General Drive-In was not disastrous. Cash flow from operations was generally sufficient to cover expenses, though depreciation charges created losses to be reported on the company's financial statements. Yet bowling clearly was not to be the vehicle for growth that the Smiths had sought. Bowling operations turned in net losses consistently through 1965, when the company began to sell off its units.

It is impossible to say whether, had he lived, Phil Smith would have acknowledged this first-ever strategic misstep and exited from the new business as swiftly as his son did. Over the course of his career, Dick Smith's decisiveness in abandoning unpromising avenues of diversification would stand out nearly as much as his boldness in pursuing the promising ones. The issues he faced as he assumed sole responsibility for the company—both the choice of theaters over restaurants and the decision to stay with or abandon the investment in bowling—surely helped to forge that strength in him. Part of Phil Smith's legacy to his son was a firm grasp of industry structure in the theater business and of the opportunities to be seized by an aggressive mover facing weak competition. In making the difficult decisions that faced him in the years immediately following his father's death, Dick Smith rounded out his valuable early training in competitive strategy.[33]

Another important part of Phil Smith's legacy was the example he set in delegating responsibility early and sharing authority readily with his successor. Dick Smith would develop his own distinctive style of leadership. Yet at its core was the characteristic that had so distinguished his father's direction of the family firm—the ability to exercise power firmly but without jealousy. As he moved forward without the benefit of family managers to help shoulder the burden of running the company, Smith's level of comfort in developing subordinates and placing trust in them provided a solid foundation on which to build the organization and to carry it through the critical transitions required for future growth.

FORGING A LEADERSHIP STYLE

Although Dick Smith was spared the crisis of authority that frequently ensues from the unexpected death of the founder in family firms, he still faced the formidable task of building a management team capable of supporting him in the exercise of his responsibilities as sole executive of a rapidly expanding business. The effectiveness of the General Drive-In management group, pulled together under his leadership in the early 1960s, would be a major factor in the company's long-term success.

In 1962 Smith began to strengthen management on various levels. He created an executive group by elevating key managers and involving them more actively in decision making. The group included the three long-time employees on whom Smith had depended most to operate and control the corporation: Mel Wintman, Ed Lane, and Sam Seletsky. Between 1962 and 1965, as a corporate ladder was created, Wintman moved up from general manager to executive vice president. Lane also moved to the top of the corporate hierarchy, becoming treasurer in 1963. They would both be elected to the board of directors in 1968. Seletsky was promoted from head film buyer to vice president for film.

On another level, two long-time family friends and business associates, Sidney Stoneman and Emmanuel Kurland, began to participate in decision making in these years. Both had been on the board of directors from the company's early years, but they played a larger role in advising Smith after the death of his father and brother-in-law. From the mid-

1960s, Stoneman's official position was chairman of the executive committee of the board, and Kurland's was secretary of the corporation. Although
Kurland confined himself mainly to offering legal opinions, during that
era both men were involved as advisers of corporate management.

Meanwhile, Smith increased the number of theater division managers
in the field from six to nine and filled in the ranks of middle management
in the home office to support Wintman, Lane, and Seletsky in handling
routine operational and control functions. Early in 1962, Howard Spiess
came in from the field to become general manager in charge of theater
operations. Another former division manager, Nicholas Lavidor, took on
responsibility for coordinating advertising. A new function, purchasing,
was added to the central office, and by 1965, the head of purchasing,
Joseph Saunders, took on the additional role of coordinating theater construction. By that time there were two separate advertising departments—
newspaper advertising under Lavidor and cooperative advertising under
Seymour Evans. The functional departments were rounded out in the
mid- to late 1960s by concessions under Stanley Werthman, and real
estate, the area of operations in which Dick Smith remained most actively
involved.[34]

William Zellen, who joined the company in 1960, advanced to become controller under Lane. Another of Lane's assistants, Morris Englander, spent most of the 1960s running the restaurant businesses. In
that capacity, he worked for Smith Management Company, the entity
that assumed responsibility for the restaurants when the new owner defaulted on its payments. When a court order failed to effect the reposses-
sion, Lane, Englander, and one of the bouncers from a General Drive-In
bowling center went to one of the restaurants and physically ejected the
non-paying purchaser. After that, the restaurants became Englander's responsibility until they were sold again, to Chelsea Industries, in 1967.
After a brief tour of duty with the new restaurant owners, Englander
returned to assist Dick Smith as manager of the real estate department
in 1969.[35]

An important addition to management in 1962 was Herbert Hurwitz. Harvard-educated, with a background in sales, Hurwitz came in as
an assistant general manager in charge of bowling operations. He was
effective in that role and even more effective in closing the business out
when it came time for that. Hurwitz advanced to assistant vice president
of the corporation by 1966 and successfully moved over to theater operations when the last bowling centers were leased, becoming vice president
for theaters in 1969.

As this management group came together around Dick Smith in the years following his father's death, the decision to divest the bowling business helped to further the coalescence of an effective team. It was not a foregone conclusion. Pinsetter manufacturers were applying pressure to keep operators like General Drive-In in the industry, and there was strong sentiment within the company in favor of trying to make a go of it based on the strong performance of the few bowling centers outside New England. However, Smith was concerned about the opportunity cost of diverting management's energies away from the theater business. He entertained "a lot of discussion" about the issue but in the end made the decision to withdraw. Overall Smith judged that the dynamic of disagreement and resolution strengthened the group, as well as his own position of leadership within it.[36]

With the theater business still growing, there was plenty of work for everyone to do. Howard Spiess recalled the collegial atmosphere in the theater group:

> Five days a week we'd come in, but we'd also always come in on Saturday. It became almost compulsory . . . and it was largely a bull session. [We] . . . would bring in some bagels and cream cheese . . . and generally, it would be Mel Wintman, it would be Dick Smith, it would be Sam Seletsky, Ed Lane and myself, and later there would be Joe Saunders, and you would sit around and talk about anything that was on your mind.[37]

Key decisions were often made in that setting—for example, to allow soft drinks and popcorn to be consumed at theater seats, a reversal of long-standing company policy that had been aimed at preserving the cleanliness and decorum of General Drive-In theaters. At the same time, it was frequently a forum for controversy and competition, especially among Wintman, Seletsky, and Lane. The two theater executives exchanged unwelcome commentary on operations in each other's areas. Lane was usually in the middle, although his position at the head of an independent control department, reporting directly to Smith, was also at times the source of friction. Moreover, the rivalries that divided them were often fed by disputes among their assistants. At times, Spiess remembered, it could be "a three-ring circus."[38]

Dick Smith presided over all of it, tolerating a great deal of conflict and competition and encouraging a full airing of views on matters of substance, but always reserving the authority to make the final decision himself. He maintained an authoritative presence in part through active involvement in the business. His grasp of key issues—real estate, finance, operations, competition—was impressive. Moreover, in an era when many theater owners seemed to view exhibition primarily as a platform for moving into film production and distribution, Smith was in the trenches, negotiating most of the company's shopping-center leases himself. At the same time, he was a willing delegator who gave his managers full authority and a great deal of autonomy in their functional areas. That combination produced a loyal, extremely hardworking, and independent-minded group of operating executives.[39]

The decade of the 1960s was a heady time for the management team, with the theater business growing by leaps and bounds. Dick Smith pulled in harness with his operating lieutenants in building a national circuit of shopping-center theaters, and he established an easy-going collegiality with them in the Saturday morning bull sessions. On a personal level, however, he kept his distance from his employees, as his father had done, never socializing with them outside the office. He was not one to attend conventions or to organize company events that included the family. In those days the management of the firm was predominantly Jewish, in keeping with the still-strong ethnic character of the industry. Yet, if there were some in the group who placed special value on that ethnic identity and who would regret its passing as the company entered new industries and added new personnel, Dick Smith offered them little support or solace. Again like his father, he was conscientious but not zealous in promoting Jewish causes. He had no particular interest in preserving the ethnic aspect of the corporate culture but viewed it simply as a fact of life in that era of his company's development.

Under Smith's leadership, the often-contentious team held together in one form or another for more than a decade, even though the company was known to be paying some of the lowest salaries in the industry. Smith himself did not draw a large salary, and that fact kept a lid on compensation at all levels of the organization. The few top executives who were compensated through Smith Management Company benefited from a profit-sharing program, and key men, Wintman and Lane in particular, were rewarded with stock options that made them quite wealthy by the time they retired. But for the most part, people were motivated by the excitement of a company moving rapidly toward leadership in its industry and by the opportunity to play a significant role in it. Individuals who helped to build the business in that era would regret its passing, as growth and diversification carried the firm and its leader far afield from their origins in the theater industry. Yet the smashing success of the shopping-center theater strategy, which they implemented, made growth and change inevitable.

THE THEATER EXPANSION PROGRAM, 1961–1973

In the 1960s the character of General Drive-In's theater holdings changed dramatically. In 1963 the company began to expand its drive-in circuit once again, through acquisitions of profitable going concerns. In that way, its chain of outdoor theaters grew from twenty-six to a peak of forty-nine by 1968, where it stayed until 1973, when the company began to lease and sell off its drive-in properties. Its group of resort and other indoor theaters dwindled slightly until the company made two acquisitions of indoor theater chains—the Mann Theater circuit in Minneapolis–St. Paul in 1970 and a group of forty-seven theaters from Loew's in 1972.

In contrast, from 1963 to 1973, the number of its shopping-center theaters surged from 10 to 319 (see Figure 2.3). In acknowledgment of the shift in emphasis, the company changed its name to General Cinema Corporation in 1964. Nine years later, General Cinema would claim the largest, most profitable theater circuit in the nation.

A driving force in the expansion program was the determination to become national in scope. That became a realistic goal when the company succeeded in establishing its credibility with the insurance firms that were financing shopping centers. Success was in sight as early as 1962 when, Smith noted in his annual report, General Cinema reached "an enviable position in the industry, where substantial real estate developers have offered us as many theatre sites in major regional shopping centers as we can absorb within the present limits of our financial resources."[40]

Having established those key relationships, the company was in a position to ride the shopping-center development boom to preeminence in the theater industry. Where competitors might carefully research the socio-economic characteristics of potential theater locations, General Cinema left that kind of analysis to others. It was one of the few companies that had no geographic restrictions on its expansion program. Its three criteria for locating a theater in a particular mall were the size of population served, the type of development, and the structure of the deal with the developer. Smith insisted on lease agreements that would allow him to realize an immediate after-tax return on investment of at least 15 percent. "And if there weren't too many other theaters competing" in the area, remembered Morris Englander, "we'd go . . . bingo. Many times in the early days the decision was made in a few minutes. Those were the fun days." That thrilling pace led to a decade of phenomenal growth of the shopping-center circuit.[41]

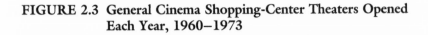

FIGURE 2.3 **General Cinema Shopping-Center Theaters Opened
Each Year, 1960–1973**

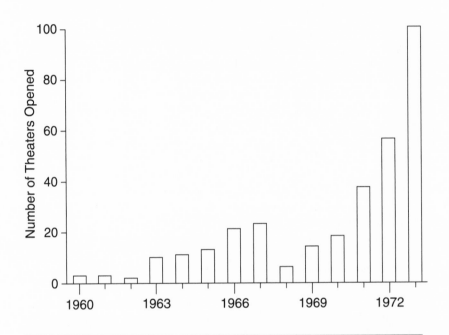

Source: General Cinema Annual Reports. Number includes "splits" of singles into twins or triples. The
1971 annual report attributes the lower rates in 1968–1970 to "lack of sufficient mortgage financing for
shopping center development."

A defining characteristic of General Cinema's expanding shopping-
center theater circuit was that all the theaters were fundamentally alike.
Their design, by architect William Reisman, stressed simplicity and comfort, and it became a trademark of the suburban cinema concept. The
most unusual feature was the so-called shadowbox screen—a simple presentation surface, with no stage or drapes. It was criticized at first, both
on aesthetic grounds and also because it eliminated the jobs of stagehands,
who in many areas were members of the projectionists' union. But in the
end it became a standard feature, touted by the company as "one of the
largest screens in the industry."[42]

In spring 1962, General Cinema (then still General Drive-In) also
took the lead in launching a twin theater, at the Peabody shopping center
in Massachusetts. This was an idea that Dick Smith had discussed with
his father before Phil Smith's death in 1961, at which time the company

already had two twin drive-in theaters in operation. The concept of the twin had broad appeal in the industry. The same film could play in both auditoriums at staggered starting times, so people could attend virtually anytime, at their convenience. Alternatively, the theaters could play different shows—for example, holding over a popular attraction while keeping up with new releases or playing children's movies simultaneously with features their parents might enjoy.[43]

To the team at General Cinema, the twin seemed to be the ideal theater type. The concept perfectly complemented the image that the company sought for its cinema theater—an integral part of the modern suburban lifestyle. Its "most important advantage," stated the annual report of 1962, was the staggered time schedule, "permitting the busy suburbanite to attend at his own convenience." Following the model of its twin drive-ins, General Cinema's twin theater was a one-story building with a single lobby, concession stand, and projection booth, centrally located to serve two auditoriums. The layout allowed substantial savings in labor costs and helped to make General Cinema's theaters some of the most profitable in the industry.[44]

The simple design for the twin opened the way to the many-screened "multiplex" theater that became the norm by the 1980s. However, General Cinema was not to be the leader in the multiplexing of America. For most of the 1960s, the projectionists' union refused to allow companies to employ a single operator for multiple screens. For a company that did a great deal of business in areas of the country that were strongly unionized, that loomed as an obstacle to multiplexing into the late 1960s. In contrast, Stanley Durwood built his American Multi-Cinema chain in the 1960s by moving aggressively to four- and six-screen units in locations where he could use nonunion labor. Yet General Cinema could still count itself the clear winner in that era. Even with two projectionists in the booth, the profitability of the twin screen fueled an expansion program that made the company undisputed "king of the flicks" by the early 1970s.[45]

NUMBER ONE IN THE INDUSTRY

General Cinema's acquisition of forty-eight theaters from Loew's Corporation in 1972 put it over the top of $100 million annual theater revenues. It thus became the biggest revenue generator in the industry, although ABC-Paramount was still larger in number of theaters. That last barrier fell in 1973, with a building spurt that added one hundred new screens and made General Cinema the leading theater circuit by all measurements. A decade before, when the theater building program was just taking off, ABC-Paramount had owned more than five times as many theaters as General Cinema. The ascendance of an independent company over Loew's and ABC-Paramount—the last two significant players of the once-dominant theater chains divested by the Hollywood majors— brought the restructuring of the film exhibition industry close to completion.[46]

In 1948 the five majors had controlled 14 percent of all theaters in the United States. By 1957, the five independent theater companies that were created in the divestiture process controlled only 7 percent of the total. Moreover, because of population shifts, their once-favored downtown locations were no longer the most desirable. The experience of the drive-ins clearly indicated that more conveniently located theaters would be able to compete for first-run film product and would eventually win the competition. That was why Phil Smith, with theaters closing all around him in the late 1950s, had been eager to undertake a building program to expand his shopping-center theater circuit.[47]

By the early 1970s, the shift in power that Smith had anticipated had come to pass, and his own company was the greatest beneficiary. As the largest theater circuit in the country, General Cinema attained preeminence in the all-important relations with the suppliers of film product. Not only were suburban shopping-center theaters routinely able to obtain first-run engagements, but General Cinema also was a favored customer of the leading distribution companies. The company's size and the size of its contribution to distributors' revenues strengthened its position in the routine negotiations for films, including "splitting" in the most competitive areas. Splitting was a device by which competition for film product had been controlled in the industry since the Paramount decision: "A process whereby exhibitors in a given market meet and determine, with the consent and approval of the film distributor, which theatres will negotiate for specific pictures, based upon the terms and conditions established by the distributor." Banned in the 1980s as a violation of antitrust regulations, the practice of splitting helped to ensure the profitability of film exhibition as long as it was in operation.[48]

In short, by the early 1970s the theater industry had resolved itself once again into an oligarchy as strong and apparently as stable as the one that had existed before 1948 but with different leading players. Not long after General Cinema established itself as industry leader, it was joined at the top by Durwood's American Multi-Cinema and United Artists Theaters. Of the companies divested from the five majors, only Loew's would remain near the top through the 1970s.

On the production and distribution side, however, the principal players remained largely the same, and their combined weight more than balanced that of the leading theater companies. In 1948 the original "Big Eight" production and distribution powers (the majors—Warner Brothers, Paramount, Metro-Goldwyn-Mayer, Twentieth Century Fox, RKO—plus Columbia, Universal, and United Artists) accounted for 80 percent of all domestic film rentals. By 1973, that figure had dropped only a little, to 76 percent, for the seven companies remaining after RKO disappeared. Over those twenty-five years, during many of which the theater industry was in disarray, the distributors were able to establish their claim to a large share of exhibition revenues, and they profited greatly from the steady rise in ticket prices. Yet the number of films released annually continued to decline through most of the 1960s. As a result, by the early 1970s, with so few films available each year, theaters were once again forced to bid for pictures before seeing them—indeed, even before they were made.[49]

The restructuring of the motion picture industry thus created two centers of power—exhibitors on one side and producer-distributors on the other—where previously there had been only one. Conflict between the two became a dominant theme of industry relations, as the distributors pushed to gain a greater share of exhibition revenues by continually increasing the cost and improving the terms of film rentals. The dwindling supply of feature films was another perennial bone of contention.

Throughout the 1960s, the number of films released each year fluctuated around 250, a figure that made theater owners extremely unhappy. Many of the major theater companies attempted to break into the production and distribution side of the industry in the late 1960s. They were motivated in large part by determination to increase the supply of films for their theaters, and also by their awareness that profits in the industry tended to flow disproportionately back to the production-distribution side. Yet that side of the industry proved to be closed to newcomers. Would-be producers such as Walter Reade Company, National General, United Artists Theatre Circuit, and Cinerama all suffered heavy losses for their efforts. That General Cinema was one of the few major theater companies that did not launch a production program in that era helps to explain why it was so far ahead of most in profitability.[50]

GENERAL CINEMA IN 1973

At the time that General Cinema established its preeminence in the theater industry, Dick Smith, at forty-nine, had run the company on his own for some twelve years. The long-term contract with Smith Management Company and the family's 30 percent share of General Cinema's stock, backed up by the 20 percent voted by Sidney Stoneman, ensured Smith's continuing control for the foreseeable future. Yet beyond the personal link between the family and the firm that he himself represented, General Cinema to all appearances was no longer a family enterprise.

In keeping with the family culture with which they had grown up, Dick Smith's sister, Nancy Lurie, left to him all decisions regarding the company and her family's stockholdings in it. His policy was never to sell stock and to keep dividends relatively low, though they increased every year, as the company continued to prosper. Both families were able to live comfortably with such an arrangement, so that most divisive of family-firm issues did not trouble General Cinema. Smith's wife, Susan, though an active partner in many of his charitable activities, played no such role in company affairs. His oldest child, Amy, was in college, and his younger children, Robert and Debra, were in their teens. The issue of succession was therefore still a wide-open question and would remain so for some time. In the mid-1970s Smith would initiate a process of professionalization within General Cinema's top management that brought in a number of potential nonfamily successors, carrying the company one step farther from its entrepreneurial origins some fifty years earlier in Smith Theatrical Enterprises.[51]

Yet, as much as the company was changing, the continuity that Dick Smith provided was perhaps its greatest asset. Phil Smith had bequeathed to his son a vision of the potential for long-term growth in the family business and a firm grasp of the fundamental elements of competitive strategy that would make that vision a reality. By 1973, the anticipated growth had been achieved many times over, though it had not followed precisely the path laid out for it in 1960. Bowling had long since been abandoned, and for most of the decade of the 1960s Dick Smith focused all of his energies and corporate resources on building the theater circuit. Nevertheless, diversification had remained a central element of corporate strategy, and in 1968 Smith undertook a diversification into soft drink bottling that radically altered the shape of his company.

The strategy of diversification was by no means unusual in the motion picture industry. By the 1970s, a number of the major studios had been acquired by diversified firms—Paramount by Gulf & Western, Universal by MCA, and United Artists by Transamerica. Metro-Goldwyn-Mayer diversified into hotels and gambling casinos, and Twentieth Century Fox into soft drink bottling, television, and record publishing. Other major exhibitors were also diversification-minded and pursued many of the same opportunities as the Smiths. United Artists Theatre Circuit ventured into drive-in restaurants and bowling alleys, among other things. The Marcus Corporation of Milwaukee invested in fast-food restaurants. Wometco Enterprises, a Florida theater company that followed a course of diversification similar to General Cinema's, went into soft drink bottling, FM radio, and television broadcasting.[52]

Yet General Cinema undertook its diversification program in 1968 on a scale that far surpassed anything that others in the industry were doing.[53] While still driving toward the completion of its national theater circuit, the company moved aggressively to establish a position close to the top of the soft drink bottling industry. That aggressiveness was also part of the legacy of Phil Smith. It was a characteristic of the firm that had become more deeply ingrained with each successive venture—into drive-ins, restaurants, bowling, shopping-center theaters—and would continue to shape General Cinema's diversification strategy as long as Dick Smith was running the company.

CHAPTER

3

DIVERSIFICATION

By proclamation of the governor, Saturday, February 26, 1966, was Joan Crawford Day in the state of Florida. On that day Miss Crawford, a member of the board of directors of PepsiCo, along with Donald Kendall, PepsiCo's president and CEO, formally opened the new $2 million facility of American Beverage Corporation's Pepsi-Cola Bottlers of Miami—"the world's finest bottling plant." It may be that most of the Miami residents who attended the plant's open house were attracted primarily by the chance to be greeted by the glamorous movie queen or by the offer of free Pepsi, Lay's Potato Chips, and door prizes. But they were also treated to a tour of the gleaming new plant, which displayed state-of-the-art equipment for every phase of soft drink bottling.[1]

In the Syrup Room, the secret-formula concentrate supplied by PepsiCo was combined with sugar and converted to syrup in batches of roughly six thousand gallons. A modern plant laboratory with electronic controls monitored the mixture, checking especially for the correct level of sweetness. In a separate room water was purified chemically, then passed through two stages of filtration and a "water polisher." Bottles were sanitized, ten thousand at a time, and inspected electronically as they moved on a conveyor line. Meanwhile the carbo-cooler combined water and syrup, carbonated and chilled the mixture, then piped it into the can line or to the bottling machines, which filled and capped 650 sixteen-ounce bottles per minute. From the Bottling Room the filled cans and bottles were moved into the packaging and warehouse area, where they were automatically packed in cartons and cases and stacked on pallets that could be moved within the plant and loaded onto trucks by fork lift. To employees, if not to the visiting public, the automation of that labor-intensive phase of operations was one of the most significant improvements on standard practice in the new plant.

From a longer-term view, the most significant aspect of the plant was its layout. Grouped together on one end of the building were the Syrup Room, the Water Treatment Room, and the room containing the giant compressors needed to power the carbonation and bottling operations. The carbo-cooler, bottle washers, and can and bottling lines occupied a single large room in the middle. The packaging and storage area and loading docks lay beyond, at the other end of the building. That arrangement allowed for significant expansion of capacity without expensive relocation of heavy equipment. It was innovative at the time and would remain a model for bottling-plant layout for decades.[2]

Another forward-looking element of the Miami plant was the inclusion of canning facilities. Though soft drinks in cans had been around for over a decade, few bottlers of major brands had yet invested in the equipment required to produce them. Most relied on the contract canning industry that had sprung up along with the new technology. Yet the potential of the new form of "convenience packaging" was clearly suggested by the fact that, of all soft drinks sold in containers (as opposed to fountain sales), the portion in cans had grown from 1.5 percent in 1955 to over 12 percent in 1965. During the same period, sales of soft drinks in containers grew from 80 to 86 percent of total soft drink sales. In short, the can line in the new plant, as much as its thoughtful layout-for-growth and the fanfare with which it was greeted by PepsiCo, clearly betokened both the leadership position of American Beverage Corporation in the beverage industry and its bright prospects for future growth.[3]

In 1965 American Beverage was the second largest of Pepsi's roughly five hundred franchised bottlers. It encompassed three major Pepsi franchises in addition to the one in Miami—in Akron, Dayton, and Youngstown, Ohio—as well as a proprietary-brand enterprise, the Golden Age Beverage Company, of Houston, Texas. It was a family business, founded in the formative years of the industry and developed to a leading position largely by the entrepreneurial foresight and drive of its second generation of owner-managers. It is hardly surprising that General Cinema would find the company an attractive candidate for acquisition.

Early in 1967 Ed Lane toured the Miami Pepsi plant. Having looked over the growth figures for American Beverage and for the soft drink industry as a whole, he would never forget his first impression of the place. "We were taken on a tour through the plant," said Lane, "and I watched the bottling operation, the little bottles going around the drum. To this day I have the same vision. I saw little green dollar signs on the bottles."[4]

Dick Smith was not specifically seeking to enter the soft drink business in the mid-1960s, but, like Lane, he recognized an unusual opportunity when it was presented to him. The business of soft drink bottling in that period was fragmented. Most bottling companies were small, family-owned franchise operations. Predictions for growth in the industry were generally pessimistic, and there was not a lot of acquisition activity. Smith saw a wide-open field with few strong participants, much as his father had seen in drive-ins and shopping-center theaters. His program to expand the theater circuit was in high gear. Yet, with the disposition of bowling operations nearly complete, the dynamic of steadily rising profits and cash flow propelled General Cinema to return to the search for a new business in which to invest.

DIVERSIFICATION IN THE CONGLOMERATE ERA

As ever, the theater business remained a high cash flow operation, even with the shopping-center theater circuit expanding at a rapid rate. By 1966, General Cinema's growing financial strength once again impelled the company toward a strategy of diversification, while the changing business environment provided a supportive context. With the conglomerate movement approaching its height in the mid-1960s, diversification by acquisition became the management fad of the day, and Dick Smith's strategy for growth placed him squarely in the mainstream. On the other hand, he pursued that strategy with a difference that would make General Cinema one of the more successful—though lesser known—diversifiers of that era.

By every financial measurement, the company was averaging better than 20 percent annual growth by the mid-1960s (see Table 3.1). Cash income increased at an average annual rate of 26 percent and financed continued expansion, largely by strengthening the company's borrowing power. Between 1961 and 1966, its long-term obligations increased from $2 million to nearly $10 million. At the same time, General Cinema took on a higher level of off-balance-sheet debt in the form of long-term leases, which rose in value from $1 million to $5 million in that period.[5]

In 1964 the company's traditional 50-cent-per-share dividend was

TABLE 3.1 General Cinema Growth, 1961–1966 (millions $)

Year	*1961*	*1962*	*1963*	*1964*	*1965*	*1966*
Revenues	$10.4	$12.8	$15.6	$20.8	$25.1	$33.7
Net Income	$0.7	$0.8	$0.9	$1.3	$1.6	$2.0
Cash Income	$1.2	$1.5	$1.7	$2.3	$2.8	$3.6

Note: Cash income is net income plus depreciation.

Source: General Cinema Corporation, Annual Report for 1966.

augmented for the first time with a 10 percent "stock dividend" (an eleven-for-ten stock split), and its shares were listed on the American Stock Exchange. The following year General Cinema split its stock again, five-for-four, and increased the cash dividend by 10 percent.

Yet very quickly the profitability of the shopping-center theaters overwhelmed Smith's ability to make prudent investments in new theaters. Outside the Smith and Stoneman families, the largest group of General Cinema stockholders were financial institutions. To remain attractive to such sophisticated investors, the company would have to provide growth, not just dividends. The wisdom of the day dictated that, if Smith hoped to sustain his company's growth at 20 percent over the long term, he would have to diversify.[6]

In the mid-1960s highly diversified giants like ITT, Litton Industries, and Textron were setting new standards for growth. Moreover, although public attention focused on the activities of the leading conglomerates, there was also a wave of unrelated diversification on a much smaller scale by companies of all sizes and types. According to Royal Little, Textron's creator, the company organized to pursue unrelated diversification was "the corporate form of today as well as tomorrow." Conglomerate managers like Little strove to perpetuate high rates of growth and profitability through aggressive programs of acquisition. In the flush decade of the 1960s many of them appeared to be succeeding.[7]

If pursuing a strategy of unrelated diversification was enough to make Dick Smith a conglomerateur, then indeed he became one. Through acquisitions in the soft drink industry, he created a company that was like a conglomerate in that it comprised unrelated businesses, with neither of its two major divisions contributing more than 70 percent of total revenues. Yet, though Smith borrowed ideas from advocates of diversification like Little, he held himself apart from the movement in a number of significant ways.

In outlook he was still fundamentally the proprietor of an owner-managed firm, as distinct from a career professional at the head of a large public corporation. The crux of that distinction lay in Smith's attitude toward growth, which exhibited on the one hand the sort of bet-the-firm confidence of the entrepreneur and, on the other, an abhorrence of growth for the sake of bigness characteristic of someone whose personal wealth depended primarily on stock appreciation, not salary. He was not interested in expanding the company beyond his ability to retain operating control. Early on Smith began to use the image of a three-legged stool to describe his vision of a diversified General Cinema—three substantial businesses providing a stable platform for long-term growth.[8]

Smith placed few limitations on the type of company he would consider as a potential acquisition but maintained high criteria for the financial terms of any transaction. Again, the operative principle was avoidance of the risk of losing control of the company. In 1967 he came close to buying a $100 million vending machine company but did not, because it would have required using a substantial block of stock to complete the deal. This reluctance to dilute ownership by using stock for an acquisition in itself clearly distinguished him from the leading conglomerate builders of the day.[9]

Smith's acquisition program was modest by their standards. Yet he was anything but timid. General Cinema's diversification into soft drink bottling must be judged one of the more successful of its era, largely because of his aggressive expansion of the new subsidiary to a position of leadership in an industry that would prove to be one of the best performers of the 1970s. After acquiring American Beverage Corporation in 1968, Smith continued with a series of acquisitions—three multifranchise companies and a dozen individual franchises—that would transform General Cinema into the largest independent bottling company in the country by 1975. This approach—quite distinct from the classic conglomerate strategy, which led to a much larger portfolio of businesses but not necessarily to industry leadership in any of them—produced results well beyond what the world would come to expect from highly diversified firms. In 1977, when the corporation joined the ranks of the *Fortune* 500, it would be in the bottom tenth of the list in terms of size but in the top fifth for net return on equity and in the top 4 percent for ten-year growth in earnings per share and total return to shareholders.[10]

Finding the third leg of the stool, however, would prove an elusive goal. Between 1968 and 1973, General Cinema purchased television and FM radio stations, initiated the start-up of a furniture retail chain, and contemplated entering motion picture production to address the perennial problem of inadequate film supply. In addition, Smith gave consideration to a wide range of possible acquisitions that were not pursued. Yet, in contrast to the move into soft drink bottling, these were far more in the nature of entrepreneurial ventures than of full-fledged diversification efforts by a highly acquisitive firm. Despite its economic performance, and for all its diversification activity, General Cinema remained a small and relatively obscure participant in the merger movement of this period.

The company also lacked the multidivisional structure and corporate staff typical of conglomerates. The professionalization of General Cinema's top management did not take place until the mid-1970s, long after the company had attained the size normally associated with that transition. Thus, both in seeking out new businesses and subsequently in managing acquired companies, it was Smith who held the responsibility for making diversification work. Managers of the new soft drink bottling subsidiary reported directly to him, as did Mel Wintman, who ran the theater business. The ventures in communications and furniture retailing were off-balance-sheet operations also linked to the corporation through Dick Smith. Thus in every respect, General Cinema's formative stage as a diversified firm strongly bore the stamp of his personal style and approach to business problems.[11]

In 1966 John McClowan of State Mutual Life Insurance, a company that Smith knew through shopping-center financings, suggested that he might be interested in talking to Julius Darsky, who was considering selling the American Beverage Corporation. "We were not extensively surveying the market for acquisitions" at that time, Smith remembered, "but when we heard of a specific opportunity I hastened to become acquainted with Mr. Darsky." Before long, Smith had become "intrigued" by the soft drink bottling business, and he embarked on what would turn out to be a year-and-a-half long effort to buy Darsky's company.[12]

AMERICAN BEVERAGE CORPORATION: THE DARSKY FAMILY FIRM

Nathan H. Darsky immigrated to the United States in 1911 and settled in Youngstown, Ohio. In 1914 he put seven dollars down on a $45 bottling machine powered by foot pedal and began producing bottled ginger ale, which he marketed as Youngstown Brand Ginger Ale. By 1930, the family firm, the City Bottling Works of Youngstown, was selling somewhat less than $100,000 in soft drinks a year. Nathan was joined in the business by his two sons, Julius and Joseph, and by his son-in-law, Carl Lockshin, in the early 1930s. In 1932 they renamed the company and their products Golden Age, and they successfully developed a regional market for Golden Age Ginger Ale. Five years later they acquired a franchise to bottle and sell Pepsi-Cola in the Akron, Ohio area.

By that time Coca-Cola, invented in Atlanta in 1886, had been produced and sold in bottles through a franchise system for nearly forty years. The sale of exclusive franchises, including the right to purchase syrup, to bottle, and to sell Coke within a limited region, had created a national product at a time when no single company could have undertaken on its own to build the plants and establish the distribution facilities that such a product required. Because franchises were sold as property, "for all time," they became the foundation of thousands of small but very profitable local and regional businesses.[13]

Pepsi-Cola was developed by Caleb Bradham in New Bern, North Carolina in 1893. It was sold by about one hundred franchised bottlers on the eve of World War I. In the postwar years the company foundered, and 80 percent of the stock of the Pepsi-Cola Company was bought in 1931 by Loft, Inc., a chain of candy stores whose owner was looking for a soft drink to sell in its soda fountains. It was not at the soda fountain, however, but in the local market that the new owners of Pepsi turned its fortunes around. Abandoning the ten-cent, 6.5-ounce bottle, an industry standard set by Coca-Cola in 1899, they offered twelve ounces of Pepsi for five cents: "Twice as Much for a Nickel, Too." That proved to be just the right appeal to depression-weary American consumers and started Pepsi on its way to becoming a significant competitor to Coca-Cola.[14]

The lesson of that marketing coup—that packaging and price, as much as brand-name recognition and loyalty, were vital in selling soft drinks—was not lost on Julius Darsky. By 1937, Darsky was general manager of the Golden Age Beverage Company. He moved to Akron to manage the newly built bottling plant and to build a market for Pepsi there, where no Pepsi franchise had existed before. Within four years his plant was selling 500,000 cases of Pepsi a year, and in 1940 Golden Age bought additional Pepsi franchises in Houston, Texas and Youngstown, Ohio.[15]

Over the next twenty-five years Darsky built his company, and his own reputation, into a position of leadership in the beverage industry. During the 1940s, he concentrated primarily on building the markets for Pepsi and for Golden Age in his territories, adding a number of new flavors to the Golden Age line. In an industry in which profit margins were low and success depended almost entirely on local factors—the week-to-week competition against other soft drinks on store shelves—Darsky excelled at getting his products prominently displayed and at using packaging, pricing, and local advertising and promotion to gain consumer recognition and build volume. He was also an innovator in plant technology, the first to install a conveyor system to move bottles around the plant and, in 1954, the first to install a can line.[16]

In the years during which he built his company, Julius Darsky was an energetic, hard-driving entrepreneur, totally committed to pushing his company to the top of the industry. He had "an eye for detail," and he made it a point to know and speak to every one of his employees by name. Not surprisingly, he was active in industry organizations as well, serving as president of the national Pepsi-Cola Bottlers Association in 1950 and of the Ohio State Bottlers Association in 1952–1953. He was the kind of man who would stand up at a convention and exhort his colleagues: "Bottlers should stop every once in a while to take stock, look for new ways of doing things and then get off their tails and go to work."[17]

Within his own company Darsky was surrounded by loyal employees and, at the top levels of management, family members. His brother, Joe Darsky, ran the Golden Age operation in Houston. The Darskys' brother-in-law, Carl Lockshin, managed Golden Age in Youngstown until his death in 1952, when he was succeeded by his son, Bert Lockshin. When the company purchased the Pepsi franchise for Dayton, Ohio in 1952, its management was taken over by Herbert Paige, a young engineering student who had risen rapidly through the ranks in Akron and who, within a few years, would become Darsky's son-in-law. Later another son-in-law, Stuart Giller, joined the company and took responsibility for operations in Akron.

Under that regime Golden Age Beverages continued to prosper. It became a public company in 1959 by merging with and assuming a majority shareholder position in American Beverage Corporation. In 1962 American Beverage purchased the Miami, Florida franchise, and by February 1966, when the new Miami plant was officially opened, American Beverage Company was selling nearly $20 million of soft drinks a year.[18]

Yet before the end of the year, American Beverage Corporation was for sale. Julius Darsky was nearing sixty, his father was in his eighties, and the fortunes of the entire family were bound up in those of the company. The corporate minutes hint at conflict within the boardroom—Herb Paige resigned all of his positions in American Beverage in January 1967—but there is no conclusive evidence as to why the family decided to sell the company when it did.[19] As the deal making progressed with General Cinema over the next fifteen months, Dick Smith made it clear that a prerequisite for his acquisition of American Beverage was agreement by the Darsky management team to stay on and run the business. He was sensitive to a certain ambivalence among the Darskys about selling the business they had built, but he was not about to relinquish the opportunity opened to him.

SOFT DRINK BOTTLING: A SOUND BET AT GOOD ODDS

There could hardly have been a business better suited to General Cinema's needs and desires in 1967–1968 than soft drink bottling. Smith's definition of compatible companies were those in "youth-oriented," "leisure-time," consumer or service industries. He was looking for a promising long-term investment for the profits of the theater division and was eager to leverage the strong financial position he had achieved to become a major player in a new growth industry. Among his company's managerial strengths he counted the ability to add some "showmanship" to the running of the business and, more prosaically, experience in controlling and coordinating the activities of many individual units spread across diverse geographic regions.[20]

The soft drink industry in the mid-1960s was just beginning to show signs of the glamour it would attain in the 1970s. The growth rate in per capita consumption of soft drinks was 6 percent per year, up from 2 percent per year in the 1950s, stimulated by the introduction of diet sodas, of various fruit flavors, and of a variety of new packages, including cans and nonreturnable bottles in many different sizes. At the same time there were some reasons to doubt that these gains represented the beginning of long-term growth for the industry. The age-group tagged as high consumers of soft drinks—children and young adults between ten and twenty-four years old—constituted an increasingly large proportion of the U.S. population during the 1960s, as the postwar baby boom generation moved through that phase of their lives. It seemed likely that total consumption might decrease as this generation matured and the percentage of ten- to twenty-four–year-olds dropped. In addition, with the introduction of canned soft drinks and the rise of contract canners, so-called private label soft drinks, particularly those marketed by large supermarket chains, had begun to make significant inroads into the market. The "Cola Wars" and the tremendous increase in consumption that they fostered were still far in the future. Many industry observers predicted that the franchised major brands could well face a declining share of a shrinking market.[21]

That was just the kind of situation to arouse the entrepreneurial instincts of Dick Smith, whose company had been built on accurate readings of cultural trends and a firm grasp of postwar demographics. Having weathered many a premature announcement of the demise of the theater industry, he could look on the more conservative forecasts for soft drinks as a source of opportunity—a chance to get good odds on a sound bet. Profit margins on soft drinks were low in that era, but the structure of the industry, with over two thousand independent bottlers in the mid-1960s, left the field wide open for a bold consolidator to establish a leading position and to improve margins through economies of scale and to increase volume through investment in marketing. Moreover, since Coca-Cola dominated the market at that time, it was possible to get better values in purchasing Pepsi franchises, if one was willing to bet on the underdog.[22]

Viewed in those terms, it is not hard to understand why, when Smith was introduced to the possibility of buying American Beverage Corporation in December 1966, he wasted no time in making contact with its owners. The asking price for American Beverage was $16.1 million—nearly nine times 1967 earnings and $2 million more than the shareholders' equity in General Cinema at the time. That was a high price for a beverage company at the time and a big pill for any acquiring company to swallow. Smith's pursuit of diversification would require both nerve and ingenuity.[23]

FINANCING DIVERSIFICATION

During 1967, the pieces of a deal were put into place. General Cinema began negotiations with American Beverage through the mediation of George Haas, a former Pepsi executive who had become an independent financier and deal maker in the beverage industry. Haas had experience in financing acquisitions of beverage plants and equipment through sale-leaseback arrangements, and that was to be the principal instrument that would allow General Cinema to acquire a company larger than itself. Twelve million of the $16 million purchase price could be recouped by selling and leasing back American Beverage's four main plants, in Miami, Akron, Dayton, and Youngstown, with their bottling equipment. Haas helped to set up a leasing company to buy the plants, and Smith arranged underwriting of the deal by a consortium of insurance companies led by Massachusetts Mutual.

Then, in December, everything fell apart. The insurance companies delayed their decision to finance the deal beyond the deadline for closing, and Darsky, though he would not renege on negotiations so long in the works, signaled his hesitancy to complete the sale by raising the price to $18.1 million. General Cinema's decision to ante up an additional $2 million to get into the beverage industry was a difficult one, but it was made somewhat easier because, by 1968, the longer-range view of where the acquisition might take the company was beginning to come into focus.

Through George Haas, Smith had made a connection to the network of Pepsi-Cola bottlers that would facilitate his acquiring additional, smaller franchises to build a soft drink bottling division around the core of American Beverage. He had also begun to organize the financial backing that would enable him to do that in a way that allowed General Cinema to make a forceful entry into its new line of business without either abandoning the program of shopping-center theater expansion or diluting the stockholders' ownership of the corporation.

Since the Great Depression, when Philip Smith had insisted on repaying his debts in full, the First National Bank of Boston had been General Cinema's principal lending partner. Yet in 1968, as Dick Smith later commented, "Our appetite was somewhat larger than our reach." To pull together the resources necessary to take a significant position in the soft drink business without cutting back on his other plans, Smith would need considerable debt financing. He had the support of Charles Moore and William Thompson, of Bank of Boston's Special Industries Lending Group, who could arrange the senior debt in the form of $30 million of revolving credit. "The revolving feature," Smith explained, "recognized the serendipitous nature of our need for funds" in a business that was seasonal and that would be making occasional acquisitions at unpredictable times.[24]

However, in order to make the bottling acquisitions he sought, Smith required an additional $20 million of long-term financing. He would have to raise that amount through a private placement. Moore and Thompson introduced him to Gilbert Butler at Morgan Guaranty Trust Company, and Smith convinced Butler to take $20 million of long-term subordinated notes, tied to an "equity kicker" in the form of common stock warrants.[25]

Issuing warrants necessarily involved reducing the proportion of ownership of existing stockholders, something Smith was loath to do. He sought to minimize that problem by issuing the warrants at a deep discount. Stock warrants were customarily offered at an exercise price higher than the current market price, encouraging the holder to wait to exercise them until the stock rose to an even higher price. Smith took the novel step of setting the exercise price at a substantial discount—$22.00 per share versus the selling price, near the end of 1967, of over $38.00. In effect, the warrants had an immediate gain built into them, an inducement to Morgan Guaranty to finance the debt with a far lower percentage of warrant coverage than was normal for such transactions. "It was hand-crafted financing," Smith later claimed, "and innovative at the time."[26]

The successful completion of those financial arrangements was a watershed event for General Cinema. By the end of fiscal 1969, the size of its operations would be three times that of 1967 in both revenues and earnings. The timing was excellent. The company entered the market for soft drink franchises at the very beginning of what would become a long-term trend toward consolidation in the industry.

Smith's strategy was to lay the foundation for economies of scale by buying Pepsi franchises in contiguous regions wherever possible and also by buying overlapping franchises for non-competing products, such as 7-Up and Dr Pepper. After closing the deal on American Beverage in March 1968, he went on to make another major acquisition: Pepsi-Cola Allied Bottlers, bought in November 1968, brought in nine Pepsi franchises in northern Florida and southern Georgia, Virginia and West Virginia, and Indiana. Also during 1968, the company bought five 7-Up franchises and six Dr Pepper franchises, all of which could be integrated into its Pepsi bottling operations. Further acquisitions during 1969 built on the core areas of American Beverage and Pepsi Allied. The purchase of the Robert H. Snyder Corporation in January 1969 added key franchises in Cleveland and Elyria, Ohio, while the addition of Pepsi franchises for Atlanta, Athens, and Gainesville, Georgia, as well as 7-Up and Dr Pepper franchises for Athens, Dr Pepper for Vincennes, and 7-Up for Charleston added significantly to the southern region and strengthened General Cinema's holdings in Indiana and West Virginia.

The soft drink entity created by those acquisitions was a strong one (see Table 3.2). Nationwide in 1970, Pepsi-Cola held a 20 percent share of the take-home soft drink market, whereas the average for General Cinema's Pepsi franchise areas was 25 percent. In addition, General Cinema was well positioned geographically to benefit from continuing growth in the industry. Indiana and Ohio were part of Pepsi's midwestern "heartland." In the South, especially the Deep South, Coke tended to dominate in market share, but high overall consumption of soft drinks, combined with high rates of population growth, made this a good area for all brands.[27]

Within those general parameters a few franchises were exceptional. Cleveland and Dayton enjoyed high market shares over large franchise populations. Miami Pepsi had a large population but was roughly even with Coca-Cola in market share and had to battle constantly to stay even.

**TABLE 3.2 General Cinema Beverages
Major Market Areas, 1971**

Franchise	Franchise Population (000s)	Per Capita Consumption of Pepsi Products (8-oz equivalents)	Pepsi Market Share	Coke Market Share
Cleveland, Ohio	2,375	124	27%	14%
Dayton, Ohio	809	198	41	17
Miami, Florida	1,310	96	19	18
Jacksonville, Florida	669	85	19	27
Atlanta, Georgia	1,473	78	16	50
GCC all regions	10,443	119	25	23

Note: Cleveland, Ohio data include Elyria.

Source: HGI corporate records.

In Atlanta, where Coke was born and made its headquarters, there was a large population of heavy soft drink consumers, but Pepsi faced an uphill struggle for market share.

In sum, for an investment of approximately $40 million over a period of less than two years, General Cinema achieved its diversification objective of becoming a leading force in the soft drink industry. The principal task of the next decade would be to build an effective operating division out of the newly acquired companies. Only in that way could the company fully realize the value in that substantial investment.[28]

STRUCTURAL RELATIONSHIPS IN THE DIVERSIFIED FIRM

Still close to his own entrepreneurial roots, Dick Smith showed a great deal of respect for the entrepreneurs whose businesses he acquired, and he attempted to give them as much autonomy as possible. He offered the key personnel of the major acquisitions—American Beverage, Pepsi Allied, and the Snyder Corporation in Cleveland—continuing control over their operations, setting them up as separate divisions. General Cinema's role was limited to maintaining financial controls, evaluating capital requests, and consulting on the timing of price increases.[29]

At the time, Smith recalled, there were two competing models for structuring relations between the home office and divisional management in conglomerates. At ITT, Harold Geneen maintained close control over operating executives by having their division financial officers report directly to the corporate office. "He was the spy, and the overseer, and the monitor for the business." In contrast, Royal Little at Textron allowed the divisional controller to report directly to his operating chief, with only a "dotted line" reporting relationship to headquarters. That approach allowed greater operating autonomy and much better suited Smith's sense of how he wanted to relate to his divisional managers.

> We were entrepreneurially oriented and had great sympathy for those that wanted to develop their own businesses. It's a real strain on operating entrepreneurs in a growth business if they've got a financial person who can kind of sit back and say, "It's not in the budget. You can't do that." . . . We were much more interested in a good relationship with the operating side of the business than with the financial side.[30]

Nevertheless, Smith's long-term objective was to create an entity greater than the sum of its original parts. That implied not just the infusion of capital or achievement of economies of scale, but also the standardization of management practices at the highest level across all the plants of the division. In the short run, the decision to structure the new General Cinema division loosely supported entrepreneurship. However, as Smith suggested in 1971, it also served his long-term objective of creating a unified management.

> I have resisted putting a single person in charge of beverages for a couple of reasons. First, I can't be sure whether there is anyone in the organization ready for the job yet. I would rather see how things go for awhile before deciding who the person ought to be. Second, we didn't know much about the business when we made the acquisitions. Having someone between us and the market might have restricted the amount of information flowing up here.[31]

In line with that thinking, the executives of the major units continued to manage their operations largely independently. Julius Darsky joined General Cinema's board of directors and served as president of the company's American Beverage Division. Robert T. Shircliff also joined the corporate board and was president of the Pepsi-Cola Allied Beverage

Division. The Cleveland franchise became a separate division under existing management, led by John H. Kerin, but Atlanta and the other Georgia franchises went under the wing of Shircliff and Pepsi Allied. The flow of information was ensured because Smith made himself readily accessible to beverage executives, and it was facilitated by the creation of a corporate staff position of beverage division coordinator and the assignment of General Cinema's corporate controller to monitor divisional financials.

Under that structure, the management of General Cinema's beverage operations would remain unsettled for a number of years, with a good deal of competition among regional division heads. As with his own theater management team, Smith was tolerant of the conflict that went along with such a situation. Rather than rush to end the confusion by selecting one person to run the division, he accepted it as part of a process that he believed would enable him to select the best person for the job. In that, Smith demonstrated a patient, deliberate approach that would become one of his better known characteristics in later years.

SHAPING ACQUISITIONS INTO A DIVISION

On one level competition between the bottling organizations centered largely on operating results. In that arena it was difficult for Pepsi Allied to compete: its "Pepsi heartland" franchises in Indiana were relatively small; its territories in northern Florida and southern Georgia presented extremely tough competitive conditions; and it was saddled with Atlanta, Coke's home town, where marketing Pepsi was like "guerrilla warfare." On another level, however, the competition was mainly between differing approaches to managing General Cinema's geographically dispersed bottling acquisitions. In that area, too, Robert Shircliff and Pepsi Allied came up short, because they could not embrace the approach clearly favored at corporate headquarters.[32]

Shircliff was a good deal younger than Julius Darsky, but like Darsky he had helped to build up his family's business from modest beginnings and had achieved considerable stature in the soft drink industry. He sold Pepsi Allied to General Cinema in 1968 in order to capitalize on that achievement and to provide funds to support what had become a diverse set of family interests. He joined General Cinema readily, because he saw an opportunity to continue his career in the soft drink industry, and he found Smith's interest in becoming "if not *the* major player, *a* major player" in the business essentially compatible with his own. However,

Shircliff and his Pepsi Allied team soon found themselves embattled against a far more aggressive American Beverage group.[33]

Despite General Cinema's initial policy of waiting and watching its new acquisitions perform, it did expect to achieve immediately some system-wide economies through cooperative effort and pooling of resources. Because American Beverage came in as the strongest force in the division, that strategy meant in effect that Allied was expected to accept its leadership in certain key areas. For example, Julius Darsky was responsible for coordinating purchasing and looking out for good deals, and a plan was soon developed to centralize the purchasing of glass under his supervision. Yet Allied managers had their own contacts and tended to feel that they could get as good a deal as anyone. For similar reasons they resisted the directive that Allied plants should use American Beverage's captive advertising agency. In both those cases the corporate office stepped in to insist on cooperation, but on a larger scale it was impossible to achieve the kind of interaction that could produce the desired synergy from the separate organizations.

Moreover, in key policy areas it was difficult for the corporate staff to make up for the lack of strong, unified leadership of the beverage divisions. After somewhat disappointing results in 1969, Smith sent a memo to plant and division managers calling for tighter control of expenses and dictating that plants be "price followers" in their local markets, reducing prices to meet competition, "only after you have seen and obtained evidence of a reduced price offer by one of your competitors." Smith suggested that they could remain competitive without price cutting by increasing various forms of advertising and promotions.[34]

Julius Darsky responded to Smith's memo by undertaking a divisional reorganization designed to tighten controls over plant operations. Herb Paige had rejoined American Beverage when it was acquired by General Cinema, and Darsky's reorganization made Paige effectively the operating officer of the division, responsible for plant operations and also for development of staff functions, including accounting systems and procedures, advertising, marketing, and market research. The objective, and Paige's chief assignment, was to create "the necessary controls to make sure that the operating policy established by the division manager is followed." Concomitant with those internal changes, Darsky explained, the division's management hoped to put an end to a situation in which "well-meant" operational advice was being given from corporate headquarters direct to plant managers. The division would improve its reporting of financial information from individual plants, but comments on operations or policy should come back only through established channels. Said Darsky: "In the past few months we have gotten away from this management fundamental, and if we are going to be responsible for exercising the proper fiscal and operating control of the Division, we must get back to basics, and follow this chain of command."[35]

The steps taken by the American Beverage group to establish a credible basis for greater divisional autonomy were timely. General Cinema's commitment to the principle of local initiative was increasingly strained by its determination to ensure that net profits be sufficient to support repayment of the debt incurred during the acquisition program. By mid-1970, when the three divisions submitted their budgets for 1971 and 1972, it was clear that that financial objective could not be achieved without greater coordination of the operating units. "The total monies requested by the Beverage Division are staggering," complained the corporate controller, "and far exceed the cash flow generated by operations." Each plant would have to eliminate all unnecessary capital expenditures and, in addition, would be required to provide extensive documentation for those it deemed essential. Further, Smith suggested that the plants should attempt to increase profitability by limiting price cutting and competing for market share with advertising and promotion instead. In response, by the end of fiscal 1970, the plants had made advertising expenditures equal to the entire year's operating profit.[36]

The lack of coordinated management had clearly led to dysfunction. As a result, General Cinema created, in August 1970, the Beverage Operations Committee (BOC) to provide a forum in which the principal executives of the American Beverage, Pepsi Allied, and Cleveland divisions would be forced to come together "to exchange ideas and arrive at common policies and unified objectives." The committee's role was to be that of an intermediary: it was to recommend corporate policy to the home office and to communicate it to the divisional managers for implementation. Its chairmanship was rotating, and it had two key subcommittees—one on industry relations, to be chaired by Robert Shircliff, the other on marketing, chaired by Herb Paige.[37]

EMERGENCE OF BEVERAGE DIVISION LEADERSHIP

The creation of the BOC was Herb Paige's golden opportunity. Paige had chosen to rejoin the business as manager of Miami operations when American Beverage was acquired by General Cinema, clearly seeing in the new company an avenue for advancement that had not been there for him in the family firm. Though Julius Darsky remained the titular head of the

American Beverage Division, Paige proved to be a talented manager, in step with Smith's ideas about where the business should go. He rose quickly within the new corporate structure.

Darsky moved into an advisory role at the time the BOC was created, and Paige then became head of the American Beverage Division. At roughly the same time, Bob Shircliff was elected president of the Pepsi-Cola Bottlers Association, to serve during 1971, so Paige was also given responsibility for the troubled northern Georgia franchises. With free rein to demonstrate what he could do in operations and a high-visibility arena in the BOC for contributing to corporate policy-making and long-range strategy, he was well positioned to become the leading contender for the top position in a unified beverage division.

The BOC provided a showcase for what quickly became American Beverage's "model" systems and procedures. By the time of its first meeting, capital expenditure was a burning issue between corporate management and the beverage divisions, inasmuch as the home office had decreed that they were not to exceed depreciation for fiscal 1971. Despite the unified protest of the division executives that this was an "inappropriate decision" that did not provide for the future growth of the business, the policy was firm. Paige, like everyone else, complied with this directive, paring his 1971 budget by $1.5 million. He also went one step further, drawing up a "model report format for controlling capital expenditures" in his division's plants. He presented this at the second BOC meeting, with both Lane and Smith in attendance, and the committee voted to require the Allied and Cleveland divisions to institute a similar form.[38]

Paige continued to strengthen his position over the next two years, while the position of the Pepsi Allied Division grew weaker in roughly the same proportions. He made an aggressive beginning in overhauling operations in Atlanta, transferring Miami's procedures for gathering information and controlling costs and instituting a new program of tracking sales volume by product and package in order to analyze market strengths and weaknesses. Within his own division, he pushed plant managers to provide more and more detailed information, "to reverse the flow of communications," to "stop unnecessary questions," and to "help you and Division analyze problems and solutions, thus focusing on profit opportunities and profit improvement." Corporate staff increasingly sang the praises of his management style and procedures, while American Beverage systems were promulgated as policy for all divisions by the BOC.[39]

With Shircliff occupied primarily with industry matters during 1971, Paige's voice was unquestionably the strongest on the BOC. As chairman of the BOC's Marketing Committee, he was charged with developing systems for sales reporting and marketing planning, and it was difficult for Pepsi Allied management to resist the trend toward centralization without seeming simply recalcitrant. In staff reports, Allied was sometimes compared unfavorably to American Beverage, and for his part, Paige never missed an opportunity to point out to corporate management Allied's failure to toe the line. In one instance Miles Dean, Shircliff's second-in-command, suggested that adding one new continuous forecasting procedure might simply be more time-consuming than it was worth. The company should be careful, he suggested, "to keep from 'overlaying' reporting systems to achieve our objectives." Behind the scenes, Shircliff vigorously protested to Smith the centralization of key functions, especially marketing, and he was opposed to duplicating resources provided by PepsiCo such as advertising. Yet, in the context of Paige's activities, defense of local autonomy was not a powerful argument against the trend toward professionalization and centralization of management.[40]

In 1972, at the fall meeting of the BOC, Smith announced that, beginning November 1, the three beverage divisions would be combined into a new company, GCC Beverages, under Herb Paige. Paige was to have full responsibility for operations and "P&L responsibility," reporting directly to Smith. In matters relating to the "tone and general direction of the business as well as acquisitions and future growth," he was to be guided and assisted by Bob Shircliff, acting as chairman of a reconstituted version of the BOC, the Beverage Executive Committee. The immediate goals of the reorganization were to effect a unification of bottling operations as smoothly as possible, while preserving "local initiative, creativity, and autonomy." The ultimate goal, as Dick Smith commented in 1976, was to make GCC Beverages "the best in the industry."[41]

At the same BOC meeting that he announced the creation of a unified beverage division, Smith informed its executive group that General Cinema was moving into the furniture business through the financing of start-up operations of a chain of warehouse-showrooms. He noted that retail furniture was then "a $10 billion industry, as compared to the $4.5 billion soft drink industry and the $1 billion theater business." Smith hoped that the venture would provide the foundation of a third major operating division—the steadying "third leg of the [General Cinema] stool." In fact, furniture retailing was only one of many avenues of diversification being pursued at that time.[42]

CONTINUING DIVERSIFICATION: QUEST FOR THE THIRD LEG

The years from 1967 through 1972 encompassed a period of high activity in General Cinema's quest for new, growth-oriented businesses.

Even as Smith pursued the main chance in soft drink bottling, he was also contemplating opportunities in the "entertainment" field, broadly defined to include radio and television broadcasting and movie production. Each of those, along with furniture retailing, appeared at one time or another to be a likely complement to the theater and beverage businesses.

In that period Smith met and formed a partnership with Alexander Tanger, a veteran of radio and television broadcasting in Boston who had struck out on his own to purchase and operate a radio station in Providence and to serve as a consultant to the state of Israel in setting up its national TV system. Smith and Tanger investigated cable TV, which had developed rapidly since its introduction in 1952, but ultimately they decided that the greatest opportunities lay in broadcasting.[43]

In the mid-1960s FM radio stations were poor relatives in an industry dominated by AM stations, despite the fact that FM provided a higher-quality signal. The potential was there to capture market share—and with it advertising revenues—from AM, but to do so would require heavy investment in equipment and programming. For that reason, it was still possible to purchase FM stations in major urban areas at reasonable prices, and that is what Tanger and General Cinema proposed to do. Though Smith was cautious in devising a relationship with Tanger that would keep the projected initial losses off General Cinema's balance sheet, this was just the kind of farsighted, beat-the-crowd opportunity that he found most attractive.

In June 1969 they completed an agreement under which Tanger was to organize and control an independent company to buy or develop broadcast facilities. General Cinema would finance the venture through loans ultimately convertible into 80 percent of the communications company's stock. Unofficially, Tanger and Smith agreed that they would only buy stations that could be reached nonstop from Boston's Logan airport. Pursuant to those agreements, between 1970 and 1973, GCC Communications, Inc. acquired stations in Philadelphia, Houston, Cleveland, Atlanta, and Chicago. None of them cost more than $500,000 except WEFM Chicago, which had the distinction of being the nation's first classical music station and was purchased from Zenith Corporation for $1 million. During the same period, GCC Communications entered television broadcasting by acquiring a struggling independent station, WCIX-TV, in Miami, Florida.[44]

Like the FM stations, WCIX was a property with great untapped potential in a high-growth area, but one that would require a substantial investment over a period of years before that potential could be realized. That need, balanced against General Cinema's capacity for investment, made the TV station—and communications in general—a good fit with the company's existing businesses. Like most diversifiers, however, Smith preferred to emphasize (though modestly) the potential operating synergies in management skills transferable from theaters to broadcasting. "We have been selling entertainment to the public for a long time," Smith noted to the New York Security Analysts in 1973, "I think perhaps more successfully than any other group in the country."

> There is certain expertise that grows in the marketing and promotion of entertainment. True enough, broadcasting is not all entertainment, and I would not want to be one who says that there is tremendous transferable expertise. But we have learned something about controlling a group of geographically dispersed and diverse operations; budgeting them, and controlling all the personalities that are engaged in the administration of these kinds of properties. I think you can overstate it, but I think there is a little something there.[45]

If General Cinema's long experience in "selling entertainment" did not exactly constitute expertise in the broadcasting field, it at least helps to explain Smith's readiness to undertake what amounted to start-up operations at a time when his company was ostensibly committed to acquisition of a third major operating division. His lifelong attachment to the entertainment industry must also largely explain the venture into film production that he initiated during that period.

In January 1972 Smith proposed to General Cinema's board to underwrite a film-financing corporation structured as a limited partnership and managed by an executive producer. In the late 1960s, when the annual output of films from Hollywood was about 250, Smith had resisted the trend among theater companies to enter film production. At that time, the drive to build the shopping-center theater circuit had been in full swing. In the early 1970s, with General Cinema's leadership in the theater industry secure, shortage of product loomed as a greater problem—the one significant constraint on the profitability that should have been the reward for its strategic coup. With the number of major motion pictures released each year then hovering around 300, the chief argument for undertaking film financing was to augment that supply and to provide insurance against more serious shortages in the future. On the other hand, Smith's proposal pointed out, there was always the possibility that, if the company could get a percentage of the profits and the films turned out to be successful, the return could be "spectacular." General Cinema's board of directors was unenthusiastic, and he faced opposition from key executives. However, Smith would continue to pursue the idea until he succeeded in putting together a film-financing venture that had a brief life in the mid-1970s.[46]

Within the corporation film financing and, to a lesser extent, communications might be viewed as Dick Smith's personal projects, but Alperts Furniture was definitely the product of a management-team effort. According to a statement of acquisition objectives drawn up by Ed Lane after lengthy discussion among the inner circle of General Cinema management, the company was looking for a substantial business with significant growth potential. They knew what they didn't want: "Research and development; complicated manufacturing processes; involved or unique technology; cyclical or stylized characteristics; cash flow rather than earnings."[47]

Fields they considered to be strong possibilities were direct mail marketing, household furnishings, and specialty retailing. The latter in particular seemed to fit the company's strengths—its established relationships with shopping-center developers, its experience in selecting locations and negotiating real estate deals, its ability to control geographically dispersed operations. In 1972 General Cinema was reported to be considering a variety of shopping-center ventures, including a chain of greeting card stores.[48]

However, the business they chose to enter was household furnishings. That was an industry that seemed at the time to be on the verge of a significant restructuring because of the phenomenal success of Levitz Furniture. Levitz had achieved a growth rate of 40 percent per year with its "Levitz concept" of selling furniture. In giant Levitz warehouse-showrooms, moderately priced furniture was displayed in household settings and sold at discount prices to shoppers, who could take their purchases home immediately out of stocks maintained on the premises. That, said *Business Week,* was "a dramatic challenge to an industry so hampered by high prices, slow deliveries, and unimaginative marketing that its average annual growth rate since 1960 has been a plodding 5.7%."[49]

Though Levitz had many imitators, the need to carry large inventories created a financial barrier sufficiently high to ensure that the industry would not become a free-for-all. It also met a number of other General Cinema criteria—it was a consumer industry drawing on a large demographic base, it could benefit from the company's financial strength and expertise in siting and real estate development, and it was geographically decentralized. The thinking was, said Ed Lane, "If Levitz could do it, we could do it."[50]

That confidence notwithstanding, General Cinema made a relatively modest investment in household furnishings, structured in such a way that kept it off corporate financial reports in the start-up phase. Herb Hurwitz investigated the ranks of retail furniture entrepreneurs and selected Frederic and Hershel Alpert. The company agreed to back the Alperts in opening a chain of five warehouse stores with the purchase of $500,000 of subordinated notes for each store. A portion of those notes was convertible into 70 percent of the equity of the Alperts' business. If Alperts, Inc., achieved its projected profitability by the end of 1974, General Cinema was obligated to convert the notes and subsequently to acquire the remaining 30 percent of the business. The first Alperts warehouse-showroom opened in Providence, Rhode Island in October 1972. Six more were planned, to be located adjacent to shopping centers in Milford, Connecticut, Buffalo and Albany, New York, and Cleveland and Akron, Ohio.[51]

Very quickly, however, Alperts would prove to be a weak third leg for the company stool. Fundamentally, both theaters and soft drink bottling were rather straightforward "conduit" businesses, in which General Cinema provided an outlet for nationally recognized products, and success depended primarily on picking good theater locations or franchise territories and running efficient operations. In contrast, furniture retailing required strong merchandizing skills—the ability to assemble from a multitude of potential suppliers an inventory with the right combination of style, quality, and price to appeal to consumers in a particular locale. In that area, General Cinema was wholly dependent on the Alpert brothers, who had proven themselves in traditional furniture retailing but, like everyone else, were neophytes when it came to implementing the Levitz concept. It is also not clear whether the real estate skills developed through the theater business, strongly oriented toward the financial aspects of space acquisition and less strong in sophisticated socio-economic analysis of market areas (for which General Cinema had traditionally relied on shopping-center developers), were the right ones for warehouse furniture retailing.[52]

Most important, perhaps, furniture retailing in the mid-1970s turned out not to be the high-growth industry it had seemed a few years before, as the ruinous combination of inflation and recession took its toll on consumer demand and margins. Inexpensive pleasures, movies and soft drinks, had a staying power in such tough times that durables simply did not. Everyone in the industry struggled under those conditions, including Levitz. The Alperts stores were unable to break into the black, and, by 1975, General Cinema curtailed plans to expand the chain beyond four stores then completed in Providence, Albany, Buffalo, and Cleveland and extended to 1981 the date for deciding on a further commitment.[53]

By that time it would be clear that any new diversification effort would have to happen on a much larger scale and in a different way. Said Smith in 1976:

> When the company was smaller, it was okay to think about starting a field from scratch, but that isn't as appropriate now as the purchase of an existing business. It should be big enough to have an immediate impact on earnings. It should have a capable management, good growth prospects, and a continuing need for investment. At the same time, General Cinema must be able to bring its competence to bear on the new business. I don't want to be dependent on the specialized skills of a few individuals.[54]

Those were tough criteria. Yet Dick Smith had some very high standards to live up to in charting the future course of General Cinema. Under any circumstances, it would be difficult to repeat the big hits scored with the moves from drive-ins into shopping-center theaters and into soft drink bottling. Yet, as the post–World War II economy matured and the wave of mergers and acquisitions begun in the 1960s rolled on through the 1970s and gained new momentum in the 1980s, the conditions that had created such opportunities disappeared. For roughly twenty years after his first soft drink acquisition, Smith would continue to search for a third major business and never quite find it. In the process, General Cinema would be transformed from what was, in 1973, still essentially an entrepreneurship—albeit one with nearly $250 million in revenues—into a professionally managed firm recognized as one of the more sophisticated players on the corporate mergers and acquisitions scene.

GENERAL CINEMA IN 1973, REVISITED

The year 1973 brought to a close a vigorous seven-year period of diversification, which, combined with rapid expansion of the shopping-center theater circuit, had made General Cinema a leader in two major industries. It was a year of triumph. But it was also a difficult year for the company—one in which doubt and caution temporarily replaced the confidence and aggressiveness characteristic of the preceding era of growth.

For one thing, a new cloud of uncertainty seemed to hang over General Cinema's businesses in the form of government intervention.

In 1973 the company settled a suit brought by the U.S. Department of Justice against its acquisition of eighteen downtown theaters in Minneapolis–St. Paul by agreeing to sell off half of them. At the same time, the soft drink industry became embroiled in litigation with the Federal Trade Commission. The FTC had brought suit against Coca-Cola, PepsiCo, and other soft drink syrup makers, attacking the franchise system under which independent bottlers such as General Cinema produced and marketed their products in exclusive territories. Finally, GCC Communications was thwarted in its efforts to obtain a license to operate its Chicago FM station, because a citizens' group had challenged the decision of the Federal Communications Commission to allow a change of the station's programming from a classical music to a popular format. In the long run, none of these legal challenges would seriously damage General Cinema's businesses. Yet at the time, federal regulation seemed to loom as a serious threat to the company's future growth.

Still more upsetting was the fact that, although 1973 revenues were up from the previous year in both theater and beverage divisions, the company's net income fell by 9 percent. Smith noted in the annual report for the year that the decline, a little over $1 million, "could be attributed entirely" to a rise of $1.5 million in its interest costs. For a while at least, he would have to refocus his attention from diversification to restructuring General Cinema's long-term debt to make it less dependent on the prime rate.[55]

However, the company would also have to address the fact that the performance of the beverage division was at least partly responsible for the disappointing financial results of the year. In 1973 General Cinema acquired American Pepsi-Cola Bottlers, with franchises in Winston-Salem, North Carolina; Springfield, Ohio; and Sacramento, California. Although its revenues rose by 6 percent, operating margins shrank, and net profit for the division fell by 4 percent. That, plus the other troubles and uncertainties of the year, added up to a prescription for pulling back and consolidating the tremendous growth that had occurred since 1966. Smith would never speak of his company as a conglomerate. Yet he would have to face many of the same structural issues as diversified firms of the conglomerate type. At the same time, he would have to shepherd his organization through the transition to professional management that such expansion of scale and scope demanded.

During the decade of the 1970s, professionalization would take place on two levels—divisional and corporate. With his appointment to head the beverage division in 1972, Herb Paige received a mandate to build a divisional staff in financial control, operations, and marketing and to standardize and integrate the operations of General Cinema's geographically dispersed bottling franchises in order to realize more fully the potential economies of scale. In fulfilling that charge, he would make the division the undisputed leader in its industry.[56]

In 1974 Smith hired J. Atwood ("Woody") Ives as financial vice president in preparation for Ed Lane's planned retirement in 1976. Thereby began the process of professionalization at the corporate level that would make possible more effective control over the divisions and provide support for Smith in strategic planning. Very soon a staff of professional managers would be ready to replace the small theater operations group that had been helping Smith to run the company since the early 1960s. Predictably, this transition and the accompanying culture change within the corporate office were not entirely smooth. The strong financial orientation of the new staff, made even stronger by the determination to marshal the resources of the company's existing business in preparation for an acquisition, set up conflicts with operating executives over the level of control from the center and the level of corporate investment in their businesses.

Those tensions persisted through much of the decade of the 1970s. Within the beverage division, Herb Paige attained a position of great strength and substantial autonomy, based in part on the strength of his personality but primarily on the spectacular growth and profitability of the business in that era. In the same period, Smith conferred on Mel Wintman full title to and responsibility for running the theater division. Wintman would also become an extremely strong and largely autonomous division executive. For several years those counterbalancing powers at the two levels of the company—the growing corporate staff and the strong division heads—struggled with each other for control. Characteristically, Smith remained aloof from corporate politics, waiting for the right direction to become clear.

C H A P T E R

4

LEADERSHIP IN SOFT DRINK BOTTLING: GCC BEVERAGES UNDER HERB PAIGE

Seasoned bottlers tended to be scornful of companies that began to diversify into soft drinks in the late 1960s expecting to improve the profitability of bottling operations through the contribution of their superior financial strength and management talent. As a group, soft drink bottlers were extremely independent—"500 free-thinking Americans," as Pepsi-Cola's James Somerall called his company's franchisees. That independence was rooted in the highly local nature of the business. "The bottler," Somerall noted, "has a 365-days-a-year fight for . . . shelf space. He lives by the total he is able to command." In that battle, national advertising, new product concepts, and marketing plans usually counted considerably less than the bottler's ability to meet or beat the competition in supermarkets, convenience stores, and gas stations each week by paying close attention to customer service and, more important, by supplying soft drinks in popular packages at a good price. Companies that bought into the industry and ignored those basic elements tended to pay for the mistake with disappointing returns. As one industry newsletter commented in 1971, poor results in newly acquired plants represented

> an internal problem common to top corporations that acquire bottling plants and get rid of the bottlers who know the business and everyone they deal with and bring in Wharton school

guys or people like that. The soft drink game is still a Hi Joe,
Hi Pete, Hi Tom business, but the conglomerates refuse to
believe this.[1]

General Cinema was able to professionalize the operations of its bottling subsidiary while avoiding those problems to a great extent because
of the skills of American Beverage chief Herb Paige. Paige shared and
vigorously pursued Smith's vision of building an elite beverage operation
through the application of professional management principles and programs. Yet he also understood and knew how to win the day-to-day battle
in the marketplace. From his background at American Beverage, Paige
had both the experience and the credentials as a bottler that would allow
him to hire "Wharton school guys or people like that" and still maintain
his credibility with the rank-and-file members of his organization, on
whom success would largely depend.

Paige achieved brilliant success in integrating the disparate bottling
operations that Smith had acquired and in transforming them into one
of the most progressively managed and profitable organizations in the
industry. To say that he did so at a time when the industry as a whole
enjoyed unparalleled growth and profitability does not diminish his
achievement. The competitive advantage that underlay General Cinema's
superior economic performance of the 1970s rested equally on the inherent profitability of the soft drink industry and the strength of GCC Beverages' position within it. The story of how Paige introduced professional
management to the gritty business of soft drink bottling is a fascinating
chapter in the company's history.[2]

LEADERSHIP CHOICE

Dick Smith had taken his time in deciding who should lead the
beverage division, and he knew the kind of person he was looking for.
When he settled on Paige, Smith gave him a mandate to professionalize
every aspect of beverage division management. By 1976, he would express
satisfaction that General Cinema had succeeded in creating an operation
more "sophisticated [than] any previously accomplished by other independent bottlers."

We had waited just long enough after the initial acquisitions
[Smith said at that time] to understand the basics of the soft-
drink business and to appraise the strengths and weaknesses

of the people who had been managing the acquisitions. Thus we were able to select Herb Paige as a strong leader and to permit the creation of a strong central management. By the time we needed to restructure, most of the people were prepared to support General Cinema's efforts to become "the best in the industry."[3]

When Paige took over, the division was under the gun to improve its profitability. Specifically, the objective set by the Beverage Executive Committee in January 1973 was to achieve after-tax profits equal to 7 percent of revenues, a standard established by the leading multifranchise soft drink bottlers, Los Angeles Coke and New York Coke. That was a challenging goal, given net profits of about 2 percent in 1970–1972, and the business conditions of the day allowed for no more than "cautious optimism" about the profitability of the industry as a whole. Margins were low and under pressure, both from inflation and from the trend in packaging to larger-sized containers, which tended to be sold at promotional prices. The industry as a whole projected no more than 4 percent growth in volume. Yet the committee estimated that growth of 6 to 10 percent would be necessary just to offset inflation.[4]

GCC Beverages' results for 1972 were fairly grim. Operating profits had fallen by 20 percent and net profit had remained virtually stagnant, though the volume of sales had risen by nearly 5 percent. The company's annual report put the best face on things by emphasizing its aggressive investment in large (32-ounce) returnable-resealable bottles, essentially writing off fiscal 1972 as a "marketing year" that would lay the foundation for future growth. Even as the report was in press, however, the assumptions underlying that investment came into question. Returnables were attractive because they allowed the bottler to recoup more on the investment in containers. The larger size—16 ounces was then the norm—was popular with consumers as an economy package, and General Cinema's leadership in introducing 32-ounce returnables helped it to win market share from private label brands in 1972. But it had little impact on the more important competition against Coke, and it went against the long-term trend toward nonreturnables, especially cans.[5]

In his first speech to the unified beverage division, Paige developed the theme "in unity there is strength," but he also delivered the message that the principle of local operating autonomy would be sacrosanct. To a great extent his success as president of the new division depended on his ability to control the tension between those two governing ideas. The soft drink business, Paige said, was "basically a local business, dealing with local competition." Yet, having promised a minimal amount of operational control from the top, he set about assembling a high-powered divisional staff whose charge was to bring the disparate operations of sixteen (soon to be twenty-one) bottling plants up to a single high standard of efficiency and profitability. The challenge then became to make the most of his staff's professional training without losing the best of his line managers' experience in the soft drink industry.[6]

THE DRIVE FOR PROFITABILITY THROUGH PROFESSIONAL MANAGEMENT

In reorganizing General Cinema's soft drink division, Paige promoted from within for line positions—plant and regional management. But he staffed the home office from outside. His first new hire was Mark Sobell, a Wharton School MBA with a strong background in marketing consumer goods at General Mills, R. J. Reynolds, and International Playtex. Sobell became divisional vice president for marketing. Subsequently, Paige hired a division treasurer, a vice president for business development and planning, a vice president for operations, and a director of information systems. All were men with advanced degrees and experience in other corporations. Over the next few years, the new home office team would usher GCC Beverages into the mainstream of professionalized management.

Since the immediate goal was to control costs and improve profitability, the first task at hand was to gather and analyze information about operations at each plant. Paige ordered the staff immediately out into the field. Remembering that period, Lawrence Gilligan, the specialist in data processing charged with developing management information systems, explained:

> The beverage division is pretty simple. Everybody does the same thing. But everybody did it differently. So . . . the charge was to do a lot of traveling, visit the plants, and gather information on how each plant ran their business. And we generally noted which plants were doing a better job than some of the other plants. We tried to develop standards [and] central operations and set policy so that we could all operate, doing the same thing the same way.[7]

The reality in the field was that, although a few plants—in particular Cleveland, Jacksonville, and Miami, which had been divisional headquarters—had computer systems in place, most did not. In March 1973 General Cinema acquired American Pepsi-Cola, with operations in California and North Carolina. Its plant in Winston-Salem kept financial records on hand-operated billing machines and ledger cards, and only a strong staff kept the antiquated system operational. Clearly, there were many opportunities for General Cinema to improve the profitability of its bottling operations. It would be roughly a decade before each plant had its own electronic management information system, but immediate gains were made by gathering information into a centralized data processing system and returning reports to plant management.

Inevitably, with the increased capability for data gathering and analysis came rising expectations for more sophisticated use of information. In the area of operations control, the staff undertook to train plant managers to make use of exception reporting of quantitative data to track and optimize the performance of production equipment. The business planning staff provided training in goal setting, risk evaluation, measurement of achievement by "key factors," and long-term planning. The treasurer's office worked with plant managers, who were accustomed to drawing up budgets and making business decisions largely on the basis of "informed judgment," teaching them to use the quantitative data at hand and to employ analytical tools such as discounted cash flow and cost-benefit analyses.[8]

Systems began to roll out of the home office in Miami at a steady rate—management information systems, inventory control systems, customized programs for internal audits. Not surprisingly, the divisional staff grew in size, and its structure became more elaborate. Of all the departments, marketing—though not the largest—was by far the most aggressive.

QUEST FOR GROWTH THROUGH MARKETING

After the "marketing year," 1972, GCC Beverages had been under the gun to control costs and increase operating margins. But by the end of 1973, slow volume growth and a loss of market share caused the pendulum to swing back toward marketing. Paige assembled division managers at a Florida resort to lay out the change in focus. "We forgot, at least temporarily, the type of business we're in," he told the group. "We are in a marketing business, and there is no way that just control of expenses can generate a healthy case sales and profit growth pattern."[9]

There was no going back on the commitment to standardization and central control in production and financial reporting. But, Paige suggested, it was important that group and plant managers' time not be devoted entirely, or even primarily, to this task. "Financial people"—home office staff and plant controllers—should attend to the financial problems of the business, so that operating managers could stay on top of those areas without constant direct involvement. Indeed, they should spend fully half their time on "sales and related opportunities."

If regional and plant managers were "on the firing line," the divisional marketing staff was there to support them. In part that support would consist simply of facilitating communication—helping local managers benefit from each other's experience and expertise. But, said Paige, the marketing staff would also provide new ideas, "in matters that require skills that you can't afford on your own staff at a plant level."[10]

At the most basic level, the staff marketers, like all the professional managers, offered information and analysis. They presented familiar industry statistics such as trends in sales volume and market share but broke them down in new ways and re-examined them in light of additional facts in order to make them more revealing. More direct assistance took the form of centrally produced or purchased, and pre-tested, promotional materials in a "catalogue" format from which local managers could pick and choose. The staff also developed programmed planning materials that guided plant and sales managers through the tasks of setting priorities and establishing goals in line with a management-by-objectives system that went into effect in 1974.

In those and other ways the marketing staff sought to bolster the resources of local managers, offering support, not control. But at the highest level, the role of the home office was to realize the full potential of the division's size. That meant allocating resources selectively to gain the highest overall return. For example, suggested Mark Sobell, the company should curtail promotional discounting in the areas of its greatest market strength, reserving the money saved for promotions in more competitive areas. Similarly, he proposed to do away with across-the-board allocation of support funds from PepsiCo and other franchisors and to channel them to those areas where they had the potential to do the most good. Sobell wanted to spend the bulk of advertising money in regions where overall soft drink consumption was highest—to "fish where the fish are."[11]

Such marketing strategies challenged the principle of local autonomy far more directly than had the imposition of controls on operations and finance. In 1976, in line with conventional management wisdom of the day, the division adopted a "bottom-up/top-down" approach to budget making, in which budgets were initially drawn up in the plants, then reviewed by divisional staff, and finally sent to corporate headquarters for approval. In contrast, the format for interaction on marketing strategy was top-down first—"the corporate overview and resolution of major priority areas"—and bottom-up second—"recognition of local market idiosyncrasies, and strategy development tailored to local needs and opportunities."[12]

In theory, marketing was the area in which local initiative and autonomy were most important. Yet as that function developed, it was the area in which the home office staff was perceived to be the most aggressive in seeking to control activity from the center. Whereas plant managers tended to welcome the support given by staff experts in operations and, even more, in finance, they resisted centralization of marketing and marketing programs that often seemed faddish, disruptive, and not sufficiently tailored to local conditions. Marketing became a point of conflict between line and staff managers.[13]

LINE VERSUS STAFF: PRESERVING THE BALANCE

Paige tolerated that conflict; indeed, he fostered it. Sales and marketing were his own areas of interest and expertise, and he encouraged aggressiveness in the marketing staff. According to Jack Bliss, Central Division manager in the 1970s, "Herb was the kind of guy that was always looking for some new bell or whistle that he thought was going to be a new, innovative thing." It was also his mandate, as division president, to bring the division up to the state of the art in marketing as in other areas. In that sense, developing new bells and whistles was an important part of his job. In 1976 Smith pointed with pride to the fact that many of General Cinema's bottling division marketing programs had been imitated by others in the industry. It suggested, he said, "That we are having some success in pioneering new ideas and techniques for the soft-drink business."[14]

Paige made it quite clear in his statements on the subject that he expected local management to be enlightened in its use of the resources offered by the divisional staff:

In this age of specialization, you have available to you specialists in each functional area of the business. To take advantage of their skills will make you a better manager and the business you run eminently more successful. Not to take advantage of them, or to resist change, which is the order of the day, is a hazardous route.[15]

However, he was just as likely to extol the significance of local control as of specialization. That was particularly true in the all-important area of promotional pricing, where profitability had to be weighed against sales volume and market share almost weekly. "Each market is different," Paige told his managers. "You know yours the best, and we depend on you to open and close the promotion valve to get the maximum number of sales from your promotion dollars."[16]

In addition, behind the scenes, Paige allowed plant managers considerable latitude to conduct their businesses as they saw fit. He was even willing, on occasion, to support individual resistance to the home office. Paige traveled regularly to the various franchises. He made it a point to get out in the field, to acquaint himself with local customers and competitive conditions, and to maintain strong personal relationships with his line managers. Said Bliss, "He walked both sides of the road":

> He told those guys in Miami, "You tell this guy that I said . . . , and you tell that guy that I said . . . ." [But] we knew when the stuff was coming in, if it was something that we didn't agree with we could always get hold of him. Then, when he'd come to the field, he'd say, "Now, if they've got a bunch of screwy ideas down there, you get back with me."[17]

In short, Paige played both ends against the middle in order to have both centralization and local initiative and control—and, presumably, to foster a tension that would prove creative. It was not a style that all managers would wish to emulate. Yet Paige carried it off, largely by virtue of his energy and the strength of his personality. He succeeded in building a team that consistently outperformed the industry.

His success was greatly facilitated by a turnaround in the industry after 1974. Then, as Paige said, "We learned that . . . we could raise prices significantly without going out of business [and] that we could improve profit performance by increasing margins and not on the basis of volume alone." With profitability rising more or less independently of volume increases, Paige could well afford to tolerate the boisterous conflict between his staff and line managers and to be flexible in mediating between them.[18]

THE SOFT DRINK INDUSTRY IN THE 1970S

Dick Smith's commitment to making GCC Beverages the best in the industry could not have been better timed. Paige's management team, running smoothly by mid-1974, began to have a significant impact on operations just as the economics of soft drink bottling started to improve. For the next five years, General Cinema would ride the crest of a surge in profitability to become one of the strongest forces in an industry increasingly dominated by fewer but stronger companies.

The key factor driving those changes was price. Despite inflationary pressures on costs, soft drink prices remained low in the early 1970s, largely because soft drink bottlers believed that demand for their products was highly price-elastic. During 1973, the cost-price squeeze intensified, as sugar prices were driven up sharply by crop failures and resulting shortages in the world sugar market. From July to September, GCC Beverages' sugar cost rose by $1.2 million. Initially, federal price controls limited the degree to which the increase could be passed on to consumers. But as the cost of sugar continued to climb during 1974 (to 70 cents per pound, roughly seven times the 1973 price), the industry was granted relief. After that, the average price per case of soft drinks rose from $2.60 in 1973 to $3.10 in 1974 and to $3.55 in 1975.[19]

Soft drink bottlers raised their prices with trepidation. Jack Bliss remembered attending a bottlers' convention in November 1973, when the first round of increases seemed imminent. "I thought everybody was going to dive off the pier into the ocean," said Bliss. "The end is here. . . . The consumer will not pay the prices we're now going to have to charge him."[20] Consumption did in fact decline slightly in 1974 and 1975. But after that it rose sharply and continued to rise, even though the new prices held and then gradually rose (see Table 4.1).

As sugar prices fell, there was a radical improvement in operating margins throughout the industry, and GCC Beverages was well positioned to take full advantage of the changing conditions. Its purchasing power protected it from the worst of the sugar crisis, and its geographical positions in the South and in the "Pepsi heartland" helped cushion it from the drop in consumption. At the same time, its operating efficiencies

**TABLE 4.1 Comparative Growth of U.S. Soft Drink Consumption
Gallons per Capita per Year, 1973–1979**

	1973	*1975*	*1977*	*1979*
Soft Drinks	31.7	31.2	36.5	38.9
Coffee	35.1	33.0	28.1	28.0
Milk	22.9	22.6	22.2	21.8
Beer	20.6	21.9	22.8	24.3

Source: Industry statistics in HGI corporate records.

enabled it to maximize the potential for profitability afforded by sustained high prices (see Table 4.2).[21]

TREND TOWARD CONSOLIDATION

The sudden rise in the rates of return achieved by General Cinema and other large-scale, efficient bottlers accelerated the pace of consolidation in the industry. The lure of high profits both attracted new investors and encouraged existing companies to expand by acquiring contiguous franchises. The economics, as *Forbes* pointed out in 1977, were simple: "Maximize volume and you maximize profit." Following that formula, many bottlers had grown, both in size and in profitability, faster than the economy as a whole through the mid-1970s. Even for smaller operations, it was a stable business, "Just a nice, relatively simple business that's ridden through depressions, inflations and sugar crises, making a pretty good average profit." That was the kind of operation, *Forbes* noted, to make "a big, acquisition-minded company misty-eyed."[22]

The competitive advantages offered by economies of scale that Smith had seen in the industry a decade before were now apparent to all. In 1977 companies as diverse as the Liggett Group, Twentieth Century Fox, Northwest Industries, and Japan's Suntory bought into the industry. In the same year Dr Pepper bought out its own franchises in Houston and Los Angeles, a move that seemed to portend a change in the major franchisors' traditional willingness to leave most of the bottling business to independents. Established players like MEI Corporation, Wometco, and General Cinema expanded their positions. The advantages that such companies gained from investments in management and technology fur-

TABLE 4.2 GCC Beverages Performance, 1973–1978

	1973	1974	1975	1976	1977	1978
Sales Volume % Increase (decrease)	3.4	2.8	(1.3)	10.6	14.0	17.4
Revenues (millions $)	$128	$157	$178	$189	$240	$315
Operating Income (millions $)	$5	$8	$17	$22	$30	$37
Operating Margin	4%	5%	10%	12%	12%	12%

Source: General Cinema Corporation annual reports and HGI corporate records.

ther fueled consolidation of the industry. "It's sheer economics," said one executive:

> the packaging proliferation, the need for machinery to produce everything from a 6½-ounce bottle to a 2-liter bottle, the pressure by consumers and the government to build plants to higher standards. It's just the maturing of an industry. After all, we used to have 300 automobile manufacturers; now we have four.[23]

Doubt about the future of the soft drink franchise system, hanging over the industry throughout the 1970s, also promoted consolidation. In 1967 the U.S. Supreme Court ruled in the *Schwinn* case that territorial restrictions in distribution were illegal on a per se basis—that is, they were presumed to be a restraint on competition in every instance, regardless of actual competitive conditions in any particular case. Based on that ruling, the Federal Trade Commission (FTC) in 1971 began to move against the territorial franchise systems of PepsiCo and Coca-Cola. Over the next nine years, franchisors and bottlers pulled together to fight the FTC's challenge, both in the courts and in Congress, where several committees took testimony on the merits of legislation to exempt soft drink franchises from antitrust law. In 1980 the so-called bottler bill would be passed in Congress, rendering moot the FTC's continuing legal battle. But in the interim it seemed at several points that the franchise system would be swept away, at the very least for soft drinks sold in nonreturnable bottles.[24]

The uncertainties in that situation clouded the prospects of smaller-scale bottlers. Their franchises protected them against more powerful co-franchisees, like General Cinema, whose large, efficient plants and distribution systems would have enabled them easily to supply soft drinks at competitive prices to broad areas beyond their franchise boundaries. Most smaller bottlers expected that, if the FTC had its way, those who could not expand would quickly be driven out of business. For many, the prudent course of action was to sell out before that happened and while the prices being paid for franchises were high.[25]

Though analysts always tempered their predictions with references to possible mandatory deposit laws, health concerns over artificial sweeteners, and the unpredictable impact of the aging of the "Pepsi generation," the consensus was that the acquisition trend would continue. With it would continue a steady inflation in prices paid for bottling companies, which in 1977 were as high as seventeen times earnings. However the franchise issue was decided, all the advantages in the industry would still belong to the large, multifranchise bottlers, of which General Cinema was unquestionably one of the strongest and most aggressive.[26]

"BEST IN THE INDUSTRY"

A number of other companies, like Wometco, had discovered the secret of combining movie theaters and soft drink bottling—"the first a highly volatile cash generator, the second highly stable and capital-intensive." But, said *Forbes,* General Cinema had "raised that discovery into the big time." By the late 1970s, GCC Beverages was one of the largest and "certainly one of the toughest" competitors in the industry.[27]

The company continued to expand through acquisitions. GCC Beverages purchased two important Dr Pepper franchises, in Atlanta and Miami, during 1975, when Coke forced its bottlers in those cities to market its own cherry cola, Mr PiBB. In 1976, Smith instructed Paige to put together a "comprehensive acquisition plan." It was "an important and continuing responsibility of the divisions," Smith said, "to identify attractive acquisitions and bring them to the attention of the appropriate corporate personnel." The following year GCC Beverages consummated two major acquisitions—of the Pepsi franchise for Washington, D.C., and Dr Pepper of Roanoke, Virginia—both of which had been in the works for some time. And still Paige's mandate from Smith was to "continue to be aggressive in seeking acquisitions."[28]

Paige did continue to be aggressive, tracking the status of neighboring franchises and maintaining a "hit list" of desirable targets. He also thought seriously about opportunities to expand through diversification. In the mid-1970s Paige investigated a number of possibilities, including wine, bottled water, and snack foods, all of which could draw on the company's existing strengths in marketing and distribution.

Besides looking outward for opportunities to expand, General Cinema made investments aimed at internal growth. The beverage division continually upgraded its information systems with new hardware and programs, such as the weekly sales forecasting system introduced in 1977, which intensified the pace of both planning and evaluation of results. The budgeting process became more rigorous, training programs were instituted, and the management-by-objectives system was moved into place. The staff operations function expanded from basic industrial engineering and quality control to developing systems to streamline and control machinery development and physical distribution. As the productive capacity of plants steadily grew, a dramatic increase in the ratio of distribution centers to plants improved the efficiency of the distribution system.[29]

The company was also a leading partner in innovation with parent Pepsi, for example in the development of the plastic bottle in collaboration with Pepsi and Amoco. General Cinema contributed to that project by helping to develop specifications, by testing the bottles on its lines, and, after the new bottle was commercialized, by sampling products off store shelves and testing for loss of carbonation. Through its effort, GCC Beverages gained a six- to twelve-month lead time over its competitors in introducing 64-ounce and 2-liter plastic bottles in 1977. In the soft drink industry, the impact of packaging on sales had been clearly demonstrated, beginning with Pepsi's introduction of the 12-ounce bottle in the 1930s. General Cinema's innovation in that area contributed greatly to its competitive strength.

At the same time, GCC Beverages was actively diversifying within its existing business by taking on new products. Throughout the industry the proliferation of new products was an important factor driving soft drink sales. In cherry colas, the battle continued between Dr Pepper and Mr PiBB; in root beers, competition was fierce between A&W, Barrelhead, Ramblin' Root Beer, and Root 66. A number of new flavors such as Mello Yellow also were introduced. As a backdrop to all of that activity, there raged the long-term battle among diet drinks, intensified by the search for acceptable artificial sweeteners. General Cinema was in the thick of the activity. The company test marketed Hawaiian Punch and Country Time Lemonade in 1977 and introduced them into most of its markets in 1978. In 1978 it took a leading position in the orange soda market with the introduction of Sunkist Orange Soda.

SUNKIST SOFT DRINKS

Development of a "famous name" soft drink line that could be nationally franchised was part of the long-term strategy mapped out for the division in 1974. The idea drew on Mark Sobell's experience at General Mills, where extensions of the Betty Crocker line, such as Chiquita Banana Cake Mix and Dole Pineapple Upside-Down Cake Mix, had proved successful. Sobell's ideas for new soft drinks included Sunkist Orange, Sunkist Lemon-Up, Mott's Apple, and Welch's Grape Soda, but ultimately Sunkist Orange was the one he pursued. In 1975 orange-flavored soda was estimated to hold nearly 4 percent of the total soft drink market, which implied annual sales of roughly 154 million cases. By 1976, General Cinema's total case sales through its bottling plants would be about 50 million, a figure that could be greatly augmented if the company could capture a share of the orange soda market from Orange Crush and the scores of other minor orange brands that made up the category.[30]

The Sunkist name, so strongly linked in consumers' minds with fresh orange juice—"like motherhood, apple pie, and a flag in this country"—was just the kind of ready-made brand advantage that would enable the company to achieve that objective. The Sunkist growers' organization was interested in selling trademark rights, but there were a number of competitors for them. The field narrowed down to PepsiCo and General Cinema in the spring of 1977. General Cinema emerged victorious and set up a new company, Sunkist Soft Drinks, Inc., with Mark Sobell as president.

After several months of intensive market research, the company began to develop its product, working closely with Sunkist to arrive at a soft drink that would replicate the color, aroma, and flavor of orange juice as closely as possible. Though Sunkist was located in Atlanta, much of the work was done in the Miami plant. Commented vice president of operations John Koss, "We had orange drinks coming out of our corks."[31]

From September 1977 to May 1978, the final product was selected from among thirty-six candidate formulations, and packaging and advertising designs and a national marketing plan were developed. General Cinema spent heavily, employing a team of consultants "the synergistic effects of which are rocking the industry," said *Beverage World* in 1979. Within a year of its first test introduction in six "lead markets," Sunkist had thirty franchises covering 20 percent of the United States. It was the leading orange soda in all its markets.[32]

THE LEADERSHIP FACTOR

The Sunkist venture contributed to General Cinema's high profile as a leader in the industry. Yet, for all its investment in innovation, in economies of scale, in marketing expertise, in expansion of its product lines, and in acquisitions, the company's strength in the 1970s derived to a great degree from its day-to-day competitiveness in the marketplace. In that arena, GCC Beverages was as tough as any organization in the business. In 1973, in its Cleveland territory, where the new owner of the competing Coca-Cola franchise sought to "buy a share of the market" through heavy discounting, General Cinema waged a fierce price war that cut Cleveland's profit margin significantly but raised its market share to a new high. In a similar struggle in Miami in 1977, *Forbes* noted, "The most visible casualty [was] Miami Coke's bottom line." In that battle it

was Coke that gained market share, but General Cinema gained a reputation as a tough competitor. In the continuing contest of wits and nerves
"in the trenches," that kind of reputation was valuable, not least as a
deterrent to future price wars.[33]

In such situations Herb Paige's long years of experience in the industry and his understanding of the importance of local factors in marketing
soft drinks made the difference. He had developed, in John Koss's words,
"a sense of the marketplace."

> He went out in the field and spent time out in the market in
> every one of these franchises and he made it his business to
> become intimately familiar with every one. . . . He knew the
> people and he knew who the competition was, and he was
> very good at being able to evaluate what the competition was
> or was not doing, and this was the basis upon which he deter-
> mined what his strategy was going to be. So, he'd make his
> profit . . . and he would also get market share. He wouldn't
> sacrifice one for the other. He would outsmart people. He
> knew when to discount and when not to discount. He knew
> what packages to discount. He was an extremely astute man
> in the real basics of the business.[34]

In fact, though many factors—booming industry, bold investment,
state-of-the-art management, and tough tactics in the field—contributed
to GCC Beverages' impressive growth in the 1970s, Herb Paige must be
given much of the credit for putting it all together and making it work.
In 1978, approaching forty-nine years old, Paige was at the peak of his
executive capacity. A tall, athletic, attractive man, he was also intelligent,
witty, and impressively well read. He was respected by his colleagues as
a tough, dynamic businessman. He had an entrepreneurial vision for the
beverage division to match Dick Smith's, and he had clearly demonstrated
the ability to follow through on their plans.

Paige exuded success. He had a flashy style—white suits, a white
Rolls-Royce, a big yacht—that stood out rather sharply against the frugal,
Yankee corporate style at General Cinema. On one occasion he attended
a winter meeting in Boston wearing a long fur coat over his white suit.
Division headquarters at Miami included an executive dining room and
gym, and Paige insisted on renting a private plane for his extensive travels
to franchise locations.

Within his own bailiwick, he was something of an autocrat who
could be moody and overbearing with his staff. He kept his desk on a
raised platform, so that even while sitting he could look down on his

visitors, and he often communicated his criticisms in sharp, sarcastic memos. Yet, on the whole, Paige was very generous and solicitous of his employees, and he rewarded loyalty well. Around the home office, at the Miami plant, he was loved by some and hated by others, with very little middle ground.

Early in his relationship with the corporate office, Paige asserted his authority to oversee operations without interference, and he jealously guarded that turf. On any number of occasions he took to task William Zellen, the corporate controller, or Brian Veasy, the corporate liaison with the beverage division, for communicating directly with his line or staff managers and thus circumventing the established chain of command. In some cases, Paige appealed over their heads, to Lane or Smith, in order to keep them in line. On other occasions, to advocate or defend a particular policy, he would send Smith a long, closely reasoned explanation of his position.

After 1976, when the corporate financial and planning functions became more professionalized and began to take a more activist role in overseeing the divisions, Paige resisted every step of the way. He preferred to run the beverage division largely autonomously and by that time had the track record to defend his right to do so. Paige was riding high on the strength of his accomplishments. That made his sudden fall all the more dramatic.

THE TROUBLE WITH HERB PAIGE

As it turned out, Herb Paige was exploiting his authority to embezzle his division's funds. That fact came to light in 1978, eight years after he began to divert rebate payments from a major supplier, Crown Cork and Seal, to his own pocket. After his scheme was exposed, it seemed incredible that it could have gone undetected so long, but Paige had devised it cleverly and eased it into place over a two-year period.

In 1970, when he took over Julius Darsky's position as head of the American Beverage Division, Paige had assumed responsibility for centralized purchasing of cans and bottles. It was standard practice for Crown Cork and Seal to make periodic "discount payments" to its customers based on volume purchased, and it had been selling cans to General Cinema subsidiaries since 1968. In October 1970 Paige told Crown Cork and Seal that General Cinema wanted all of its rebate checks to go to a single subsidiary—Pasha Service Corporation, a front he had created to channel the funds to his own account.

On the surface the new arrangement did not bring about any notice-able change in can-purchasing arrangements. Paige continued to produce quarterly rebates on can purchases, in at least one instance by transferring funds received by Pasha via a cashier's check payable to Pepsi-Cola Bot-tling Company of Miami. In January 1973 Crown Cork and Seal changed its rebate procedure for most companies and began to incorporate dis-counts directly into invoices. Although Crown Cork and Seal continued to make payments to Pasha, Paige informed plant controllers that the rebate checks would be discontinued in favor of accounting by invoice only. Over the years, as the scale of General Cinema's operations grew, the size of the rebates grew also, to the point that, in 1978, Paige received four payments totaling over $2 million. By that time Crown Cork and Seal had paid a total of $5.9 million to Pasha, still apparently believing it to be a subsidiary of General Cinema.[35]

As clever as it was, the scheme relied on Paige's independence in negotiating with Crown Cork and Seal in the purchase of cans. He en-joyed that independence in large part because he had won Dick Smith's trust by showing himself to be a dynamic, capable, and successful division executive. His position was greatly strengthened from below by a corpo-rate policy and practice that dictated strict confidentiality regarding pur-chasing agreements. The divisional policy manual stated: "The confiden-tial nature of our pricing arrangements will insure fair treatment of all suppliers and assure the continuing willingness of all our suppliers to bid competitively." That policy supported Paige's request that rebate pay-ments be recorded "by journal entry only with as little explanation as possible." Presumably, after January 1973 he invoked that policy to keep from plant controllers the information they would have needed to discern whether their Crown Cork and Seal invoices reflected the discounts they were supposedly receiving on can purchases.[36]

But Paige's personal style—the same characteristics that helped him to win the position of division president, to keep his staff and divisional managers in harness together, and to go head to head with competitors in price wars and come out victorious—also helped defend him from challenges from below. He did not readily accept questions of his judg-ment or authority in any area, and he communicated his views in strongly worded memos that left little opening for reply. It is not surprising that, though plant managers occasionally questioned the order to purchase all of their cans and bottle caps from Crown Cork and Seal, they did not pursue the issue. Paige's raised desk and autocratic manner around the home office undoubtedly had a similar effect on his staff, and his aggres-sive defense of his turf kept corporate controller Zellen at arm's length.

At the time Paige joined General Cinema, it had been suggested that the cause for his resignation from American Beverage Corporation had been dishonesty. He was then in the process of paying back some questionable "loans" from corporate accounts. When Woody Ives started work in 1974, he was mildly surprised to find that Paige as divisional vice president was not also a corporate officer or director. It was even more surprising that Paige did not have authority to sign checks for his own division. All of that had changed by 1978. As the head of the company's largest division and its third highest paid officer, he had as much status and authority as anyone in General Cinema. In the words of William Zellen, "it was like this guy could do no wrong."[37]

After 1978, as many unsavory details of Paige's lifestyle and financial affairs were brought to light during the lengthy course of proceedings against him, it was easy enough to ask why his flamboyance and obvious wealth had never aroused the suspicion of Smith and others at General Cinema corporate headquarters. However, as *The Wall Street Journal* noted when the charges against Paige were made public, "A more unlikely target for such a charge could hardly be imagined." His taste for fancy cars and flashy clothing may at times have "raised a few eyebrows," and his executive manner may have been criticized as "highhanded," but such traits in an active and respected member of his community and, above all, an effective and highly successful division president, were hardly to be taken as cause to suspect corruption.[38]

The autonomy and great authority that Paige enjoyed within General Cinema—which enabled him to override the controls and silence the questions that might have exposed his embezzlement scheme years before it was actually discovered—derived primarily from the unassailable fact of his division's success. In retrospect, one is tempted to explain his energetic defense of that autonomy as wholly self-aggrandizing and self-interested. Yet to do so would be to miss a central point about this chapter of General Cinema's history: the extent to which successful organizational transformations tend to be dependent on an aggressive leader.

Eventually, two General Cinema employees, division treasurer Stanley Harris and assistant treasurer Bernard Zitofsky, did step forward, with some trepidation, to raise questions about Paige's activities. Woody Ives had recently given up smoking in the summer of 1978, when Harris "dropped the bomb" of his suspicion that something was amiss in the soft drink division's purchasing program. He smoked a pack that night in Harris's room at the Colonnade Hotel in Boston, as he repeatedly reviewed the questions that had been raised and decided to inform Smith and the company's law firm, Ropes & Gray. Smith, too, would always remember the moment he learned of the problem, because it coincided with the marriage of his daughter Amy, and Paige was one of the wedding guests.[39]

After Harris's initial meeting with Ives, there began a long period of investigation into Paige's affairs—a time of great tension and anxiety. Harris reluctantly returned to Boston on two occasions to repeat the reasons for his suspicion, first to Smith and later to Paul Galvani, the Ropes & Gray attorney assigned to the case. Since Harris had no proof, it was decided that the audit committee of General Cinema's board of directors would attempt to determine whether there were irregularities by making a comparison of can prices paid by the Washington, D.C. franchise before and after its acquisition in May 1977. In the meantime, it was also discovered that the company from which General Cinema had been leasing a plane for Paige was owned by Paige. He was suspended by Smith on the grounds of that deception in October 1978.

The tension increased during the fall, as the audit committee slowly moved forward with the task of analyzing General Cinema's complicated system of can purchasing. One weekend, Zitofsky agitatedly called Ives in Boston to say that four men had barged into the Miami office and were loading Paige's files into a panel truck. It took Ives an hour and a half to arrange for General Cinema's accountant and some Pinkerton detectives to go to the office; by that time, Paige's office had been cleared out. However, in the end, the investigation led General Cinema to Crown Cork and Seal and thereby to Pasha. In January 1979 Paige was forced to resign. In June General Cinema filed suit against him in Dade County, Florida.

Crown Cork and Seal denied complicity in the Paige affair but accepted responsibility by agreeing to repay General Cinema the full amount diverted by Paige. The company could not escape the damage to its reputation for honest dealing caused by the revelation. The president, John Luviano, was forced to resign under a cloud of suspicion. When the settlement with General Cinema was announced, the Securities and Exchange Commission (SEC) brought suit against both Paige and Crown Cork and Seal for violations of federal securities laws. Crown Cork and Seal settled its suit in September 1981 with a consent decree under which it agreed to institute tighter controls and then joined General Cinema in its suit against Paige.

In June 1982 Paige himself settled with the SEC, agreeing to place over $800,000 in an escrow account, eventually to be repaid to General Cinema. A year later he pleaded guilty to a criminal charge of mail fraud, based on the activities of Pasha Service Corporation. While he was serving a two-year prison term, the judge in his civil case awarded General Cinema triple damages, plus interest—over $26 million—under a little-used Florida civil theft law.[40]

GCC BEVERAGES AFTER THE FALL

At a hastily called Sunday meeting at Smith's home in October 1978, Robert J. Tarr, Jr. was tapped to take over the beverage division. Tarr had joined General Cinema as director of corporate planning in 1976 and had recently become corporate treasurer. He was thirty-five years old, a graduate of the U.S. Naval Academy and the Navy's nuclear submarine program, of Harvard Business School, and of the Fletcher School of Law and Diplomacy at Tufts University. Tarr had worked in the finance department of Paine, Webber, Jackson and Curtis with Woody Ives, who had recruited him for General Cinema's corporate staff.

Other than serving as an officer on a submarine, Tarr had no general management experience. After appointing him acting president of GCC Beverages, however, Smith stepped back and gave Tarr full authority to run the division. Perhaps the fact that much of Smith's own business education had been gained in the years when his father had supported him in much the same way—and had taken a similar leap of faith in entrusting Mid-West Drive-In's expansion program of the 1950s to a young, unproven son—gave him the confidence to place General Cinema's largest operating division in the hands of a neophyte. The move would prove to be a brilliant stroke. It was the making of Tarr's career and in the long run would provide General Cinema with a strong operating officer and future CEO.

Tarr's arrival on the scene dramatically changed the balance of power within the division. Within the first few days, he gathered the regional group vice presidents together and told them, in essence, that they had to run the business while he got out and learned it. "I recognized pretty early," he said, "that I had to have their support." By early 1979, when he was appointed president in his own right, he was ready to translate that insight into formal policy. At the annual managers' meeting, remembered John Koss,

> Mr. Tarr . . . made one very significant statement which has driven the operation of this company ever since that time. He said that he wanted to transfer the authority and responsibility from the [home] office to the field level, and the group VPs had the responsibility out in the field of running their group operations.[41]

In 1980 divisional headquarters was moved from Miami to Boston. Despite incentives offered by General Cinema, only 30 of the 125 home office staff members made the move. Most of them were unwilling to exchange the Florida climate for that of Boston, and they had little difficulty in finding other jobs in the industry. Tarr took the opportunity to reduce the size of the division staff, effectively completing the decentralization. In the process, he had won the support of three strong group vice presidents—Jack Bliss, Gary Schirripa, and Lamar Russell—all of whom had respected and worked closely with Paige but who grew to respect Tarr even more and welcomed the lessening of the authority of the home office staff.

Those men would help Tarr guide GCC Beverages into the 1980s, a decade that brought slower growth in the soft drink industry, rapid acceleration of the trends toward consolidation, and fierce competition for market share. In addition, the consolidation movement was to take a new twist with the entrance of parent Coke and PepsiCo into the bidding for available franchises. There would be no slack in the operation such as Paige had been permitted and no more attractive deals on new franchises. As one analyst accurately predicted in 1979, in the 1980s the basic business decision for bottlers would boil down to a choice between "market share and margin maintenance." Bob Tarr, with his tough, naval officer's style and strong financial background, was often able to wring a little of both from the beverage organization.[42] One can only speculate on how Herb Paige might have fared, if he had been simply a brilliant manager and not also corrupt.

AFTERMATH

Paige's downfall was a watershed event for General Cinema, with repercussions on many levels. After 1978, Smith veered away from the Textron model that had made sense a decade before, restructuring reporting responsibilities so that divisional controllers were accountable both to their operating executives and to the corporate controller's staff. Through that and other measures, a rigorous system of checks and balances was put into place, ensuring that no operating chief could ever again override control measures in the way that Paige had done. The degree of trust and autonomy that Paige had enjoyed was far from unusual for a successful executive in a small firm but no longer a viable situation for the company. As much as anything, the enhanced system of controls signaled General Cinema's awareness of the responsibilities attached to its increasing prominence as a major public corporation.

In other ways as well, the Paige affair once and for all brought to an end the era in which General Cinema could be managed like a small, proprietary enterprise. Most important, perhaps, it prompted Smith to abandon the informal, personal style in which he had overseen the theater and beverage divisions. "I was perfectly happy," Smith later said, "to have a good personal business relationship with the heads of the operating entities . . . and I was willing to invest lots of autonomy in those leaders because I felt I had my hands on the businesses." All that changed after 1978, with an attendant loss of independence for all division heads.[43]

Yet the change was one that had been in the making for several years. In 1972 Paige had been given a mandate to build a professional staff for the beverage division, and he had proven to be something of an empire builder in carrying it out. Professionalization of the corporate office did not begin until 1974, and it took a couple of years to reach the point at which the corporate staff was ready to assert a greater degree of authority over divisional strategy and management. Paige cooperated, but reluctantly and only to a limited degree. The period 1976 to 1978 was one in which, once again, Smith was in the position of presiding over conflict among his subordinates about company policies and strategic priorities.

Paige was usually at the center of the debate. When the finance-oriented corporate staff went head to head with divisional managers over capital budgets, for example, he was an authoritative spokesman for the operations point of view. Moreover, since he had joined the company in 1968, Paige had become the most powerful member of the old guard— that group of loyal lieutenants who had helped Smith build the company and who were used to the informal style of decision making that had afforded them a strong sense of participation in setting the company's future course. To a great extent the conflict of the mid- to late 1970s was about the professionalization of corporate culture. Paige's freedom to continue acting much as he always had helped to sustain the old, personal-ized style of interaction in the corporate office.

Conversely, Paige's abrupt departure in disgrace undermined the po-sitions he had defended and the corporate style he had come to represent. Very quickly General Cinema moved along the spectrum of diversified firms from being, in Paige's own words, "a modified holding company" to maintaining one of the more activist corporate offices. Within a few years the rest of the old guard would retire, and the company would be launched on a path toward a new identity in which theaters would be a minor factor and soft drink bottling would entirely disappear.[44]

C H A P T E R

5

PROFESSIONALIZATION OF THE ENTREPRENEURIAL ENTERPRISE

The decade of the 1970s was a critical period of transition within General Cinema, during which the company developed a divisional corporate structure with a professionalized top management group befitting a company of its size. On one level, these changes may be viewed as the result of the increasing scale and complexity that accompanied growth. Since the turn of the twentieth century, countless U.S. firms had made similar adaptations to the need for more formal, rigorous control of operations and for more formalized planning, especially strategic planning. Indeed, General Cinema went through this transition quite late relative to other companies of comparable size—a fact that may be accounted for largely by the simplicity of theater operations, the power of the shopping-center theater strategy, and the rapidity with which the company expanded in the years immediately following the diversification into soft drink bottling.[1]

The precise manner in which the transition was accomplished, however, and the character of the firm that emerged from it, bore the distinctive stamp of Dick Smith. The success of the strategy for long-term growth through diversification—formed jointly with his father and pursued unswervingly for more than a decade—had, within the space of a few years, placed him in a league of corporate executives quite different from the one he had inhabited as the head of a theater company. By the mid-1970s, Smith realized, General Cinema had reached a size at which

future growth through diversification would have to come in large incre-
ments in order to have an impact. The company would have to cultivate
the support of external stockholders and bondholders, mostly financial
institutions, who would be needed to finance the firm's ambitious strategy.
Just as Phil Smith had realized how the stature to be gained by going
public would help put the company on a higher trajectory of growth,
Dick Smith now determined that General Cinema would have to look
like a "blue-chip growth company" in order to become one.[2]

In the business environment of the 1970s, the best way to establish
such an image—as well as the reality—was to develop a strong corporate
staff with professional training in general management. In the 1960s the
number of major U.S. corporations led by individuals with advanced
degrees in management, especially finance, had risen dramatically. Underlying that trend was the information revolution brought about by the
spread of computers. Increasingly the business community expected investment decisions to be based on sophisticated analysis of detailed financial data, and companies promoted people with ability in that area. This
was especially true of conglomerates, which were pursuing a strategy of
unrelated diversification by acquisition. For them, skills in portfolio management, cash management, strategic analysis of industries, and deal making were deemed essential. Those trends and expectations provided the
context for the professionalization of General Cinema's management at
the corporate level.[3]

Following Smith's well-established pattern, the process of professionalization at General Cinema, though fraught with conflict and competition, was a deliberate one, in which he presided over a thorough airing
of contending views. Moreover, although the result was a corporate structure and a high-powered, activist corporate office on the conglomerate
model, Smith modified the model in significant ways. Most important,
perhaps, he remained fully involved in the direction of the firm and
through his direction ensured that growth would not be pursued in ways
that risked dilution of his family's stake in ownership and control.

A defining feature of the managerial firm—of which the conglomerate form is a variant—is the separation of ownership from control. Yet
professionalization at General Cinema did not have that effect. Far from
assuming a titular role and handing management over to professionals,
Smith assembled a team and worked with it in a way that strengthened
his own leadership. Thus, by virtue of his own capabilities, and his capacity for development, he was able to convey to his company the organizational capabilities associated with the managerial revolution while maintaining the corporation's fundamental character as an entrepreneurial
enterprise. The differences in approach that distinguished General Cin-

TABLE 5.1 General Cinema Growth, 1967–1973 (millions $)

	1967	*1973*
Revenues	$42	$246
Total Assets	$30	$179
Stockholders' Equity	$14	$64

Source: General Cinema Annual Reports.

ema's program of diversification in the conglomerate era would remain undiminished as its period of transition ended and it re-entered the mergers and acquistions arena in the 1980s.[4]

IMPETUS FOR PROFESSIONALIZATION

Within a very short period, growth and diversification had transformed General Cinema from a small company into a substantial corporation more than five times larger (see Table 5.1). In the mid-1970s its portfolio of businesses included, along with theaters and beverages, furniture retailing, radio and television stations, and a nascent venture in film financing. In both accounting and operating terms, however, furniture and communications were no more than investments, while General Cinema's relationship to its beverage division was indeed something like that of a holding company, with the corporate office lacking the information and personnel necessary to play a significant supervisory role in the division's management. In 1973 net profits were down despite rising revenues—a clear signal that the rapid expansion of the enterprise had outstripped its managerial capabilities.

At the time, General Cinema's two roughly equal-sized core businesses were both well beyond the stage requiring direct involvement by the chief executive. Yet Smith still participated in day-to-day decision making in the theater business and, outside routine financial reporting, he alone bore the responsibility for supervising the beverage division. The theater business was managed too actively from the top, GCC Beverages not actively enough. Smith needed to free himself to focus on his strategy for acquiring new businesses and, at the same time, to control the operations of existing businesses sufficiently to ensure their contributions to fulfilling that strategy. The company's financial strategy, heavily dependent on bank debt and thus at the mercy of the prime rate in an era of rising interest rates, was in need of rethinking. Those kinds of issues drove the processes of reorganization and professionalization at General Cinema in the mid-1970s.[5]

Other forces for change were related less to the stages of corporate evolution than to the natural life cycle of its leader. Smith turned fifty in 1974. At the time, he was effectively chief executive, operating, and financial officer of the firm. Like his father before him, Smith had also risen to a prominent position in a number of civic and charitable organizations, in particular the Dana Farber Cancer Institute—an organization that had its roots in the Jimmy Fund, which had been one of Phil Smith's philanthropic interests. Dick Smith served as president and chairman of Dana Farber from 1973 to 1981 and as vice chairman thereafter. His wife, Susan Smith, worked alongside him in that endeavor, as founder and leader of a women's fundraising auxilliary, the Friends of Dana Farber. In the mid-1970s, with the organization in the midst of a large capital fund drive, Smith was spending a quarter of his time on his duties in that position.

For various reasons, therefore, Smith began to feel the need for support in his executive responsibilities, especially in the formulation of business and financial strategy. He was also mindful that he was now the head of a large public corporation, with responsibilities to many stakeholders. As his long-time friend and adviser (and major stockholder) Sidney Stoneman frequently pointed out, it was only prudent to begin to expand the corporate staff to a point that would make General Cinema less dependent on Smith's personal leadership. Stoneman was insistent that he begin to develop a potential successor.

By the age of fifty, Phil Smith had been working closely with his son for two years and was well along in grooming him for eventual leadership of the company. At the same age, Dick Smith was the only family member active in General Cinema's management. His middle child, Robert, would join the company in 1987, but in the mid-1970s Robert and his younger sister, Debra, were still in high school. Amy, the eldest, graduated from Harvard University in 1974 with a bachelor's degree in visual studies. Although she, like all the children, had always followed the doings of the firm with enthusiasm, she became interested in participating only with the decision to launch a film-financing effort. For two years, Amy worked with Herb Hurwitz in that venture and took business school classes in the evening. In 1977 she enrolled at Harvard Business School to work full time toward an MBA degree, which had become a prerequisite for advancement within the firm. Dick Smith had developed strong views on family participation in the management of General Cinema. "Daughter or not," he commented, "she'd have gotten nowhere without professional skills."[6]

By 1979, however, when Amy received her degree, General Cinema was on its way out of film financing and so did not hold the same interest for her. She had married a fellow Harvard Business School student, John Berylson, in 1978 and was pregnant with their first child. In keeping with the family culture, she chose to focus her attention on husband and children and to channel her extra energy and her managerial skills into public service and philanthropy.

The question of a potential family successor at General Cinema would thus remain dormant through the 1980s. As he moved through the process of professionalizing top management—which began with the hiring of Woody Ives in 1974—Smith remained aware that he was also providing for the future leadership of the company.

SEEDS OF CHANGE: THE ARRIVAL OF WOODY IVES

When Dick Smith began to look for a replacement for Ed Lane, who had announced plans to retire in 1976, the list of qualifications he drew up succinctly described the attributes of a professional manager: an MBA in finance from a "recognized" business school, a "broad cultural education," and experience at the "policy level." As it happened, Smith did not have to go far afield to find such a person. He found the person he wanted on his own board of directors.

J. Atwood (Woody) Ives had been educated at Yale University and Stanford Graduate School of Business and had started his career with Price Waterhouse in California. He moved back East in the mid-1960s, where for two years he worked closely with Royal Little at Narragansett Capital. He joined Paine, Webber, Jackson and Curtis in 1966 and became vice president and head of its New England corporate finance group in 1970. That same year, Ives replaced Maurice M. Wheeler—a limited partner of Paine Webber and a General Cinema director since 1960—on the General Cinema board.[7]

Woody Ives had first met Dick Smith as a client when Paine Webber was helping General Cinema with one of its financings. He had quickly come to appreciate Smith as one of the sharpest financial minds around. "Dick was a very sophisticated financial person," Ives recalled, "who was one of the few clients that we didn't have to modify our sort of Wall

Street lingo to talk to. He knew exactly what we were talking about and was usually a half-step ahead of us."[8]

The admiration was mutual. In tapping Ives, then only thirty-three years old, to be a director in 1970, Smith praised him as "one of the bright young stars" at Paine Webber. Ives proved to be an active director, helping to evaluate acquisition opportunities and participating in the start-up of the furniture retailing business.[9]

In 1974, when Ives was asked to join the company's management, the existing corporate group included Smith, as chairman and president; Mel Wintman, executive vice president; Ed Lane, financial vice president; Herb Hurwitz, senior vice president; and Bill Zellen, treasurer and controller. All were more or less actively involved in running the core theater business, while Smith, Lane, and Zellen provided the company's link to its large subsidiary, GCC Beverages. Smith served as the company's liaison with Al Tanger in the communications business. Hurwitz was responsible for oversight of Alperts Furniture, and he was working with Smith on plans to launch the venture in film financing. All of these men would be profoundly affected by Ives's arrival on the scene.

Even before his first day of work, Woody Ives had an impact. In negotiating his contract he secured a salary so high by General Cinema standards that Dick Smith had to increase his own compensation and to give Lane, Wintman, and Hurwitz substantial raises as well. Ives negotiated an agreement to be sent by the company to Harvard Business School's Advanced Management Program. Still more significant in the long run, Smith granted Ives a loan of 100 percent of his salary to purchase General Cinema stock. Wintman and a few other key employees had been given stock options on occasion, and in 1973 the company had developed a "phantom stock" plan under which bonuses were partially deferred and translated into fictional shares that paid dividends and could be vested after three years. However, the Key Executive Stock Purchase Loan Plan, modeled on Ives's arrangement and put into place early in 1975, for the first time opened up the opportunity for executives to purchase significant amounts of General Cinema stock. In short, simply by joining the firm, Ives had begun to change it, beginning by bringing the compensation of the corporate staff into line with that of professional managers of other companies of comparable size in the mid-1970s.[10]

For his part, Ives experienced a certain culture shock on joining the top management group. Before taking the job, he had felt some concern about working in a family firm and one that was decidedly Jewish in the composition of its top management. "I was very concerned," Ives recalled, "about going into a family company where, if you weren't a family member, your days were numbered or your position limited." He was also fearful that he might be expected, as in some Jewish firms, to contribute time and money to Jewish causes. Sidney Stoneman, whom Ives consulted on these issues, laughed at the thought that Dick Smith might require an employee to contribute to the Combined Jewish Charities. "That's not the way he operates," he assured his fellow board member. "I believed Stoneman," said Ives, "and Stoneman was absolutely correct."[11]

Indeed, once he arrived—fresh from his Harvard courses—Ives found that the cultural barrier he faced was not determined by family ownership or ethnicity but by the informal, non-professional approach to management that prevailed in the corporate office, which was still at that time essentially the management group for the theater business. Meetings were convened and decisions were made ad hoc, in an atmosphere that seemed as conspiratorial as it was collegial. There was a great deal of competition, sometimes outright conflict, among the members of the management group, and Dick Smith still made every important decision by himself. "I didn't know if this was the littlest big company or the biggest little company," said Ives. "It was clearly a pretty big company that had a very proprietary, small-company approach to how it was run." This was an uncomfortable situation for an ambitious young vice president, who expected to advance his career on the basis of job performance, not personal relationships.[12]

To a great extent the cause of those conditions was structural. Whereas Herb Paige, as head of GCC Beverages, enjoyed a great deal of autonomy in running his business, Mel Wintman's position as general manager of the theater business was very different. Everyone else in the corporate office had both longtime experience and a continuing role in that part of the business. Herb Hurwitz was a strong second-in-command, and Dick Smith was still active in deciding day-to-day issues, especially in making the key long-term decisions regarding new theater locations. The financial function for theater operations was performed by the corporate financial group under Ed Lane, who reported directly to Smith (just the structure that Smith had rejected for the bottling businesses when he first acquired them). Those parallel lines of authority inevitably had led to ill-will between the two sides, operating and financial, that extended down through the organization.

Thus, when he started work, early in 1975, Ives stepped into an informal but highly politicized office culture in which structural ambiguities encouraged individuals to compete for Dick Smith's attention. Ed Lane was still in the middle and tended to play the role of peacemaker— often a difficult one, since his subordinates, from Bill Zellen on down the line, were usually at odds with film buyers, theater managers, and Herb Paige. Herb Hurwitz was influential in that period because he was working closely with Smith on the film-financing project. He tended to share and encourage Smith's risk-taking tendencies, whereas Mel Wintman was "the office realist." Paige did his own thing in Miami, but as his division grew rapidly in size and profitability, his views increasingly carried weight in Boston, and he became a corporate officer in 1975.[13]

By injecting Woody Ives into that milieu, Smith effected an opening-up on several levels. The list of Ives's responsibilities ensured that he would be a pivotal member of the corporate office. They encompassed, among other things, oversight of financial strategy, including investments in film and real estate; "review and critique" of all financial statements and plans; analysis and execution of acquisitions and dispositions; and development of a management information system. In addition, next to Smith himself, Ives was to be the most visible member of the group to the outside world, with responsibility for public relations in all financial and legal areas and for relations with the directors.[14]

When, shortly after he joined the company, Ives began to propose procedural and then structural changes that would bring General Cinema more in line with current management practice, Smith was receptive. One of the first things to change was the informal and unstructured mode of interaction among the top management group. At Ives's suggestion, they began holding regularly scheduled weekly meetings, then setting agendas and recording decisions on action items.

Meanwhile, there was yet another proponent of change on the scene, a Harvard Business School professor named James McKenney, whom Ives brought in as a consultant to help develop corporate information systems. An integral part of that process was to review the operations of General Cinema's two businesses and to analyze the relationships between the operating units and the corporate office. Naturally enough, McKenney soon became involved in advising General Cinema on the key organizational issues that faced the company. Ives and McKenney proposed a restructuring of the company that would set the theater business off as a separate division, and that step was taken in October 1975. The next step was to develop a more systematic approach to planning and division review—a new operating role for the corporate office.

THE ROLE OF THE CORPORATE OFFICE IN THE DIVERSIFIED FIRM

By the mid-1970s, there was a large body of thought to draw on in considering how a diversified company should be structured and managed. One could, for example, study the practice of active managers, as reported and commented on in the popular business press and in the teaching cases used in schools of management. In addition, a growing body of empirical work by faculty in business schools offered both theory and concrete examples of how diversified firms functioned. Any new wisdom on the subject was quickly disseminated by management consultants, who were either academics themselves or ready translators of the latest academic theories.

The governing paradigm of the era was "strategy and structure," drawn from the seminal work of Harvard Business School historian Alfred D. Chandler, Jr., published in 1962. Chandler argued that the so-called multidivisional structure that had evolved in U.S. business over the course of the twentieth century represented the most advanced bureaucratic form of the times. Its defining characteristics—and greatest advantage, Chandler asserted—were the freeing of corporate chief executives from routine operational decision making and the creation of supporting staff functions that provided the detailed information and analysis necessary for strategic planning and implementation of strategy, primarily through allocation of resources.[15]

The concept of corporate strategy was just coming into focus in academic and popular literature when Chandler's *Strategy and Structure* appeared. His work contributed to a growing pressure on company leaders to devote their energies to making strategic decisions—to seizing long-range opportunities rather than to solving current operational problems. Chandler's simple yet novel dictum, "structure follows strategy," offered a theoretical explanation of observed business practice, even as it highlighted structural issues as a primary concern of corporate leadership.[16]

By the mid-1960s, the conglomerate movement was in full swing, and academics were scurrying to evaluate the strategy of diversification by acquisition into unrelated industries and the structural variations that flowed from it. At the same time, a great deal was spoken and written about the management of conglomerate companies by the companies' managers themselves. Those executives were repeatedly called on to justify their motives and methods before numerous congressional committees and government agencies. They were followed closely and interviewed frequently by the business press. All in all, they proved to be articulate and effective advocates of the distinctive form of multidivisional corporation that the conglomerate represented.[17]

The key differences between the conglomerate structure and the older form of multidivisional organization lay in the character of the corporate office and its role in the enterprise. The conglomerate corporation maintained no staff in any of the principal operating functions—manufacturing, marketing, purchasing, or R&D—in contrast to multidivisional firms that had diversified largely by internal expansion into related businesses. As a result the size of the corporate staff in a conglomerate tended to be quite small relative to other companies. It also tended to have a distinctly financial, as opposed to an operating, orientation. Such an organization allowed much greater autonomy to division executives. Yet the creators of conglomerates argued that a small corps of generalists at the top of a highly diversified, decentralized organization could extract superior performance from operating divisions, not by managing them, but by ensuring that they were well managed. Indeed, that was the principal justification for acquisitions in unrelated industries.[18]

By the mid-1970s, however, conglomerates were decidedly out of favor, having proven themselves to be, in many cases, unwieldy and underperforming giants. In Chandler's second major book, *The Visible Hand,* awarded a Pulitzer Prize in 1977, he spoke of the new business form with some skepticism. The strongly financial and legal corporate staffs of conglomerates, Chandler noted, were not well equipped to monitor and evaluate, much less to improve, divisional performance. They could not "nurse sick divisions back to health" or "introduce new processes and products regularly and systematically into the economy." The managers of conglomerates were not quite like bankers, because they still had ultimate responsibility for the performance of businesses in which they invested. That caveat aside, Chandler argued, they had become "almost pure specialists in the long-term allocation of resources."[19]

Indeed, as closer study of highly diversified firms revealed, the relationships between the corporate office and its operating divisions was one of the thorniest that top managers in such companies had to face— precisely because of their different perspectives on the question of how resources should be allocated. Put simply, the interests of the two often came into conflict, as division managers attempted to maximize their own performance, whereas the corporate staff strove to maximize the performance of the company as a whole. For example, as one staff officer responsible for planning in a large conglomerate commented, the divisions "always want to spend money for development if they are allowed to. . . . We might do better from a corporate viewpoint to put this money elsewhere." Said another, "Division managers will always say you are milking the business, not making the proper provision for the long range, and so forth. . . . There aren't any easy answers to any of this."[20]

Dick Smith's diversification strategy and the company he had built differed significantly—not least in size—from the leading conglomerates. He was not eager to have that unpopular term applied to General Cinema.

Nevertheless, as the professionalized corporate office began to take shape and to define a role for itself, the company would become increasingly like a conglomerate in its structure and approach to management. He would be forced to wrestle with all the dilemmas attendant upon that change.

At issue, Smith realized, were not only individual careers, but also some basic questions relating to the management of existing businesses and the strategy of diversification. In 1975, as the transition was just beginning, Smith cooperated with Harvard Business School in the preparation of a teaching case on General Cinema. He told the Harvard interviewer that he had set "a very high standard" for growth—15 to 20 percent annually. Yet, Smith made clear, there were key decisions yet to be made, which he stated as follows:

> (1) the proportion of future growth to be achieved by acquisition as distinct from internal growth; (2) the specific directions and operating philosophies which flow from [the chosen] acquisition policy; (3) the parameters for trading off financial conservatism for leveraged earnings growth; (4) development of [General Cinema's] own unique professionalism required for the effective management of a company clearly moving on from its entrepreneurial stage.[21]

In essence, those issues became a battleground of contending ideas at the corporate level. The way in which they were decided largely determined the future course of the company.

Transitional Structure: Management by Committee

In setting out to build a professional corporate executive staff and to ensure an orderly succession at General Cinema, Smith was sensitive to the claims of long-time General Cinema employees to a place in whatever corporate leadership group was to emerge. Ives became chief financial officer in 1976. Herb Paige was the leading candidate for chief operating officer, although he lacked both experience outside the soft drink bottling business and professional management training. Mel Wintman, Herb Hurwitz, and Bill Zellen had similar limitations. Smith was determined to include them but equally set on creating a professional top management team. He clearly stated as much in a reorganization memo in June 1976:

The basic intent of present thinking is to move the company in an orderly fashion from its paternalistic and entrepreneurial beginnings to a more professional style of management; a style which will be more consistent with a growing multidivisional enterprise and provide for its future development and continuity by orderly and consistent planning, personnel development and professional administration.[22]

The reorganization created a transitional structure designed to give the division managers an opportunity to grow into general management through participation in it. It established a committee system at the corporate level, which brought the operating executives into the key processes of corporate strategic planning and division review. At the same time, Smith put each of the operating units—the beverage division, the theater division, the communications group, the furniture group, and the film-financing group—on notice to develop a business plan and budget and to prepare for regular corporate reviews of their operations.

The new committee system blurred the distinction between divisional and corporate leadership. Smith and Ives sat on two key committees with Wintman, Paige, and Hurwitz—Corporate Strategic Planning (CSP) and Corporate Division Review (CDR). The corporate financial staff—Ives, Zellen, and Bob Tarr, then director of corporate planning—also sat on the CDR committee and played an important role as staff to the CSP committee. With Smith, they formed a third committee, Financial Planning, which was charged with setting the company's overall financial strategy and helping translate it into divisional and corporate budgets and acquisition guidelines. James McKenney also attended most meetings as secretary to the CSP, in a role designated alternatively as "catalyst" for change and "teaching aid" for managers as they worked to implement change.[23]

Smith viewed the committee structure as a first step toward bringing the operating executives into the corporate office. At the first CSP meeting, he urged Wintman, Paige, and Hurwitz to begin identifying and developing subordinates who could take over routine operations of their divisions and free them to spend more time on corporate affairs. He envisioned that participation in the committees would help them to develop a broader view of the entire corporation through exposure to the other businesses and through discussion of overall strategy. At the same time, as division heads within the new structure, they would be subjected to the financial discipline that, by the mid-1970s, had become synonymous with professional management.

The professionals—Ives, McKenney, and later Tarr—took a somewhat different view of the committee structure. They welcomed it as a means of transcending the highly personalized, one-to-one relationships that Smith maintained with his operating executives. The CDR in particular allowed the corporate staff to analyze and comment on divisional operations in a setting that afforded facts as much weight as personalities. Moreover, because of Smith's stated desire to professionalize management, they were able, to a great extent, to set the terms of discussion within the CSP and CDR committees. In support of the committees' deliberations, the financial staff provided economic forecasts, financial criteria for acquisitions, guidelines for divisional reporting, and recommendations on how General Cinema should evaluate requests for capital funds. They also worked with Smith to formulate a financial strategy, which essentially set the parameters of discussion of broader corporate strategy.

The transitional structure gave Smith time not only to assess his management group and to choose a corporate team from among them, but also to ease into a definition of the relationship between the corporate office and division management. At least in principle, the arrangement left open a full range of options, from a system in which operating executives played a major role in setting overall corporate strategy while maintaining varying degrees of autonomy within their divisions to a top-down form of direction from the corporate office. As the committees began to function, some predictable differences arose over just where on that spectrum General Cinema belonged. The issue was not one to be resolved in a few meetings; indeed, it could not be decided in the abstract. Rather, as appropriate for a diversified firm, the character of the corporate office and the definition of its role evolved in tandem with and in response to the full articulation of corporate strategy.[24]

DEBATE OVER STRATEGY AND POLICY, 1976–1978

The first session of the CSP met at Smith's home in July 1976. In that and subsequent meetings, discussions covered a wide range of practical and philosophical issues related to the future of the firm. Those discussions were informed by and ultimately merged with separate discussions by the same group in different combinations, in different committee venues. The Financial Planning Committee—Smith, Ives, Zellen, and Tarr—began to develop a financial strategy focused largely on preparation for an acquisition but having significant implications for ongoing operations.

As a major acquisition became more of a certainty, it took on greater importance in strategic thinking, not least in the sense that it became a strong competitor for corporate funds. Allocation of resources was thus a central theme of discussion in the committees, while debate over the imposition of professional management systems and values formed a strong subtext.

An important element of the acquisition strategy was an effort to win favor in the financial community in order to gain an A or BAA bond rating, to attract institutional investors, and to push up the price of General Cinema stock. That effort demanded that General Cinema project the image of a solid growth company—that is, one with a stable balance sheet and a regular pattern of earnings growth. Preservation of capital assumed a high priority among corporate goals, and constraint in capital spending became important both as an end in itself and as a means of limiting growth to a level that would appear to be sustainable over the long haul. It became important that General Cinema should not be—and should not appear to be—a high-risk growth company with volatile earnings. The strategy assumed that risk was unavoidable in making an acquisition, but that spending in existing businesses should strictly adhere to corporate criteria for return on investment.

As the strategy emerged, it created conflict over capital spending in the beverage division, where Herb Paige tended to view growth primarily as a marketing problem. Paige had established a practice of setting goals for volume growth and then spending the capital necessary to achieve them. On that basis, he expressed confidence that beverage division earnings could grow 15 percent annually, even without adding new franchises. However, the corporate financial strategy dictated that capital expenditures be held to the level of depreciation, and the depreciation base in the beverage division was shrinking as a result of a program, initiated in 1975, to convert a large portion of the truck fleet from owned to leased vehicles. Under those constraints, Paige had increasing difficulty defending his 1977 and 1978 capital budgets, even though division earnings were growing by 25 to 30 percent a year in that period. There was a concern, as Smith expressed it, that Paige's approach amounted to "buying future profits now with an accelerated high rate of capital investment."[25]

None of the operating executives was comfortable with the concept of managed growth. "Why not," Hurwitz asked, "let the businesses do what is natural rather than try to show stable continuous earnings?" Paige said much the same thing, arguing that, when the beverage division had achieved some momentum in volume growth, the necessary investment should be made to "take it while it was available." The rejoinder from Smith and Ives was that investors looked for a consistent pattern of growth and would reward it by paying a higher price for General Cinema stock.[26]

Still, there was resistance to both the philosophy and the discipline of "management by the financials." By the third meeting of the CSP, early in 1977, Smith insisted that operating executives present their long-range plans "in the language of business, that is, in terms of necessary capital, financial needs, and funds flow over an extended time horizon." In the discussion that followed, Hurwitz argued that other factors—"markets, people, legal, and other important institutional factors"—could be just as significant in the formulation of a strategic plan. Wintman seconded that argument. "Each business operates within a set of constraints unique to its business," he suggested. Strict dependence on financial criteria such as return on investment might keep the company from making investments that might have strategic significance—for example, protecting General Cinema's position in a particular theater market. The group accepted such ideas in principle, but the financial criteria for evaluating the businesses continued to govern in practice.[27]

This development put some operating executives at a disadvantage. For example, Al Tanger, who by his own admission had little facility for thinking in financial terms and no staff to support him in doing so, found it increasingly difficult to win support for his plans to develop the radio and television stations. "Not being a financial person," Tanger recalled, "it was always difficult for me to explain how these results would come in over a long period of time. I was up against all of these financial wizards!"[28]

Perhaps the most troubling issue for the operating executives, however, arose when the corporate staff began to set division profit goals as well as capital-spending limitations. The first time this happened to Paige, he criticized the corporate analysis as a "top-of-the-mind" exercise that did not take into account the real capital needs of individual plants. Both Wintman and Paige, on different occasions, became concerned when the staff adjusted divisional performance to factor in or out the effects of presumably one-time occurrences. Similar events would happen again sometime in the future, Paige argued, and if they were to be factored out of the budgeting process, they would appear later as unhappy surprises. He complained that the combination of high profit goals and low capital expenditures would not only run down the physical plant, but would also result in a shift of profit responsibility from operating managers, where it belonged, to the financial staff.[29]

In fact, as the long-term strategy came into focus, there was a shift in thinking about where General Cinema's future growth would come from. At the first CSP meeting in 1976, Smith had suggested that, if the theater division continued to add seventy screens a year and the beverage division continued to increase case sales by roughly four million cases per year, 80 percent of General Cinema's target growth could be generated internally. However, by mid-1978, the financial staff had developed projections about earnings that suggested that, of all the sources of income in the company's portfolio, investment income on cash reserves would be the most promising growth area of the company into the early 1980s (see Table 5.2).

The division heads continued to grumble. Tanger and Paige protested to Smith that General Cinema was beginning to look like a bank, but they could not successfully counter the main premise of the financial strategy, that a major acquisition would be needed to sustain 15 percent annual growth into the 1980s. In fact, the beverage division's exceptionally high rates of growth between 1975 and 1978 had expanded the earnings base to the point of making it difficult to achieve targeted growth, especially with capital expenditures held to depreciation. At the same time, the cost of acquiring new franchises was becoming prohibitive, because soft drink bottling had by now become a popular target for acquisitive companies. Taking those factors into account, Paige had to acknowledge that the beverage business might mature as early as 1981.[30]

As corporate strategy focused increasingly on future acquisitions, General Cinema moved toward a more top-down mode of direction. The creation of the CDR committee opened the door for the corporate staff to analyze and comment on divisional operations. Bob Tarr's charge as director of corporate planning was to implement "modern budgeting systems and capital budgeting systems and all of those things that were missing" in the financial administration of the divisions. To the financial staff, Herb Paige's "bottom-up/top-down process" for capital budgeting—in which each plant manager developed a "wish list," justified by need, either to maintain the existing level of business or to expand beyond it—was appropriate for a much smaller operation, not for one that had become like the beverage division, a business with capital budgets of $20 to $25 million. By 1978, they had established a new set of procedures, under which each plant was to be held accountable for achieving a 20 percent return on assets. Sales goals for each plant were to be derived from established trends in return on investment, and additional capital investment would be approved as necessary to achieve those goals. The new system was sophisticated enough that neither division was able to implement it without the assistance of the corporate financial group, and it was thus a wedge that could open the door to control of the divisions by the corporate office.[31]

The effort to implement the new systems for analyzing divisional

TABLE 5.2 General Cinema Earnings Growth Rates, 1978–1986, as Projected in 1978 (percent)

	1978	1979	1980	1981	1982	1983	1984	1985	1986
Beverage Division	28	10	10	10	10	10	10	10	10
Theater Division	46	0	5	5	5	0	0	0	0
Communications	22	20	15	15	15	15	15	15	15
Investments	—	100	64	52	42	33	28	21	21
Profit before Income Taxes (PBIT)	22	9	25	20	15	10	10	10	10

Note: PBIT assumptions included Sunkist as an expense until 1981, a contributor of revenues thereafter; film financing as an expense throughout.

Source: Exhibit B-2 in CSP committee minutes for May 24, 1978, in HGI corporate records.

finances and procedures for controlling allocation of resources met with predictable resistance, and the dynamics of the CDR were, in Bob Tarr's words, "not very pleasant." Mel Wintman took the position that sophisticated financial planning and control were just not appropriate for a business as simple as theaters. Herb Paige defended the existing systems that he and his staff had used for a number of years, during which the beverage division's performance had been outstanding. Yet both Bob Tarr and Jim McKenney believed that, though GCC Beverages had grown and prospered with the soft drink industry, it could well have been even more profitable with tighter control and more efficient management. Just about the time that Paige's embezzlement scheme was uncovered, the CSP committee was about to consider a consultant's report that took a similar view of the division's operations.[32]

Paige's abrupt departure dramatically accelerated the pace of change in the relationship between the corporate office and the divisions. His long-term embezzlement of funds clearly justified the creation of a far more rigorous system of control. Also, in a more subtle way, the scandal shaped the evolution of the corporate office by its impact on the collective corporate attitude toward divisional management. There would be little tolerance in the future for executives attempting to play the role of strong, independent division heads. Thus Paige's departure marked the end of the era of transition and hastened the change from the old guard to the team of professionals that ultimately took control of General Cinema's corporate office. Just as compelling to Wintman and Hurwitz, however, was the state of their businesses. Changing industry conditions made theater operations an uphill battle in the 1970s, with doubtful prospects for the 1980s, and film financing from the beginning struggled with the problem that no one could quite envision how it fit into General Cinema's portfolio.

FILM EXHIBITION IN THE 1970S

The 1970s were difficult years for movie theater operators. Although the number of theaters in the country grew steadily, the number of films released each year declined (see Table 5.3). As a result, the balance in the relationship between exhibitors and distributors shifted in favor of the latter. Distributors were able to claim a larger and larger share of box office revenues. They also began to require theater owners to bear much of the risk associated with the release of new films by making them guarantee

TABLE 5.3 U.S. Theater Industry, 1964–1978

	Theaters	Films	Admissions
1964	12,740	242	1,024
1965	12,825	279	1,032
1966	12,930	257	975
1967	13,000	264	926
1968	13,190	258	979
1969	13,480	251	912
1970	13,750	306	921
1971	14,070	313	820
1972	14,370	312	934
1973	14,650	267	865
1974	15,384	268	1,011
1975	15,969	215	1,033
1976	15,976	206	1,044
1977	16,554	186	1,063
1978	16,755	199	1,133

Source: Gary R. Edgerton, *American Film Exhibition and an Analysis of the Motion Picture Industry's Market Structure, 1963–1980* (New York: Garland, 1983), pp. 27–28, 47.

substantial returns independent of actual box office receipts. They even employed blind bidding and blind selling in competitive areas.

Between *The Sound of Music* in 1965 and *The Godfather* (1972) and *The Exorcist* (1973) was a long dry spell with few big movie hits. Then, in 1975, *Jaws* became the first film ever to surpass $100 million in box office receipts. *Jaws* established a new formula for promoting movies that included a massive advance effort and then simultaneous release to at least a thousand theaters around the country in so-called saturation bookings, tie-in books, soundtracks, and souvenirs. The widespread application of that formula made movies more expensive but also potentially more profitable. Only *Star Wars* (1977) scored a hit comparable to *Jaws*. Yet on average, twenty-six films per year grossed $10 million or more in the period 1975–1979, whereas in the years 1970–1973 only eight films per year had reached that level of success at the box office.[33]

The advent of the 1970s blockbusters had an impact on the industry not unlike the introduction of CinemaScope in the 1950s—between 1973 and 1978, attendance rose by 31 percent, reversing the effects of an eight-year period of steady decline. That fact had a great deal to do with the optimism of theater owners in the era about the long-term health of their industry, an optimism that fed the continuing boom in new theater construction. Yet the steady increase in the number of theaters, combined with a low supply of film product, made it a sellers' market for feature film rentals, and the conditions for the buyers worsened over the course of the decade. That trend was exacerbated by the production studios' efforts to protect their large investments in producing and promoting new films.

During the 1970s, the terms for film rental became increasingly onerous for exhibitors. In was not uncommon in major film releases for distributors to demand a share of the first week's box office revenues equal to 70 percent of gross or 90 percent of net admissions after house allowances, whichever was larger. From the mid- to late 1970s, the distributors' share of total box office receipts rose from about 35 percent to nearly 40 percent. By the end of the decade, less than 2 percent of theater profits were derived from admissions, although the average price of a theater ticket rose from $1.55 to about $2.35 between 1970 and 1979.[34]

Even more burdensome on the theater industry were the demands of distributors for hefty advance guarantees on film rentals. In 1969 the Justice Department negotiated stipulations to the Paramount consent decree that permitted blind bidding on three films a year, with an escape clause that allowed theaters to rescind their bids within two days of viewing a film. In 1975 those limited restrictions were lifted, and blind bidding became a widespread practice. By the end of the decade, advance guarantees were typically required for as much as two-thirds of the total film rental. Distributors argued that such guarantees were required in part as protection against slow payment of rental fees, but in fact the system transferred to exhibitors much of the risk associated with high production and advance promotion costs incurred in the quest for blockbusters.[35]

Blind bidding was anathema to theater owners. In 1975 conditions were bad enough that Richard Smith took the highly uncharacteristic step of confronting the producer-distributors directly. In a letter to the heads of the major companies, Smith argued that onerous terms for film rentals threatened "the most serious crisis in history" for the theater industry. Although General Cinema theaters were still profitable, Smith said, "Virtually every dollar earned is the net result of concession sales while motion picture exhibition results in a small loss. . . . [O]ur records indicate that the vast majority of the important pictures have been exhibited at a loss or, at best, a breakeven."[36]

The situation got appreciably worse with the Justice Department's decision in April 1977 that film product "splitting" constituted bid rigging and was in violation of the Sherman Antitrust Act. The elimination of that practice—by which theaters in a given market area agreed on

which of them would compete for specific pictures—was far more injuri-
ous to smaller-scale theater operators than to national chains such as General Cinema. Yet, in combination with blind bidding, open competition
for films substantially increased the costs of film rentals for all companies.
It reduced General Cinema's theater division margins by 3 percent in the
first year. After 1977, the company had to count on close to 60 percent
of box office receipts going to distributors.[37]

The conflict between exhibitors and distributors reached new heights
for General Cinema near the end of the decade, when the company filed
suit against Disney distributor Buena Vista. The dispute was over the
distributor's attempt to make minimum per capita charges a standard part
of its film rental contracts. Buena Vista had argued for many years that it
was short-changed by contracts based on a percentage of box office receipts, because theaters charged less for children's admissions and frequently showed Disney pictures at bargain matinees. The minimums instituted in 1977 were so high that theaters would have had to do away
with bargain pricing in order to make acceptable margins. Mel Wintman
believed, and Smith concurred, that this policy would be disastrous for
the exhibition side of the industry. "As the leading theater chain at the
time," said Smith, "we thought we had to stand up and do something
about it." After a year-long struggle during which General Cinema refused
to pay charges based on per capita minimums and experienced increasing
difficulty winning bids for Disney films, the company took Buena Vista
to court, charging that per capita minimums amounted to price fixing.[38]

Buena Vista in turn launched a countersuit against General Cinema
for its participation in product splitting, which the distributor claimed
was a clear violation of antitrust law. Their suit became one of three major
cases on the issue of splitting to be prosecuted by the federal government
on behalf of film distributors. On the local level, distributors had long
condoned product splitting as a relatively effortless way to ensure orderly
dissemination of their films. But the major production companies and
their distribution subsidiaries were officially opposed to the practice, and
the Justice Department's decision to ban splitting in 1977 was influenced
by that opposition. The decision against General Cinema in a California
federal district court became the definitive statement on splitting, which
was judged a per se violation of antitrust law. After that round of litigation
on the issue, the government would attack splitting in criminal, rather
than civil, suits.[39]

The irony in the battle between General Cinema and Disney was that
they were each other's best customers. Since the days of Mid-West
Drive-In, the Smiths had oriented their theaters toward family fare and
had done very well with that approach. It was also ironic because both

Phil and Dick Smith had always conscientiously avoided conflicts with suppliers. That General Cinema had become embroiled in such a situation was testimony to how badly industry relations had deteriorated in the 1970s. When the decision went against General Cinema in California, Mel Wintman and others in the company wanted to pursue an appeal. Smith's final decision was to accept a large out-of-court settlement, and to insist on patching up the relationship with Disney as quickly as possible. Disney was also ready to end the conflict—having prevailed over General Cinema in the original suit and established its right to charge per capita minimums, Disney abandoned the practice.

COMPETITIVE PRESSURES

While battles between exhibitors and distributors over blind bidding and product splitting got most of the attention in the industry press, competition among theaters was also increasing. Theaters continued to proliferate, leading one General Cinema executive to admit that the exhibitors had become their "own worst enemy." General Cinema continued to add theaters along with the rest of the industry (see Table 5.4). Between 1970 and 1979, the circuit had grown by one-and-a-half times in number of theaters and more than tripled in number of screens.

General Cinema moved steadily forward with multiplexing in those years, but with its emphasis on twins and triples, it stood at a disadvantage in those markets where competitors had six, eight, or even twelve screens. One competitor, American Multi-Cinema, developed a rather simple strategy that consisted mainly of finding out where General Cinema planned to build a new theater and then building a larger multiplex nearby. In those larger complexes, it was possible to play most or all of the current releases at one time, which maximized their marketing impact. General Cinema film buyers, on the other hand, had to work harder and to be selective. Even if the canniest buyer might succeed in anticipating precisely which movies would be the big box office hits of the season, the sheer variety of current films at the giant multiplexes created a kind of "carnival effect" with a drawing power that a twin or triple could not easily match.[40]

All those factors combined to place heavy pressure on General Cinema's theater profits in the 1970s. Revenues became volatile, surging to a record high in 1975, dropping back in 1976, then rising sharply again in 1977. Many of General Cinema's theaters became uncompetitive, especially drive-ins and the single-screen indoor theaters that had been acquired from Loew's and Mann theaters in 1970 and 1972. Those were

TABLE 5.4 General Cinema Theater Circuit, 1970–1982 (number of theaters by type)

	Total	Single	Twin	Triple	Quad	Quint	6-Plex	8-Plex
1970	198	152	45		1			
1971	215	153	58	2	2			
1972	284	191	86	5	2			
1973	289	142	129	14	4			
1974	307	116	159	26	6			
1975	305	82	173	40	10			
1976	319	61	189	55	11	3		
1977	329	43	188	76	18	4		
1978	335	32	181	95	23	4		
1979	337	23	169	104	35	6		
1980	347	21	156	114	41	13	2	
1981	350	15	150	111	56	13	5	
1982	350	13	143	109	56	15	13	1

Source: Theater records provided by Howard Spiess.

eliminated between 1976 and 1978. In the following year, twelve shop-ping-center theaters, with a total of nineteen screens, were either sold or closed. The write-offs associated with those theater closings combined with higher film and operating expenses to depress earnings still further. Whereas profit margins had averaged 12.6 percent from 1968 through 1972, the average fell to 8.3 percent in the years 1973–1978.[41]

THEATER DIVISION MANAGEMENT

There were also significant changes in the management of General Cinema's theater business in the 1970s. Some were evolutionary adapta-tions related to growth and geographic expansion. Others were more radical, resulting from the corporate restructuring that established GCC Theatres as a separate division in 1976. In the harsh economic climate of the industry as a whole, alterations in organizational relationships and management policies exacerbated deep-rooted tensions among key divi-sional functions—operations, film buying, and finance.

Before the reorganization, the theater circuit had become so large that the functional department heads in Boston began to have difficulty handling all the issues that seventeen district managers could raise about construction, purchasing, advertising, concessions, or theater operations. The problem was most acute in the area of operations. There a sort of de facto regional organization took shape when Howard Spiess and Stan Werthman divided the responsibility for troubleshooting day-to-day is-sues, with Werthman taking the region west of Chicago, and Spiess taking the region to the east. That experiment worked well, and in 1974 three district managers were promoted to the position of regional director, one for the East, one for the Midwest, and one for the West. A fourth region, for the South, was added soon afterward.

Top managers of the theater organization were divided over the ques-tion of whether the offices of the regional directors should be located in the field or in the home office in Boston. Wintman and Werthman, both of whom had earned their spurs in concessions, wanted regional managers to be out where they could keep closer contact with the action in the field. Spiess and Hurwitz demurred, believing it more important for man-agers to remain in the central office where policy was made. The latter view prevailed for the first five years, but in 1979, when two new regions were created, separate offices were set up in Atlanta, Chicago, Detroit, Dallas, and Los Angeles.[42]

Regardless of where the regional offices were located, control of the

theater business remained highly centralized under strong functional department heads who remained in the Boston home office. When GCC
Theatres, Inc., was created in the restructuring of 1975, those individuals
became vice presidents, reporting directly to Mel Wintman. In addition,
at that time the division took over responsibility for its own financial
direction, accounting, and control. During 1977, Bill Zellen transferred
from the corporate office to head the new financial function. He was
promoted to senior division vice president for finance in 1979. Morris
Englander became vice president for real estate, although that function
remained closely linked to the corporate office and Dick Smith (see
Figure 5.1).

The field organization officially reported to the home office through
Operations, but the other departments were also out in the field function-
ing more or less independently. As in the past, relationships among functional groups continued to be more competitive than cooperative.

Film buying was organized regionally from the beginning, with separate offices in major cities around the country reporting to the head film
buyer in Boston. The underlying principle of that structure was that audience preferences for different types of movies varied greatly, depending
on the cultural and socio-economic characteristics of a particular area.
Film buyers had to know their areas extremely well, to anticipate how a
particular film would fare, and to structure a bid accordingly. They enjoyed a great deal of independence but also had to suffer a lot of criticism
from the theater management side about the product they supplied and
the prices the company had to pay.[43]

When a divisional financial department was established, a new position was created, titled "film economist." Film economists reported to the
vice president for finance but operated in the regional film-buying offices.
The purpose was to provide information on how specific films had performed in different areas under differing conditions of timing and promotion—a set of numbers to provide underpinning for what was essentially
a judgment call. Designed to support film buyers, the program tended to
be viewed as a control function and as such it was very divisive. The film
economist function was eliminated after a few years, but even without it,
finance remained an extremely powerful function, parallel to operations
and film buying. In 1979 the offices of treasury and control alone were
large enough to provide one staff member for every three theater managers in the field.[44]

In short, the setting off of GCC Theatres as a separate division did
not eliminate the parallel lines of responsibility and authority that had fed
conflict in the home office since the 1950s. It did accomplish the goal of
bringing everything under Wintman's control, but holding it all together

FIGURE 5.1 Theater Division Senior Management Staff

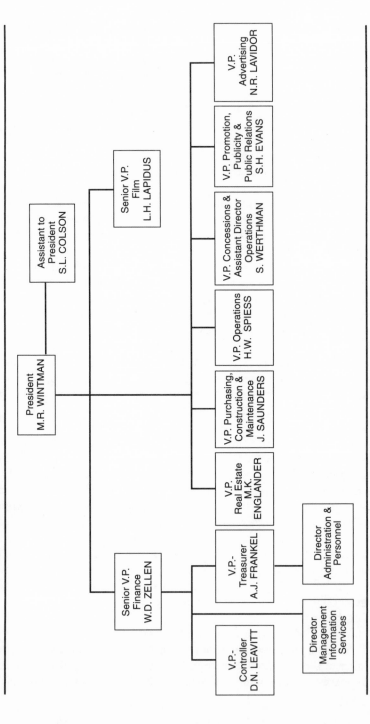

Source: GCC Theatres, Inc., "Tables of Organization," October 1979, in HGI corporate records.

was a difficult assignment for the new division chief. Dick Smith had been able to keep people in harness together. His was an overwhelmingly authoritative presence, both outside and inside the company, and yet he had always been able to remain above controversy. By contrast, Wintman had been in the thick of the fray for decades and was strongly associated with theater operations, as distinct from film buying or finance. He was able to control his strong department heads only by being extremely assertive. Thus many in the theater division came to view him as autocratic, arbitrary, and heavy-handed, although he had his fans as well—people who were convinced that the business could not have survived without the tight controls that he imposed.[45]

After the 1976 reorganization, the division came under increasing pressure from the corporate office to develop management information systems, more sophisticated budgets and economic analyses, and a management-by-objectives program for rewarding achievement of financial goals. A cost-cutting program was adopted near the end of 1977 that involved, among other things, reducing expenditures for advertising and trimming payroll costs. The latter goal was to be achieved by cutting back on the number of ushers, cashiers, doorkeepers, and, in extreme cases, projectionists, with a concomitant expansion in the duties of theater managers. Although it was recognized that such policies contributed to low morale among managers, they were seen as essential to maintaining the profitability of the business.[46]

There were also positive steps to be taken to improve profitability. The most important of those was increasing volume and margins in concessions. General Cinema experimented with selling such different types of food as pretzels, and such non-food items as cigarettes (although in 1976 the company would be the first major chain to ban smoking in theaters). Gamerooms with electronic game machines and novelties related to film promotions also became important items in concession sales. Taken together, the measures to cut costs and raise revenues were successful. The theater division's profit margin rose in 1979 to a little over 10 percent, a level that would be sustained through the early 1980s.[47]

FILM FINANCING

While the management of GCC Theatres focused on slashing costs and building concession revenues, Dick Smith continued to look into the prospects for financing films. Inadequate film supply, he believed, was the root cause of the sagging fortunes of film exhibition. Of the roughly 150 movies released per year by the major studios, Smith calculated that only 25 to 30 were popular enough to make a positive contribution to theater profits. When the number fell below that, as in 1976, the theater division faced declining revenues and profits even though the size of the theater circuit increased. If General Cinema through its own efforts could bring only a handful of successful movies into circulation, it could eliminate the one major constraint on the profitability and growth of the business.

An eternal optimist about the prospects of film exhibition, Smith was encouraged by movie-going trends in the 1970s. Having spent, by his own accounting, some thirty years in the business of entertainment, he saw hope in what seemed to be a "return to basics." Americans had been displeased by movies of the previous decade, which dealt with controversial subjects and advanced the film-makers' political or social causes. Such pictures might win critical acclaim, he argued, but the opinions of film critics had "little to do with determining the commercial success of films in most of our markets." Rising attendance levels in the era of the blockbuster demonstrated the vitality of the medium when it abandoned the "artistic perimeter of society" for the mainstream, said Smith. "Producers are making films now for pure entertainment purposes and they are bringing back audience segments too often excluded by controversial subject matter in the past."[48]

There was a great deal of "pure entertainment" in the flamboyant career of Sir Lew Grade, General Cinema's first partner in film production. The son of Russian immigrants to Great Britain, Grade's early life was spent in a London slum. He first made his mark at the age of twenty as "the World Champion Charleston Dancer." He went on to become a theatrical agent and television producer. His 1950s series *Robin Hood* was one of the first to provide filmed instead of live TV programming. That and many of his other shows were syndicated worldwide. Grade was the principal owner and chief executive of Associated Television Corporation, Ltd. (ATV), a diversified firm and the largest producer of programming for Britain's commercial television network. He had been knighted in 1969 and unofficially was dubbed the "supreme impresario" of British television.[49]

Grade prided himself on his ability to select programs with popular appeal. No snob was he: "My tastes," he said, "are the average person's tastes" and his track record seemed to prove the point. In 1971 Grade determined to expand on that record in television by moving into production of feature films. He had just the image to make a splash in movies. His trademark was an extra long, custom-made Cuban cigar, of which he reputedly smoked fifteen a day. He lived in luxury in a London flat, invariably traveled around town in a Rolls-Royce, and helped promote

Philip Smith (1899–1961), founder.

The first Mid-West Drive-In theater, opened in 1938 in Cleveland.

Advertising for the opening of the first Mid-West Drive-In, Cleveland, 1938.

Phil Smith in his Boylston Street office, about 1940.

Opening the Cinema Framingham, 1951: Phil Smith (far left) and Dick Smith (far right) with representatives of the shopping-center developer, National Suburban Centers.

Phil Smith (standing, second from left) with Massachusetts governor Christian M. Herter (seated, left) and baseball star Ted Williams (seated, right) to promote the Jimmy Fund, about 1955.

The Mid-West Drive-In management team, late 1950s (seated, from left):
Mel Wintman, Sam Seletsky, Phil Smith, Dick Smith, Ed Lane.

A Richard's Drive-In Restaurant in the 1950s. Every unit had the same architecture, menu, and operating procedures.

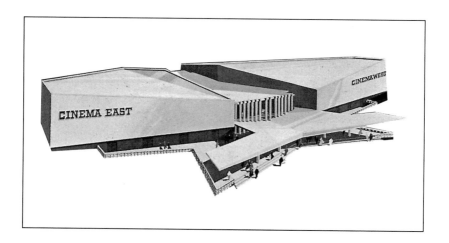

Theater innovations of General Drive-In, early 1960s: the twin theater and the shadow box screen.

General Cinema officers in 1965 (from left): Ed Lane, treasurer; Sam Seletsky, vice president-film; Sidney Stoneman, chairman of the executive committee; Dick Smith, president; Mel Wintman, executive vice president; Emmanuel Kurland, secretary.

Signing to close the acquisition of American Beverage Corporation, 1968 (seated, from left): Julius Darsky, Dick Smith; (standing, from left): Ed Lane, Joseph Darsky.

General Cinema Corporation division managers, 1972

Theater Operations Group (from left): Nathan Lavidor, Stanley Werthman, Mel Wintman, Seymour Evans, Howard Spiess, Herbert Hurwitz.

Beverage Group (from left): Robert Shircliff, John Kernin, William Zellen, Herbert Paige, Miles Dean, Jack Bliss.

The Corporate Strategic Planning Committee in 1977 (from left): Herb Hurwitz, senior vice president and president GCC Films, Inc.; Mel Wintman, executive vice president and president GCC Theatres, Inc.; Dick Smith, president, chairman and CEO; Herb Paige, senior vice president and president GCC Beverages Inc.; Woody Ives, senior vice president-finance.

Paul Del Rossi was appointed president of General Cinema Theatres, Inc. in 1986.

Bert Einloth was appointed president of General Cinema Beverages, Inc. in 1986.

The Office of the Chairman, 1987 (clockwise from upper left): Woody Ives, Dick Smith, Bob Tarr, Sam Frankenheim.

Robert J. Tarr, Jr. was appointed chief executive officer in 1992.

Richard Smith in 1992.

rumors about his skill at reaping huge profits from his varied business ventures. Grade launched his film-making career with gusto, claiming in 1974, "I intend to produce more feature films than any major studio in the world. I am only 68 and just beginning. By the time I am 70, British films will rule the world."[50]

Lew Grade's plan to make lots of movies with broad audience appeal meshed well with General Cinema's objectives in film production. His approach to financing was also attractive. It included selling TV exhibition rights in the United States and foreign distribution rights before the movies actually went into production. Such pre-sold rights could limit the producers' profit from a blockbuster; however, as Smith pointed out, the approach would also avoid "much of the volatility of production and yet [supply] the maximum number of quality popular films to a product-starved industry." In 1975 General Cinema created a subsidiary, GCC Films, Inc., and launched Associated General Films (AGF) as a joint venture with Grade's ATV. By the end of 1976, AGF had six movies in various stages of production, all of which had prominent directors and major actors in starring roles: *Voyage of the Damned, Cassandra Crossing, The Domino Principle, Cross of Iron, The Eagle Has Landed,* and *March or Die.*[51]

As laid out in Smith's public statements, General Cinema's film-financing program was eminently sensible. Indeed, many other large theater companies launched similar programs at much the same time. The industry's two major trade organizations, the National Association of Theatre Owners and the National Independent Theatre Exhibitors, also attempted to enter film production in the 1970s. Nevertheless, there was a great deal of debate within the company about the purpose and the desirability of the venture. From the beginning, the board of directors was highly skeptical of the wisdom of entering film production and placed a firm limit on how much could be invested. Smith persevered, however, and gave line responsibility for making a go of film financing to Herb Hurwitz. Hurwitz became president of GCC Films, although Smith himself continued to play an active role in the project.[52]

In 1976 Hurwitz developed a business plan, including a mission statement that envisioned the business developing into a full-fledged division of General Cinema. For the next two years, the Corporate Strategic Planning Committee spent much of its time discussing the issue of how film financing fit into General Cinema's emerging corporate strategy. Did it represent vertical integration into production and, eventually, distribution? Was its main purpose to support the theater division or to grow into a new line of business? Could five to eight additional films a year save the theater industry? Was film financing to become the company's long-sought-after third leg? Although they soon decided the last question in the negative, the group was never able to reach consensus on the strategic significance of the venture.

During 1977, they became embroiled in a dispute with Lew Grade over whether or not General Cinema was to participate in key decisions. It was decided to let Grade go his own way if he chose to do so, and near the end of the year he bought out the company's interests in all but two AGF films. Only *Capricorn I,* the seventh and final movie produced by the partnership, enjoyed much success at the box office. GCC Films was at a disadvantage in the joint-venture relationship. It would lose money if a film did poorly and only break even if it did moderately well, whereas ATV was essentially protected from losses and stood to gain much more from successful films. Such a relationship was not one to make General Cinema's board very happy. Still, the company's losses in the end were minimized by the sale of its share of the business to Grade. The venture was written off as a $300,000 learning experience that would guide GCC Films' continuing activities in film financing.[53]

Even as the relationship with Grade moved toward termination, GCC Films was working to establish new ties among producers and distributors. In announcing the plan to sell out to Grade, Smith noted that General Cinema would be "pav[ing] the way for expansion of our film financing activity with American partners." The company was beginning to receive more and better scripts for review, and the CSP was moving toward a willingness to support outright film production. In 1977–1978 GCC Films started five films, two completely on its own and three with partners. At the same time, General Cinema began discussions with Columbia Pictures Industries aimed at working out a closer relationship in film production and distribution.

COURTING COLUMBIA

By the spring of 1978, Dick Smith had grown more concerned than ever about the future supply of motion pictures. Of all the major production companies, only Columbia had demonstrated any intention of expanding its program, and the major distributors seemed to be pursuing diversification more actively than ever, in an apparent effort to reduce their exposure in the film business. By 1981, Smith predicted, "there could be as few as forty to fifty pictures available, which would be a severe threat to the theater exhibition business." He staunchly favored expanding the activities of GCC Films to the point of producing up to twenty movies a year.[54]

Working with Columbia was an attractive option, because it would link General Cinema not only to production but also to a powerful distribution network. In 1978 Columbia distributed one of the films made by AGF and signed advance contracts to distribute three more GCC Films then in production. As *Variety* noted in linking General Cinema to Columbia in 1977, Columbia's president, Alan J. Hirschfield, had "long been on record in favor of production finance arrangements from exhib[itor] sources." The Paramount court decision requiring a rigid separation between production-distribution and exhibition, Hirschfield argued, needed reconsideration in light of changed economic conditions in the industry. Columbia had already entered film-financing arrangements with Time Inc. and Electrical and Musical Industries (EMI) and was looking to expand outside support of its ambitious film production program.[55]

However, discussions with Columbia foundered on an embezzlement scandal involving its studio president, David Begelman. Hirschfield sought to remove Begelman from his job. Yet, after an extended conflict with his board of directors, Hirschfield himself was forced to leave Columbia in summer 1978, while Begelman was kept on. "The talk about joint venturing pictures with them was terminated at that point," remembered Richard Smith. "We backed away from wanting to do anything with [Columbia] outside of buying stock in their company." (It was just at that point that Smith was beginning to confront his own embezzlement scandal, which he would handle in a very different way.)[56] Subsequently, General Cinema adopted another approach in its relationship to Columbia, still aimed at increasing the supply of feature films but more indirectly as a major stockholder. During 1978, the company began to acquire Columbia shares on the open market. On January 2, 1979, Smith announced that General Cinema held 4.6 percent of Columbia's stock and proposed to expand its position to 20 percent with the approval of the Columbia board.

The situation at that time was complicated. In December Kirk Kerkorian, the controlling owner of Metro-Goldwyn-Mayer, had commenced a tender offer for 20 percent of Columbia's shares at $24 per share. Columbia's board had agreed to support Kerkorian's bid under certain conditions, one of which was that the board would withdraw its support if another offer was made at a higher price. The executives at General Cinema now saw an opportunity to gain a larger position in Columbia by helping the company defend itself against Kerkorian. Smith indicated he would be willing to pay more than $24 for the Columbia shares in order to do that.[57]

Columbia promptly rebuffed the General Cinema offer. As *Variety* commented at the time, that decision came as no surprise to the industry at large:

[I]t quickly became almost conventional industry wisdom that
a purchase by the nation's largest exhibitor chain (over 800
theatres) of a substantial share of a production-distribution
company would violate the spirit if not the letter of existing
antitrust legislation.[58]

Off the record, Columbia officials expressed concern that if General
Cinema owned one-fifth of its stock, Columbia's ability to negotiate with
its largest single customer for film would be undermined. After a decade
of conflict between the two sides of the industry, a major producer-
distributor and the nation's largest theater chain seemed strange bedfel-
lows. Although General Cinema was convinced that the relationship could
be a positive one and would not violate antitrust rules, it was a vain hope
that Columbia would welcome being rescued from Kerkorian. Still, it was
because of General Cinema's offer that Columbia was in fact able to gain
the upper hand with Kerkorian, negotiating a deal that authorized Kerkorian to make a new tender offer for 25 percent of its stock but that
imposed a three-year waiting period on the offer. Before that time was
up, Columbia was acquired for an even higher price by Coca-Cola.[59]

General Cinema's interest in film production waned after the unsuccessful Columbia offer. GCC Films undertook no new production ventures in 1979, and Smith announced that the business would be discontinued at the end of that fiscal year. None of the nine films that had
been produced had been a significant box office success, and the board of
directors simply could not continue to support what seemed to be such
a losing investment. It was decided that the two remaining movies in
production, both wholly financed by GCC Films, would be written off.
The company took a loss of about $5 million in liquidating its film-
financing subsidiary, not counting whatever opportunity costs GCC Theatres had suffered in playing the company's movies. As one theater executive noted, production could be a bad business for a theater company: "if
you own a film, then you put it in your theatre to pay it off, and then it
bombs, you lose not once but twice."[60]

Herb Hurwitz, feeling frustrated, left the company in 1979, although
he would remain a consultant and a director through 1985. "We thought
we were knowledgeable because we ran theaters," he said in retrospect.
"We thought we knew what films made money, but we turned down a
lot of pictures that made money." Hurwitz was very critical of Smith and
others for what he viewed as a lack of entrepreneurial daring in pursuing
film production. He believed that General Cinema should have launched
a hostile takeover of Columbia. As for Dick Smith, by 1980, he had
decided that, if General Cinema ever again felt compelled to undertake

film production, it would not do so as an entrepreneur. "We'd buy ourselves a film company," he said, "and do it right."[61]

TOWARD THE 1980S

Early in 1978 Dick Smith had announced to the CSP committee that he was considering creating a new top management structure, an office of the president, and he had once again urged the operating executives to identify their successors in preparation for joining that group. Roughly one year later, the idea was put on the shelf. By then both Hurwitz and Paige were gone. Bill Zellen had also ceased to be a corporate officer in 1977, when he went into the theater division. Of the old guard at headquarters, only Mel Wintman remained. Not until Wintman's retirement in 1983 would Smith revive his idea, creating an Office of the Chairman with a different, younger cast of characters.

In the interim, General Cinema continued to expand its corporate capabilities, developing the staff and information systems necessary to give closer oversight to the operating divisions, and to formulate business and financial strategy in a more systematic way. Although Dick Smith had initiated the professionalization of his company's top management group, its expansion had an internal dynamic of its own. When Woody Ives had sought approval to hire Bob Tarr as director of corporate planning in 1976, Smith had said, "Okay, go ahead. But do you really think you can keep him busy?" Smith very quickly came to value and rely on the kinds of analysis that Tarr was able to produce, and Ives proceeded to expand the corporate staff in other ways. In 1978 he hired Anthony Trauber as corporate controller, while Smith hired Samuel Frankenheim as corporate counsel, with the charge to build an in-house legal department. In 1980 Ives brought in James Moodey as treasurer. Each of these men brought considerable corporate experience. They were attracted by the opportunity to build, from the ground up, essential administrative functions for what was by then a *Fortune* 500 firm.

Coming into General Cinema, those professionals found a company that relied heavily on outside accountants and lawyers. Its financial control system had long been computerized, but it was oriented entirely toward recordkeeping and provided little management information about how the businesses actually operated. Such arrangements had worked for many years but were clearly inadequate given the company's increasing scale and complexity.

The new cadre of corporate officers brought the key functions in-house. There were some economies in that, but the most important benefit by far was in gaining the ability to deal with major issues proactively. The control function provided the foundation for division review and allowed the top corporate management team, for the first time, to play an active role in reviewing beverage division strategy. The expanded treasury function brought greater order to General Cinema's borrowing and investments and also broadened its financial relationships, making the company less dependent on a few key lenders. The establishment of an in-house legal staff made it possible to take a more systematic approach to the company's routine legal issues and to deal with special problems on a more "managed" basis.

In short, the professionalization of the corporate office gave General Cinema the essential organizational capabilities required by a large—and acquisitive—diversified firm. If Dick Smith had not fully anticipated the rapid growth of his corporate staff, he quickly came to appreciate its strengths, as he turned his attention from structural and staff issues to the pursuit of his acquisition strategy in the increasingly superheated environment of the 1980s.

The men who had worked with Smith on the entrepreneurial ventures spawned in the late 1960s and early 1970s, each of whom had at one point envisioned that the new business might become the proverbial third leg, viewed these developments with disappointment and dismay. Herb Hurwitz—a casualty, at least to some degree, of the string of unsuccessful ventures (bowling, Alperts Furniture, and film financing) with which he had been associated—in the end saw the professionalization of the corporate office as leaving few opportunities for someone like himself, whose greatest contribution over the years had been a willingness to tackle new and risky projects. He also mourned the loss of the firm's Jewish character and the passing of the corporate culture that had existed when salaries had been low but the excitement of building the enterprise had run high. The company, he said, had changed, "from a close-knit family with people knowing what was going on . . . to a more structured hierarchy with divisional review and corporate strategic planning." As compensation, pensions, and other benefits had become more heavily weighted toward the top, General Cinema, he believed, had ceased to be a "people-oriented" company. "The corporate family feeling was completely destroyed." Ed Lane, though he observed most of the changes from retirement, felt much the same way. "The personal touch left when we became bigger," Lane said. "You could no longer be a small family, which is what we were."[62]

Al Tanger was another operating executive unhappy with the turn of events at General Cinema. To be sure, the communications properties, and the radio stations in particular, had never been widely popular within the company. The financial staff, beginning with Ed Lane, as well as some of the directors, disliked the broadcasting properties because, although they were appreciating in value, they contributed little to the company's profits. Herb Paige thought that broadcasting in general was too volatile a business for the company to be in, and no one was comfortable with the degree of government regulation to which the business was subject. Moreover, Tanger's 20 percent ownership of the radio properties and his insistence on keeping his office separate from company headquarters—anomalies left over from the days when things had been more freewheeling—became increasingly unacceptable as General Cinema began to look and act more like a large, publicly owned corporation.

In the past, Tanger had depended for support on the vision he shared with Dick Smith of a potential future for the company in communications. "When Dick gave you the opening to do these things," he remembered, "you were able to develop the properties in the right way, and you were playing for the long-term pull." Smith's decision to trade off the kind of flexibility that had allowed him to launch the venture in communications for the greater organizational capabilities gained through professionalization of top management (with the hope of a much larger-scale diversification down the road) left Tanger in a weaker position. Between 1975 and 1977, General Cinema sold off radio stations in Houston, Cleveland, and Atlanta, grossing $8.5 million on an investment of $3.1 million. Although the company would remain in the field for another ten years, consolidating GCC Communications in 1978 and even acquiring a new radio station (WHUE in Boston), Tanger understood by the mid-1970s that the company would ultimately withdraw from the business.[63]

In his view, communications and film financing were terrible missed opportunities for General Cinema. In both cases, he believed, Dick Smith had demonstrated remarkable foresight in seeing the potential in industries "years ahead of most people." But, said Tanger, "He seems to make the commitment, then the financial people drag him off, because they don't understand these businesses." In fact, from the other side of the home video revolution, which virtually assured the profitability of any movie coming out of Hollywood, the fact that those financed by GCC Films were not successful at the box office does seem insignificant. "It has been proven," said Tanger in 1989, "that what he was doing, [making] these lousy movies, was forward-looking."[64]

Smith too would come to believe, in retrospect, that there had been significant trade-offs in some of the business decisions made when he was no longer making diversification decisions on his own. From the beginning, he and Tanger had talked enthusiastically about the opportunities in cable television. In 1979 Smith put together a deal with Comsat to invest $60 to $75 million in satellite transmission of cable TV, only to have it killed by the board of directors, largely on the strength of opposition from Ives and Hurwitz. "Al Tanger wanted to take us into cable TV," recalled Smith, "but we didn't have the resources or the motivation to do it when it would have been early enough to have been an important diversification." That was a "road not taken" that he would regret. As for the decision on film financing, Smith said,

> We looked for our returns in the operations rather than the creative side, and that was fine for the '70s and '80s. In the '90s, world-class entertainment companies who control the software are great enterprises, and if we had been one of those, perhaps it might have been a different kind of future than the one that we found.[65]

Despite such reflections on what might have been, the steps Smith took to create a professional and strongly financial corporate office were far more in tune with his long-standing, long-term strategy for General Cinema than the entrepreneurial ventures launched and abandoned in the 1970s. Determined to make an acquisition large enough to balance his two existing core businesses, and equally determined to avoid equity financing of that acquisition, which would have diluted his ownership position, he sorely needed a top management team capable of supporting him in the formulation of the financial, business, and acquisition strategies by which he could achieve those goals. No corporate leader, however brilliant, can expect to marshal the resources for an acquisition, analyze opportunities, and handle the complexities of deal making without the support of a sophisticated in-house staff.

In the 1980s stinging critiques of the professionals managing U.S. corporations, voiced by a broad spectrum of business observers, would echo the criticisms of the emerging corporate office mounted by the operating heads of General Cinema's businesses in the 1970s—that they were unfamiliar with and insensitive to practical operating concerns, overdependent on financial measures of performance, and over-focused on the short term.[66] Similar complaints would continue to come from theater and beverage division personnel as long as General Cinema owned those businesss. They were serious issues, which Dick Smith took seriously. Indeed, he was sensitive to the assertion that the company was "managing by financials," which was made by consultants brought into General Cinema in the late 1980s to assist the diversification program. Seeing that as a potential danger to the long-term health of the firm, Smith and other members of the top management team would take steps to change the corporate division review process in an effort to mitigate the problem.[67]

At the same time, within the context of this company's story, these issues can be recognized also as products of unavoidable tensions in a diversified, acquisitive firm. In 1978 General Cinema was investing heavily in the introduction of Sunkist Orange Soda. In the 1980s there would be investments in state-of-the-art bottling and distribution facilities for the beverage division and a large-scale expansion and remodeling program in the theater division. It would be hard to argue that the company was "milking" its divisions. Nevertheless, by 1980, the corporate office had decided that the best opportunities for long-term growth lay elsewhere. For operating managers that was a bitter pill to swallow, but, as in all such businesses, subordination of the interests of individual divisions to those of the company as a whole was a founding precept of strategy formulation.[68]

In the 1980s the strategic focus would be on completing an acquisition. The path that General Cinema trod through the "merger mania" of those years would be distinguished far more by the ways in which the company differed from most large corporations of the day than by the ways in which it was the same. Chief among the differences was the way in which the company's top management combined high-powered professional skills with the business values of an owner-managed, entrepreneurial enterprise.

CHAPTER

6

PATIENT OPPORTUNISM IN AN AGE OF EXCESS

For General Cinema Corporation, prospects for diversification became considerably more complicated as raids, leveraged buyouts, and "strategic restructuring" through divestitures created a high-stakes free-for-all in the market for corporate assets. The wave of acquisitions that began in 1975 and billowed in the 1980s was increasingly characterized by hostile takeovers and bidding wars. Those contests drove prices to premiums of 50 to 100 percent above market value, compared with a range of 10 to 20 percent in the 1960s. By the mid-1980s, deals exceeding $1 billion were common. The long bull market in equities, from 1982 to 1987, further contributed to the spiraling costs of acquisitions, as stock prices soared to record highs. The creation of an extensive market for high-yield "junk bonds," accompanied by a general loosening of credit, sustained a high level of merger and acquisition activity at ever higher prices. Those conditions severely limited the kinds of opportunities that had enabled General Cinema to pull together its soft drink bottling business in the late 1960s and early 1970s.[1]

Still, diversification had been the core of the company's strategy since the 1950s, and it remained an appropriate avenue for growth in a business that produced a large and consistent cash flow. In the late 1960s the conglomerate movement had formed the backdrop for Dick Smith's pursuit of diversification by acquisition. Now, in the era of hostile takeovers, he began to look like another corporate raider. But, as before, there were significant differences, deeply rooted in the character of General Cinema.

A defining characteristic was a management outlook more typical of a private company run by owner-managers than of a professionally managed public corporation. In the early 1980s Smith organized an Office of the Chairman that included Woody Ives, Sam Frankenheim, and Bob Tarr. Through a generous program of stock options and loans, these men came to have most of their personal wealth tied up in General Cinema stock. Working closely with Smith to formulate and implement strategy, they shared his sense of ownership in the enterprise. With this team in place, the goals of General Cinema's acquisition program remained essentially as they had been since the late 1960s: to add one, or at most two, substantial operating divisions that would fit with theaters and beverages to ensure long-term growth, and to finance the acquisition program in a way that would not risk their losing control.

The style of the executive group was also largely congruent with Smith's personal style. For a high-powered team of corporate managers, active on the mergers and acquisitions scene, they were notably unostentatious. "Tightfisted Yankees" was a phrase applied to General Cinema's executives more than once in the business press. Its "austere" headquarters, next to a General Cinema theater in a suburban Boston-area shopping mall, was frequently the focus of comment. In keeping with that image, General Cinema managers eschewed "greenmail" and made it clear that they were not out to strip the assets of acquisition targets; they were looking for a business that General Cinema could operate and grow.[2]

With those clear-cut objectives and conservative style came a limited willingness to do battle in the takeover wars. The theoretical guidelines for choosing a potential acquisition were very general: it should be a business in a consumer industry and one that the corporate team could understand. With such a wide field of possibilities, there was little motivation to wage an all-out battle for a particular prize. General Cinema was profitable and growing at a respectable rate throughout the 1980s, so there was little pressure on management to rush forward with an acquisition program. They could afford to be selective and price-sensitive.

As the company attained a higher profile—with a run at Heublein in 1981 and a "white-knight" rescue of Carter Hawley Hale three years later—its distinctive style and "creative financing" gained it a reputation for shrewd but unconventional moves. Within a growing cadre of analysts and institutional investors who followed its activities, General Cinema was valued for the strength of its core businesses as well as for its patient, cost-conscious approach to diversification. Indeed, Smith and his management team received the ultimate stamp of approval in 1984, when the stockholders, roughly one-third of whom were institutional investors, voted in favor of creating a "super stock" vested with extraordinary voting powers designed to thwart an unwanted takeover attempt.

Yet, when the acquisition effort continued for nearly a decade without accomplishing the stated goal of stabilizing the corporation on a third leg, many observers began to wonder about the direction of General Cinema's diversification program and even about the true character of the company. In the late 1980s the dominant image of Dick Smith on Wall Street was not of the head of an operating company, but of a canny investor playing largely with his own money. Smith himself at times contributed to that view. In 1984 commenting on the run at Heublein and the Carter Hawley Hale deal, he told *Business Week* that, for the moment at least, "the investment activity" was ahead of "operating activity" at General Cinema. Similarly, in a 1985 speech on General Cinema's financial history, he said, "I may be a reasonably successful operating executive, but I have the soul of a financial opportunist."[3]

As the 1980s wore on, however, the success of General Cinema's investments made it ever more imperative that an acquisition be completed. If the company's growing cash hoard were not deployed in the development of a new core business, there would be little reason to refrain from distributing it among shareholders and becoming an investment company in reality. No matter what image he projected, that was not an outcome acceptable to Dick Smith.

It was not for lack of trying that General Cinema failed to achieve its acquisition goals in the 1980s, but for lack of acquisition opportunities that met its stringent criteria. The chances to gain first-mover advantages, as in the theater business, or to consolidate a leading position in a fragmented industry, as in soft drink bottling—and to do so on a scale appropriate for the company in the 1980s and at a reasonable price—were virtually nonexistent. Smith and his team could envision other avenues of competitive advantage, but the openings to them were few and far between. Even without the excesses for which conglomerates are infamous, their experience would suggest that unrelated diversification is not an easy or sure route to long-term growth and profitability.

In 1987 General Cinema seized an opportunity to separate a distinguished set of high-end specialty retail stores from Carter Hawley Hale and created a new business, the Neiman Marcus Group. At General Cinema's annual meeting in March 1988, Dick Smith welcomed stockholders "to the first annual meeting of the new General Cinema"—finally rounded out to three major operating divisions. Yet within a year, the company's largest division, GCC Beverages, would be sold to PepsiCo for $1.75

billion, and the question of whether General Cinema could serve its stock-holders best by distributing its cash or by continuing to search for a new "third leg" would be reopened. As he turned sixty-five in 1989, Smith reached the point in his career when it became important to resolve that question, left hanging after a decade of taking the patient approach to acquisitions.[4]

THE RUN AT HEUBLEIN

General Cinema's approach to Heublein arose from the beverage division's long-standing interest in the wine industry. A number of soft drink bottlers had diversified into wine distribution in the 1970s—for example, Coke, New York. Herb Paige had investigated large-volume wine distribution to restaurants, among other things, as an avenue of diversification for GCC Beverages. In the early 1980s, as Smith and Ives began seriously considering acquisitions, they took a new interest in the wine business, because it appeared that, through distribution in grocery stores, wine was on the verge of becoming a mass consumer product, more akin to soft drinks than to liquor.

However, buying a stake in the domestic wine industry would be far more difficult than establishing a position in soft drink bottling had been in the late 1960s. Although there were many small wineries that conceiv-ably could be consolidated into a larger entity, there was no franchise system, as in soft drinks, to guarantee its competitiveness. On the con-trary, the industry was dominated by a few major wine companies—substantial corporations much larger than General Cinema and not inter-ested in selling out. When overtures were made through a third party to Gallo, a private company, word came back that one of the Gallo brothers had asked, "General Cinema—who is that? Should we buy them?"[5]

With $2 billion in sales in 1981, Heublein was the second largest company in the industry, after Gallo. A distributor of liquor and specialty foods, Heublein had acquired United Vintners in 1968 and had greatly improved its sales and profitability through aggressive marketing and new product development. Heublein's stock soared to a price thirty-five times its earnings in the early 1970s. However, subsequent acquisitions of Hamm's Beer and Kentucky Fried Chicken—businesses that required skills other than distribution and marketing—were far less successful, and in the late 1970s Heublein's stock price fell to a third of its former high.[6]

By 1981, when General Cinema began looking at the company,

Heublein's results had improved, but its stock price did not reflect the underlying value of its assets. The thinking at that point began to shift. General Cinema could not acquire whole a company more than twice its size, but it could establish a minority position in Heublein at an attractive price. From that position it could conceivably bring to bear its strength in beverage marketing to help realize the potential growth in the wine business. With that thought in mind, between December 1981 and February 1982, General Cinema acquired nearly 10 percent of Heublein's shares on the open market, for $35 to $40 per share.[7]

Smith then initiated a dialogue with Heublein's management and suggested essentially what had been proposed to Columbia a few years before: General Cinema would establish a large but not dominant stockholder position and contribute to the management of Heublein through participation on its board of directors. That was the plan that Smith subsequently labeled "investment with involvement"—a plan of which Heublein's chief executive officer, Hicks B. Waldron, took a dim view, to say the least. "[Smith] told me that they didn't have the money to go out and buy a big liquor or fast-food company," Waldron told a biographer some years later. "So they decided to buy a piece of a big company. . . . And he was just cocky enough to say that he thought he could help manage the company better."[8]

Waldron's resistance quickly transformed General Cinema's initiative into a public test of wills (see Figure 6.1). Behind the scenes, a range of possibilities was discussed. One of those was the sale of part or all of the wine business to General Cinema. However, as they got close enough to Heublein to understand its businesses better, Smith and Ives began to see that the wine business would require huge investments, much of which would be tied up in inventory. As an agricultural business, it was also seasonal and subject to the vagaries of nature—elements of risk quite foreign to the owners of theaters and soft drink bottling plants. Buying the wine business by itself was therefore not an attractive option for General Cinema. On closer inspection, however, the food segments of Heublein's portfolio began to look more interesting. Another deal was discussed, in which General Cinema would buy the entire company but help Heublein's management finance a leveraged buyout of the liquor distribution business, which included principally Smirnoff vodka but also national brands of sherry, rum, tequila, and scotch.[9]

While talks were in progress, General Cinema steadily raised its stake in Heublein, but in May 1982 the company announced that it would stop at 18.9 percent. In the business press that was interpreted as a gesture of good faith. It had been widely assumed that the stock purchases would

FIGURE 6.1 General Cinema–Heublein Timeline

February 3, 1982	GC announces it has purchased 2.1 million shares (9.7 percent) of Heublein "for investment purposes" and intends to purchase more than 15 percent of Heublein's stock.
February 22, 1982	Heublein announces it has filed suit in federal court in New York to nullify GC's purchase of its stock and block further purchases, charging that GC's goal was a takeover of Heublein and that GC had violated antitrust law by failing to disclose its intentions earlier.
March 1, 1982	Heublein announces it has purchased 3.5 percent of GC's stock (380,800 shares) and files its intention to acquire more.
March 12, 1982	GC buys 1,060,800 of its own shares, receives board of directors' approval and an expanded credit agreement to buy back as many as 3 million shares (27 percent) if necessary to thwart a takeover by Heublein; GC announces it will resume buying Heublein stock.
March 17, 1982	Heublein secures a temporary restraining order against the FTC restriction on its buying more GC stock; requests a list of GC stockholders "to question [them] about the propriety of their company's purchases of both Heublein and General Cinema Stock."
March 18, 1982	GC stockholder Harry Lewis files suit in Delaware seeking to block further stock repurchases.
April 15, 1982	GC files notice with the SEC of further purchases of Heublein stock, bringing its share up to 12.8 percent and its investment to $104.4 million.
April 27, 1982	GC files notice with the SEC that it has purchased another 325,400 shares of Heublein stock, bringing its stake to 14.3 percent; states intention to raise the stake to as much as 25 percent.
May 28, 1982	GC informs SEC it has purchased additional Heublein shares, bringing its stake to 18.9 percent but that it has no "present intention" of continuing its purchases; Heublein contradicts GC's statement that talks are in progress between the two companies.
July 29, 1982	R. J. Reynolds announces agreement to acquire Heublein in a two-part tender offer in which it will pay $63 per share for 52 percent of Heublein's outstanding shares and then trade RJR common and preferred stock worth $56.83 for each remaining Heublein share.
August 2, 1982	GC announces it cannot tender its Heublein stock under SEC rules but will be able to trade for RJR stock once the merger is completed.
October 13, 1982	Heublein stockholders vote in favor of RJR acquisition; Heublein files suit in federal district court seeking to force GC to return the profits it will make in exchanging its Heublein stock for RJR stock.

Source: Compiled from articles in *The Wall Street Journal* and the *Boston Globe*.

go forward until General Cinema owned 20 percent of Heublein, at which point it could have consolidated its holding into earnings statements. In fact, by July, Smith believed he had succeeded in negotiating a deal for investment with involvement that included an agreement to halt the purchases of Heublein stock. Yet, shortly thereafter, Waldron announced that Heublein would be acquired by R. J. Reynolds (RJR) for $63 per share.[10]

At no time, apparently, had Hicks Waldron believed what General Cinema said about its intentions. In a lawsuit filed immediately following completion of the sale of Heublein to RJR, Waldron claimed that General Cinema had planned all along to take over his company and its management. However, as most commentators noted, that was an improbable scenario. With the junk-bond financing of takeovers still a tool of the future, there was as yet no thought at General Cinema that such a multibillion-dollar acquisition might be possible for a company its size. Moreover, both Smith and Ives at the time were still of the opinion that hostile takeovers were unethical. (In 1980 Smith had signed an advertisement condemning takeovers that was part of Mallencrodt's defense against Avon.) Said Smith of Heublein: "We wanted to be friends. They just didn't believe us."[11]

General Cinema profited from its investment in Heublein, receiving 2.6 million shares of R. J. Reynolds common stock and over one million shares of RJR 11.5 percent preferred stock for its Heublein shares. Nevertheless, Smith did not consider the outcome a victory, and in the aftermath he and Woody Ives began to rethink the concept of investment with involvement. Given the likely fears of entrenched managements in a takeover climate, it no longer appeared to be a viable alternative to a strategy of outright acquisition. The idea that Hicks Waldron might actually have welcomed their input seemed naïve in retrospect, and the idea that General Cinema might attempt a hostile takeover began to seem less unlikely. When they raised that issue with General Cinema's board of directors, Smith and Ives were somewhat surprised to find them in unanimous agreement: a hostile takeover was acceptable as long as it was in the best interests of General Cinema shareholders.[12]

General Cinema came away from its aborted Heublein relationship with its financial position stronger than ever. In April 1983 the company issued $100 million of 10 percent subordinated debentures exchangeable for 60 percent of its RJR common stock. Shortly thereafter, GCC Communications sold its Miami television station, netting $40.1 million after taxes. The proceeds from those transactions made it possible to repay the $220 million bank debt incurred in the purchase of Heublein and General Cinema stock, and General Cinema's debt-to-equity ratio fell to 0.54 to one, the lowest point in twenty years. Early in 1984 General Cinema issued another $78 million in subordinated convertible debentures for its remaining RJR common stock. For an investment in Heublein of about $157 million, the company had realized an immediate return of $178 million, postponing capital gains tax until exchange of the debentures. In addition, General Cinema continued to hold RJR preferred stock worth over $100 million, from which annual dividends could be expected to contribute substantially to future revenues. Under then-current law, 85 percent of such intercorporate dividends were excluded from taxation, and the interest General Cinema paid to its bondholders was fully deductible.[13]

These financings demonstrated precisely the kind of creativity in which Ives and Smith took great pride. Yet equally, they provided a measure of their commitment to the search for an acquisition. General Cinema was sacrificing the chance to earn far greater investment profits down the road for an immediate, dramatic gain in financial strength and flexibility. There was little doubt in the corporate office that they could do better for stockholders in the long run by using that money to buy a new operating company than by maintaining a passive investment.[14]

Taking everything together, General Cinema could afford to spend as much as $500 million in a takeover bid. Nevertheless, Dick Smith told a group of financial analysts, General Cinema's management was in a good position to be patient:

> Our overall financial strength and the momentum in our existing businesses enable us to be very comfortable, very careful and very deliberate in the search for our next major investment or operating business. . . . You will not see General Cinema bidding on every deal that makes the news. On the other hand, I can assure you that we are invited to consider almost every opportunity that does occur.[15]

Indeed, seeking out and evaluating opportunities had become the main business of General Cinema's top management. In 1976 Smith had told a Harvard Business School interviewer, he was handling the diversification effort on his own, calculating that, since he was looking only for a single new business, it made little sense to establish a functional group for that task. Much had changed since then, both within the company and in the business environment. Smith recognized that the ability to analyze and negotiate potential deals would be as important as the financial resources to fund them. In late 1983 he put the finishing touch on nearly a decade of organizational restructuring and development by creating a four-person Office of the Chairman (OOC)—the team that would guide General Cinema into the 1990s.[16]

CREATION OF THE OOC

Dick Smith was experienced in dealing with strategic issues in a collegial setting from working with his father in the formative years of his career, and that experience guided him in creating and working within his new Office of the Chairman. Smith's pattern for many years after his father's death had been to talk issues through with his operating managers and then make decisions himself. He had some trusted advisers, Sidney Stoneman in particular, but he had really handled the strategic thinking for the firm on his own and had been comfortable with that. Now, in part because of Stoneman's urging that he develop a successor and in part because the strategic issues facing the company were far more complex, Smith was prepared to share the responsibility for charting the future course of General Cinema.

Two central precepts informed his decision to establish an Office of the Chairman. One was the belief that a process of open discussion and disagreement, by bringing different perspectives and professional strengths to bear on business problems, tended to produce sound decisions. From the early days of his management of the theater business, Smith had tolerated (some say encouraged) disagreement among his subordinates—strong, independent department heads, who often differed over how things should be done—and had relied on that dynamic to inform his decisions. The second precept was that the process of arriving jointly at decisions could provide the individuals involved a unique opportunity to learn from each other and, if the issues addressed were of strategic scope and significance, to grow to their maximum potential for corporate leadership. He had experimented with that idea in creating a committee structure in the mid-1970s.

In 1978 Smith had broached the idea of an Office of the President. The candidates for membership in the group at that time were Ives, Wintman, Paige, and Hurwitz. In the years between the first articulation of the concept and its implementation, not only the personnel had changed; Smith's concept of the top management group had evolved as well. The issue of developing potential corporate leaders was still important. Yet the need to pull together a team to shape corporate strategy was in some ways more pressing. General Cinema emerged from its run at Heublein with increased resources and a higher profile. Its range of options was greatly expanded, but so were the complexities of formulating strategy and responding to opportunities.

By the early 1980s, the candidate group had become quite different. Woody Ives remained at the center as chief financial officer, but of the three original operating officers only Wintman remained in the firm, and he was close to retirement. Smith waited to create the OOC until after Wintman retired and then tapped Bob Tarr, who had earned his stripes in general management through six years of running GCC Beverages. He rounded out the group with Samuel Frankenheim, the company's general counsel.

In bringing together Ives, Frankenheim, and Tarr, Smith began to think of a team whose members represented distinct professional and intellectual disciplines—finance, law, and general management. Those would be the key functions, he decided, both in managing the company that General Cinema had become and in shaping its future character and direction. "In choosing to form the OOC," he later commented, "the idea was to include only the most significant functions from an overall strategic managerial point of view. . . . Those functions are more significant than the operating managerial competence associated with the running of a single division well."[17]

It was a departure from long-standing practice for Smith to look to a lawyer for contributions to business decisions. Emmanuel Kurland had served as corporate secretary since the creation of Mid-West Drive-In in 1937 and was effectively the company's general counsel, but he had made it a practice seldom to advise his clients in their business operating decisions. "He was the kind of lawyer who doesn't exist much anymore," observed Sam Frankenheim, "in the sense that most corporate lawyers or business lawyers are not a bit shy about business advice to their clients." Smith had been comfortable and satisfied with that style. "So it's kind of odd in a way that I should be here," reflected Frankenheim, "because I am just the opposite in the way I look at things."[18]

In his own view, it was the Heublein episode that made Frankenheim a candidate for the OOC. Throughout, General Cinema relied heavily on the legal advice of Skadden, Arps, Slate, Meagher, and Flom, a law firm specializing in takeover battles. Frankenheim was the liaison with Skadden, Arps and worked closely with Smith and Ives for nearly a year as events unfolded. "We literally met, or at least talked on the telephone, every day during that period." During that experience, Smith began to value the kind of input Frankenheim could offer in formulating and evaluating strategies. The legal discipline, as he came to appreciate it, was one that dictated attention to process, including careful appraisal of all of the negatives, as well as the positives, of a proposed course of action. Such a perspective added a dimension to the discussion of corporate strategy that, in Smith's opinion, nicely balanced the financial and operating points of view.[19]

Like Frankenheim, Bob Tarr was included in the OOC because he had earned Smith's respect. Presented with an unusual opportunity to make his career as head of GCC Beverages, Tarr had demonstrated the good sense to begin by learning the bottling business from the division's strong corps of experienced line managers. In return, he had helped many of them to develop as managers by pushing them to assume fiscal responsibility for their operations. Though he was fast becoming an operating manager, Tarr's first area of expertise was financial control, and he had instinctively judged his best opportunity to improve the division's performance to lie in building skills and attitudes within the organization to complement his own. "They were always well-qualified sales and marketing executives," he said of the beverage division managers. "Some of them were well-qualified production and operations executives. But the financial piece was one that was missing, and once that came together, the general managers really became well rounded."[20]

In the GCC Beverages school of financial management, the budgeting process, in particular the capital budget, was the core curriculum. When Tarr took over leadership of the division—and especially after the 1980 move of divisional headquarters to Boston—the activities of line managers were opened up to oversight through the corporate division review (CDR) process as they had never been under Paige. In proposing capital projects, managers competed against each other for a fixed amount of available funding, and they did so on the strength of their analyses of expected returns. Those who succeeded in winning funding for major projects then provided a "post-completion review," comparing projected returns to actual results within the first two years. The reviews became a central part of the advocacy process by which funds were allocated. In the words of corporate controller Anthony Trauber, the "post-completion review of resulting IRR/ROI establishes credibility for current and future requests." From the corporate point of view, the main thrust of the budgeting process was to ensure, through careful analysis, the highest possible return on those investments. Yet the system also fostered a selection process for managers that favored strong financial skills.[21]

By opening up the organization in that way and pushing corporate priorities down into the ranks, Tarr helped transform General Cinema from the "modified holding company" it had once been into an actively managed diversified firm. The transformation was completed with his return to the corporate office as chief operating officer. In the OOC, the discipline of general management would be represented by his tough, strongly financial approach to operations. General Cinema's operating managers might chafe at this numbers orientation, but Tarr was universally respected as someone who had learned the beverage business inside-out and had run it himself for a number of years.

THE CULTURE OF THE OOC

The four members of the OOC—Dick Smith, Woody Ives, Sam Frankenheim, and Bob Tarr—all felt great pride and pleasure in the way it functioned. People who came in to consult or negotiate frequently commented on the unusual dynamics of meetings with General Cinema's top management group, who would not just offer different viewpoints but would directly challenge each other's positions. The members of the OOC liked being unusual in that way. As much as anything, though, they valued the distinction of being a team of owner-managers.

The resolution of disagreements stemming from different perspectives and roles was the central dynamic of the OOC culture. Yet underlying and supporting it all was an assumption of complete unanimity on the ultimate goals of the group's activities—an assumption resting on the fact that each member of the OOC had at least three-fourths of his personal wealth tied up in General Cinema stock. Beginning with Woody Ives in the mid-1970s, corporate officers—and eventually all senior managers—benefited greatly from a program of liberal stock options and loans for stock purchases. As the value of General Cinema stock rose dramatically through most of the 1980s, General Cinema top managers all became wealthy men, with a powerful incentive to keep in mind the interests of the stockholders—of whom Smith himself was the most significant—in every business decision.

Dick Smith, Woody Ives once quipped, had always "felt about the stock the way a peasant does about his land"—he would go to any lengths to avoid selling it or diluting its value. Feeling as he did, Smith understood the motivating force of stock ownership. What he created was not an extended family group—relationships among the members of the OOC were open and close, but they were professional rather than personal. Yet he established the foundation of common interest, which is the great pillar of strength in successful family management teams. "We were employees," said Woody Ives, "whom Dick motivated to think as shareholders. It's more beneficial to me to have General Cinema stock go up five points than my bonus, by a long shot. That gets me thinking . . . I'm spending my money, as well as Dick's and other shareholders', when I'm spending money."[22]

Dick Smith has recommended the OOC structure for top management to other organizations when he has been in a position to do so. Yet it was undoubtedly as much the individuals involved as the structure itself that made it work at General Cinema in the mid-1980s. Smith had laid the groundwork years before in his treatment of senior executives. In the 1970s Ed Lane had opposed Smith's film-financing plan on the board of directors. He had advised Smith of his views in advance, and, though Smith was not particularly pleased, he had agreed that Lane should speak his mind. In more dramatic fashion, Woody Ives, after agonizing over his opposition to Smith's cable deal with Comsat, flew home on the Concorde from a European vacation in order to be on hand to speak against the plan to the board of directors. Again Smith, with dismay but without hesitation, urged Ives to voice his concerns. With Comsat officials waiting in the wings to seal the deal, Ives, together with Herb Hurwitz, spoke against the proposal, and the board voted to send it to a committee for further study—a move that effectively killed it.[23]

If that experience convinced Dick Smith of the need to push for consensus in the future, it also confirmed Woody Ives's opinion that he had made an excellent decision in coming to work for General Cinema. Both men were temperamentally well suited to working in a top management team. Ives was strong enough to stick to his guns and also to accept the same behavior from others when he was in a position of seniority. During the brief period that Bob Tarr had reported to Ives in the corporate office, from 1976 through 1978, they had developed a strong collegial relationship. Though ten years younger and a new hire, Tarr could disagree with his boss without fear of hard feelings and was free to communicate his views to Smith without interference.

Though Ives recognized the penalty Mel Wintman had paid for being the perennial naysayer in discussions of strategy, he was willing to play that role himself to some extent, because he saw that Wintman's negativism had at times provided a necessary balance to Smith's optimism. Within the culture of the OOC, as it developed during the years when the main strategic focus was on finding a third operating business, that kind of role playing was legitimized and even formalized in Smith's thinking about the interaction of the different disciplines represented in the group. "I want everybody to be a dreamer, and everybody is a dreamer here," said Smith. "But my function is to keep stimulating dreams and to keep thinking about what might be." It became Bob Tarr's role to flesh out the dream with ideas about how potential acquisitions could grow or be better managed, whereas Woody Ives and Sam Frankenheim were responsible for uncovering any financial or legal reasons why the deal might not be good for General Cinema in the long run. In that sense, according to Smith, they were "cast in the role of poking holes in each new kite as it tries to fly."[24]

All in all, that dynamic provided a positive experience that forged the OOC into a close-knit group. For roughly four years (until the creation of the Neiman Marcus Group pulled Bob Tarr more into the orbit of operations), they discussed policy and strategy in regularly scheduled weekly meetings and handled each issue or opportunity that arose as a team. Observing what he had wrought, Dick Smith would judge the OOC a resounding success. "There are four people here who could be CEO of this company," said Smith in 1990, "and that has evolved over a period of time. I don't think that any one of them, including myself, would have been capable of doing the kind of job they could do today if they hadn't had these years of interacting as peers on all problems and strategies and considerations."[25]

Along the way, Smith could well have pointed out, the team lived through exciting times, and wrought tremendous changes in General Cinema. Bob Tarr likened the experience of working with the OOC to playing basketball with the Boston Celtics' championship team of the 1980s: ". . . like Larry Bird playing with Kevin McHale—he knows where to throw the ball, and that the other guy's going to be there." Everyone in the OOC agreed that the episode that really pulled them together and proved what they could accomplish was negotiating the Carter Hawley Hale deal in the spring of 1984.[26]

PHIL HAWLEY'S WHITE KNIGHT: THE OOC IN ACTION

Only in Massachusetts, "cradle of the American Revolution," do they celebrate Patriot's Day, the anniversary of the battles of Lexington and Concord. It makes for a welcome day off in April, when people can take a little extra time to relish the rites of spring, perhaps by watching, or even running in, the Boston Marathon. For Dick Smith and his associates, however, there would be no such holiday in 1984. On Friday, with a long weekend coming up, Eric Gleacher, head of mergers and acquisitions at Morgan Stanley, called General Cinema with the suggestion that they talk to the management of Carter Hawley Hale (CHH), one of the nation's largest department store companies, about a possible rescue from a hostile tender offer from The Limited, Inc.

At lunch, the OOC team decided that the opportunity was worth at least one holiday weekend, so Ives, Tarr, and Frankenheim rushed off to catch a plane to Los Angeles, where CHH had its headquarters. Smith had a dinner engagement in Boston and could not arrive until the next afternoon. In the meantime, each of his colleagues closeted himself with a CHH counterpart, as Bob Tarr recalled:

> Sam went off with the legal considerations, Woody went with the financial, I went off with the operating people. We got back and caucused any number of times and had meals together. By the time Dick arrived, we all had good views about our respective responsibilities and were able to brief him so that he was well prepared to take the baton, because then we were down to nut cutting.[27]

The deal was done by Monday. General Cinema paid $300 per share for a million shares of a newly issued preferred stock convertible within a year to 11.1 million shares, roughly 22 percent, of CHH common stock. In addition, General Cinema got a six-month option to buy CHH's Walden Book Company, a national chain of shopping-center bookstores (Waldenbooks), for $285 million. It had all had been approved in a hastily convened telephone meeting of General Cinema's board on Sunday. General Cinema's lending banks expanded its line of credit to cover the $300 million and wired the money out of New York, because Boston banks were closed for Patriot's Day. Ives, Tarr, and Frankenheim had worked seventy-two hours around the clock and enabled Smith to put together a deal that was extremely advantageous to General Cinema. "I still marvel," said Tarr, "at flying back on the airplane and saying, 'we just could have spent close to $550 million in 72 hours.' I never imagined we'd be able to do that."[28]

Their accomplishment validated Smith's vision of what an interdisciplinary team could contribute to the extremely complex decision making involved in acquisitions. It also afforded them the opportunity to test the central assumption of "investment with involvement"—that they could create value for General Cinema stockholders by working with CHH management to improve the performance of the company and thereby enhance the value of its stock. Following the unsuccessful attempt to negotiate a deal with Heublein, they had kept alive the investment-with-involvement idea as a possible alternative. In fact, they had been working with Eric Gleacher on a possible deal with Storer Broadcasting in which General Cinema would have purchased a 25 percent interest in Storer and taken a number of seats on its board, with the long-term objective of learning more about the cable broadcasting business and possibly taking it over completely. The OOC had looked hard at that option and turned it down, but shortly thereafter the problems of CHH's management gave them a chance to put the concept of investment with involvement to a test.[29]

The CEO of CHH, Philip Hawley, had been under the gun to improve operating performance for some time when his company came under siege by The Limited, Inc., a dynamic women's clothing retailer one-third its size. When Hawley became president of CHH in 1972, he had begun to expand the company from its already strong base, which included Broadway department stores in the Southwest and southern California, Texas-based Neiman Marcus, and San Francisco's Emporium. Over the next eight years, he acquired a number of leading department store chains, including Bergdorf Goodman, John Wanamaker, Thalheimer Brothers, and Canada's Holt Renfrew. Hawley had achieved a particularly notable success in reviving New York's high-fashion Bergdorf Goodman from a period of "dowdy" stagnation, and he poured money into expanding CHH's so-called specialty division, which included Neiman Marcus and Waldenbooks. Yet throughout, he labored under an inability to make the sprawling chain as profitable as it should have been.

Indeed, business analysts uniformly viewed Hawley as an executive who was always on the verge of making a big breakthrough in performance, which for one reason or another never materialized. CHH earnings declined steadily from 1980 through 1982. In 1983 CHH earned only $67.5 million on sales of $3.63 billion, compared to The Limited's earnings of $70.9 million on sales of a little over $1 billion.[30]

Early in April 1984 The Limited's CEO, Leslie Wexner, had made an attractive but unsolicited tender offer for CHH: $30 per share for 56 percent of the stock, then selling at about $20 per share, and an exchange of Limited stock, then trading at about $22 per share, for the remaining 44 percent. After the deal with General Cinema was announced, Wexner raised his bid to $35 per share, all in cash. Hawley was widely attacked for his all-out resistance to takeover by The Limited. The SEC brought suit over a stock buyback program, rating agencies considered downgrading CHH bonds, and the New York Stock Exchange threatened to delist its stock. Yet, as *Forbes* pointed out, Hawley steadfastly maintained his belief that the department store chain was just about to turn the corner and that he was helping CHH stockholders and employees by protecting them from Leslie Wexner—"An opportunist . . . looking to grab CHH's stores just before Hawley could complete their turnaround."[31]

Regardless of the legitimacy of Hawley's resistance to The Limited (ultimately none of the punitive actions against CHH was sustained), his problems created an opportunity for General Cinema. The OOC team recognized that fact and quickly turned it to advantage. From the outset, they made it clear that General Cinema was not interested in paying $300 million merely for a stake in department stores. The deal began to go forward only after CHH agreed to the option on Walden Book. Smith negotiated the option down from $450 to $285 million, knowing that it would be valuable whether or not the option was exercised. There were other potential buyers for Waldenbooks, one of the two largest bookstore chains in the country.

It was virtually a no-risk deal for General Cinema. The convertible, preferred stock paid an unusually high dividend, 13 percent in the first year and 10 percent in subsequent years. The breakup value of the company, in real estate alone, comfortably exceeded its level of indebtedness, so the holders of preferred stock could expect to get paid off no matter what became of CHH. The dividends were insured by a sinking fund, so in the worst case, the $300 million investment could be considered a fixed-income loan. At the same time, there were substantial tax advantages to the preferred stock, since the interest on debt incurred to purchase the stock was tax-deductible, and 85 percent of the dividends received were tax-free under an IRS loophole that would later be partially closed.[32]

At the same time, the deal left open a wide range of opportunities for General Cinema. The terms of the agreement ensured that the conversion price of the preferred stock would not be inflated by the effects of The Limited's tender offer. It allowed General Cinema to designate a day within the first year as the starting point of a thirty-day period that would be the base for determining an average price for CHH stock. The conversion price was to be set at 115 percent of that average price. It ended up being about $23 per share.

Originally General Cinema's preferred stock gave it control of 22 percent of the voting power in CHH, some eleven votes per share. But, borrowing heavily, Hawley bought roughly half of his company's outstanding stock on the open market, which raised General Cinema's voting position to nearly 37 percent. General Cinema also gained seven seats on the CHH board. The agreement barred General Cinema from raising its stake in CHH for seven years—by which time, the press was quick to point out, Hawley would reach retirement age. However, if CHH received and rejected a new tender offer for a majority of its stock, General Cinema would be free to attempt to gain a majority of CHH stock or, if 40 percent of CHH's shares were tendered, to sell its stock to the new bidder.[33]

In the first few months after the deal closed, the OOC mounted an intensive examination of Walden Book, relying on consultants but actively

participating in the process. Specialty retailing in shopping-center locations was a business General Cinema had had in mind for many years,
and the team had many ideas about what questions should be asked. In
the end, they decided that the Waldenbooks chain did not hold the kind
of potential for growth or improvement of operations that would justify
the $285 million exercise price. In July K mart bought it for $295 million
plus a $5 million payment to General Cinema for giving up its option. A
few days afterward, CHH stockholders voted overwhelmingly to ratify
the deal with General Cinema and to install a new slate of directors,
including Smith, Ives, Tarr, Frankenheim, and three of General Cinema's
independent directors. The OOC settled down to practice its first "investment with involvement" and returned to its search for the elusive third
leg.[34]

THE CONTINUING QUEST

The whole idea of investment with involvement had been born of
the "frustration," as Woody Ives put it, "of not being able to find things
to buy and own and operate 100 percent." The main focus of the OOC
remained the search for a new operating business that would have the
kind of impact on General Cinema that the bottling acquisitions had made
fifteen years earlier. The task did not become any easier. Smith had put
together a powerful executive team, and they had launched themselves
into the high-profile business of mergers and acquisitions. But it was a
highly competitive, high-stakes, and increasingly high-risk game that more
often required help from outside the firm. Whereas Smith had formerly
relied on his board of directors to help him develop leads on potential
acquisitions, now General Cinema circulated a statement of acquisition
objectives to investment banks. The greatest difficulty lay in finding a
business to buy at a price that would provide an acceptable level of return
on the investment.[35]

The run at Heublein and, especially, the CHH deal brought General
Cinema into public view as it had never been before. As the business press
took a more active interest in the company's quest for an acquisition, its
image became one of a company that was, and took pride in being, different. In 1980 Dick Smith had declared General Cinema to be "acquisition
minded and definitely growth oriented." Four years later, with a far
greater financial capability to undertake an acquisition but no deal in the
offing, Smith said, "Most other companies would have bought something
by now. . . . But we're not like most companies." Any business acquired

would have to increase not just General Cinema's size, but its potential for profitability and growth. And it would have to be a good deal. Said Smith: "We're just not willing to pay the super premiums."[36]

As the "merger mania" of the 1980s raged on around them, General Cinema's management confirmed the public image with actions as well as words. Though the company amassed an impressive war chest, it made few forays into battle. Smith became known as a "finicky buyer" with unusually high acquisition criteria. Yet the conservative approach was validated by a dramatic rise in the trading price of General Cinema stock throughout the mid-1980s. When polled for opinions, analysts familiar with General Cinema presented a consistent picture, at the center of which was the image of owner-managers with a rigorous regard for shareholder value. "When you buy General Cinema," said the head of one investment firm, "you're investing in Dick Smith and his team knowing their goal is to maximize value for all shareholders including themselves."[37]

General Cinema stood out in the crowd not only for its approach to acquisitions, but also for the way its portfolio of existing businesses was managed. In the mid- to late 1970s, Woody Ives later remembered, he had courted business analysts and investors, talking "ad nauseam" about General Cinema's financial attributes—in particular the strength and consistency of its operating earnings and cash flow, which supported an aggressive use of leverage at the corporate level. By the early 1980s, a major shift in focus had occurred within the financial community, from accounting measures of performance such as net profit and earnings per share to economic criteria such as free cash flow and the level of risk associated with corporate strategies. General Cinema had been a strong performer under the old measures but looked even better when emphasis was placed on enhancing shareholder value through cash earnings and stock appreciation. The company's core operations produced strong and steady cash flows throughout the 1980s (see Figure 6.2). Its cash reserves grew steadily through short-term investments and were augmented by dividends from RJR and CHH stock.[38]

General Cinema's liquid assets—and Dick Smith's reputation for keeping his eye on the ball—were further enhanced by the sale of Sunkist to the Canada Dry division of R. J. Reynolds in October 1984. By that time, Sunkist had a respectable share of the orange soda market and was a profitable business, but it had not developed quite as Smith had hoped. In the late 1970s it had seemed that orange soda was a product with untapped market potential and that, with a premier name like Sunkist, General Cinema could establish a strong position within it. By the 1980s, it appeared that the market was smaller than predicted and the competition was tougher, with new entrants coming into the field with new

FIGURE 6.2 General Cinema, Operating Cash Flow, 1968–1988

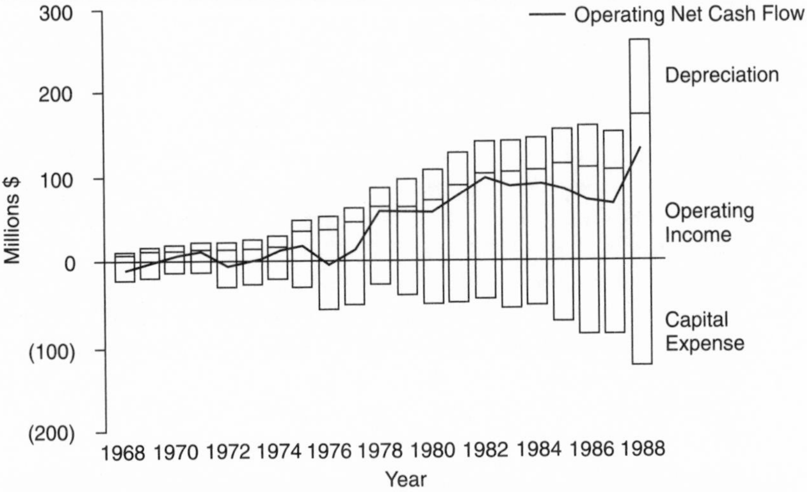

Note: Operating net cash flow = total operating income + total depreciation − total capital expense.
Source: General Cinema Annual Reports, 1968–1988.

orange products—Coke's Minute-Maid soda and Pepsi's Orange Slice. Anticipating the impact of those factors, General Cinema sold Sunkist at the peak of its performance, netting $37 million on an investment of $20 million.[39]

Like Sunkist, GCC Communications was performing well in the early 1980s—in 1981 it contributed just 3 percent of revenues but 6 percent of profits. However, Al Tanger had built the company's stations to the point where there was a far greater profit to be taken by selling than by operating them—this in an era of the company's history when General Cinema was known for its readiness "to sell anything that the market values higher than it does." A few radio stations had been sold in the mid-1970s, but the 1982 sale (completed in 1983) of the big money-earner, Miami's WCIX-TV, was the major step toward dismantling the division. By 1986, General Cinema had sold radio stations in Chicago, Philadelphia, and Boston, as well as the Buffalo television station obtained as partial payment for WCIX.[40]

The company posted capital gains of $83 million on the sale of those communications properties. Adding that to the gains from the Sunkist sale, plus hefty dividend income from RJR and CHH stock, plus core businesses that had produced, as *Barron's* put it, "two decades [of] . . . legendary cash flow," General Cinema was richer in cash than ever before.

It would have been a prime candidate for takeover had management not taken measures to protect itself.[41]

SUPER STOCK AND ITS BENEFITS

In the late 1970s the company's by-laws and certificate of incorporation had been changed to create a class system for election of directors and a rule requiring a two-thirds majority vote of stockholders to remove directors, approve mergers, or further alter the certificate and by-laws. Since Dick Smith and Sidney Stoneman then controlled about one-third of General Cinema's stock, those were deemed adequate defenses for the time.[42]

That perception had changed abruptly in 1982 when Hicks Waldron appeared to be launching what would later come to be called a "Pac Man" defense of Heublein. General Cinema ensured its independence at that time by buying back a large block of its own stock—which raised the holdings of the Smith and Stoneman families to 47 percent—and by securing authorization to buy back more if necessary. Subsequently, the company issued a new preferred stock designed to afford a greater degree of protection. The Series A preferred stock offered a perpetual dividend advantage of twelve cents per share and was fully convertible into General Cinema common but carried no voting rights. It was expected to trade at a premium over the common stock, but it did not perform as predicted in the market.

Therefore, during 1984, Smith and the OOC proposed creating a so-called super stock, which would pay a lower dividend than common stock but would carry extraordinary voting powers. The proposal was considered and approved by a special committee of the independent members of the board of directors and subsequently by a special meeting of stockholders in December. Class B stock could cast ten votes per share in the event of an outside individual or party's gaining 20 percent of the common stock. Otherwise, it carried one vote per share but voted separately as a class on any extraordinary action such as a merger or a change in the certificate of incorporation.[43]

During the month of January 1985, all holders of common stock had a one-time-only opportunity to trade it for Class B stock. After that, Class B stock could not be transferred except within families, although it could at any time be reconverted, share-for-share, into common stock. Once the exchange was complete, Dick Smith, his sister Nancy Lurie Marks, and their families owned virtually all of the nearly twenty-two million shares of Class B stock outstanding. If the ten-vote rule were invoked, they would control more than 80 percent of the votes, but even without that, they were in a position to veto a merger they opposed. With this change, Sidney Stoneman was able to liquidate a large part of his sizable holding in General Cinema stock after nearly fifty years of helping the Smiths to build, and then protect, the company. (He remains, however, a significant shareholder.)

The creation of the Class B stock constituted a resounding vote of approval of Dick Smith's twenty-three years of leadership at General Cinema. In the view of the outside directors, who studied and approved the measure, Smith's large equity stake in the firm and the continuity he had provided in management had been strongly positive elements in its success. They supported his acquisition strategy and were willing to support measures to protect the company from takeover, if that was what Smith and the OOC required to continue with the same aggressiveness.[44]

While the plan was in the works, Ives sounded out the company's major stockholders, personally visiting or telephoning everyone who held fifty thousand shares or more. Most of those were institutional investors and some were on record as strong advocates of shareholder rights. Indeed, opinion in the financial community was sharply divided over whether the threat of takeover tended to have a positive or negative effect on corporate management. Yet virtually all of General Cinema's institutional stockholders agreed to support the measure. Said one to Ives, "you're one of the five companies in America who could come in and ask me to do this and I'd do it."[45]

From Dick Smith's point of view, protection from hostile takeover was essential if General Cinema was to be "a creditable player" in the arena of mergers and acquisitions. The control block created by the Class B stock, he argued, was "an incredible company asset," enabling General Cinema "to look at large as well as small deals and to take chances on deals that will pay off in the long run rather than the short run." The company made good use of that asset once it was created.[46]

For example, late in 1986 General Cinema accumulated an 8 percent stake in Cadbury Schweppes, a 150-year-old British candy and beverage company three times its size. In January 1987 Smith made public the company's position and filed a statement of intention to acquire as much as 25 percent of Cadbury's stock. The OOC had begun to study Cadbury the summer before as part of a broad evaluation of companies in beverage industries. Cadbury had recently suffered losses in its North American divisions, and its stock price was down—"a screaming value," Dick Smith said later, compared to the company's underlying assets. No matter what developed, Smith argued, it was a smart investment for General Cinema.[47]

During 1987, General Cinema raised its holding to around 18 percent, and in 1988 the company attempted to start a dialogue with Cadbury. "Investment with involvement" was bandied about with little expectation of its being accepted after a cool reception in England. From the beginning, General Cinema was cast in the role of hostile invader. The General Cinema team saw potential for growth in the candy business and attractive possibilities in Cadbury's soft drink franchises. Those included Canada Dry and Sunkist, which Cadbury had agreed to buy from RJR in 1986. Cadbury could just as easily have found GCC Beverages an attractive target, had it been possible to consider a takeover of General Cinema. As it was, the OOC was free to play a waiting game, while the value of its Cadbury stock soared.[48]

By the grace of the Class B stock, the company was also able to weather periods when its own stock price was running well below the break-up value of its underlying assets. Such a period followed hard on the heels of the creation of the Neiman Marcus Group in August 1987. In the stock market crash of October 1987, General Cinema stock lost more than 50 percent of its value. Many companies that suffered similar losses bought back large blocks of stock in order to raise earnings-per-share and thwart a possible takeover. In contrast, General Cinema was able to maintain its cash and borrowing power for acquisitions and near the end of the year spent $234 million to raise its stake in Cadbury Schweppes. Smith and the OOC greeted the adjustment of stock prices as an opportunity to find some good values in potential acquisitions. They moved confidently into an era of transition that would involve not only taking up the reins of its long-awaited third operating division, but also adjusting to long-term changes in its core businesses.[49]

CREATION OF THE NEIMAN MARCUS GROUP

Plans to separate Carter Hawley Hale's specialty retail units from its department store business began to take shape in 1986. During its two-year involvement, General Cinema had encouraged Hawley to sell off some assets—Holt Renfrew in 1985 and Wanamaker in 1986—in order to strengthen his balance sheet. Those steps, combined with Hawley's own program of changes in operating policy, had contributed to noticeable improvements in performance. However, the company remained heavily burdened with debt, including its $30 million annual dividend on General Cinema's block of preferred stock. Except for a brief surge following the sale of Holt Renfrew, CHH stock struggled along at $25 to $30 per share—five to ten points below The Limited's tender offer and well short of the company's probable break-up price. Phil Hawley still had to deal with the threat of a hostile takeover, and General Cinema held the deciding vote on whether a takeover attempt would succeed.[50]

His continuing dilemma created a new opportunity for General Cinema. Having had a couple of years to familiarize themselves with the business, the OOC team had been able to envision a competitive strategy for CHH's specialty store division. During those years Neiman Marcus, Bergdorf Goodman, and Contempo Casuals all posted revenue gains more than twice those of the department store division. Yet Smith, Ives, Tarr, and Frankenheim believed they could perform even better as a separate entity freed from CHH's substantial debt. In the Bergdorf and Neiman names they saw valuable but—especially in the case of Neiman Marcus— underdeveloped assets requiring more vigorous financial and operating management and, most important, an increased level of investment aimed at polishing up the stores' images as leaders in high-end, high-fashion retailing.[51]

Phil Hawley was willing to part with those assets in order to gain takeover-proof control of CHH's department stores and independence from General Cinema. In his view, the potential for growth in that division was just as great as in the specialty stores. Hawley had many good ideas about how to boost market share and earnings, and he could justify spinning off one division as a move that would sharpen the focus of CHH's management on making the other a stronger competitor in its segment of the industry.[52]

The restructuring of CHH was spurred on by a new tender offer from The Limited, now in partnership with shopping-center developer Edward J. DeBartolo. First made in late November 1986, the offer started at $55 per share but was "sweetened" to $60 per share as an inducement to General Cinema to accept the takeover. Yet by the time that occurred, the details of the complex restructuring plan were already well enough worked out to provide a viable alternative to The Limited-DeBartolo offer. When the plan was announced, that offer was withdrawn.[53]

Near the end of December, General Cinema bought another large block of CHH stock to ward off further takeover attempts while the restructuring was in progress. The company purchased CHH stock again in August 1987, bringing its total stake to just under 50 percent. In September, CHH stockholders received one share in the newly created Neiman Marcus Group and one share in the smaller CHH, plus $17 in cash, for every share in the old Carter Hawley Hale. General Cinema surrendered its CHH common and preferred stock for a 60 percent equity position in the Neiman Marcus Group, plus a cash payment of $124 million. Special provisions, effective until 1993, limited General Cinema's voting power in the new company and constrained its ability to take over the remaining 40 percent of the Neiman Marcus Group (see Figure 6.3). Nevertheless, the OOC team could congratulate themselves on paying a rock-bottom price for effective control of a $1.2 billion company, unencumbered by debt, its major businesses virtually assured a position of industry leadership by the exclusive Neiman Marcus and Bergdorf Goodman names.[54]

After September 1987, each member of the OOC took up an executive position in the Neiman Marcus Group comparable to the one he held at General Cinema. As Bob Tarr remembered that time, they felt a little like dogs that had been chasing a car and unexpectedly caught it. Yet, if the complexity of specialty retailing seemed daunting compared to soft drink bottling and theaters, in broad strokes their strategy for the business followed a tried-and-true formula. As Smith had done in the late 1960s, they began immediately to look at further acquisitions that would strengthen the position of the Neiman Marcus Group in its industry. In 1988 the Neiman Marcus Group acquired Horchow Mail Order, Inc., to add to already strong Neiman Marcus and Bergdorf Goodman catalogue businesses; over the next year they looked at Bloomingdales and came close to buying Saks Fifth Avenue.

At the same time, they invested heavily in the ongoing businesses, especially Neiman Marcus. Despite having been on the CHH board for more than three years, General Cinema executives met with some unpleasant surprises when they took control. On his first complete tour of Neiman Marcus, Bob Tarr was appalled at the condition of some of the stores. Very quickly the new management mounted a large capital spending program aimed at expanding the Neiman chain and remodeling existing stores. Other investment programs focused on raising the levels of service and fashion "excitement," the better to compete for the affluent female consumers who provided most of Neiman's revenue. Other types of investment were less visible to the outside world, but no less important. As soon as General Cinema took control in fall 1987, Bob Tarr threw himself into the operations of the new business, much as he had done in the beverage division a decade before. As in the beverage business, he found that to run the Neiman Marcus Group the way he wanted would require developing "well-rounded retail executives"—individuals who could cover the bases equally well in merchandizing, operations, and finance. "There was a tremendous amount of work to be done assimilating that business," Tarr said, "getting it organized, populating it with the right management teams, inculcating a General Cinema type of culture and control system environment."[55]

FIGURE 6.3 Creation of the Neiman Marcus Group

GCC Stake in CHH	GCC Stake in NMG	Special Provisions
1 million shares CHH 10 percent preferred stock →	12.2 million shares NMG common + 1 million shares NMG 6 percent preferred convertible into 8 million shares NMG common	59.9 percent equity share of NMG but until 1993 limited to only 44 percent of voting power because of "adjustable voting" characteristic of preferred stock; until 1993, GC cannot buy more CHH shares unless it makes a tender offer for all shares, in which case tender must be approved by 50 percent of NMG stockholders
4.1 million shares CHH common stock (purchased in December 1986 and August 1987) →	4.1 million shares NMG common + 4.1 million shares CHH common, sold to CHH for $13.66 per share + $17 per share ↓ $124.6 million in cash	

Source: General Cinema Annual Report for 1987.

This new business was a far cry from movies and soft drinks, the essence of which, as Dick Smith once described it, was to provide inexpensive pleasures to the great American public. Yet the operative elements of competitive strategy were fundamentally the same. The cachet of the Neiman Marcus and Bergdorf Goodman names provided what was essentially a franchise in high-end retailing, ensuring, as long as that industry segment remained healthy, that General Cinema's investments would pay off down the road in profits and cash flow.[56]

In the short run, however, these investments depressed earnings, and that fact, combined with rising doubts about the future of the retail industry, hurt the new company's stock and put considerable pressure on its management. The value of the Neiman Marcus Group stock, pegged at $38 per share at the time of its creation, fell to $15 per share in the stock market crash of October 1987. It would trend further downward into the early 1990s under the effects of a severe recession, high consumer debt, and a move by Americans away from the flamboyant consumption of the 1980s—all of which seemed to bode ill for high-end retailing. General Cinema's 60 percent ownership would enable the Neiman Marcus Group to take the long view, adhere to its strategy, and ride out the fluctuations in its stock price. In much the same way, the security from takeover enabled General Cinema to withstand a difficult period of adjustment in its theater and beverage businesses.[57]

CORE BUSINESSES: GCC THEATRES

The 1980s were something of a roller coaster ride for GCC Theatres, with dramatic changes within both the industry and the organization. In 1977 a much-publicized study by Arthur D. Little predicted that cable television and videocassette recorders (VCRs) would become the major outlets for motion pictures by the mid-1980s and that, as a result, there would be a significant contraction of the theater industry. In fact, the effects of those innovations, though substantial, did not play out just that way. In the short run, the principal impact of cable and video distribution was to eliminate what had long been the greatest constraint on theater profitability—the shortage of film supply. By providing more reliable returns to producers and distributors, cable and home video underwrote a higher level of productivity in the film industry. The number of major studio films produced each year rose from 110 in 1977 to 146 in 1984 and continued to rise throughout the 1980s. In response, far from contracting, the theater industry launched a building boom, adding a thousand new screens every two years in the mid-1980s. With theater attendance steady at around one billion patrons a year, the end of the decade would find the nation badly overscreened and an industry shake-out in full swing.[58]

GCC Theatres was led through this difficult period of transition by Paul R. Del Rossi, who became head of the division in 1983, when Mel Wintman retired after thirty-three years with General Cinema. Del Rossi had grown up in the Boston area and was well acquainted with General Cinema theaters—but strictly as a moviegoer. He had majored in history at Harvard and, after graduating in 1964, had enjoyed a brief career in professional baseball as a pitcher (a lefty) with New York Yankee AAA farm teams in Virginia and Ohio. Deciding that his career prospects might be better elsewhere, Del Rossi moved on to Harvard Business School and completed an MBA in 1969, with a specialization in financial management. Like most of his classmates of that era, he then looked for a job in management consulting. He worked for Arthur D. Little for a few years, then formed his own consulting company, and finally in 1978 joined the financial strategies group of the Boston Company, where Dick Smith became one of his clients. Smith had been urging Mel Wintman to develop a successor for some time and made the connection for Del Rossi, who joined GCC Theatres as executive vice president in 1980.[59]

The first few years on the job were devoted to learning the business, and Del Rossi emerged from that period with the conviction that significant changes were needed. In part those changes simply entailed leadership passing from one generation to another. By 1983, the entire group of senior theater executives—the men who had helped Dick Smith and Mel Wintman build the business in the 1960s and 1970s—was close to retirement. Coming up behind them was a younger generation eager, as Del Rossi was, to try some new approaches to the business. The most dramatic organizational change was the reversal of the centralization that had occurred in the 1970s. Del Rossi moved his regional directors out of Boston and greatly reduced the home office staff. At the same time, he emphasized the importance of operations in the field by making the rounds of the theater circuit himself—something Mel Wintman had rarely done since the drive-in days. Within the home office, Del Rossi promoted a very different style of management, which broke down functional barriers (built up over many years by strong department heads) and strove for broad participation and consensus in decision making.

At the same time, there was a general feeling—among oldtimers and up-and-comers alike—that strategic change was in order, that General Cinema had entered the 1980s at a competitive disadvantage. In the all-out effort to maintain profits through the late 1970s, theater maintenance budgets had been casualties of cost cutting, and the physical plant had suffered accordingly. Howard Spiess remembered a feeling of sadness at the time of his retirement in 1982. "We no longer operated the best theaters," said Spiess. "We operated good theaters, but not the best."[60]

In addition, the strategy of expanding the circuit, which had guided General Cinema's rise to preeminence in the 1960s, had continued to run more or less on automatic pilot through the 1970s. By "riding the coattails" of the leading shopping-center developers, the company had built theaters in a number of mall locations around the country that simply did not have strong market potential. Subsequently, as the pace of mall development slowed, GCC Theatres had begun to lose ground to competitors who were building aggressively in promising locations outside major suburban shopping centers. Moreover, in the theaters it built, General Cinema continued to lag behind the cutting edge in multiplexing—in 1980 its new theaters averaged only four screens per unit.[61]

To remedy these more fundamental problems, Del Rossi proposed a major program of building and remodeling, which the company launched in 1984. Home video was a concern, and General Cinema commissioned a study of its potential impact on the theater business. But the predominant mood in the mid-1980s was one of optimism about the industry. Having long argued that the only significant constraint on the theater business was film supply, Dick Smith believed that, with the number of films increasing every year, attendance would also rise. The company's annual report for 1984 described a building program that would enlarge General Cinema's circuit not only in new, high-growth Sunbelt areas, but even in its existing territories, long presumed to be mature. "An expanded film supply," the report stated, "can support more screens in any given market area."[62]

Meanwhile, General Cinema attempted to hedge its bets with a foray into the video business. In December 1985 the company purchased Super Video, Inc., a recent start-up that rented videocassettes through supermarket outlets. The commissioned study, a two-year program of surveying theater patrons, had shown that a large majority owned VCRs but suggested that the negative impact on theater attendance had nearly peaked. Theaters, it seemed, competed primarily with other out-of-home forms of entertainment and could coexist peacefully and profitably with home video. A separate market study conducted for Super Video indicated that just under one-fourth of supermarket shoppers owning VCRs would rely on the supermarket as a primary source of video rentals. It looked like a solid niche in a dynamic new industry.[63]

General Cinema's OOC tapped middle managers from its beverage division to run Super Video, assuming that their skills and experience in selling through supermarkets would provide an advantage in the new business. This proved to be a miscalculation, as the differences in the two businesses overrode the similarities. General Cinema's large and powerful bottling entity could control the cost of its products to a degree that Super Video could not approach. In addition, because of its territorial franchises, GCC Beverages did not have to compete against other companies selling the same products in its market areas. In contrast, there were no significant barriers to entry in the video rental business, and the film studios dictated the cost of obtaining their product. As the number of video outlets increased, price became a key competitive factor, and the pressure on margins was tremendous.

Blockbuster Entertainment Corporation, launched in Texas in 1985, would demonstrate just what could be accomplished with an aggressive national strategy in this fragmented and fast-growing industry—much as Dick Smith had done in soft drink bottling some fifteen years before. The franchised video "superstore" concept, backed by a national distribution center with sophisticated proprietary software for inventory management, would propel Blockbuster to dominance in just a few years. General Cinema in the mid-1980s lacked the interest and the will to invest on that scale in the emerging video industry. By October 1987, the OOC had determined that the company could not expect to earn a satisfactory return on its investment. Super Video was discontinued and later sold, with the cost of the experiment netting out to about $9 million after taxes.[64]

That was a disappointment, but a minor one compared to the frustration experienced in the theater business in the late 1980s. Theater attendance, which had grown between 1980 and 1983 from about 1 billion to 1.2 billion, peaked in 1984, an unusual year of four blockbusters—*Ghostbusters, Beverly Hills Cop, Indiana Jones and the Temple of Doom,* and *Gremlins.* After that, attendance dropped back to 1 billion, where it would stagnate for the remainder of the decade. As it turned out, a broad selection of movies was not sufficient to bring people out to the theater. They had to be good movies, well advertised and well promoted. Said Dick Smith, after a disappointing season in 1985:

> The application of sound consumer marketing practices . . .
> is absolutely necessary for most pictures to have a chance of
> becoming a box office success in view of the number of alterna-
> tive films competing for patrons. The industry must develop
> efficient techniques to increase the frequency of patron atten-
> dance by creating excitement around *every* picture.[65]

Such entreaties notwithstanding, the major change in the producer-distributor end of the industry came not in new marketing practices but in a return to vertical integration, as antitrust policy underwent a major transformation during the administration of Ronald Reagan. By the mid-1980s, the federal government had made it clear that it would not frown on major studios buying into the theater business, nor would it contest a suit against the 1948 consent decrees if one were to be brought. In 1983–1984 Paramount, Warner Brothers, MCA, Columbia, and Disney had all bought into or launched cable video channels. In 1986 Columbia bought the Loew's theater chain from Lawrence Tisch for $160 million, as well as the much smaller New York circuit of Walter Reade. MCA bought 50 percent of fast-rising Cineplex Odeon for $162 million. Neither Columbia nor MCA had been constrained from vertical integration by consent decrees, and now, in any case, the antitrust climate was changing to allow such mergers. Subsequently, Paramount and Warner Communications joined forces to create their own theater subsidiary, Cinamerica, the ninth largest chain in North America in 1991.[66]

As the process of reintegration accelerated the building and renovation boom in theaters, General Cinema in 1986 lost its position as the largest circuit in the nation. Thereafter it would quickly fall to fourth in size after United Artists (bought by Telecommunications, Inc., in 1986), Cineplex Odeon, and American Multi-Cinema. Correspondingly, attendance declined steadily at General Cinema theaters from 1985 through 1990, except for 1989, which produced a crop of high-grossing films led by *Batman, Indiana Jones and the Last Crusade,* and *Rainman.* Although operations remained profitable with the help of increased ticket prices and concession sales, profits fell each year. The division would post its first-ever operating loss in 1990.[67]

Going into the 1990s, the theater business carried some heavy baggage acquired in the building boom of the mid-1980s. During those flush times, it had been impossible to negotiate long-term leases at the reasonable rates General Cinema had long enjoyed, especially in major markets where competition for prime theater locations was intense. Through the 1960s and 1970s, the company could count on a new theater becoming profitable within the first year of operation. By the late 1980s, theaters were taking two to three years to build up patronage levels to the point of profitability. That was especially true in major markets, which were the most overscreened; one long-time theater man called them "The piranha pools . . . the Houstons, the Dallases, the Miamis, Atlanta. In the old days [they] made a lot of money for General Cinema, but now you've got a theater on every corner."[68]

As its building program proceeded, General Cinema disposed of its most uncompetitive theaters. By 1990, when some eighty screens were sold or closed, the circuit stabilized at about 1,450 screens, nearly three-fourths of which were new or recently remodeled. As a result General Cinema would be better off than a number of its leading competitors, who achieved much of their growth in the 1980s by buying existing theater chains. Such companies found themselves saddled with a large number of older theaters at a time when the studios were regaining the upper hand and attempting to ensure that their films would be played only in the most modern, comfortable settings.[69]

A divisional reorganization in 1990 reduced staff levels in both home and regional offices. By that time, there was strong sentiment within the corporate office that the theater division should have been sold in the mid-1980s, when it would have fetched an excellent price. Given the economic and structural changes in the industry, it appeared doubtful to some that the business would ever again be able to provide returns that were up to General Cinema's standards. Dick Smith, they feared, was exercising his heart over his head in deciding that theaters should remain part of the company's portfolio.

On the other hand, after the investments of the 1980s, GCC Theatres seemed positioned to survive a looming shakeout period and to win the battle for market share in a mature industry. The theaters would require a minimum of new capital and could once again deliver significant cash flow back to the company. And at any rate, when the OOC began discussing the idea of selling the beverage division, divestiture of GCC Theatres was out of the question.

LONG-TERM TRENDS IN THE BEVERAGE DIVISION

From the late 1970s, GCC Beverages was a strong cash producer for the corporation. Yet competitive conditions were tough—and became increasingly tougher—in the 1980s, as Coke and Pepsi settled down to fight the cola wars in earnest. With a solid lead in fountain syrup sales and a larger market share overall, Coca-Cola had for many years been content to allow Pepsi to grow in the domestic take-home market for soft drinks and had focused instead on building its international sales. That strategy changed abruptly after 1980, when Coke substantially lowered the price it charged its bottlers for syrup, bringing it down to some ten cents per gallon below the cost to Pepsi bottlers for finished syrup. In addition, Coke (having been outspent by Pepsi by almost two-to-one in the late 1970s) began spending heavily on advertising and promotions aimed at gaining a larger share of the take-home market. As *Beverage Industry* noted in 1981, the competition between Coke and Pepsi had been going on for years, "But only recently has it escalated to the point where it is virtually daily news in many of our leading periodicals." When Coke took up the battle for supremacy in the take-home market, bottlers' margins become the main casualty.[70]

Coke's aggressive tactics put pressure on Pepsi bottlers in a number of ways. Diet Coke, introduced in 1982, rose within two years to be the fourth most popular soft drink after the two sugared colas and 7-Up. Although Pepsi could take some comfort in knowing that much of Diet Coke's market share was "cannibalized" from regular Coke, the fact remained that Coke had established a clear lead in the fastest-growing segment of the soft drink industry. Coke was also out in front in adopting high fructose corn sweeteners, which for several years gave it a cost advantage over Pepsi. Most problematic was Coke's increased emphasis on price-off promotions. Between 1980 and 1985, the percentage of Coca-Cola products sold at a discount rose from 51 to 57 percent. In 1985 the average price per case of Coke, adjusted for inflation, was 19 percent lower than it had been in 1976, yet the proportion of Coke's revenues spent on marketing and advertising had nearly tripled. Table 6.1 shows just how brutal competitive conditions had become.[71]

In addition, in the recession of the early 1980s, the rate of volume growth in the soft drink industry as a whole fell to less than half that of the previous decade. In General Cinema's franchise areas it was even lower, averaging only 3 percent in the period 1980 through 1985. Though the business tended to be "recession resistant," as Smith liked to note in his annual reports, it was not recession-proof, at least not in the recession of this period, which fell with disproportionate severity on the heavy industries of the Midwest. Between 1979 and 1984 the population of General Cinema's Cleveland franchise area declined by over 100,000, that of the Dayton area by over 50,000. Those two key strongholds of the "Pepsi heartland" had traditionally been the most reliable contributors to growth and profits. Losses there could not be offset by the modest gains made in other franchises. GCC Beverages' case sales fell by 5.3 percent in 1981 and did not regain their 1980 levels until 1984 (see Table 6.2).

In these years, GCC Beverages remained profitable largely through aggressive control of costs. Though the cost of soft drink concentrate rose at a rate well above inflation—consuming about 10 percent of revenues in 1980, over 15 percent in 1985—the increase in direct cost was largely offset by containment of the costs of sweetener, packaging, and labor. In the 1980s the potential economies inherent in General Cinema's franchise system were fully realized, not least by using its great purchasing power to obtain the most competitive prices for raw materials. The company invested heavily in its transportation system, both to enhance its centralized purchasing function and to support greater consolidation of production. As one after another of its plants became too aged to operate profitably, General Cinema consolidated production into fewer, more efficient plants that could serve large geographic areas through a network of distribution centers. For example, in North Carolina in 1984 three plants with five production lines were consolidated into a single, state-of-the-art facility with three lines. By the end of the decade, similar consolidations would be made in northern Florida and northern Ohio.

As greater savings were wrung from the system, the managerial ethos of GCC Beverages came to be defined largely by the notion that soft drink

TABLE 6.1 GCC Beverages, Competition and Prices, 1980–1985

	1980	1981	1982	1983	1984	1985
GCC discounts/revenues (per case)	12.5%	13.0%	14.6%	17.1%	19.7%	20.8%
GCC price/case (constant $)	$5.94	$6.16	$5.85	$5.74	$5.50	$5.41
GCC market share percentage points advantage (disadvantage) Pepsi v. Coke	4.5	3.5	1.3	(0.7)	(0.1)	2.9
GCC profit before taxes in millions $ (constant $)	$59.2	$58.2	$57.5	$58.7	$60.2	$74.3

Source: HGI corporate records. Prices and profits adjusted to 1982–1984 dollars using the Consumer Price Index from U.S. Department of Commerce, Bureau of the Census, *Statistical Abstract of the United States, 1989* (Washington, D.C., 1990), p. 462.

TABLE 6.2 GCC Beverages, Trends in Volume and Case Sales, 1979–1985

	1979	1980	1981	1982	1983	1984	1985
Major Brands Volume Growth							
National	2.8%	4.4%	3.2%	5.0%	5.8%	4.1%	3.8%
GCC Areas	3.5%	4.2%	2.3%	2.9%	4.7%	3.0%	7.0%
GCC Case Sales							
Actual (millions)	81.0	82.5	78.1	78.6	81.5	88.2*	101.0*
± Percent	7.1%	1.8%	−5.3%	0.6%	3.8%	8.2%*	14.6%*
8-oz equivalent cases							
± Percent**	n.a.	5.1%	−3.9%	0.4%	3.8%	10.0%	13.5%

*1984 and 1985 data reflect acquisition of the Ft. Myers, Florida, franchise in November 1984; gains in case sales without Ft. Myers were 7.5% in 1984 and 10.5% in 1985.

**Corporate and industry records often cite 8-oz equivalent cases, which more accurately reflect total liquid volume sold and are therefore more closely comparable to the volume growth data generally used to describe industry trends. However, sales by volume are strongly influenced by container mix and in these years were driven upward by the popularity of the 2-liter bottle. Because discounting activity tended to focus on this container, its dominance in the mix was not necessarily beneficial to the bottler.

Source: HGI corporate records.

bottling was a "penny business," one in which a reduction in costs of even a few cents per case could have a sizable impact on profitability. That approach, however rational, produced frustration among the more marketing-oriented executives, as well as among those who would have liked to invest more in human capital and who believed that GCC Beverages was no longer the "people" company it once had been. Nevertheless, the emphasis on cost reduction gave General Cinema the highest operating margins in the industry from the mid-1980s on.[72]

With annual volume increases well under 10 percent for most of the decade, however, and prices remaining relatively stable, cost savings alone could not generate growth. For that, acquisitions of new franchises were required. Yet, GCC Beverages acquired no new territory for seven years after its purchase of the Washington, D.C. franchise in 1977. As a result, by 1984, General Cinema ranked last among the top five beverage companies in sales growth for the year and next to last in five-year average growth. On both measures it was well below the industry medians.[73]

In internal analyses of performance, the division compared itself primarily to MEI Corporation, a Minnesota-based company that had entered soft drink bottling in 1972 and was the third largest Pepsi bottler by 1984, with franchises primarily in the West and Midwest. From 1979 through 1984, MEI far outdistanced GCC Beverages on all measures of growth, with 70 percent of its growth derived from soft drink acquisitions and 30 percent from acquisitions in the food industry, principally the nut and candy distributor Los Angeles Nut House. At the same time, by buying franchises contiguous to its existing territory, MEI was able to consolidate operations and to achieve efficiencies that made its operating performance nearly equal to General Cinema's. Though smaller than GCC Beverages in franchise population served, MEI surpassed General Cinema in bottling revenues by a small margin in 1984.[74]

The thrust of such analyses was to suggest that the beverage division could contribute far more to corporate GCC if it were allowed to expand through acquisitions. Yet after 1977, the company was simply not willing to pay the prices required to purchase franchises large enough to have an impact on its already huge bottling operation, and it was outbid for a number of franchises, including some in areas contiguous to its own, in North Carolina, Virginia, and West Virginia, in California, and in the area surrounding Washington, D.C. With Herb Paige gone, there was no "true believer" within top management to make a case for the long-term prospects of the industry, as Dick Smith could make a case for continuing investment in the theater division. There was no one to argue in favor of paying a price that, under existing conditions, seemed already to reflect the full value of the business. The view from within the division suggested that the beverage business had become a stepchild in the corporate portfolio, yet General Cinema's strategy was clear-cut, and the company gained high marks in the financial community for its portfolio management. In positioning itself for a major acquisition, the corporation was borrowing against the cash flow and equity built up in the beverage division. The OOC was not disposed to forgo that leverage in support of a program of territorial growth or diversification by GCC Beverages.[75]

The fortunes of the division peaked in the years 1985 and 1986 with the achievement of growth rates in case sales reminiscent of the mid-1970s, just as the cost-control initiatives of the 1980s came to full fruition. At the end of 1984 General Cinema acquired a valuable new franchise, for Ft. Myers, Florida, which added to its growth in case sales in 1985. By that time, however, changes in the behavior of Coca-Cola and PepsiCo had begun to foreclose the opportunities for further territorial expansion.

CHANGING RELATIONSHIP WITH PEPSICO

At the end of 1985 PepsiCo abandoned its traditional policy of leaving the distribution of its product largely to independent bottlers and inaugurated a new era of vertical integration in the industry with the acquisition of MEI Corporation. Within the next two years, Pepsi would expand control of its bottling operations from 21 percent to nearly a third.[76]

In 1986 Coca-Cola began to move in the same direction, purchasing its own largest independent bottler, Chattanooga-based JTL Corporation, and the huge soft drink division of Beatrice. Coke then combined those two acquisitions with its own franchise operations to create Coca-Cola Enterprises (CCE), a public company of which Coca-Cola retained 49 percent. By mid-1988, CCE was bottling about 45 percent of all Coca-Cola products sold in the United States and was competing directly with GCC Beverages in most of its major markets, including Ohio, California, Miami and northern Florida, northern Georgia, and Washington, D.C.

This new entry into soft drink bottling stiffened the already tough competition in the industry. Though technically an independent public company, CCE aggressively pursued the interests of Coca-Cola. Its tactics included discounting furiously to drive up volume sales and market share, even to the detriment of its own bottom line.[77]

For most of the 1980s, Coca-Cola was also active in the proliferation of new soft drink products. For over a century, there was only one product named Coke. Diet Coke broke the ice in 1982, and within four years there were seven varieties of Coca-Cola, including "new" Coke and "classic" Coke, Cherry Coke, and the caffeine-free and diet versions of all of the above. In 1985 Coca-Cola introduced Minute Maid Orange Soda, a direct competitor with Sunkist. Pepsi countered to some extent with a better-tasting version of Diet Pepsi, reformulated with aspartame, and with the juice-added Slice line, which achieved a growth rate five times that of the industry as a whole within a year of its introduction. Coke overtook Pepsi in the take-home market in 1986, while Coke and Pepsi together increased their combined share of the total soft drink market to nearly two-thirds, at the expense of minor brands such as 7-Up, Dr Pepper, Schweppes, and Royal Crown.[78]

These developments strained the relationship between General Cinema and Pepsi. Coming off a banner year, 1985, when volume, profits, and market share were all up, GCC Beverages attempted to lead the industry in a new direction—one more favorable to bottlers—by unilaterally implementing a "two-tier" pricing system, in which diet and juice-added drinks were sold at a premium, reflecting their higher ingredient costs. The strong market demand for juice-added drinks seemed to offer an opportunity to rationalize the pricing of soft drinks and thereby to relieve some of the pressure on bottlers' margins that had been building up as the result not only of higher ingredient costs, but also of the higher production and marketing costs associated with the increased number of soft drink products.

As Bob Tarr explained to security analysts in announcing the new system, General Cinema hoped to set a new standard for the industry by moving forward "with some resolve."

> We are going to take a leadership position in introducing this system. Where we have to be competitive, we will certainly be competitive to preserve market share. However, we are not going to look at a short-term opportunity with additional funding from the parent company [support from PepsiCo for marketing Slice] and miss a long-term opportunity by not taking the leadership position. The consumer can understand why this is necessary.[79]

As sensible as that approach was in business terms, the two-tier pricing system put General Cinema totally out of sync with the rest of the industry. For the most part, neither its competitors nor its fellow Pepsi bottlers followed suit, and its grocery store customers strongly opposed the program, some to the point of refusing to advertise or display value-added products. PepsiCo's official position was that their bottlers were free to set prices, "according to local conditions." But it was generally assumed in the industry that Pepsi opposed two-tier pricing, and its passive resistance undoubtedly helped to doom the project. Within less than a year, GCC Beverages had largely abandoned two-tier pricing, its market share down in several key franchises. At the top of its list of items for "strategic focus" in 1987, division management placed "regain momentum, blunt Coke's growth, [and] restore importance within Pepsi family."[80]

The failure of that bold experiment underlined the degree to which the interests of the syrup makers and their franchisees had diverged by the mid-1980s. It clearly defined the limits of General Cinema's position as the largest independent Pepsi bottler. Moreover, coming off the negative experience of two-tier pricing, GCC Beverages was confronted with the even harsher reality created by the formation of CCE.

In competition against a nationwide bottling system effectively controlled by parent Coke, PepsiCo was at an extreme disadvantage so long as it had to work with large independent bottlers like General Cinema. Its problems derived not only from the conflict of interest over pricing, but also from limitations on its ability to profit from market segmentation. For example, Pepsi could not achieve national distribution of Slice because multifranchise Pepsi bottlers with a financial stake in 7-Up or Sunkist could not be expected to switch to a new, competing lemon-lime or orange soda. General Cinema sold Slice in only 50 percent of its market territory. The same problem would confront Pepsi in marketing a cherry cola that competed with Dr Pepper or a root beer in the market against established brands like Hires, Barrelhead, or Frostie, all of which General Cinema bottled in at least one of its franchise areas. To Pepsi executives, who firmly believed that product innovation was the key to future growth, that was a significant constraint.[81]

General Cinema was equally constrained. It could not expect to acquire new franchises, at any price, without confronting Pepsi head-on. Though GCC Beverages remained the largest independent bottler, the new rules of competition between Coca-Cola and PepsiCo relegated all bottlers to second-class status in the industry, a position that did not suit the company's self-image. Moreover, though the business had remained profitable in the 1980s, it had ceased to grow at a rate equal to the company's long-stated goal of outperforming inflation by a substantial margin (see Table 6.3).

In short, for many reasons, the sale of GCC Beverages to PepsiCo, proposed by Pepsi in 1988 and consummated in March 1989, was the best possible outcome for both parties. Nevertheless, it was a painful step. "From an emotional point of view," said Dick Smith, "it hurt a lot to sell

TABLE 6.3 GCC Beverages, Year-to-Year Percentage Increase (Decrease) in Revenues and Operating Earnings (adjusted for inflation)

	1980	1981	1982	1983	1984	1985	1986	1987	1988
Revenues	(0.4)	(2.2)	(4.4)	1.5	3.9	12.9	4.6	2.2	2.3
Earnings	3.0	(1.0)	(2.3)	(0.1)	1.3	21.1	5.5	(0.8)	(2.1)

Source: General Cinema Annual Reports. Data adjusted by Consumer Price Index to 1982–1984 values.

Pepsi, because we had built it up over twenty years. I guess we learned from that that nothing is forever in business." Said Bob Tarr: "My biggest heartbreak was to watch that team go and suddenly become disbanded."[82]

The sale of the beverage division would drastically diminish the operations of the company, leaving only theaters and the Neiman Marcus Group, just 60 percent owned. "Although we had some other interests," Smith recalled, bottling "was the major locomotive that was drawing the rest of the company along." Once it was sold, the pressure to complete an acquisition became tremendous. Still, PepsiCo was willing to pay a premium price—$1.75 billion, nearly nineteen times 1988 pre-tax earnings—in order to consolidate a captive bottling network comparable to Coca-Cola's. General Cinema would be able to exit the soft drink industry a clear winner, with a huge infusion of cash to devote to acquiring a new operating business with greater long-term growth potential than its beverage division. "We didn't want to make the Pepsi deal," said Smith, "but it became apparent that that was the best thing to do. Did we show in that deal that we would part with anything if it was in the best interests of the shareholders? Yes, we certainly did that."[83]

WHITHER GENERAL CINEMA?

Dick Smith turned sixty-five the year the beverage division was sold, yet there was no talk of reducing his involvement in the affairs of the company. From his perspective, the mission on which he had embarked some twenty years earlier was still incomplete, and he was more than ever determined to leave behind a General Cinema with at least three substantial operating divisions and strong prospects for continued growth. At 9.5 percent, the 1989 rate of interest on the proceeds from the sale to Pepsi, the investment return would easily exceed the operating earnings of the beverage division. But, Smith reasoned, if he had wanted to create an investment company, he would have taken General Cinema private in 1984 rather than creating the Class B stock that protected its independence as a public company.[84]

That protection would become increasingly important as the search for a new operating division dragged on for nearly four years. The Class B stock also took on added significance in this period, as Dick Smith was joined in the ranks of top management by his son, Robert Smith, and a son-in-law, Brian Knez, husband of Smith's youngest child, Debra. Since the creation of the OOC in 1983, owner-management had been an important facet of the company's self-image and of the face it presented to the world. That, far more than family ownership, had been the dominant theme in the creation of the super stock a year later. However, as the long search for an acquisition pushed General Cinema into what can only be called an identity crisis, the issue of the Smith family's special relationship to the firm moved much more into the foreground.

From 1961, when Phil Smith and Morris Lurie died, until 1985, when Robert Smith came to work at General Cinema, the family connection was latent, existing only in the active involvement of Dick Smith. Throughout that time, Smith also exercised on his own the family's voting power in the company, held jointly with his sister Nancy Lurie Marks, who continued to follow their long-established pattern in deferring to his judgment. During those nearly twenty-five years, Smith had come to view General Cinema as a public company, not a family firm, and he had adopted policies for the family that clearly aimed at protecting the enterprise he had built.

One of those was his insistence that any family member seeking a place in General Cinema's top management must have the professional training that would be required of any candidate for such a position. Smith took another important step along similar lines in 1986 with the definition of the "Smith Family Group" (see Figure 6.4) and the execution of the Smith-Lurie/Marks Stockholders Agreement covering disposition of General Cinema Class B stock. This agreement provided that family members who chose to convert their Class B stock into GCC common in order to make their assets more liquid would, before doing so, give others in the family an option to buy the Class B shares. The arrangement protected the family's interest but also served to insulate General Cinema from the changing dynamics of family relationships and interests.[85]

In balancing the interests of family and firm, Dick Smith sought to preserve the relationship that had served both well for so many years. An important part of that relationship, in his eyes, was the active involvement of family members as owner-managers. Like his father before him, therefore, he welcomed both his son and his son-in-law into the business. As family members—having acquired the proper credentials—they would have opportunities to participate in top management at a young age. And, Smith believed, they would bring to the job a level of commitment that no nonfamily professional could quite match. Developing them early was, "in a sense, long-range executive planning for the company."[86]

In keeping with the traditions of his own upbringing, Smith had been careful to avoid making any of his children feel that they had to make careers in the company. On the other hand, much like his father, at home he communicated an excitement about the business that drew every-

FIGURE 6.4 The Smith Family Group, December 1986

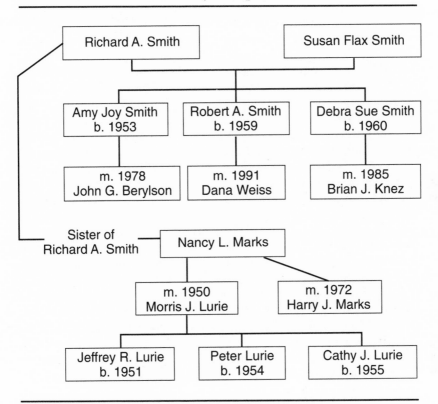

one in. General Cinema was part of his children's growing up. Birthday parties featured current movies in the family's screening room, and on one memorable evening in 1964 all the Smith children gathered around to help choose the company's first official logo (the G and two Cs shaped and arranged to resemble a movie projector) from a selection of design prototypes. At the same time, Dick and Susan Smith created a family culture in which philanthropy and volunteer work were valued equally with professional achievements and were pursued with comparable dedication. Around the dinner table of his childhood, Robert Smith remembered, detailed discussion of company affairs was discouraged, whereas his parents' work for Dana Farber could be followed in great detail. Dick Smith joined the Harvard Board of Overseers in 1988. Following his model of active involvement, Amy, Robert, and Debra all became active on the boards of the schools they had attended and of various charitable and civic organizations. Robert alone would follow his father into the management of General Cinema.

Robert Smith was twenty-six when he started his career at General Cinema in 1985, but he had long been rather precocious in the interest he showed in the business. Early on he had taken to reading the contents of his father's briefcase on evenings or weekends, and by fifteen or sixteen, he recalled, he could piece together a company's financial situation from reading its annual reports, and he had a grasp of General Cinema's main lines of business. At about the same age, he had his first regular summer job in a Stoneman theater on Cape Cod.

Like his father, the younger Smith attended Harvard, graduating in 1981 with a degree in economics and government. He worked one summer in a Pepsi bottling plant and wrote his senior thesis on the beverage business. After college he spent two exciting years with the management consulting firm Bain & Company during a period when its business was growing more rapidly than its staff and a junior researcher enjoyed some unusual opportunities to take on challenging work. In the end, though, Robert Smith decided he would rather run a business than analyze it as a consultant. So, after briefly considering attending law school, he entered Harvard Business School and prepared to work at General Cinema.

Also like his father, Robert Smith took a special interest in the real estate transactions that were central to the theater business. He worked on that area in summer jobs during his business school years and then full-time when he joined the division in 1985, just as the theater expansion program was getting under way. In 1988 he joined the corporate office as vice president for development. In that capacity, he participated in real estate decisions for the theater division and for the Contempo Casuals and Neiman Marcus stores. Reporting to Bob Tarr, the younger Smith then began to get more involved in overseeing the operations of some of the NMG divisions. He was elected to the board of directors in 1989.

Brian Knez had much the same reason as his brother-in-law to start working at the family firm. He was working his way up in the Boston law firm of Choate, Hall & Stewart when he married Debra Smith, but he was envious of his corporate clients who dealt with business issues as managers, not as advisers. In his last year of law school at Boston College, Knez had founded a discount travel business, Last Minute Travel, with a friend, and they had built it to $1 million in revenues before selling out. In General Cinema he saw an opportunity to get back into business as a career, and he joined the company's beverage division in 1987. The first year he rotated around to various departments, learning the ropes, and in 1988 he went to work as assistant to the division president, Bert Einloth.

When the sale of GCC Beverages was completed in early 1989, Knez moved over to the corporate office. There he ran the two small bottling operations—in Ft. Lauderdale, Florida and Staunton, Virginia—that the FTC had ruled could not be sold to Pepsi. Gradually he would be drawn into the expanding effort to acquire a new operating business.

With its buying power greatly enhanced by the sale of the beverage division, the OOC would be able to cast its net more widely than ever before in considering potential acquisitions. Yet evaluating the broad range of possibilities that existed and finding attractive deals within it would remain a difficult task. Moreover, with Bob Tarr virtually consumed by the complexities of Neiman Marcus, with Dick Smith near retirement, and with two new family members participating in strategic discussions, the OOC was itself entering a period of transition.

In short, although the 1980s had been a decade of high excitement and impressive achievements for General Cinema, it ended inconclusively. From the moment the deal with Pepsi was sealed, Smith and his team would redouble their efforts to complete another major acquisition—a goal that proved remarkably elusive. The actual character of "the new General Cinema" that Smith heralded at the stockholders' meeting of 1988 would remain a matter of speculation for several years thereafter.

C H A P T E R

7

PATIENCE REWARDED:
ACQUISITION OF HBJ

General Cinema moved its acquisition effort into high gear following the sale of GCC Beverages, just as the nation as a whole began a painful period of transition from the 1980s into the 1990s. The collapse of the junk-bond market, widespread distress in the banking industry, and a slowing economy finally brought an end to the era of high activity in mergers and acquisitions. In the aftermath, the focus shifted to sorting out the problems of companies that had taken on heavy burdens of high-cost debt either to acquire, or to resist acquisition by, other firms.

Since the mid-1970s, the corporate group at General Cinema had pursued a financial strategy aimed at building the capability to purchase a major new operating business, and they had been actively looking for opportunities for some six years. In 1989 the company's financial strength was greater than it had ever been. After the sale of the beverage division and subsequently of the stake in Cadbury Schweppes, General Cinema was one of the few companies with cash to spend on a large transaction. Ostensibly, the options were wide open. Yet it would remain a difficult task to find a company to buy that was not fully priced.

Some of the pressure to complete an acquisition was external. After many years of healthy appreciation, General Cinema's stock had leveled off, reflecting investors' uncertainty about the company's identity and direction as well as doubt about the industry conditions affecting theaters and high-end retailing (see Figure 7.1). In addition, with the sale of its

**FIGURE 7.1 General Cinema Corporation
Stock Price Performance, 1972–1991**

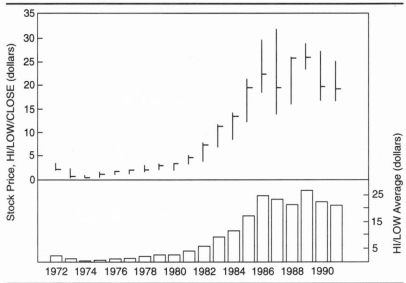

Note: Prices are adjusted for all stock splits and dividends.

Source: COMPUSTAT PC Plus database.

largest division, General Cinema had begun to look more than ever like an investment firm—an image that, for many reasons, it did not wish to project.

However, the greatest pressure was internal. Dick Smith was determined to keep the company on the long-term path he had charted for it of continuing growth built on a healthy mix of strong operating businesses. His vision for the company guided—and drove—his corporate management through what would turn out to be a long and difficult process that led ultimately to the acquisition of Harcourt Brace Jovanovich (HBJ). Only when that deal was completed would Smith be satisfied that he could pass the leadership of the company on to a new generation.

THE ACQUISITION SEARCH

In the early 1980s General Cinema's search for a new operating division had involved just a few people—Dick Smith, Woody Ives, and the treasurer, Jim Moodey. In the mid-1980s the OOC had been the acquisition team, with Moodey's support. In 1989 the team expanded further to include two additional staff members reporting to Moodey, along with Robert Smith and Brian Knez. Bob Tarr no longer worked with the group on a day-to-day basis, but he participated in key discussions and decisions. The acquisition process necessarily became more formal as the group expanded, with smaller teams taking on the investigation of specific issues or opportunities and then reporting back to the larger group.

As the team had evolved, so did its ideas on potential avenues for diversification. The core ideas remained constant: any new business should be in consumer goods or services; and most desirable was a conduit business, involving distribution of products developed and manufactured by someone else. On the other hand, many of the precepts developed earlier to guide the search—for example, that General Cinema would not go into a fashion-sensitive business, or invest in foreign assets, or consider a cash-consuming (as opposed to cash-generating) business—had been abandoned by 1989. The group was determined to stay away from high-technology industries but aside from that would consider almost anything. Such open-endedness proved to be both a blessing and a curse.

The General Cinema team looked at virtually every potential acquisition, usually from a variety of angles. The company announced publicly that it was holding the after-tax proceeds of the sale of its beverage division, over $1 billion, in cash and short-term investments and that it was "aggressively" seeking a new operating business in which to invest those funds. Its debt-equity ratio was a mere 0.3 to 1, with nearly all of its borrowing in fixed-interest subordinated notes and debentures. That left the company with the flexibility to take on substantial amounts of senior debt (the type preferred by commercial banks) in order to make a big acquisition. At an annual shareholders' meeting early in 1990, Dick Smith speculated that General Cinema could comfortably make a $3 to $4 billion acquisition with cash and senior bank debt, and that for an "exceptional opportunity" it would be willing to take on additional subordinated debt in order to complete a much larger deal. Then, in October 1990, after four years of uncertainty over where the investment would lead, General Cinema sold its large stake in Cadbury Schweppes for about $500 million after taxes and costs, boosting its "cash hoard" to $1.6 billion. With a depression in the bond market and the onset of recession, few companies enjoyed that kind of financial strength and flexibility, and few were as active and open in mounting their merger and acquisition programs.[1]

To a limited extent, General Cinema's openness could be accounted for by the need to demonstrate to the Securities and Exchange Commission (SEC) its commitment to redeploying the company's short-term investments in an operating business as quickly as possible in order to avoid regulation as an investment company. To a much greater extent, the openness was a fundamental aspect of the corporate team's opportunistic acquisition strategy and its approach to dealing with advisers. Whereas many acquiring firms preferred to work with only one or two familiar advisers, General Cinema made a point of getting the word out to all the financial and banking houses offering acquisition services that they would consider all ideas and would pay well for those they were able to use. As a result, in 1989–1990, General Cinema looked at roughly the same list of companies with virtually every investment banker in New York. Yet the M&A team examined each new proposal methodically and rigorously and as much as possible with open minds, understanding that, as Dick Smith said, "The easiest thing in the world is to shoot down a new idea."

> It's a cinch. There are always some warts or problems with a new idea. Any one of us could have killed any prospective deal, unilaterally, without any problem. But that wasn't the process that we wanted. What we wanted was, "Well, OK, these are the problems. What are the opportunities?"[2]

Would-be deal makers visiting corporate headquarters in Chestnut Hill could see as they signed the guest book that they were adding their names to a growing list of their competitors. They knew that General Cinema was likely to have an existing file on any company they brought up for consideration. They also knew that the ideas they presented would be picked over in minute detail and examined critically from every conceivable aspect for whatever strategic opportunities they might pose for General Cinema.

One of Smith's objectives in creating the OOC had been to develop an executive team capable of that kind of analysis. Between 1983 and 1988, the four-man OOC had met regularly and dealt with virtually every decision of strategic importance together. Since the creation of the Neiman Marcus Group, Bob Tarr had been pulled away from the OOC to deal with operational issues, and the others had perforce focused more on the M&A activity. In addition, on the occasions when Robert Smith and Brian Knez joined the group, as Woody Ives observed, a "whole new set of dynamics" came into play. Those changes sometimes created frustration and a sense that communications had broken down and that the "give and take from different disciplines that was constructive" had been lost in the day-to-day decision making in the corporate office.[3]

When consultants came in for major presentations, however, it was the core OOC group with whom they had to deal—a group whose approach to dealing with outside advisers was highly evolved. Except on rare occasions, the OOC did not meet in advance of a presentation, specifically in order to avoid establishing a single "company position" on an issue. "More ideas flourished," argued Smith, "if the climate was there for different approaches." People who made proposals to General Cinema had to respond to four strong individuals, each coming from a slightly different perspective. And in the end, the members of the OOC could feel comfortable that they had examined every idea as thoroughly as possible.[4]

General Cinema's acquisition search stimulated a great deal of activity on Wall Street. Smith and his management group were known to be determined, sophisticated investors who would not shy away from an opportunity that required an unfriendly posture or the use of some complex or unusual financial instrument. They had proven as much on a number of occasions. That fact, combined with the company's financial strength, motivated quite a few investment bankers to think creatively about General Cinema's diversification problem.

All of that input, plus an internal effort to identify opportunities, broadened the range of ideas that came up for consideration. The corporate group looked at many very large companies, whose acquisition would have required taking on a great deal of debt, but which might have proven to be vehicles for long-term growth through restructuring—the sale of some divisions that did not fit with the core business and later acquisitions of other businesses that did. They also looked at much smaller companies that might, on the model of General Cinema's success in soft drink bottling, form the nucleus for further growth by acquisition in industries where no large entities had yet emerged to dominate the market. Supermarkets seemed to fit that bill and became for awhile an area of particular focus. One regional supermarket chain might provide a platform for growth by acquisition on a national scale, so the thinking went. The company went so far as to seek a meeting with the management of American Stores in Salt Lake City, but it soon became apparent that there were no great operating efficiencies to be gained by combining regional chains.

Over the course of many months, the corporate team heard full-blown presentations on a wide range of industries. Specialty chemicals and insurance merited a second look. The credit information business seemed interesting enough to prompt a study of Equifax, one of the big three in the consumer segment of that industry, along with Trans Union and TRW. But in the end General Cinema had little to bring to the critical technology element of that business. When the savings and loan crisis developed, they looked seriously at the idea of buying up troubled S&Ls.

All the while an internal group led by Jim Moodey was approaching the problem from a longer-term perspective. They brought in *Megatrends* author John Naisbitt in an attempt to understand where the next great consumer wave was going to emerge. Out of that effort came a passing interest in child and geriatric day-care and the hiring of another consultant on emerging industries in the areas of environment, waste, and energy. General Cinema also commissioned a corporate culture study from The Boston Consulting Group as a means of addressing the diversification problem more fundamentally, in relation to the company's own organizational capabilities.

Yet overall, the dynamics of the acquisition search were such that developmental efforts tended to be pushed aside whenever a new opportunity coming in from the outside was judged to merit serious consideration. That was true, for example, in late 1990 when the company announced a bid to buy the public's shares of the Neiman Marcus Group, a bid it later withdrew, based on the market's negative reaction to the price offered. Another time-consuming, and ultimately disappointing, effort was the attempt to acquire Saks Fifth Avenue for the Neiman Marcus Group. General Cinema again went as far as making a bid, but it lost out to a foreign investor who was willing to pay far more than Smith and his management team believed the company was worth.

In both those cases, though General Cinema failed to achieve its goals, its tough-mindedness regarding price was to prove invaluable in the negotiations it would later conduct for HBJ. In the short run, however, as such initiatives came to naught and the intense effort to examine any and all options stretched out month after month, confidence and morale in the corporate office came under tremendous pressure. "It was an awful and in many ways debilitating process," remembered Dick Smith. "You couldn't really come to work at this company and think of anything else, very much, except what are we going to do with it. As Bob Tarr used to say, 'What are we going to be when we grow up?' That was the critical thing."[5]

DARK DAYS

Beyond a doubt, there was a governing concept of what General Cinema should be. It was provided by Dick Smith, who had developed, refined, and nurtured a vision for the company over decades. Yet, as the diversification effort dragged on into 1990, others in the corporate office would find it increasingly difficult to remain committed to that vision.

The problem was compounded by the fact that neither of General Cinema's existing businesses was performing very well, and its stock remained more or less stagnant at 1986 prices.

The central element of Smith's vision was that General Cinema should always be an operating company managing diversified businesses. The roots of that idea stretched back to Phil Smith's pattern of investing the cash flow from his theaters in other not entirely unrelated forms of enterprise—amusement parks, restaurants, and bowling alleys—and reflected the belief that the best way to build the family's fortune was through investment in a mix of growth businesses. As a guiding principle, that had proven extremely robust over the thirty years since public stockholders had gained a stake in the firm.

However, as General Cinema's rigorous, methodical search for an acquisition continued with disappointing results, the commitment to finding a new operating business came under increasing pressure. Everyone in the corporate office understood that General Cinema was at a disadvantage in an unrelated diversification. Though the company had great financial strength, freedom from fear of takeover, and a firm grasp of what constituted good management, it would also need a distinctive competitive strategy for an acquired business in order to justify paying the high entry fee into a new industry.

Early in 1989 General Cinema circulated a "Statement of Acquisition Objectives," addressing that issue (see Figure 7.2). Of particular interest in the acquisition search, the memo indicated, were businesses in which competitive advantage could be gained by redefinition, consolidation, or expansion—all strategies with which the OOC felt familiar and comfortable. In 1960 Phil and Dick Smith had placed the company on a path to leadership in movie exhibition by redefining its business from drive-ins to shopping-center theaters. Roughly ten years later, in soft drink bottling, Dick Smith had created an industry leader with a strategy of consolidation in a fragmented industry. Both in operating that business and ultimately in selling it, General Cinema had enjoyed tremendous returns on his investment. A third strategy—as yet unproven, but still promising—had been to buy industry leadership, as in the Neiman Marcus Group properties, and then to make the investments required to improve and expand on that position. The acquisition strategy embodied in the statement of objectives thus assumed that the potential for operating synergies lay mainly in opportunities for General Cinema's executives to implement a competitive strategy that they knew from experience they could execute well. That was a reasonable answer to the critical question, what could General Cinema "bring to the party"?[6]

Still, two years of hard searching with little result planted a seed of

**FIGURE 7.2 General Cinema Corporation
              Statement of Acquisition Objectives**

Acquisitions to be considered must have a clear rationale for the creation of increased profit and cash flow potential, with high return on total invested capital.

The following categories of value creation opportunity will receive special emphasis in the Company's search and selection process, and may be used as a guide.

> Redefinition formats: Companies with a unique asset position (e.g., brands, market share, distribution strength, or manufacturing competence) which can be transferred or extended in new growth directions.
>
> Consolidation formats: Fragmented businesses or industries which, if consolidated, will provide economies of scale, entry barriers and pricing leverage.
>
> Expansion formats: Companies with under-exploited product or brand leadership whose potential can be expanded with increased marketing or distribution support, for example:
>
> line extensions
>
> channel extensions
>
> geographic extensions
>   regional to national
>   foreign to domestic
>   domestic to foreign

Source: HGI corporate records.

doubt: General Cinema, with the overwhelming financial orientation of its corporate office, just might not have the depth of operating experience to envision strategic opportunities for other companies. "It's something we look at periodically," said Woody Ives in early 1990, "we individually, or we as a group."

> If we can't redeploy these assets prudently and get value for spending the money, or if we haven't got a strategic plan for the business that we buy to make it worth more than we pay for it, then maybe we ought to consider some other things— either act truly as an investment company or a holding company, or buy in stock and take the company private.[7]

Such ideas surfaced for debate on occasion. An even more divisive issue was the question of how large an acquired business had to be. As the team worked its way through the many proposed deals and came up with no real prospects, the level of frustration rose. A number of promising looking small- to mid-sized companies simply could not make it through the initial screen for serious consideration.

For his part, Smith believed firmly that the acquisition had to be large enough to absorb a substantial portion of the proceeds from the sale of the beverage division. He was also determined that the acquired company hold a prominent position in its industry. General Cinema had been disappointed in its prior efforts to build businesses from scratch, and the prospect of going back to repeat on the same scale what he had accomplished in the beverage industry twenty years before held little appeal for him. He wanted to build on that achievement, not replicate it. "I didn't believe," Smith commented, "that a small idea was ever going to deliver the shareholder value that was necessary to replace and enhance what we had with the soft drinks. So, we held out for a larger, but not gigantic, idea."[8]

As the acquisition team looked around at the many companies laboring under immense burdens of debt taken on in the 1980s, it began to appear that the most important thing General Cinema could bring to an acquired company was the ability to use its large cash holdings to restructure a weak balance sheet and its relatively low cost of capital to finance growth, including in particular growth by acquisition. Supermarkets had not panned out, but the idea of looking for a substantial company in a strong position in its industry that could serve as a "platform" for future growth by acquisition remained viable. This notion now became central to Smith's thinking.[9]

Growing tension in the corporate office did not necessarily mean that the members of Dick Smith's team disagreed with him in substance. As professional managers, and even as stockholders, they simply found it difficult to muster the patience required to delay redeployment of General Cinema's assets, waiting for those ideas to bear fruit. At the same time, they grew increasingly uncomfortable with the continuing investments in ongoing businesses, which some thought went too far in sacrificing near-term returns for long-term growth potential. Unhappy that GCC Theatres had not been sold in 1985–1986 when the business would have brought a premium price, the financial staff in particular agonized over the postponement of staff reductions and the continuation of a $200 million remodeling and expansion program through the 1990 fiscal year, despite steadily declining operating earnings that took the division into the red in 1990. Similarly, they fretted over continuing a high level of investment in the Neiman Marcus Group despite the prospect of an extended slump in the retail industry. Dick Smith might feel confident that General Cinema's investments would be recovered eventually, but in the short run its earnings were suffering and its stock was being penalized.

The acquisition of HBJ would resolve the question of what kind of company General Cinema was to become. Yet it would prove to be a long and arduous process that only heightened tensions within the corporate office. HBJ was a venerable company with a solid franchise in a growth industry and clear opportunities for synergistic acquisitions. It was also a company that was badly wounded by an extended period of financial distress and uncertainty. As negotiations dragged on for nearly a year, it became increasingly clear that General Cinema was looking at substantial investments to turn the company around and an uncertain horizon for return on the investment. Through most of that time, it was Smith's vision of General Cinema's future—and often little more—that sustained the corporate management team in its effort to complete the acquisition of HBJ.

HBJ ON THE HORIZON

The publishing conglomerate Harcourt Brace Jovanovich first appeared on the screen in Chestnut Hill in 1989 in connection with its effort to sell its theme parks division, consisting primarily of four Sea World parks. General Cinema was not interested in that business but had for some time considered publishing an attractive field. Because reputation counted for so much in signing authors and selling textbooks, the industry had high barriers to entry. But it afforded great opportunities for established companies to grow rapidly through acquisitions, since the gains to be realized from consolidating additional publishing franchises were immediate and substantial. General Cinema had previously been discouraged from looking seriously at publishing because in the mid- to late 1980s, companies were changing hands within the industry for twelve and fifteen times cash flow. However, when the Sea World opportunity was offered, General Cinema sent its refusal back to HBJ with the message that it would be very interested in discussing the possibility of a friendly deal for the company as a whole.

By the end of 1989, HBJ was at a low point in its seventy-year history. After twenty-five years of dramatic growth and diversification, the company faced the prospect of paying down a huge debt incurred in defending itself against takeover. William Jovanovich had been running the business since 1954, when it was a private corporation named Harcourt Brace, with $8 million in revenues and 125 employees in two publishing divisions—textbooks and trade books. Jovanovich had never held a controlling interest in the company; in 1989 he owned 2 percent of its stock. Yet the company's name had been changed to Harcourt Brace Jovanovich in 1971 in recognition of his leadership, under which it had grown, largely by acquisitions, into a diversified publishing and insurance firm with annual revenues of $350 million. His move into theme parks with the purchase of Sea World in 1976 had been controversial at the time, but a decade later HBJ was a highly successful conglomerate with a strong balance sheet and rising profitability.

The reward for such success in the 1980s—when companies were most commonly spoken of in terms of their breakup values—was to become a takeover target. In May 1987 HBJ received a proposal from Robert Maxwell's British Printing & Communication Corporation to buy the company for $44 per share of common stock, about $1.7 billion in all. That was roughly twelve times HBJ's 1986 cash flow and a premium of $14 to the most recent trading price of its stock. However, the stock had been trading as high as $39 within the previous four months, and a number of the company's recent investments were expected to have a major positive impact on earnings in the near future.[10]

HBJ had just acquired one of its oldest rivals, Holt, Rinehart and Winston, through the acquisition of the educational and professional publishing division of CBS in late 1986. That move had made it the leading publisher of elementary and high school textbooks, a field that was anticipating significant growth through the 1990s, based on demographic trends. The years 1988 and 1989 were to be big marketing years for new texts in reading and math, and HBJ could look forward to a major boost from adding Holt's textbook programs and consolidating administrative functions. In addition, the theme parks division was soon to open a new Sea World in San Antonio, Texas. All of the mystery surrounding Robert Maxwell and the financial structure of his media empire made him a rather unappealing suitor to begin with. Given what the HBJ directors knew about their own company's financial condition and its future prospects, they believed they had solid reason to reject his offer on the grounds that it was simply too low a price.

Unfortunately, they had to mortgage those future prospects rather heavily in order to make the rejection stick. For William Jovanovich, it was absolutely essential to keep HBJ intact, and he was confident that, if that could be achieved, the company's growing cash flows would be adequate to retire the necessary debt. With the help of First Boston Corporation, HBJ undertook a complicated recapitalization plan (see Figure 7.3), which had various features aimed at achieving higher values than those offered by Maxwell. HBJ stockholders received a premium to Maxwell's $44-per-share bid: $40 in cash plus one share of a new 12 percent preferred stock for each share of common stock. Based on the trading prices of HBJ common and preferred, that was worth about $60 per share when the deal was done.

To finance the recapitalization, HBJ took on roughly $3 billion in long-term debt, structured in a way that envisioned repayment through continued growth but gave the company a six-year window in which to achieve the necessary growth. That was accomplished primarily by the sale of a large block of 14.75 percent "zero coupon" and pay-in-kind (PIK) debentures (see Figure 7.4). Cash interest payments on those bonds would not have to begin until March 1993, but the burden of debt on HBJ's balance sheet would increase steadily as the value of the zero coupons built toward maturity and the number of PIKs outstanding grew with each in-kind interest payment.

Additional financing was provided by the sale of $500 million of 13.75 percent senior subordinated debentures and by $1.9 billion in variable-rate bank debt under a credit agreement with a bank syndicate led by Morgan Guaranty, including $250 million in revolving credit for working capital. The credit agreement required some asset sales, and near the end of 1987, HBJ sold off a number of minor operations—business periodicals, trade shows, a school supply distribution business, and two television stations—and used the proceeds ($370 million, before taxes) to retire part of the bank debt. All in all, the deal left the company independent and largely intact, but highly leveraged.

The following year, operating earnings were up in all divisions. But the gains were not as great as they needed to be to keep pace with interest payments, and they were partially offset by the loss of earnings from the divested businesses. In the second half of 1988, rising interest rates pushed up the cost of servicing the variable-rate bank debt, including the remaining $1.4 billion term loan and the company's borrowings for working capital. HBJ began to miss the targets set for it in the recapitalization.

First Boston then came up with a refinancing plan that included the sale of $100 million in HBJ stock, two new classes of publicly traded bonds, and a private placement of convertible debentures (see Figure 7.5). The plan stretched out the debt and provided for retirement of the high-yield preferred stock held by First Boston. But 1989 proved to be a disastrous year. After growing at an annual rate of 47 percent from 1985 through 1988, operating income from publishing dropped sharply. That disappointing performance was largely attributable to school publishing, where the merger with Holt, Rinehart and Winston, plus heavy invest-

FIGURE 7.3 HBJ 1987 Recapitalization

1. Special dividend to stock-holders and some holders of convertible debentures (40.5 million shares)

2. Repurchase of 4.3 million shares of HBJ common stock and $18.8 million in convertible debentures for $264 million

3. Transfer of stock to HBJ employee stock ownership plan (ESOP):

> Issued 10 shares of 10-year convertible preferred stock to HBJ ESOP, converted into 4.7 million shares HBJ common stock.

> Sold 4.8 million shares of HBJ common stock to HBJ ESOP for $49.3 million and guaranteed loan to pay for it.

> Sold 10 million newly issued shares of common stock to HBJ ESOP, paid for mostly by its proceeds from special dividend.

SPECIAL DIVIDEND,
PER SHARE:

$40.00 special cash dividend

1 Share HBJ Common Stock

1 Share HBJ 12% Preferred Stock

- $13.50 liquidation preference over HBJ common stock

- Non-voting except in certain circumstances

- Pay-in-kind dividend through June 1993

Total value (based on high-low stock trading prices, July 1987–July 1988): $65.00–$49.50

4. Sold 40,000 shares of Redeemable Exchangeable Escalating Rate Preferred Stock to First Boston Securities Corporation for $83.6 million.

DETERRENTS TO FURTHER TAKEOVER ATTEMPTS
CREATED BY RECAP

1. Exchangeable preferred stock issued to First Boston constituted 14.4 percent of voting power and could vote separately as a class on "certain business combinations and other matters."

2. In case of a takeover attempt, the exchangeable preferred stock had rights to demand redemption at a premium.

3. HBJ ESOP held 24.3 percent voting power of HBJ common stock and 20.8 percent of common and exchangeable preferred voting together.

4. Under the bank agreement providing term and bridge loans and revolving credit for working capital, the maturity of those loans could be accelerated in case of threats of a change in management.

Source: GCC/HBJ Joint Proxy Statement.

FIGURE 7.4 Financing of HBJ 1987 Recapitalization

1. **Credit Agreement with bank syndicate:**
   $1.7 billion in variable rate bridge and term loans; revolving credit agreement for working capital up to $250 million

2. **High-Yield Bonds:**
   $500 million in 13.75 percent senior subordinated debentures due 1999

   $507.5 million in 14.75 percent discount (zero coupon) debentures due 2002 (sale price $250 million)

   $250 million in 14.75 percent pay-in-kind (PIK) debentures due 2002

3. **Sale of Non-Core Operating Businesses**

Source: GCC/HBJ Joint Proxy Statement.

ment in a new reading program, had created such high hopes just two years before. As explained by HBJ's annual report, the problem was not simply that the volume of textbook sales had fallen short of expectations, but also that production and marketing expenditures had grown entirely out of proportion as the company had attempted to meet all of the varying needs and requirements of major school systems around the country. In correcting the situation, the company was forced to write off nearly $95 million in inventory, printing plates, development costs, publication rights, and costs of restructuring its HBJ and Holt school divisions to eliminate redundancies in marketing. Added to a drop in earnings from operations of some $45 million, the write-offs brought the reduction in operating income from publishing to a staggering 96 percent.[11]

To exacerbate an extremely bad situation, HBJ's theme parks and insurance businesses also lost ground in 1989. Earnings from theme parks declined slightly, with lower attendance levels at parks generally around the country. At the same time, owing primarily to changes in accounting rules, operating income in the insurance division fell by 40 percent. In September HBJ entered into a deal with Anheuser-Busch Company to sell its theme parks and some related landholdings for $1.1 billion. That was an impressive price for a business that Jovanovich had built up from an investment of $49 million in 1976.[12] With the proceeds, the company was able to pay off all of its borrowings under the credit agreement, reducing long-term debt by nearly $1 billion from 1988. Yet that provided only temporary relief, as the debt represented by the zero coupons

FIGURE 7.5 HBJ 1988 Refinancing

1. **Stock Sale:** 10.5 million shares of HBJ common stock for $100 million

2. **New Public Debt:**
    $200 million in 13 percent senior notes due 1997

    $200 million in 14.25 percent subordinated debentures due 2004

3. **Private Placement:** $53.6 million in 9.75 percent convertible subordinated
    debentures

Use of Proceeds

1. **Retirement of Redeemable Exchangeable Escalating Rate Preferred**
    Stock sold to First Boston Securities Corporation in 1987 Recap

2. **Refinancing of Bank Debt:**
    Term loan reduced from $1.45 billion to $880 million

    Limit on revolving credit for working capital raised to $350 million

    Maturity of loans extended and some covenants made less restrictive

Source: GCC/HBJ Joint Proxy Statement.

and PIKs continued to grow on the balance sheet, while income taxes of some $197 million on the gain added to HBJ's operating losses for the year. Operating cash flows decreased in 1989 and again in the following year (see Table 7.1).

HBJ FOR SALE

Inevitably, HBJ's inability to meet the targets set for it in the 1987 restructuring placed a great deal of pressure on management at all levels. The company's financial position put HBJ's remaining businesses at a disadvantage against competitors, not least by creating questions about the future that made it harder to win new customers and retain valued employees. During 1990, HBJ moved haltingly toward the difficult decision to offer itself for sale. With changing leadership, the scales ultimately

TABLE 7.1 **Deterioration of HBJ's Financial Condition 1986–1991**
(selected data in millions $)

Year	1986	1987	1988	1989	1990	First Half 1991
Long-Term Debt	788	2,270	2,557	1,655	1,818	1,990
Shareholders' Equity (deficit)	531	(1,382)	(1,398)	(1,377)	(1,464)	(1,581)
Interest Expense[1]	22	164	314	351	255	132
Operating Cash Flow (before taxes and interest)[2]	179	225	267	176	145	63[3]

[1]Includes cash and non-cash interest due on debt securities. [2]Includes earnings and depreciation from businesses discontinued in 1987 and 1989. [3]Cash flow for the comparable period in 1990 was $77 million.

Source: GCC/HBJ Joint Proxy Statement, pp. 22, F3; HBJ Annual Report for 1989, pp. 12, 42, 44; and HBJ Annual Report for 1988, pp. 14, 39.

tipped in favor of selling HBJ in its entirety. In early 1991 General Cinema emerged as the favored buyer.

In the annual report for 1988, William Jovanovich vigorously denied "the big lie repeated in the press" that the company's bankers were pressing for his resignation as CEO. Nevertheless, he did in fact relinquish that post in December 1988, though he remained chairman of the board. Ralph Caulo, formerly executive vice president for school publishing and recently named president of HBJ, succeeded Jovanovich as CEO. In the wake of 1989's disappointing results in elementary and secondary textbook publishing, Caulo resigned, as did eight top executives in the school division. William's son, Peter Jovanovich, then became president and CEO. Father and son would run the company together for less than a year, however. In May 1990 William Jovanovich retired after thirty-six years as head of the company.

Peter Jovanovich's career at HBJ had been made largely by his success in sorting out problems. He had started in publishing with Macmillan in 1972 selling college textbooks—the same way his father had started at

Harcourt Brace some twenty-five years earlier. By the late 1970s, he was a vice president of Macmillan and head of its trade department. In 1980 he moved over to lead HBJ's trade department, and three years later he was sent to London to help out with what were viewed as public relations problems resulting in heavy losses in that branch of HBJ's scientific book and journals unit, Academic Press. What Jovanovich found were essentially operating problems. He was able to turn the business around, and from that success he moved on to become president of Academic Press and, in 1985, head of HBJ's university and professional publishing division.

HBJ tended to be viewed by the outside world as a family firm, though it was certainly not that in ownership or tradition. William Jovanovich had come into power originally because of a falling-out between the firm's founding owners, Alfred Harcourt and Donald Brace, over Harcourt's desire that his son should succeed him. After that incident, the company had adopted rules against nepotism so unbending that, when Peter Jovanovich joined HBJ, his status was officially that of a consultant for several years, until the board of directors voted to make an exception allowing him to become an employee. By the time he was appointed CEO, the younger Jovanovich had expanded on his success at Academic Press by overseeing growth in the university and professional division— including the integration of Holt, Rinehart and Winston's operations in that area—that resulted in a fourfold increase in operating profits. Nevertheless, there were many people who believed that, barely forty, Peter Jovanovich would never have gotten the position without the family connection. As the crisis at HBJ continued to unfold, it seemed more likely that only someone motivated by family loyalty would be crazy enough to want the job.[13]

When Peter Jovanovich took up his new post in 1990, the burden of debt on the company loomed large. HBJ would be required to make cash interest payments of $128 million that year, but in 1993 that figure would more than double. From January to May, HBJ worked with First Boston on an approach that involved selling off parts of the company and attempting to buy in a large portion of the outstanding public debt and preferred stock at a discount to its face value. By June, a majority of the board of directors had become convinced that no such partial approach would solve HBJ's problems and that the options under consideration would have to be expanded.

Reaching that conclusion was a watershed for HBJ. Following the retirement of William Jovanovich, board member John Herrington, only recently returned to his law practice after four years as Ronald Reagan's assistant secretary of energy, then became chairman. Herrington's charge was to guide the company to a resolution of its predicament. He ended HBJ's relationship with First Boston and brought in new financial advisers—Smith Barney, Harris Upham & Company. With them and a small committee of outside directors, Herrington revisited the options available to HBJ. Out of their discussions came a decision to offer the company for sale.

The critical underpinning of that decision was the growing conviction of Peter Jovanovich and his supporters on the board that HBJ would be ruined by any partial solutions, which would run the risk of either falling short or falling through and would lead ultimately to bankruptcy. As HBJ's struggle with its overleveraged condition dragged on without resolution, the job of CEO had begun to devolve into little more than firefighting, aimed at keeping the organization intact. The company continued to invest in its businesses, and 1990 was shaping up to be a good year—publishing income would be up, and program development for new curricula in math and reading would be launched in the school division. Yet those positive steps had little effect on the public image of HBJ, laboring under its debt.

The debt, remarked Peter Jovanovich, "was a cloud that covered up all the good." As long as that cloud remained, the company faced an uphill battle to avoid losing customers, authors, and employees to the competition. The struggle to keep the company intact began in earnest with the publication of an article, headlined "Can Harcourt Brace Survive Its Debt?" on page one of the *New York Times* business section in April 1990. "School districts just don't buy books from bankrupt companies," said Jovanovich. "College professors don't sign contracts with bankrupt companies." Each additional news report and article on HBJ's troubles gave competitors a fresh opportunity to approach key personnel—not just in publishing but in all HBJ's businesses—with enticements to jump what appeared to be a sinking ship. Eventually half of the CEO's time had to be devoted to working personally with employees to persuade them to stay.[14]

It was largely that struggle to keep the company together that convinced Peter Jovanovich and through him HBJ's board not only that bankruptcy would destroy HBJ, but also that the threat of bankruptcy would seriously erode the company's value. With that in mind, they rejected the options of attempting another refinancing or restructuring, including selling off parts of the company, in favor of an attempt to sell HBJ as a whole. At the beginning of November 1990, the board began to solicit proposals from third parties. Out of forty potential buyers contacted, nine went as far as signing agreements to obtain confidential information about HBJ. In mid-January 1991 three, including General Cinema, made proposals.

GOING FOR THE DEAL

At General Cinema, the proposal put forward to buy HBJ represented months of intense analysis and soul-searching. After waiting for two difficult years for an opportunity like HBJ to come along, General Cinema's OOC had swung into high gear to evaluate the potential acquisition. They had first learned of it in spring 1990 through First Boston. When John Herrington decided to recruit new advisers, First Boston's HBJ account team had been left with extensive knowledge of HBJ and its situation and with a feeling of frustration that the company was in such trouble after all of their efforts to keep it whole and independent. It was clear that the best thing they could do for HBJ at that point was to find a buyer who would keep the company together. That had brought them to General Cinema.

A lot of work by a lot of people went into getting from that initial contact to the plan for merging the two companies. Very quickly, the OOC had pulled together a large team to analyze HBJ's operations and at the same time to determine what it would take to buy the company. High-yield bond specialists from Salomon Brothers came in to work with First Boston on the critical task of putting together a bid for HBJ stock and bonds. Providing support in analyzing HBJ's operations were management consultants from McKinsey & Company, insurance specialists from Tillinghast, and a "boutique" publishing consultancy, Moseley Associates. The New York law firm Simpson Thacher & Barlett, which had worked with General Cinema on M&A activities since the Carter Hawley Hale deal in 1984, was charged with handling the extremely complex legal details involved in acquiring HBJ.

Those were high-powered consultants, but General Cinema was not a company simply to put itself in the hands of its advisers, no matter how experienced and capable they might be. First Boston's William Reid described what it was like to be one of General Cinema's consultants:

> At every meeting up at General Cinema—and this was repeated 25 or 30 times—we would walk into a very large board room, and there would be three or four or five of us on one side of the table, and then an entire management team from

General Cinema would come in and sit down on the other
side of the table. Then we would meet with them for eight
solid hours on the transaction. We would go through presentations and models and analysis page by page by page, and we
would be absolutely grilled on what we were thinking: Why
do you believe that? Why did you pick this number? It was
completely participative, run by Dick Smith. He went through
every scintilla of analysis and got deeply involved in what was
going on.[15]

"Completely participative" meant, typically, that Smith, Ives, Tarr,
and Frankenheim, leading the discussion on General Cinema's side, would
each come at an issue from a slightly different angle. After working closely
as a team for some seven years, the members of the OOC had perfected
the art of creative disagreement. Sometimes, their advisers felt, the General
Cinema group was simply uncomfortable when people agreed with each
other, as if that suggested they had not analyzed the issues rigorously
enough. The approach tended to push consultants to give their maximum
effort, but in the end there was a certain reward in having worked with
a client so engaged in and committed to the process. Moreover, given the
complexity and difficulty of the HBJ deal, nothing less than the maximum
effort would have served.

There were no easy answers to the questions the team had to address.
Given its complicated debt structure, HBJ would be brutally difficult to
acquire. Would it be worth the effort? The acquisition would bring a
complex organization with numerous distinct lines of business (see Figure
7.6). The critical question was, after the years of looking, did General
Cinema want publishing to become its core business for the foreseeable
future?

Publishing was a $15 billion industry in 1989, and HBJ was the
second largest U.S. publishing company, after Simon & Schuster (a subsidiary of Paramount Communications). The industry had grown at a
respectable pace through the 1980s, with price increases exceeding the
rate of inflation. There had been a fair amount of consolidation, especially
in educational publishing, and General Cinema's consultants anticipated
more in the future, as less profitable middle-sized publishers succumbed
to takeovers, leaving a few large powers and a number of small "niche
players." Publishing was protected by high barriers to entry, not just in
reputation and image, but also in high fixed costs and substantial investment requirements. In educational publishing, for example, the costs of
product development and printing plate could take years to earn a return.
Thus, there were opportunities for economies of scale, but also substantial

FIGURE 7.6 Harcourt Brace Jovanovich, 1991

Publishing

HBJ School Department (Orlando, Fla.): publishes for grades K–8 in fields of reading, language arts, spelling, mathematics, social studies, science, handwriting, art, music, and health

HRW School Department (Austin, Tex.): publishes for grades 7–12 in English grammar and composition, literature, science, health, mathematics, social sciences, and foreign languages

HBJ College Division (Fort Worth, Tex.): publishes for junior colleges, four-year colleges, and universities in 19 fields, including English, history, economics and finance, computer science, foreign languages, engineering, and the sciences

HBJ Trade Department (San Diego, Calif.): publishes fiction, non-fiction, children's books, and accounting books

The Psychological Corporation (San Antonio, Tex.): publishes aptitude, diagnostic, achievement, and performance assessment measures for elementary and secondary schools, clinical practitioners, and certain professions

Academic Press, Inc.: an international publisher of books and scholarly journals for the natural and physical and social sciences

W. B. Saunders Company, including **Grune & Stratton, Inc.:** international publishers of books and periodicals in medicine, nursing, veterinary medicine, dentistry, allied health professions, and bioscience

Harcourt Brace Jovanovich Legal and Professional Publications, Inc.: publishes books and tapes in the conduct of state bar review courses for lawyers; conducts examination preparation courses in accounting, law, and business; through **Law Distributors** sells graduate-level books

Johnson Reprint Corporation: publishes reprints of scholarly journals and books and large-scale facsimiles of works of literature and art

Weber Costello, Inc.: manufactures and distributes school supplies

Drake Beam Morin, Inc.: an international provider of outplacement counseling and instruction for executives

Insurance

The Farm Division: underwrites and markets life and accident and health insurance to rural dwellers

The General Agency Division: underwrites and markets life and accident and health insurance nationwide

The Credit Insurance Division: underwrites and sells credit life insurance and credit accident and health insurance through group policies issued to automobile dealers, credit unions, banks, and other financial institutions

Source: HBJ/GCC Joint Proxy Statement, pp. 98–99.

risks. More than 95 percent of all books published sold fewer than twenty thousand copies, the consultants told General Cinema, and only one in five could be counted a real success.[16]

For the industry as a whole, the prospects for continued growth and profitability were positive, including a strong potential for growth in international markets. Unlike theaters and soft drink bottling, publishing was an industry with weak suppliers. The printing industry was highly competitive, and book authors were not powerful as a group, although the best ones could be selective in choosing a publisher. The greatest challenges lay in developing new products for and marketing to increasingly diverse groups of buyers in key segments of the industry. Indeed, as General Cinema learned, book publishing could not be understood "as a whole." HBJ competed in five distinct industry segments—college, school, testing, medical and scientific, and trade. Envisioning a future in publishing required an evaluation of HBJ's position and prospects in each.

HBJ was strongest in testing and professional publishing. In the former, its subsidiary Psychological Corporation was the leading for-profit publisher of clinical and educational tests and did not compete directly with the leading publisher, the nonprofit Educational Testing Service. As a result its high market share was stable, its operating margins among the highest in the industry. Margins were also high and stable in medical and scientific-technical publishing. In 1990 HBJ's W. B. Saunders Company held an 11 percent share of the $1.2 billion medical publishing market, including both journals and books. Its scientific and technical publishing subsidiary, Academic Press, in 1990 held 5 percent of a slightly larger market in its field. Between them, some 25 percent of sales were in international markets and both, said McKinsey, were "favorably positioned against market requirements and key trends." HBJ's legal publishing business was the leading publisher of law school study aids, but it drew most of its $35 million of revenues from running the nation's largest bar exam review program. General Cinema's advisers judged this to be a profitable business that required little, if any, corporate input to remain stable but had little prospect for growth. HBJ's trade division, which had only one percent of its market and operated at breakeven in 1989, also required little analysis. Its contribution to the business lay in its long-standing reputation as a publisher of "renowned literary figures" and children's literature—a distinctive asset in marketing school and college English texts. These parts of the business—both the strong and the weak—were straightforward to analyze, but they were not the main event. The analysis of HBJ's major divisions, college and school publishing, were much more complicated, the conclusions much less clear-cut.

With $3.5 billion in revenues, the college market was the largest of the industry segments and traditionally one of the more profitable ones. In market share, HBJ was the fourth largest publisher in the field, yet here again it was difficult to generalize. In combination with its Holt Rinehart and Winston (HRW) divisions, HBJ had solid market share in English literature, social science, and humanities, but these were the least attractive fields in terms of growth and profitability. In more promising areas, its position was mixed: through Dryden Press and Saunders College (both acquired with HRW from CBS Publishing in 1986), HBJ was strong in business and scientific publications; but in computers, math and engineering, and education its position was relatively weak. Competitive advantage in the college market, the consultants asserted, came from leadership within disciplines. That required editorial strength and reputation, development of ancillary products that transformed a basic text into an "educational package," and marketing. HBJ's position was strong but had been deteriorating since the late 1980s, mainly from lack of investment in new product development and a failure to integrate its acquired divisions, but also apparently from a declining ability to attract the top editors and authors who held the keys to discipline leadership. In this part of the business the negative impact of HBJ's financial problems was a great unknown: To what extent was its college division "damaged goods"; and, alternatively, to what extent did its problems in this segment mask underlying strengths and offer opportunities for General Cinema to effect major improvements in performance?

Similar and equally thorny questions plagued the analysis of HBJ's school divisions. This was the second largest publishing segment in terms of revenues ($2 billion in 1989), and HBJ ranked second in it, after Simon & Schuster. Here again, the business had suffered greatly from HBJ's debt troubles. Inadequate investment put HBJ well behind in the race to develop a secondary school math curriculum responsive to changing pedagogy in that field. The problem had been much worse in the elementary school division, where submission of "old programs with minimal revisions" had caused HBJ's market share to drop by nearly 30 percent between 1987 and 1989. At the same time, the fundamental strength of the combined HBJ/HRW school division was undeniable. At the secondary level, in particular, HRW had brought leadership in science and mathematics, which made a perfect fit with HBJ's traditional strength in English and social studies. In elementary, the company had marshaled its resources for a major, and highly innovative, revision of its reading curriculum, which, through cooperation with HBJ's trade division, would include many of the contemporary classics of children's literature. Said the publishing specialists, Moseley Associates, after all the problems were exposed, one remained "enormously and favorably impressed by the overall excellence of the combined HBJ/HRW School programs and products."[17]

Thus the "damaged goods" question was largely one of judgment—the evidence was not conclusive. To complicate matters further, the most troubling industry trends appeared in the educational segments, where HBJ's competitive position was already the most in doubt. School markets, suggested the McKinsey team, were becomming far more complex as student populations became more diverse, as all students arrived in school less comfortable and facile with the medium of print, and as parents and local governments paid more attention to curriculum. School systems were demanding, for example, bilingual curricula, content relevant to local conditions and concerns, classroom materials that incorporated computers and other high-tech equipment, and pilot programs to test how well such innovations would work. These changes could be expected to put increasing pressure on margins in this segment and would require new skills in product development, marketing, and sales.

Margins were also coming under pressure in college publishing. Top authors were seeking higher royalties, teachers and students were looking for fresher, more varied materials, and competition was driving marketing and publication costs higher. Used-book wholesalers and, to a lesser extent, photocopying services had arisen as competitive threats, and looming on the horizon was an emerging technology that promised totally customized in-store publishing. There were opportunities as well as threats for publishers in the applications of computer and communications technologies. Moseley Associates took pains to point out "the gap between the promise and implementation of technology." On the other hand, as McKinsey emphasized, an innovation like customized text publishing (scheduled to be piloted in 1991 in a joint venture by McGraw-Hill, Kodak, and the printer R. R. Donnelley) "could drastically change the face of industry competition and cost structures."[18]

The balance between threats and opportunities in these industry trends, the obvious damage to HBJ versus the potential to win big in a successful turnaround, the chance to gain (or lose) relative standing in the industry as it continued through a consolidation phase—all these were factors to be weighed in the decision to pursue or not pursue an acquisition. The projection for the bottom line, developed by General Cinema's investment bankers, was not favorable. Their model predicted a return on investment of roughly 12 percent over a ten-year period. "That was not," said Dick Smith, "a return that would have satisfied our group as a whole, on a financial basis." Yet Smith was ready to argue that, although the model appropriately incorporated conservative assumptions about the investments that would be required to get HBJ back on track and the operating results they could expect in return, the effect of those assumptions was additive. "The conservatism and hedges in the financial model," Smith believed, cumulatively gave "a more pessimistic picture of the prospects than was the likely reality."[19]

Taking in the scene of all of General Cinema's advisers in this deal—with financial, legal, strategic, and specialized industry expertise—plus all of the highly trained and experienced members of the expanded corporate staff, every one putting his best effort into analyzing the competitive advantage to be gained from the HBJ acqustion, the contrast could hardly be greater to the image one has of the company's diversification into soft drink bottling. No less a momentous decision for General Cinema, that had been decided one morning when Dick Smith walked into Ed Lane's office with the news that Julius Darsky was willing to sell American Beverage Company, but only at a higher price. "Ed," Smith asked, "would you pay $2 million more for the beverage division?" "Positively," said Lane. Smith walked back to his own office and made the deal.[20]

That contrast neatly captures twenty years of dramatic change, in the company and in the business environment. Yet in the end, just as before, the decision on HBJ came down to Dick Smith, his business instincts, his entrepreneurship, and his vision for the future of General Cinema. The younger generation of executives who would run the new business—Bob Tarr, Robert Smith, and Brian Knez—as well as others in the corporate office supported going for the deal. But the analysis did not clearly point that way, and in light of the economic projections there were strong arguments advanced against it. Those projections would get more pessimistic as negotiations with HBJ's bondholders dragged on for nearly a year, both because the bondholders were winning better terms and because the publishing businesses were deteriorating. However, having worked through the analysis to a decision—and seeing the alternative as buying in a large block of General Cinema stock and contracting its activities—Smith adhered to his view that the publishing business held a promising future for the company, and his commitment would see the team through the ordeal of acquisition.

HBJ ACQUISITION: PHASE I

General Cinema's proposal was attractive to HBJ's management for many reasons. It was an all-cash offer, not contingent on financing, either for the acquisition or for subsequent working capital needs. The fact that—given General Cinema's financial strength and reputation—this deal among all the offers made had the greatest likelihood of being successfully completed was also a major consideration. In addition, General Cinema proposed to buy out HBJ's debt and its common and preferred stockholders at a premium to the current trading price of both stock and bonds. That compared favorably with the other two proposals, both of which involved leaving HBJ a publicly traded company and buying out the preferred stockholders and most or all of the debt holders with a combination of newly issued common stock and the proceeds from the sale of new debt securities. In either case, HBJ would have emerged with debt to third parties on its books and the need to continue to borrow to finance working capital.

Another positive element was the fact that General Cinema's executives were known to be looking for a new core business, one that they could grow by investment, including investment in acquisitions. They were not publishers and so were more likely to preserve the organization, rather than to try to merge it into existing publishing operations, a step that would inevitably involve substantial layoffs for HBJ's staff. For those reasons, understandably, HBJ employees tended to look favorably on acquisition by General Cinema.

As HBJ was in the process of considering various third-party proposals, Peter Jovanovich received an invitation to meet with the investment banker Leon Black, a major holder of one class of HBJ bonds. Black suggested the alternative of a prepackaged Chapter 11 bankruptcy that would have amounted to a leveraged buyout by HBJ management, which he would support. At the time, such deals were not the common phenomenon they have since become.[21] Jovanovich firmly rejected the proposal, holding fast to the conviction that HBJ's businesses would be irreparably damaged by a bankruptcy of any duration. Separately, Dick Smith was urged by some of his advisers to give serious consideration to a deal in which HBJ would undergo a prepackaged bankruptcy prior to acquisition—an approach that would surely have cost General Cinema much less in the long run. Yet in the process of getting to know HBJ, Smith had come to share that company's fears about bankruptcy. In choosing among the proposals it received, HBJ had correctly assessed General Cinema as a company—perhaps the only company—with both the wherewithal and the will to solve HBJ's problems outside a bankruptcy court.

The first official meeting of the acquisition process took place in mid-January 1991 in the Manhattan office of General Cinema's legal advisers, Simpson Thacher. It was to be a marathon meeting to negotiate the terms of a merger agreement. General Cinema had requested that Smith, Ives, Tarr, and Frankenheim meet personally with Herrington and

Jovanovich, along with their respective teams of lawyers and bankers. Among the terms proposed by General Cinema were some rather stiff conditions, including a termination fee of $30 million plus expenses if the merger failed to go through and a so-called crown jewels option, to buy two of HBJ's most profitable publishing units, W. B. Saunders and Academic Press, if the merger failed.[22]

The meeting was carefully scripted, as each side had anticipated exactly what the other planned to say. Yet the day began surprisingly, when Peter Jovanovich pointedly abandoned his script to give Dick Smith an HBJ watch. It was a gesture, said Jovanovich, that his father had always made at the beginning of a new business relationship, and it was meant to signify his belief that General Cinema was the right buyer for HBJ. Afterward, Smith's advisers debated how the gift should be interpreted— as a sincere act or as an unusually clever bit of scripting on the other side.

As the negotiations proceeded, General Cinema agreed to increase the total amount it would offer for HBJ's bonds, to abandon the termination fee, to limit HBJ's liability for General Cinema's expenses to $5 million, and to accept an option for Academic Press only. The merger agreement was executed and announced on January 24, and there were celebrations all around. As it would turn out, though, that first step was deceptively easy. It would be eleven long months before the merger was finally consummated.

In the time leading up to HBJ's acceptance of a merger plan, the General Cinema team had developed some basic assumptions that shaped its approach to buying out the holders of HBJ's debt and equity securities. First, they calculated that, although HBJ stock had no intrinsic economic value, it was worth some monetary consideration attributable to its voting rights. In a bankruptcy proceeding, the stockholders would most likely have gotten nothing after HBJ's liabilities were paid. Yet in order to avoid bankruptcy for HBJ, General Cinema had to win approval of the merger from HBJ's stockholders. Moreover, just to get the deal off the ground, the initial offer would have to give enough consideration to the stock so that HBJ's board would approve the merger as being in the interests of the stockholders, the largest of which was the company's own employees' retirement plan.

The second key assumption was that success in buying out HBJ's public debt securities at a fraction of their face value would depend on an insistence that 90 percent of the bonds in each class would have to be tendered in order for the deal to go through. Given General Cinema's credit rating, any bonds not tendered would come through the merger essentially as investment-grade securities, in effect providing a reward for uncooperative bondholders, who would become "free riders." The size of that group had to be kept to an absolute minimum, or the majority would never agree to tender their bonds at a discount. The 90 percent was written into the merger agreement, ensuring that the target would not change once the deal got under way.

Those assumptions set the ground rules that, at the most basic level, would make the deal possible. But the rules did little to reduce the complexity of the issues to be resolved and provided no assurance that General Cinema would be successful at the end of the day. Out of a total anticipated acquisition price of $1.46 billion, the original merger agreement called for $174 million to be paid to HBJ's stockholders: $1.30 in cash for each share of common and preferred stock. Bondholders were to be offered an aggregate of $914 million, in prices ranging from 93 to 32 cents on the dollar across the five tranches of HBJ's public debt. After reaching agreement with HBJ's board, the next step was to commence tender offers to the bondholders. That stage of the proceedings, said Dick Smith, was like "fencing with a marshmallow."[23]

PHASE II: NEGOTIATIONS WITH HBJ BONDHOLDERS

Once the HBJ acquisition reached the stage of negotiating with the bondholders, the core team on the General Cinema side consisted of the four members of the OOC, Bob Friedman of Simpson Thacher, and General Cinema's investment bankers from Salomon Brothers and First Boston—Caesar Sweitzer and high-yield bond specialists Greg Meredith and Bill Reid. Over the next eight months, in innumerable meetings and endless conference calls, at all hours of the day and night, that group would work through each step in the convoluted process of putting together an agreement with HBJ's bondholders. The deal was like "a three-dimensional chess game," said Bill Reid. Each move, every likely countermove, and all possible responses would be thoroughly debated by the General Cinema team.[24]

Going in, they understood that there were many layers of conflicting interests and jealousies within the bondholder group. About the only thing they all had in common was a determination to see the stockholders' share of the total deal reduced. The major lines of division fell between the different tranches of debt, among which there was a hierarchy of seniority that provided the basic structure of General Cinema's initial offer (see Figure 7.7). Depending on the particular bond they owned and what they had paid for it, some people would make huge gains in tendering at the prices General Cinema offered. Others would suffer big losses, and many would be somewhere in between. Yet in the end, virtually everyone would have to agree that the deal made sense—though many bondholders might wish to be among the free riders, few could actually do so.

Some bondholders had bought HBJ debentures at par when they were first issued. Subsequently, over the two to three years that the bonds had been traded on the open market, they had been acquired in different amounts at varying prices by institutions and individuals with varying characteristics and investment philosophies. Many investors had ventured into high-yield, or junk, bonds for the first time in 1988, fleeing the stock market after the crash of October 1987. Junk-bond funds had blossomed, and bond prices generally had risen steadily into 1989. People who bought HBJ bonds in that period had paid relatively high prices, since the bonds had traded up with the market as a whole, peaking in September 1989, virtually at par.

During 1990, the tide had run in the opposite direction. Drexel Burnham Lambert, the investment banking firm most associated with junk-bond financing, filed for bankruptcy early in the year, and in April its star employee, Michael Milken, pleaded guilty to various charges of fraud. The country had begun to slide into recession, and the high-yield bond market started a sharp decline, as the prospect of wholesale defaults and bankruptcies by companies overburdened with 1980s debt began to loom on the horizon. Bondholders who bought HBJ securities in that period had done so at a small fraction of their earlier prices. Theirs was a speculative investment with much greater potential for gain.

In fact, the largest single block of HBJ bonds was held by Apollo Investments, one of a number of so-called vulture funds that had been created during 1990 for the express purpose of reaping big gains from the problems of companies in HBJ's situation. Vulture fund managers specialized in buying up controlling blocks of relatively senior bonds with an eye to converting the investment into equity or selling out at a big profit when companies began to default on their debt and were forced to restructure. Vulture investing very quickly became notorious for its aggressive tactics and extremely high stakes—the "greenmail of the 1990s," one observer called it. Apollo's manager was Leon Black, who had tried to sell the prepackaged bankruptcy idea to Peter Jovanovich. He was one of the more high-profile players in the arena. Apollo was better financed than most vulture funds (thanks largely to a $1 billion investment by the French bank, Crédit Lyonnais), and Black had a reputation for ruthlessness. As a former top deal maker at Drexel, he had helped put together financings for many of the companies whose bonds his

FIGURE 7.7 GCC Initial Proposal for Purchase of HBJ Public Debt and Equity

HBJ PUBLIC DEBT SECURITIES

$200 Million

13 percent
Senior Notes
1988 Refinancing

Trading Prices:
Sept. '89: $1.09
Dec. '90: $0.76

GCC Tender Offer:
$0.93

$500 Million

13.75 percent
Senior Subordinated
Debentures
1987
Recapitalization

Trading Prices:
Sept. '89: $0.99
Dec. '90: $0.58

GCC Tender Offer:
$0.77

$200 Million

14.25 percent
Subordinated
Debentures
1988 Refinancing

Trading Prices:
Sept. '89: $1.01
Dec. '90: $0.26

GCC Tender Offer:
$0.45

$250 Million

14.75 percent
Subordinated
Pay-in-Kind
Debentures
1987
Recapitalization

Trading Prices:
Sept. '89: $0.66
Dec. '90: $0.11

GCC Tender Offer:
$0.40

$507 Million

14.75 percent
Subordinated
Discount
Debentures
1987
Recapitalization

Trading Prices:
Sept. '89: $0.66
Dec. '90: $0.11

GCC Tender Offer:
$0.32

HBJ EQUITY SECURITIES

61 Million Shares

HBJ
12 percent Preferred
Stock
1987
Recapitalization

Trading Prices:
4th Quarter '90:
$1.12–$0.34

GCC Original Offer:
$1.30 per share

73 Million Shares

HBJ
Common Stock
1987 Recap and
1988 Refinancing

Trading Prices:
4th Quarter '90:
$1.38–$0.41

GCC Original Offer:
$1.30 per share

Source: GCC/HBJ Joint Proxy Statement; IDD Information Services, Tradeline.

Apollo fund was now buying up at pennies on the dollar. The HBJ acquisition was to be the first major deal in which Black would be a central figure—Apollo held a controlling block of HBJ's 14.75 percent senior subordinated debentures. Many people were watching to see just how he would fare in negotiations with General Cinema and with the other HBJ bondholders.[25]

Given the diversity of HBJ's bondholders, the General Cinema team expected that negotiations over the tender offer would be complicated and difficult. They could not have anticipated the changing economic conditions that would work to give full play to the competing interests, dooming the tender offers to failure on the first round. Through the fall of 1990, as General Cinema had been developing its bid for HBJ, U.S. troops had been moving in force to the Persian Gulf in response to Iraq's midsummer invasion of Kuwait. The economy had gone into a state of suspended animation, and stock and bond prices had fallen steadily into the new year. With hostile troops massed on either side of the border between Kuwait and Saudi Arabia and the United Nations' January 15 deadline for Iraq's withdrawal looming, the financial markets had gotten off to their worst start in many years. That was when General Cinema was deciding how much to offer for HBJ's stock and bonds.

By mid-February, however, when the tender offer actually began, Iraq had been bombed into submission in a matter of days, consumer spending was rising on a brief surge of postwar psychic relief, and the financial markets were rallying toward what would turn out to be one of the best single quarters in a decade. "When we started," remembered Salomon's Greg Meredith, "there was going to be a fairly large cash price for a distressed company in a distressed market." Indeed, there had been hope that the deal might be welcomed by the holders of HBJ securities as a promising alternative to the uncertainties they faced if the company went into bankruptcy. "All of a sudden," said Meredith, "there was a cash bid for a distressed company in a rallying equity market and a rallying high-yield market." As the opportunities for short-term gain outside the deal expanded, the threat of an HBJ bankruptcy in 1993 appeared more distant, and the incentive to the bondholders to accept General Cinema's offer diminished proportionately.[26]

Shortly after the offer commenced, in mid-February, a number of bondholders with large positions in various tranches formed a committee and hired legal advisers and a financial adviser, Lehman Brothers, to support them in considering General Cinema's proposal. Although the members of the committee together controlled only around 20 percent of all the bonds, no deal could be struck without them. They represented the first hurdle, and from the beginning it was clear the hurdle would be a high one.

The total amount to be paid from the bonds was only part of the problem General Cinema faced in reaching agreement with the bondholders' committee. General Cinema could and did agree to pay more, but just how the added money was to be divided was a question that only the members of the bondholders committee could decide, since any one of them had the power to block the deal. Playing out the role expected of him, Leon Black demanded that the price offered for the senior subordinated notes be raised substantially. At the same time, another leading force on the committee, Ken Urbaszewski of Kemper Financial Services, insisted that the zero coupons and PIKs (tranches in which Kemper held the largest position) should also get a substantial increase. Urbaszewski not only wanted the offer to be increased in the aggregate, but also the bonds Kemper owned to be allotted a larger proportion of the total consideration.[27]

General Cinema extended the deadline for the tender offer on several occasions over a period of three months and increased its offer by $40 million. Yet, given the structure of the deal, they could not simply accede to the demands of the leading bondholders. If the senior subordinateds, zeros, and PIKs got a big increase, every other bondholder group could then be expected to demand a proportional increase, and that would take the total well above what General Cinema was willing to pay for HBJ. Indeed, after months of negotiation, the parties remained some $130 million apart. Most members of the committee were pressing for a deal, but it became clear that there was not enough willingness to compromise within the group to make it happen. "Every time it looked like we were willing to be flexible about something," remembered Dick Smith, "somebody would want more. . . . There wasn't a firm position on the other side—no one could say yes or no. On our side, we were handicapped by being able to say yes or no."[28]

Discussions then began within the General Cinema team about the need to walk away from the deal. Everyone felt that the only way to make the bondholders engage seriously in an effort to resolve their differences was to convince them that General Cinema was ready to let HBJ go rather than continue to compromise. They agreed that the company would announce the withdrawal of its tender offer on Friday, April 26.

Greg Meredith was at Salomon Brothers' desk on the bond trading floor that morning, with the assignment of demonstrating to all interested parties that the deal was off. On the phone as the announcement was due to come over the wire, Meredith slammed down the receiver just loudly enough to be sure that everyone around him could tell he was upset.

Then Salomon freed up HBJ bonds, and he watched to see what effect the news would have on the trading price. Said Meredith:

> The bonds started to trade down, and then a press release came out of the company [General Cinema] stating that, if the bondholders could get their act together, the company would be happy to reopen negotiations. Basically any of the weight to our statement that we were walking away just disappeared. The bonds immediately turned around and flew right back up.[29]

Back in General Cinema's offices in Chestnut Hill, there had been considerable disagreement over whether to issue that statement leaving the door ajar for the bondholders' committee. In the end, though, Dick Smith had decided that he was not willing to let go of the HBJ deal, primarily because there was simply no good acquisition alternative in sight. The stock market had continued to rise, and interest rates were moving down, so HBJ was actually worth a little bit more than it had been in January. By the same token, acquisitions in general and hostile takeovers in particular had become more expensive. Opportunities for a friendly acquisition, as HBJ was, were few and far between. If General Cinema had cut off the deal entirely, Smith reasoned, they would have lost contact with HBJ, opening the way for another buyer to come in, or at least making it very difficult to put the deal back together at a later date.

The prospect of going back to the open-ended acquisition search that had occupied General Cinema for two years was alarming. "I was beginning to worry that we were just going to have a shell of a company at the end of this process if we didn't get HBJ," said Smith. "That didn't make HBJ worth any price but it did make it, on a relative basis I thought, more attractive than it had been in January."[30]

At the same time, the fact that General Cinema had walked away from the deal "straining to look back over its shoulder," as one bondholder put it, was not the kind of tactic likely to speed the deal to a successful resolution. General Cinema's investment bankers were distraught over the turn of events. They insisted that the company maintain "radio silence" after that. HBJ and General Cinema declined to exercise their rights to terminate the merger agreement, but absolutely no action or communication was allowed until the bondholders broke the silence. Eventually, the bondholders realized that the deal was not going to go forward unless they did something to make it happen, but in the meantime, it would be an excruciating two months for Dick Smith.[31]

THE IMPASSE BROKEN

The wait was particularly difficult because of the adverse effect on HBJ of the growing threat of bankruptcy. The pressure on its customers, authors, and personnel to defect to competitors intensified greatly as the prospects for acquisition by General Cinema dimmed. It became more and more difficult for Peter Jovanovich to keep his organization intact. Bob Tarr, Robert Smith, and Brian Knez were continuing to visit HBJ's operations and were reporting back to General Cinema that school publishing, especially, was beginning to suffer from the uncertainty of the company's future. All of the increase in HBJ's value that Dick Smith had seen from January to April was threatening to evaporate by June.

At the same time, however, the increasing likelihood of an HBJ bankruptcy put some pressure on the recalcitrant members of the bondholders' committee to consider how negotiations with General Cinema might be revived. Depending on just how badly its businesses were hurt by its tenuous financial position, HBJ could have gone into default on its debt by the end of the year, or it might have struggled on and thereafter filed for protection under Chapter 11. If HBJ went into bankruptcy, the bondholders could legitimately claim to be the owners of the business. Yet there was always a degree of uncertainty in losing control to a court-supervised proceeding. Moreover, the bondholders could see as clearly as General Cinema that the value of what they would own would deteriorate if HBJ finally fell into financial ruin.

In the end, it was Leon Black who took the initiative to break the impasse. Smith had been making weekly calls to his advisers to ask if there was something he could do to get things moving. Nevertheless, he had succeeded in maintaining public silence and thereby in conveying to the outside world that General Cinema was not going to accede to the bondholders' initial demands. Eventually Black began to make some calls, fishing for information about Smith's willingness to restart discussions. Then, through a mutual acquaintance, he arranged to meet with Smith in Boston. Over lunch, Black succeeded in convincing Dick Smith that he was committed to playing a positive role in completing the deal.

Out of that meeting came a rough agreement as to what form a workable deal might take. Black was in a very senior position in HBJ's

financial structure and stood to make a huge profit under any circumstances. In a bankruptcy, he could expect to get close to face value for the
large block of senior subordinated notes he had acquired in 1990–1991
when they had traded in a range from 71 to 58 cents on the dollar. He
could with some justice demand much more than the 77 cents in General
Cinema's first tender offer. Yet in order to have the deal succeed, he would
have to moderate his claims. Many bondholders, especially those in the
more junior tranches, were looking at tremendous losses, and (given
the requirement of 90 percent bondholder approval) they could block the
deal as effectively as he.

For his part, Dick Smith had to come up with a large part of the
$130 million that had divided General Cinema and the bondholders' com-
mittee at the breakup of the first round of negotiations. Smith concluded
that the bulk of that would have to come out of the consideration to be
offered to HBJ's common and preferred stockholders. That step posed a
major risk to General Cinema, in Smith's view, because ultimately the
stockholders would also have the power to kill the merger if they did not
like the terms. Stockholder resistance could drag the proceedings out,
increasing the likelihood of greater deterioration in HBJ's businesses. In
the worst case, the deal could be voted down at the end of the day, and
all of General Cinema's investment in time and money would be lost.

Going into the negotiations with the bondholders committee at the
beginning of the year, Smith had been convinced that General Cinema
could never agree to a reduction in the payout for HBJ equity. "But in
the end," he said, "it was a case of either get the deal done that way or
don't get it done at all." By June, it had become clear that bondholders
who were going to have to accept substantial losses simply would not
tolerate a payment of $1.30 per share for stock that traded at an average
price of $0.72 in the second quarter of 1991 and would most likely have
no value at all if HBJ went bankrupt.[32]

The face-to-face discussion between Smith and Black was the essential
breakthrough. In Dick Smith's mind, the struggle to put the HBJ deal
together had become like trying to get a picnic laid out on a windy beach.
Said Smith, "Leon Black was, for me, the first corner and the essential
corner to getting that beach blanket down." Up to that point, there had
been no one among the leading bondholders with whom General Cinema
could really negotiate. Indeed, "it was very rewarding for the bondholders
not to have a firm position and not to have a leader." Smith respected
Black for coming forward and stating clearly what it would take to win
his support for a deal, and that respect laid the foundation for negotiations. "My judgment of the man was very important," Smith argued,

because Leon, having been in Drexel Burnham with Milken
and so forth, was held with some wariness by a lot of people,
including some of our advisers. I rode over that and said,
"Well, no. Here's a man that a guy can look in the eye, and
we can come to agreement." It didn't mean that we didn't have
differences in point of view, and we did; and it didn't mean
that he didn't get paid very well, because he did. But that was
his job. [Black] had integrity, and that was critical to me.[33]

Nevertheless, as the legions of advisers to the various parties involved
in the deal told each other, it was not "soup" yet. The next step, Black
suggested, was to talk to Ken Urbaszewski at Kemper. Kemper's large
investment in HBJ zero coupon and PIK bonds was concentrated mainly
in Kemper's High-Yield Bond Fund but was spread in smaller amounts
across a range of funds, including some that were primarily equity funds.
There was some strong sentiment running through Kemper's main office
in Chicago that in acquiring HBJ, General Cinema was getting a good
bargain on assets that would be worth a great deal in the long run.

Kemper wanted a tender offer that provided some vehicle for its
equity-oriented funds to share in that anticipated appreciation in value.
After a month of furious activity among its financial and legal advisers,
General Cinema came forth with a proposal for such a vehicle, which
they called contingent payment obligations, or CPOs. The CPOs, Greg
Meredith said, were like "a shadow piece of equity." They were characterized mainly by having certain put and call options, with the option prices
to be determined by the value of HBJ at the time of exercise.[34]

There were still other members of the bondholders' committee to be
brought on board, each one needing to be convinced that the deal offered
the best opportunity to maximize the value of his investment. It was
strictly a "linear problem," commented Caesar Sweitzer. They would succeed in bringing one holdout on board—inevitably with an increased
offer for that particular class of bonds—and then they would have to move
on to the next. Discussions continued for weeks without the bondholders'
committee coming together in support of a deal. Finally, by mid-August,
General Cinema was again at the point of having to walk away from its
offer in order to get some meaningful action. "We decided that the money
that was there was there," said Greg Meredith.

The committee was as together as it was ever going to be, and
on that basis it was time to set a deadline and tell them this
deal can happen, but you have to make it happen. And if you

don't make it happen by this date, then well and truly Dick Smith is going away and never coming back.[35]

In the end, of course, only Smith himself could deliver that message. The deadline was set for 9:00 A.M., Friday, August 16. All that week, there was a flurry of calls between advisers but no substantive negotiations, as the bondholders focused on trying to determine whether Smith was really ready at that point to give up on the HBJ deal if General Cinema's offer were not accepted. Finally, Leon Black attempted to reach him directly by phone. Throughout the day on Thursday, Smith's advisers prevailed on him to resist returning Black's calls, but Dick Smith considered that extremely impolite. At 11:00 P.M.—with Meredith in his New York office, Reid in a Los Angeles airport hotel, having missed his flight home from a business trip, and Smith at his summer home on Cape Cod—they agreed that he would place a return call to Black. They did not bother to script the call—after all the work and compromise of the previous two months, it was not a difficult task for Smith to convey that he had finally reached the limit of his patience.

After that, the deal with the leading bondholders became soup rather quickly, with Leon Black leading the way to get the committee lined up behind it. The key to success was Black's willingness to trade some of his senior subordinated notes for less favored bonds in order to spread the gains and losses somewhat more evenly and to play an active role as broker in similar swaps among other bondholders. Smith had indicated he would extend the deadline into the afternoon on Friday but absolutely no longer. Endless phone conversations continued through Thursday night and well into the next day, but by afternoon the deal was done. Lehman Brothers announced for the bondholders' committee that they would "react favorably" to General Cinema's revised tender offer, including the offer of the CPOs. "Essentially," said Greg Meredith, "the deal was put together in about a 15-hour period after being alive for eight months."[36]

FROM SOUP TO NUTS

Within the ten days after the deadline passed, General Cinema secured the approval of HBJ's board of directors for its revised merger proposal. Letters of agreement were executed, binding the major bondholders to tender all of their bonds at the commencement of a new offer for HBJ's public debt securities under the revised terms (see Table 7.2). Two big hurdles then remained. First, a large number of bondholders

TABLE 7.2 GCC/HBJ Original and Final Merger Agreement and Tender Offers

	Original Merger Agreement and Tender Offers Total Value: $1.46 Billion	Final Merger Agreement and Tender Offers Total Value: $1.56 Billion
HBJ Common Stock	$1.30 per share in cash	$0.75 per share in GCC Class B stock
HBJ 12 percent Preferred Stock	$1.30 per share in cash	$0.75 per share in GCC common stock
HBJ Senior Notes	93% of principal amount[1]	100% of principal amount[2]
HBJ Senior Subordinated Debentures	77% of principal amount[1]	91% of principal amount[2]
HBJ Subordinated Debentures	45% of principal amount[1]	47.5% of principal amount[2]
HBJ Subordinated Discount Debentures (zero coupons)	32.4% of principal amount at maturity	40.975% of principal amount at maturity
HBJ Subordinated Pay-in-Kind Debentures	40% of principal amount	47% of principal amount[4]

[1]Plus accrued interest through March 15, 1991. [2]Plus accrued interest through September 28, 1991. [3]Including pay-in-kind debentures issuable on March 15, 1991 in respect of interest. [4]Including pay-in-kind debentures issuable on September 15, 1991 in respect of interest, plus a cash payment of 47 percent of interest accrued from September 15 to September 28, 1991.

Source: GCC/HBJ Joint Proxy Statement, pp. 32, 40, 46–47.

who had not been party to the negotiations had to be brought on board if General Cinema was to get 90 percent of each class of bonds. Second, two-thirds of HBJ's common stock and a majority of the preferred had to be voted in favor of the deal. After more than a year of effort, General Cinema's attempt to acquire HBJ would come down to the wire with that very last vote.

As the tender offers commenced, Leon Black once again was key in bringing the deal together. General Cinema's investment bankers could provide information on who had tendered bonds and who had not, but the impetus for the deal at this stage had to come from within the bond-

TABLE 7.3 Progress of Tender Offers for HBJ Publicly Held Debt: Percentage of Bonds Tendered at Deadline Date

Tranche/Date	9/27/91	10/4/91	10/11/91	10/23/91
Senior Notes	90.1	91.8	91.8	92.0
Senior Subordinated Debentures	84.4	84.7	84.7	90.2
Subordinated Debentures	78.3	78.6	81.1	90.0
Subordinated Discount Debentures (zero coupon)	89.0	89.2	89.2	90.0
Subordinated Pay-in-Kind Debentures	89.1	89.1	89.1	90.0

Source: General Cinema Corporation, "News Release," September 30, 1991, October 7, 1991, October 14, 1991, and October 23, 1991, in HGI corporate records.

holder group, which looked to Black to lead the way, since Apollo stood to gain the most from having the deal go through. From September 28, through two deadline extensions to October 14, there was some furious horse trading among bondholders from one tranche to another. But the total amount of the bonds tendered was still short of the requisite 90 percent in all but the most senior notes (see Table 7.3). Close to exhaustion, the bankers joked grimly that the last 20 percent of the bondholders were struggling to end up in the last 10 percent.

The free rider problem was making it impossible to get the deal finalized. On Friday, October 11, the day General Cinema's second deadline extension was due to expire, HBJ's zero coupon bonds traded at 71 cents on the dollar—30 cents more than the tender offer price. On Monday, when General Cinema announced a final extension and threatened not just to withdraw the tender offers but to cancel its merger agreement with HBJ, some $2 million of the same bonds reportedly traded hands at $0.61. Such purchases were made with the express purpose of holding out for free rider status, and they presented a tremendous problem for the bankers trying to identify the holdouts and bring them into the fold. "The smartest thing you could do," said Bill Reid, was to "buy the bonds and not answer the telephone."[37]

As had happened so many times before, the deal with HBJ's bondholders came down to the last few minutes of the final deadline day. For the last time, Dick Smith made it absolutely clear that he was not going to extend the deadline again. This time people believed him, and a fourteen-way swap of bonds finally brought the tenders in all tranches up to 90 percent.

Then it was up to HBJ to put the final piece of the puzzle in place. Peter Jovanovich, with HBJ's executive vice president and chief financial officer, Robert Evanson, and their advisers at Smith Barney had a month to do that before the stockholders' meeting scheduled for Saturday, November 23. "That was like a political campaign," said Jovanovich—identifying the stockholders, getting them on the phone, and trying to persuade them to vote for the merger.[38]

The holders of HBJ's preferred stock presented the most difficult problem. Those securities, issued in the 1987 recapitalization, carried a $13.50 liquidation preference over the common stock that would be wiped out in the takeover. There was an economic logic to that aspect of the deal, driven by the fact that neither class of stock stood to get anything if the company went into bankruptcy, but the stockholders were understandably disappointed to be getting only $0.75 per share for stock that had sold around $10.00 per share shortly after it was issued. Dividends on the preferred stock had been paid in kind before 1991, when all dividends ceased.

A committee was formed to pull together everyone holding preferred stock who was thinking about voting against the deal. In contrast to the situation among the bondholders, there were not many investors holding blocks of preferred stock large enough to block the deal by themselves. So, for Peter Jovanovich and the others, the task was simply one of going through the arguments time after time—that HBJ would get no better deal; that without some alternative solution it would be likely to go bankrupt; and that bankruptcy would destroy the company—in order to patch together a majority of supporters. On the day before the meeting, affirmative votes were just short of 50 percent.

One of the few stockholders capable of putting HBJ over the top with a single vote was the Resolution Trust Corporation (RTC), the federal agency that had been formed to sort out the savings and loan debacle. The RTC held 11.75 percent of HBJ's preferred stock, which it had acquired early in 1991 with the assets of the failed Columbia Savings & Loan. On Thursday, they had indicated an inclination to vote no. Friday morning, Jovanovich and Herrington decided that their only chance to obtain a majority was to fly down to Washington to make their case to the RTC in person. Over a pay phone on the shuttle they learned that a committee was to meet at 11:00 A.M. to make a final decision on how the RTC's vote would be cast. They arrived at 11:30 to find the meeting had been postponed so that they could talk to the official responsible for RTC dispositions, William Roelle.

According to Roelle, the RTC was determined to hold out for a higher consideration for the preferred stock. Jovanovich pointed out that, since two-thirds of the common stock had to be voted in favor of the merger, the entire transaction would be threatened by a last-minute deal that sacrificed the common in favor of the preferred. However, most of his arguments centered on the likely consequences of bankruptcy to HBJ and its employees. Roelle indicated he was still inclined to withhold the RTC's approval. Given HBJ's capital structure, it was literally true—as the bondholders had frequently said in negotiations—that the bondholders owned the company. Yet when it came down to the final stockholders' vote, the RTC was in a position to gamble that the bondholders would be willing to make one last deal in order to conclude the sale they had been negotiating for nine months. Jovanovich and Herrington had to wait an hour and twenty minutes for Roelle to return from the meeting to inform them that the committee had faxed its proxy to New York, voting no. "Believe it or not," said Peter Jovanovich, "it was raining."[39]

They left Roelle's office discouraged and distraught, making sure he understood that, for ten cents a share, the RTC was risking the jobs of thousands of HBJ employees as well as the value of its preferred stock. The stockholders' meeting convened at 10:00 A.M. the next morning in a ballroom on the fifty-fourth floor of a New York hotel. Jovanovich postponed the polling until noon, by which time the stockholders were angrily demanding that the meeting proceed. There was an hour of argument for and against the merger, and then the polls opened at 1:00 P.M.

As the voting proceeded, Jovanovich received a call from the RTC. The committee had reconvened on Saturday morning and had kept in touch with developments in New York through RTC representatives attending the stockholders' meeting. Rather than risk having the merger go down to defeat with a minority of the preferred stock voting in favor, they had decided to change their vote. The final count was 61 percent of the preferred in favor of GCC's acquisition of HBJ. On Monday, November 25, the day the deal finally closed, Roelle called Peter Jovanovich one last time to let him know that, in the end, it was his argument about the human cost of bankruptcy that had swung the committee's vote.

With the HBJ deal concluded, Dick Smith could look at General Cinema's portfolio of businesses with the satisfaction that he had succeeded by dint of sheer persistence in making an acquisition with all of the attributes he cared most about. It was big, but not too big. It absorbed most, but not all, of the proceeds from the sale of the beverage division and shares in Cadbury Schweppes, and it did not burden the company with debt.

In the end, General Cinema had paid what it considered to be a full price for HBJ, based on the analysis conducted in the fall of 1990. But the analysis had not accounted for the value of the company as a platform for future publishing acquisitions, which Smith considered to be of crucial significance. Most important, perhaps, the purchase of HBJ had brought General Cinema a leading franchise in a growth industry—a business that, with good management, investment, and financial discipline could appreciate greatly in value over the long term.

CHAPTER

8

THE NEW GENERAL CINEMA DEFINED

The acquisition of HBJ brought the end of an era at General Cinema. Dick Smith passed the title of chief executive officer to Bob Tarr, retaining his position as chairman of the board. After eighteen years as chief financial officer and twenty-one years as a director, Woody Ives left the company late in 1991 to become CEO of Eastern Enterprises, a utility holding company. Sam Frankenheim left shortly thereafter to join Boston's venerable law firm Ropes & Gray. After a decade of M&A activity, General Cinema was shifting, in Tarr's words, "from a deal company to an operating company," with all that implied for the makeup and role of the corporate office.[1]

AN OPERATING COMPANY

It had been four difficult years since Smith had announced, prematurely, the advent of "the new General Cinema." Now he could look forward to retirement from day-to-day executive responsibilities with the satisfaction that he had succeeded in bringing the company to the point that he had long envisioned. At the annual stockholders' meeting in March 1992, Bob Tarr described in detail the businesses and prospects of the enterprise as it had finally emerged from its lengthy period of self-redefinition.

"First and foremost," said Tarr, the acquisition of HBJ had "once

TABLE 8.1 General Cinema Operating Businesses
Contributions to Revenues and Earnings
Consolidated Results for 1991

	Revenues	Earnings[1]
Neiman Marcus Group	50.0%	32%
HBJ—Publishing	25.0%	47%
HBJ—Insurance	12.5%	17%
GCC Theatres	12.5%	4%

[1]The HBJ earnings presented do not reflect the charges associated with the merger and restructuring. Both of HBJ's businesses reported net operating losses for 1991.

Source: General Cinema Annual Report for 1991, pp. 22–23; and General Cinema 1992 First Quarter Report, pp. 17–18.

again rendered General Cinema a true operating company." Consolidated 1991 revenues were $3.6 billion, with HBJ's businesses contributing close to 40 percent.[2] Discounting the heavy costs of the merger, HBJ contributed an even larger share of operating earnings (see Table 8.1). Overall, Tarr pointed out, operating margins were low, just over 5 percent of revenues, but the "upside potential" in that situation was great. The large capital-spending programs in both GCC Theatres and the Neiman Marcus Group were virtually complete; and an investment of $130 million in HBJ, planned for 1992, could be expected to begin a revitalization of its businesses after five years of financial crisis. General Cinema could look forward to becoming an "earnings growth company," as it had not been since the sale of the beverage division. "It has been an exciting year for us all," concluded Tarr, "and we are energized by the prospects we envision for the new General Cinema in the years ahead."[3]

For Bob Tarr, simply settling down to operations was the most exciting prospect of all. With sound expectations for improved performance over the long term, the businesses nevertheless presented many challenges. Tarr would face those together with a reconstituted team in the corporate office, including a new CFO and a new corporate counsel, both to be recruited in 1992. Robert Smith, as group vice president, was to have responsibility for GCC Theatres, Contempo Casuals, and the mail order division of the Neiman Marcus Group, as well as continued responsibility for real estate. Brian Knez was to serve as corporate vice president, overseeing HBJ's university and professional publishing division.

Regarding General Cinema's new core business, there was reason for cautious optimism. As commentators on the HBJ acquisition pointed out, the $1.5 billion purchase price reflected the fact that General Cinema was "buying into a turnaround situation."[4] Throughout the protracted negotiation process, Tarr, Robert Smith, and Knez had continued to visit and communicate with HBJ, and they had observed the deterioration in its competitive position, especially in school publishing, during that time. Yet, they had also been able to see that Peter Jovanovich was continuing to make sustaining investments in the businesses and was having some success in keeping key personnel on board. They were able to contribute to the damage control effort by their show of commitment to acquiring and, over the long term, to investing in HBJ. All of that amounted to a significant advantage from the operating perspective—they had been welcomed into the business; they knew what had to be done; but they also knew that the businesses were fundamentally sound. There would be, they reasoned, no unpleasant surprises of the sort that Bob Tarr had experienced on his first complete tour of Neiman Marcus stores.

In four-and-a-half years of running the Neiman Marcus Group, Tarr had worked hard, logging countless miles of travel, to get effective management teams in place and, in his words, to "inculcate a General Cinema type of culture and control system environment." Consistent with his approach in the beverage division a decade before, Tarr focused on recruiting and developing well-rounded managers, strong in operations and finance as well as in merchandising. Under his direction, the Neiman Marcus Group invested in new information systems, inventory control, and accounting practices aimed at laying a foundation for "high-quality" earnings in future years.[5]

The protection of General Cinema's Class B stock afforded Neiman Marcus and Bergdorf Goodman the luxury of resisting the price cutting that became endemic in the industry during its long recession. In contrast, they were able to focus on building strong relationships with important fashion designers and on remodeling stores. It was a strategy aimed at bolstering the image of exclusivity that would, Tarr believed, set them apart from every other retail chain and provide the key to profitability when the industry finally began to revive.

Similarly, despite a highly volatile earnings record, Contempo Casuals—the youth-oriented women's wear shopping-mall chain of the Neiman Marcus Group—was able to invest in developing an in-house design and production capability. That was an essential step toward becoming competitive in an area of retailing dominated by powerful chains like The Gap and The Limited, where keeping prices down and responding quickly to fashion trends were the keys to success. With the new capability in place, Contempo Casuals was able to launch a new chain and catalogue, Pastille, for women's fashion aimed at a somewhat older

age group. Another large investment went into the mail-order division of
the Neiman Marcus Group, which had been through some difficult times
since the acquisition of Horchow Mail Order, Inc., in October 1988.
Horchow had been reorganized and combined with the more successful
catalogue operations of Neiman Marcus, which were moved in 1989 into
a large new, highly automated distribution facility in Texas. With those
investments in place, the Neiman Marcus Group could reasonably anticipate that a revival of the retail industry would send its revenues and profits
soaring.

Long-term prospects for the theater business were less certain but
still positive, also as a result of heavy investments made between 1985
and 1990. The bulk of that expenditure had gone into expansion and
remodeling of the circuit. Combined with dispositions of unprofitable
theaters, the program had left General Cinema with not the largest, but
the most modern and best capitalized national theater chain. At the conclusion of the capital program in 1990, the division had been reorganized,
with a reduction in staff of nearly 50 percent. Like hundreds of other U.S.
companies, GCC Theatres achieved much of that reduction by eliminating
layers of middle management and by providing vastly improved information systems to help those who remained handle their increased responsibilities. Twenty-six geographic divisions were reduced to ten, and instead
of thirty-five film buyers there were twelve. At the same time, salaries
were raised—making General Cinema competitive within the industry for
the first time in its history—and restructured on a pay-for-performance
model.

For all that, it would remain an uphill battle to achieve any kind of
consistent earnings growth given the heavy overscreening of the industry.
Since the mid-1980s, annual attendance had remained steady at between
1 and 1.2 billion, while the number of theaters increased from 15,000 to
23,000. With its strong balance sheet, modern circuit, and streamlined
management structure, GCC Theatres could look toward the inevitable
industry shakeout with relative confidence. But it would have to come up
with some innovative concepts to increase its profitability.

Some of those were in the works by 1991, including the development
of an advance seating reservation system and the sale of fast food from
Taco Bell and Pizza Hut in theater concession stands. More fundamental,
perhaps, was a shift in film-buying strategy away from aggressive bidding
and toward building strong relationships with a few film suppliers—for
example, with Disney, with whom General Cinema had a positive relationship dating back to the late 1940s, interrupted only briefly by their legal
battle in the 1970s. Finally, theater division management began to define
its business more broadly, as entertainment, and to look for opportunities

in new technologies, such as ride simulation, and new venues, such as shopping malls and retail stores. Said Robert Smith, in the business language of the 1990s but very much in the spirit of his grandfather and father—who had never wavered in viewing theaters as a source of opportunity—"We are trying to leverage our senior management operating skills and diversify our portfolio of entertainment businesses."[6]

In short, General Cinema, with its new mix of businesses, was an operating company sitting on a large potential for future growth. This was a very different situation from the one in which Bob Tarr had gained his first experience in the corporate office. Then, the overriding concern had been portfolio management, and the corporate role in operations had been primarily one of control. "It used to be an adversarial relationship with the divisions," said Tarr. "It was us and them. But now that's different. We're into these businesses, and I want the corporation to have ownership . . . to feel responsible for results . . . really, to be sponsors of these businesses in any way possible to help them grow."[7]

The goal he set for himself and his two junior operating executives was to be good "corporate partners" with the divisional officers reporting to them. That meant investing in human resources and supporting creativity and entrepreneurship. "We're not going to save our way to prosperity, we're going to have to grow our way," said Tarr. "We need people who can think in terms of increasing the number of transactions and increasing the number of units per transaction." That thought represented a 180-degree turn for the COO of the 1980s, who had frustrated his divisional executives with the attitude that personnel represented costs, not capital. As a symbol of the many changes in process since the HBJ acquisition, it captured much of the essence of the new General Cinema.[8]

At the same time, amid all the change, there would be significant continuities. The transition from Dick Smith to Bob Tarr was a smooth one, just as Smith's own succession to leadership some thirty years before had been; and, as before, the change would bring a reaffirmation and strengthening, rather than a reversal, of the overall direction and basic characteristics of the company. "Stylistically," Tarr was quick to point out, he would be different from Dick Smith: "He went to Harvard, and I went to the Naval Academy—you can extrapolate the differences from there." But the fundamentals would be the same.[9]

In thinking about how operations would be managed, for example, Tarr's model was the General Cinema in which he had grown up, with few divisions and a small corporate office. "The success of this company," he suggested, "has been to have strong divisional presidents and short lines of communication and, to the extent you can, to eliminate both politics and bureaucracy." Within the corporate office, Tarr would also strive to preserve the "freewheeling open environment" that he, and others, judged to be such a healthy part of its culture: "The constant interaction and the challenging, on a high plane—in a constructive, not a destructive way—I think that has been part of the success of General Cinema." This mode of leadership, he realized, would test his own mettle. "Sometimes," Tarr allowed, "you'd like to jump across the table and say 'that's insubordinate!' But you don't dare do that, because you don't want to stifle the good ideas." Following in the path laid out by Dick Smith would not be easy.

In the management transition of the mid- to late 1970s, the shift had been from an operating to a financial emphasis. The corporate office had limited capital spending and had set aggressive profit goals for the divisions in order to establish a stable pattern of earnings growth and build resources for future acquisitions. Those policies had become a battleground, and the outcome of the battle had largely determined the makeup of the top management group. In the late 1980s, the emphasis had shifted back again. As before, the process was not without some conflict, and it had its impact on the corporate office. Now, however, the points at issue were complicated in a way they had not been a decade before by the more open and forceful articulation of family concerns in discussions of business strategy.

FAMILY INTERESTS AND PROFESSIONALISM: A DELICATE BALANCE

The professionalization of corporate management in the 1970s had played a central role in transforming General Cinema into a major corporation. Since then, the tensions inherent in family control of a professionally managed public corporation had remained dormant. Indeed, General Cinema had distinguished itself as a company in which all of its senior managers thought and acted, in Dick Smith's words, "as owners, not just as corporate stewards." Dick Smith, Woody Ives, and Bob Tarr together had crafted the financial strategy and operating policies that had led to General Cinema's consistently strong performance through most of the 1980s. With Sam Frankenheim, they had made the company a respected presence on the mergers and acquisitions scene. Their accomplishments—and their perceived attention to shareholder value—had brought General Cinema to the attention of the financial community and had sent its stock soaring, from an average price of under $5.00 per share in 1978 to $25.00 per share in 1986.[10]

Growth in shareholder value had formed the basis for stockholder approval of General Cinema's Class B stock in 1984. Investors had understood at that time that Dick Smith would buy in stock and contract the company rather than continue to pursue diversification and growth at the risk of losing control. In accepting his terms for proceeding, they had accepted the proposition that the interests of the public shareholders would be well served along with those of the Smith family.

Sam Frankenheim, who had played a large role in crafting the provisions of the Class B stock, and Woody Ives, who had helped to sell the idea to General Cinema's institutional investors, had both fully accepted that proposition when it was put forward. They had become increasingly uncomfortable with the situation, however, as the HBJ acquisition dragged on—with the economic model forecasting lower returns with each passing month—and as GCC Theatres and the Neiman Marcus Group continued to swim against the tide of depressed industry conditions, with disappointing results and dim prospects for earnings improvement in the near term. They feared that, in Dick Smith's determined pursuit of his long-term vision for the company he wished to leave to future generations, family interests had begun to diverge from those of the public shareholders. The fact that General Cinema's stock had leveled off between $20 and $25 per share since 1986 strengthened those concerns. "Everybody likes to think that American companies should be operating more for long-term benefits than short-term benefits," commented Frankenheim.

> But General Cinema has also been a company that planned for the long term while watching profitability in the short term. I may be wrong, but I think that . . . a lot of the public shareholders—whose idea of long term, if they're really long term, is three, maybe four years—may suffer the same kinds of impatience that they have experienced over the last five or six years, because the company has yet to demonstrate its ability to fully exploit the assets that it owns.[11]

Smith understood the dilemma of his professional managers. Yet, in his view, building shareholder value over the long, long term was one of the defining strengths of the company, a strength that derived from family control and active family leadership. "Your shareholders are in several classes in terms of horizons," he said, "but the longest of them doesn't extend to the time horizon of the family." If focusing on that horizon caused some discomfort in the corporate office, Smith was willing to live with that.[12]

Indeed, the family perspective had asserted itself ever more strongly, as Robert Smith and Brian Knez were drawn into corporate councils. They were early and vocal supporters of the HBJ deal and had quickly moved "off the paper" (the conservative economic model) in assessing the value of HBJ and its prospects. Young Smith and Knez had been attracted to General Cinema in the first place by the potential challenges of operations. Still in their thirties, they were generationally disposed to take a long-term view toward investments in the businesses they looked forward to running. Moreover, both young men were working closely with Bob Tarr. As COO, Tarr had played a large role in building the management teams and shaping the strategies of the theater division and the Neiman Marcus Group. He shared Dick Smith's commitment to seeing them through the adverse conditions in both industries, and, still in his forties, he too could look forward to running them for years to come and to enjoying the fruits of success when it arrived.

The freedom of General Cinema's top executives to challenge Dick Smith had become a hallmark of the firm among outsiders who experienced the dynamics of the OOC in action. "This was not a soft and mellow group of people in those conversations," noted Salomon Brothers' Caesar Sweitzer, who had observed them on numerous occasions. Yet, as he and others had discovered, after all the disagreement, once a decision was made, everyone fell in line and supported it wholeheartedly. "Here you had a group of four individuals," said Sweitzer, "who could get in a room and discuss an issue, and apply great intellect, great passion, and great ego to the situation, and still end up clearly as very good friends with a lot of respect for each other."[13]

By the end of 1991, the friendship and respect remained, but the unanimous support of every decision could no longer be maintained. The business issues had become too divisive, while the dynamics of the OOC had changed with the addition of Smith's son and son-in-law. Woody Ives had long before expressed concern about joining a family firm, but he had not felt that General Cinema truly was a family firm until Robert Smith and Brian Knez assumed larger roles. Among professional managers there was, quite simply, a philosophical opposition to moving young family members too quickly into top management positions, which made the situation difficult for the old guard in the corporate office. Completely independent of the actual merits or accomplishments of Robert Smith and Brian Knez, there would always be an assumption of nepotism to be dealt with in relations with the outside world.[14]

For some years, there had been an understanding among the members of the OOC that Bob Tarr would become CEO when Smith was ready to relinquish that position, and that Smith would not be ready until he had successfully acquired a third major business. Indeed, that had been a goal to which all were committed. The successful conclusion of the HBJ deal freed Ives and Frankenheim to look outside General Cinema for one more challenge before retirement. Dick Smith might disagree with their departing view of the company but, characteristically, he took pride in having an executive team of such calibre that its members could move with ease into the top ranks of a leading law firm and utility company. He could count as an achievement the fact that he had created and for so long sustained a hospitable environment for talented nonfamily executives such as they.

To be sure, the issues that had divided the OOC remained concerns in the corporate office of the new General Cinema, but they were now viewed in a more positive context. General Cinema had indeed lost a number of shareholders who had become impatient with its disappointing year-to-year results, said Bob Tarr. There had been a fair amount of ex-plaining to do in regard to the theater and retail businesses, but "those [stockholders] that stayed knew and appreciated what we were doing." Moreover, some new shareholders had been attracted by the fact that the large capital investments, especially in the Neiman Marcus Group, were now in place. Said Tarr, "they want to get on the ride from here forward."[15]

In the 1970s General Cinema had attracted a following in the market largely on the basis of rising earnings and free cash flow from the bottling business. In the 1980s the following had broadened, in part on the strength of people's faith in Dick Smith's investment savvy. After some trying years, Tarr knew, it was now up to him to reward the faithful and develop a new following based on the performance of General Cinema's current mix of businesses—on "consistently improving every year in a reliable way, so that we can get the stock price up and give the sharehold-ers a fair return."[16]

His view of the family issue was equally practical. He asked for, and Smith agreed to, an employment contract designed to ensure that he would feel free to act independently as CEO. That done, Tarr set out to run General Cinema as a public corporation. "It's too big a company for a family to manage," he said. "It's too complex. We have to rely on outside management, and if we're going to attract professional managers—and I view myself as a professional manager; I'm a 'hired gun'—we're going to have to run a meritocracy and reward good performance and provide career paths for that management." The appearance of nepotism was an issue in hiring and keeping professionals, Tarr conceded. Yet there again, the solution to the problem would come from the firm's performance. If the factual evidence indicated that General Cinema was being run professionally and provided career opportunities for nonfamily members, the initial appearance would be unimportant. "I think we're going to be judged," said Tarr, "on what we do and how we run the company."[17]

Dick Smith firmly believed that family ownership and active involvement were among General Cinema's greatest resources and that bringing the next generation into the firm was a vital achievement. With all the advantages that education and training in the corporate office could confer, they were able, he believed, to contribute to the company in ways that nonfamily managers could never quite match. "When these young people dedicate their careers to the company," Smith noted, "they're dedicating the life of their careers—thirty or forty years, not five or ten, until they move on to the next position." The classic advantages conferred by owner-management, he suggested, would also apply. These family managers would not be focused on taking money out of the company in salaries, bonuses, or corporate perquisites. They would gain much more from increases in General Cinema's stock price and dividends, which would come only through long-term creation of profits and cash flow. Said Bob Tarr, "If anybody has an interest in this company's value appreciating, it's those two."[18]

FAMILY OWNERSHIP AND SHAREHOLDER VALUE

For his part, after thirty years at the head of the corporation, Dick Smith took pleasure in stepping back from the responsibilities of CEO with the prospect of continuing family participation in the direction of the firm. Having brought his son and son-in-law into the fold, and having taken them through all of the financial, strategic, and organizational issues of the enterprise in a critical period of transition, he could close the circle on an executive career that he had begun by learning from his own father and working with a brother-in-law. Indeed, Smith had been much like his father in his openness to succession planning. His approach to development of the company's future leaders—by providing challenging responsibilities and exposure to the full range of issues to be faced at the executive level—was virtually the same approach Phil Smith had taken decades before. Yet, with the company radically altered in both scale and scope, the issues he had faced were far more complex.

The collegial atmosphere of the OOC and the generous program of stock options and executive loans had been important steps, consciously taken, toward creating an environment conducive to keeping family and nonfamily executives working harmoniously and with common objectives. Having mentored Bob Tarr and helped to shape his career, Smith could feel comfortable with the succession he had planned and could warmly support Tarr's commitment to maintaining high professional standards in hiring and promotion. Finally, in General Cinema's Class B stock, Smith believed he had created a unique security that—in contrast to many forms of super stock, which were blunt instruments ensuring control under all circumstances—was expressly designed to preserve the delicate balance needed to sustain both family and professional involvement.

At the end of 1991 the Smith family owned virtually all of the Class B stock but a negligible amount of the common and preferred. In total, their stake in the corporation was just under 30 percent. To retain control, they were required to keep together a block of at least 12.5 percent—any less, and the Class B stock would revert to common. The Smith family agreement provided that, if some family members wished to liquidate a major part of their holdings, others would have the option to buy the Class B stock before it could be offered for sale. Such an arrangement acknowledged that in future generations not all the cousins could be expected to take an interest in General Cinema. Smith wanted those who wished to stay involved to be able to do so. At the same time, he believed it important to protect the company from control by any group, family or nonfamily, who did not have a significant financial stake in the enterprise.

The Class B stock provided only passive control. The family could veto any takeover with the ten-vote-per-share provision; but on all other issues, the Class B stock carried only one vote per share. They could not independently mandate changes, since the public shareholders could veto amendments to the corporate charter, voting separately as a class. The terms of the Class B stock also required General Cinema to maintain majorities of independent directors on the board and on its key committees. "The point was," said Dick Smith, "that this wasn't just a license for the Smith family to control the company forever, without being involved and without being professionally governed. The family can, and will I suspect, provide some of the future leaders of this company, not all. That's the unique General Cinema mix of professional and family involvement."[19]

With the Class B stock, Smith felt he had created an institutional framework robust enough to sustain that special characteristic of the firm over future generations. As he looked forward to retirement, he could also take satisfaction in having institutionalized his family's values of social responsibility in the General Cinema Foundation. The company had long made routine annual gifts in relatively small amounts to a wide variety of Boston's civic and charitable institutions, some of which had first begun receiving support from Phil Smith. In 1980 Dick Smith had initiated a two-for-one matching gifts program for employees that encouraged contributions to any type of non-political, non-religious public cause and provided extra support for organizations where employees volunteered their time. In 1987 he brought in outside advisers to consider a more focused approach to corporate giving, with larger grants targeted to areas where they could have greater impact.

When the beverage division was sold in 1989, Smith took the opportunity to endow the General Cinema Foundation with some of the proceeds. He made the OOC its board of trustees, and that group ran it very much as they ran the corporation, imposing rigorous standards of financial discipline on the organizations they chose to fund. When Robert Smith and Brian Knez joined the corporate office, they became foundation trustees as well. Out of the group's deliberations—and drawing on Dick Smith's long-time interest and experience in medical research and education—would come two innovative grants programs aimed specifically at areas that other funders tended to overlook. While many other companies were forced to cut back on charitable giving in the tough economic climate of 1989–1991, General Cinema continued its funding programs steadily, becoming one of the top half-dozen corporate donors in the Boston area. Along with other forms of corporate giving, and the Smith family funds, it would constitute a major force in the charitable community (see Figure 8.1).[20]

Facing the future with new businesses and new leadership, General Cinema was nevertheless set firmly on the course that Dick Smith had charted for it. The corporate foundation, like the Class B stock, gave structural solidity to the balance between private ownership and public responsibility that, in his mind, made General Cinema unique. Some thirty years before, he had inherited from his father a thriving core business and a vision of what the enterprise could become. Building on that legacy, Smith had achieved long-term growth with a strategy of diversification by acquisition, placing General Cinema in a select group of successful conglomerates. He had also succeeded, where many others had failed, in maintaining family control of the business as it grew into a multibillion-dollar company without taking it private. His own legacy to the firm was a healthy mix of businesses with solid prospects for future growth and a clearly defined governing philosophy—that the enterprise would prosper so long as the family continued to serve the interests of General Cinema's public shareholders as well as its own.

FIGURE 8.1 Corporate and Family Philanthropy

Harcourt General Charitable Foundation (created in 1989)

Representative grants:

City Year
Boys and Girls Clubs
Wang Center for the Performing Arts, renovation and restoration
    campaigns
Museum of Fine Arts, Boston, Hollywood in History exhibit (1987)
The Boston Symphony
The Boston Ballet
WGBH: *Long Ago and Far Away* (funded jointly with the Neiman Marcus
    Group) a children's fairy tale series linked to school reading assignments
New Investigator Awards in medical research (created in 1992): grants of
    $100,000 over two years, four per year, to support researchers not yet es-
    tablished in their fields, for work on AIDS, cancer, diabetes, and heart
    disease
The Fund for Educators (created in 1993): three-year grants of up to
    $50,000 per year for teacher development in the Boston city school sys-
    tem, targeted for collaborative teacher development programs not funded
    by the school system

The Richard and Susan Smith Family Foundation (created in 1970)

Representative grants:

Dana Farber Cancer Institute
Children's Hospital, the Smith Family Emergency Trauma Center
Project Bread
Combined Jewish Philanthropies
Facing History and Ourselves
Harvard Hillel
Beth Israel Hospital

GROWTH THROUGH DIVERSIFICATION: THE MAKING OF HARCOURT GENERAL

In 1992 the new General Cinema settled down to its first full year
of operations. During the year, Bob Tarr got his executive teams in place
in the new divisions. Peter Jovanovich left to join a rival educational
publisher, Macmillan–McGraw Hill, and Tarr recruited Richard T. Morgan (the former head of Macmillan–McGraw-Hill) to lead publishing

operations. Subsequently Morgan and Tarr appointed new heads for most of HBJ's publishing units. Later in the year, Frederick M. Dawson became chairman of insurance operations. In 1992 General Cinema borrowed $300 million in senior notes and debentures to finance the retirement of HBJ's high-yield debt and to refinance its own subordinated debt at a lower rate of interest. With new management and new capital investments of more than $100 million in publishing operations, 1992 operating earnings rose by some $40 million (roughly 36 percent) over the previous year. Budgets developed in 1992 projected a further investment of $130 million in 1993 and continued high levels of spending thereafter, aimed at recapturing lost market share in the educational segments and at expanding international operations in the scientific-medical-technical publishing businesses. General Cinema also invested some $20 million in HBJ's insurance business, strengthening its capital structure and raising its ratings, an important step toward improving its market position in future years.[21]

In contrast, the years of heavy investment in the retail and theater businesses ended in 1992. Over the previous five years, the Neiman Marcus Group had had an infusion of $370 million. Much of that investment had gone into expansion of the Neiman Marcus and Contempo Casuals chains and into remodeling of Neiman Marcus stores in the most competitive markets. It had also gone into the creation of Bergdorf Goodman Men, a separate store across the street from Bergdorf's renowned location on Fifth Avenue in New York City. Less visible investments had been those in new management information systems and a new distribution facility for the mail-order lines. Similarly in theaters, capital spending for relocating and remodeling to strengthen the company's competitive position in the most promising markets had been balanced by investments in operational improvements.

The result in theaters was a 25 percent improvement in operating earnings, despite flat revenues in a "lackluster film year." The circuit would be ready for much more significant gains when *Jurassic Park* and *The Firm* hit the theaters in the summer of 1993. In 1992 Neiman Marcus, NM Direct, and Bergdorf also saw earnings improvement well in excess of revenue gains. Contempo Casuals, continuing to struggle to position itself in an extremely tough segment of the retail market, posted a loss for the year. That part of the business would remain a question mark, as the shakeout of the retail industry continued in the middle and discount segments, but prospects for Neiman Marcus and Bergdorf, on the high end, would brighten as the national economy slowly improved through 1993.

At the end of 1992, well along toward assimilating the new core business, General Cinema renamed its publishing subsidiary Harcourt Brace & Company. Shortly thereafter, General Cinema renamed itself Harcourt General, Inc. These steps recognized the dramatic changes that had occurred and set the enterprise squarely on its future course.

As for any company, General Cinema's decision to change the face it presented to the world had layers of meaning. Most obvious was the emphasis on the publishing business, which contributed more than half the company's operating earnings in 1992 and was the focal point of its strategic direction. Getting those basic facts to the surface within the financial community was essential, in Bob Tarr's view, if the company was to develop "a following" and be rewarded in the market for its improvements in performance. The company's stock, he knew, would suffer "the conglomerate discount" if it could not simplify its story so that analysts and investors could grasp the corporation as a whole, understand its strategy, and evaluate its position, performance, and prospects in the industries in which it competed. In the mid-1980s skills in portfolio management—for which General Cinema had consistently been praised—were highly valued. In the early 1990s attention shifted to levels of corporate investment aimed at improving the competitiveness of business units over the long term. As Harcourt General, the company could more easily get out the story of its performance in that regard.[22]

On another level, the name change symbolized the shift in emphasis from deal making to operations. That too had ramifications for how the company was perceived in the outside world. By the early 1990s, the business community had settled down to the realization that the foreseeable future was one of slow economic growth and fierce competition—a world in which competitive strategy and operating performance would count for everything. At the same time, within the company, the formal acknowledgement of this critical shift was full of symbolism. The change encompassed the succession of Bob Tarr as CEO, along with broader changes in the personnel of the corporate office that reoriented its capabilities away from acquisitions skills toward the skills required for running businesses. With those changes completed, Harcourt General turned away from the strategy of growth through diversification that had produced it.

Dick Smith had always understood that operating businesses profitably was the real work to be done in building wealth. That conviction had guided and sustained him through the difficult final stages of the acquisition effort that led to the making of Harcourt General. On the other hand, diversification had preoccupied him for most of his thirty-plus years of leading the company, and over the course of that career he had gained the not inconsiderable distinction of being one of the few corporate executives to make a success of the conglomerate form. The sources of that success, and all that it entailed, form the basis of this story and make it worth the telling.

Harcourt's roots must surely be traced back to Phil Smith's firm grasp of the fundamentals of industry analysis and competitive strategy in an era long before those were explicated and broadly understood. Its foundation was laid with the overwhelmingly successful shopping-center theater strategy, for which he was largely responsible, and with his vision of how the theater business could fund both internal growth and diversification through its strong and consistent cash flow. Building on that foundation, Dick Smith's consolidation strategy in soft drink bottling lifted the company to a new plane in terms of size and aspirations. Smith consolidated the gains in theaters and beverages with reorganization and professionalization of management in the 1970s. Those changes provided the financial resources and top management skills required for the renewed diversification effort of the 1980s, which led first to acquisition of the Neiman Marcus Group and ultimately to HBJ and Harcourt General.

Told in that way, the main lines of the story make it all look rather easy. The real story lies in just how difficult it was to succeed with a strategy of unrelated diversification. As counterpoint to the smashing success in beverages, the disappointing outcomes in bowling, furniture retailing, and supermarket video belie the notion that Dick Smith and his management team had somehow developed the skill of "picking winners" into a reliable corporate asset. The ordeal of the OOC in the 1980s suggests that, with the dramatic inflation of prices paid for companies, it became questionable even that there were winners to be had in the open market for corporate control.[23]

In retrospect it seems that General Cinema's greatest assets in the acquisition quest were Dick Smith's patience and the high level of preparedness within the corporate office to seize whatever opportunities arose. The company's methodical approach to the search—which ensured that it would get a chance to consider virtually any potential acquisition—combined with the analytical, decision-making, and deal-making skills concentrated in the OOC and with General Cinema's financial strength and flexibility, provided the formula for success. They were ready, then, when takeover threats to Carter Hawley Hale brought about the opportunity to create a new—and unique—retail entity, the Neiman Marcus Group. And they were ready when HBJ's debt problems opened the way (albeit a way fraught with difficulty) to acquire a venerable company with a strong position in an attractive industry. If serendipity played an important part in General Cinema's success, it may be added that luck tends to favor those who are prepared to recognize it and to pursue the opportunities it creates.[24]

As he picked a careful path through the M&A madness of the 1980s, Dick Smith took great pride in those characteristics of the company that made it different, including patient opportunism and deal-making skills, in particular financial expertise. Yet those were not the most fundamental differences.

In its prolonged acquisition search, General Cinema had presented the unusual spectacle of a public company run by owner-managers pursuing a strategy of unrelated diversification—a combination that to many would seem, on the face of it, a contradiction in terms. In that era of growing disillusionment with U.S. corporate management—as, in industry after industry, American business lost market share in the face of increased global competition—conglomeration and the active, sometimes frenzied, market for companies that it had spawned topped most lists of corporate evils. As the critique evolved, it focused increasingly on the separation and insulation of management from ownership as the root cause of the problem. Pursuit of bigness for the sake of career (and salary) enhancement, deployment of cash in acquisition programs instead of in the building of competitive strengths, and myopic focus on short-term profits were failings attributable to that "central weakness of the public corporation—the conflict between owners and managers over the control and use of corporate assets." By the early 1990s, owner-management would be hailed as the central element of new corporate forms that appeared to be changing the way business was done.[25]

Many of the welcomed changes associated with these new organizational forms—for example, the use of debt rather than equity financing, the alignment of managerial interests through large equity stakes, the willingness to shrink corporate size to serve shareholder interests— represented ideas and attitudes that Dick Smith had been demonstrating for decades. Over the years, as General Cinema had become larger and Smith had taken on a higher profile in his acquisition search, the consistency of his outlook and approach contrasted ever more sharply with the business environment as it changed around him. It is somewhat ironic that what had seemed conservative and idiosyncratic from the late 1960s, through the 1970s, and much of the 1980s would be the model for corporate behavior in the 1990s.

On the other hand, Dick Smith, along with many others, would conclude that the changes in attitude underlying that shift in perception had been engendered largely by the pressures brought to bear by active acquirers such as he. "To the extent that takeovers forced managements to become more efficient, and sometimes to restructure their business holdings, they were healthy for the country," said Smith. "A lot of this is creative destruction" (a term coined by the economist Joseph Schumpeter, whose course Dick Smith had taken as a Harvard undergraduate). "I believe that it did more good than harm."[26]

In his long pursuit of growth through diversification, Smith had played the role of conglomerateur and, later, of corporate raider with distinction. Similarly, in carving out positions of industry leadership in theaters, soft drink bottling, retailing, and publishing, he achieved some enviable successes. To a great extent, Harcourt General is the culminating product of his career, spanning the past fifty years of American business history. In charting a consistent course through dramatically changing times, that career sheds light on those times and on what the changes have meant for everyone.

NOTES

Chapter 1

1. On the economic significance of the industry and the importance of exhibition, see Douglas Gomery, *The Hollywood Studio System* (New York: St. Martin's, 1986), pp. 6–14; and Mae D. Huettig, *Economic Control of the Motion Picture Industry* (Philadelphia: University of Pennsylvania Press, 1944), presented in abridged form in Tino Balio, ed., *The American Film Industry* (Madison: University of Wisconsin Press, 1985), pp. 285–292.

2. See Harcourt General, Inc., Annual Report for 1992.

3. Marc Sandberg, "Contribution to the History of the Work of Serge Sandberg (1879–1981): Pioneer of the Movie and Patron of the Arts in France," unpublished manuscript (Paris, 1989), translated from the French by Viviane Wohl-Ackerman, MS provided by the Smith family. Mel Brooks is quoted in Jason E. Squire, ed., *The Movie Business Book* (New York: Simon & Schuster, 1983), p. 29.

4. Quotations from Neal Gabler, *An Empire of Their Own: How the Jews Invented Hollywood* (New York: Crown, 1988), p. 5; and Russell Merritt, "Nickelodeon Theaters, 1905–1914: Building an Audience for the Movies," in Balio, ed., *American Film Industry*, p. 88. See also Robert C. Allen, "The Movies in Vaudeville: Historical Context of the Movies and Popular Entertainment," in ibid., pp. 57–82; and Gomery, *The Hollywood Studio System*, especially chapter 1.

5. Gomery notes, "Perhaps 'Hollywood' was the greatest corporate creation of the studio system." *The Hollywood Studio System*, pp. 193–194.

6. Gabler, *An Empire of Their Own*, p. 6. Much of Gabler's book is devoted to a psychological analysis of Zukor, Laemmle, Mayer, and other Hollywood Jews, which fleshes out his interpretation of their unique role in the movie industry and, more specifically, in the production of films that idealized American culture and middle-class American values. The very different and in some ways more useful analysis of the production side of the studio system by Douglas Gomery starts from the premise that the content of movies was determined primarily by each studio's efforts to differentiate its product from those of competitors. See Gomery, *The Hollywood Studio System*, chapters 2–10.

7. From a profile and interview with Philip Smith: Joseph Downes, "Hamburg Palace on Commonwealth Ave Will Be Duplicated Across the United States," *Boston Sunday Post* (September 30, 1956).

8. Ibid.

9. For descriptions of the National Theater in 1911, see *Boston Globe* (August 10, 1911).

10. Richard A. Smith, interview with Bettye H. Pruitt and George D. Smith, June 21, 1988 (hereafter cited as Smith Interview, I). On the effect of the depression on the movie industry, see Douglas Gomery, "U.S. Film Exhibition: The Formation of a Big Business," in Balio, ed., *American Film Industry*, pp. 226–227.

11. Smith Interview, I; and Nancy L. Marks, interview with George D. Smith, January 17, 1989 (hereafter cited as Marks Interview).

12. Smith Interview, I.

13. Gomery, *The Hollywood Studio System*, p. 8.

14. See the *New York Sun* (June 7, 1933); *Business Week* (August 5, 1933); and a brief history written for the fiftieth anniversary in *The Washington Post* (June 5, 1985).

15. Quoted in Downes, "Hamburg Palace on Commonwealth Ave."

16. *Boston Post* (April 26, 1942), and *Boston Globe* (February 7, 1960).

17. *Detroit Times* (May 27, 1938); quotation from *Cleveland Press* (June 4, 1938), clippings in Smith family scrapbook.

18. *Variety* (July 19, 1961). Smith himself used the same numbers for 1940 in a 1956 interview: *Boston Sunday Post* (September 30, 1956).

19. Weekly attendance statistics from U.S. Census data in U.S. Department of Commerce, Bureau of the Census, *Historical Statistics of the United States, Colonial Times to 1970,* Part I (Washington, D.C., 1975), Series H, pp. 862–877; *Fortune* (April 1936), p. 222; *The Economist* (January 4, 1936).

20. U.S. Bureau of the Census, *Historical Statistics,* Part II, Series Q, pp. 148–162.

21. Sidney Stoneman, interview with Bettye H. Pruitt and George D. Smith, May 4, 1988 (hereafter cited as Stoneman Interview). Other theater operators, E. M. Loew and Max Rothstein, pioneered drive-in theaters in New England.

22. *Cleveland Press* (June 4, 1938). See also, *New York Herald Tribune* (June 8, 1933); *Variety* (October 24, 1933); and *New York Times* (August 14, 1938).

23. Early income statements are retained in the files of Harcourt General, Inc. (hereafter cited as HGI corporate records). Industry statistics are from American Association of State Highway Officials, *Policy on Drive-In Theaters* (Washington, D.C., 1949), p. 4, which estimated fifty drive-ins by 1941. Other estimates put the number at sixty: see *Time* (July 14, 1941); and, for a retrospective view, *Variety* (July 19, 1961).

24. See Frank H. Ricketson, Jr., *The Management of Motion-Picture Theaters* (New York: McGraw-Hill, 1938); Carlie Beach Roney, "Show Lady," *The Saturday Evening Post* (February 16, 1939), pp. 23ff.; and Richard Thruelsen, "Movie-House Manager," ibid. (November 15, 1947), p. 34.

25. Stoneman Interview; "Industry Case Digest," *Theater Owners of America* 4 (May 11, 1949); and Emmanuel Kurland to First National Bank of Boston, April 5, 1950, Exhibit 1.2 in a loan application (1950), in HGI corporate records.

26. Small speakers that could be hung inside the car window were installed in a Hollywood drive-in in 1937, but those would not become widely available until the late 1940s. See *Detroit News* (June 18, 1938). On the development of directional blast speakers and their adoption by drive-in theaters, see *Literary Digest* 122 (July 22, 1933): 19; *Variety* (October 24, 1933) and (June 22, 1938); and *New York Herald Tribune* (May 2, 1937).

27. On Nate Barger, see *Time* (July 14, 1941).

28. Hollingshead's charge, made in a 1965 interview, is recounted in a retrospective article on the origins of the drive-in theater, *Boston Globe* (June 6, 1983).

29. *Variety* (July 6, 1938).

30. Huettig, "Economic Control of the Motion Picture Industry," pp. 296ff.; and Michael Conant, *Antitrust in the Motion Picture Industry: Economic and Legal Analysis* (Los Angeles: University of California Press, 1960), table 17.

31. Smith Interview, I.

32. Howard Spiess, interview with George D. Smith, December 29, 1988 (hereafter cited as Spiess Interview, I).

33. Conant, *Antitrust in the Motion Picture Industry,* pp. 99–100.

34. Spiess Interview, I.
35. On the industry's postwar ills, see Balio, ed., *American Film Industry,* p. 401; and Gary R. Edgerton, *American Film Exhibition and an Analysis of the Motion Picture Industry's Market Structure, 1963–1980* (New York: Garland, 1983), p. 27.
36. Smith Interview, I. Figures on numbers of theaters from Edgerton, *American Film Exhibition,* p. 28; and Jack H. Levin Associates, *A Study of Influences on Drive-In Theatres in 1952* (New York, 1952), in HGI corporate records.
37. Gomery, "U.S. Film Exhibition: The Formation of a Big Business," pp. 220–223. See also Russell Merritt, "Nickelodeon Theaters," pp. 100–102; and Gabler, *An Empire of Their Own,* pp. 5–7.
38. For an outsider's sense of *Variety*'s viewpoint, see John Durant, "The Movies Take to the Pasture," *The Saturday Evening Post* (October 14, 1950), pp. 25, 85–89. The term "ozoners" became *Variety*'s standard term for drive-ins in the 1940s and 1950s.
39. Smith Interview, I.
40. Marguerite W. Cullman, "Double Feature—Movies and Moonlight," *New York Times Magazine* (October 1, 1950), p. 68; and John Durant, "Movies Take to the Pasture," p. 85. On the development of small speakers, see *New York Morning Telegraph* (April 7, 1941).
41. Cullman, "Double Feature—Movies and Moonlight," p. 72.
42. Durant, "Movies Take to the Pasture," p. 85. Similar descriptions abound in the periodical literature of the late 1940s and early 1950s; see, for example, William Ornstein, "Growth of the Roofless Theatre: 750 Drive-Ins Today Do Big B.O.," *Variety* (January 5, 1949), p. 30; Fred Hift, "Drive-In Movies Booming—They Even Offer Laundry Service," *New York Herald Tribune* (April 10, 1949), p. 1; and Thomas M. Pryor, "Movie Novelty Develops into Big Business," *New York Times* (September 4, 1949).
43. Ibid.
44. *Variety* (January 4, 1950). See also, "NW Indies Split Over What Product, Clearance Should Be Given Ozoners," *Variety* (November 16, 1949), p. 34.
45. *Variety* (November 29, 1950), p. 3. Drive-in plaintiffs are quoted in ibid. (August 17, 1949). On consent decrees, see *Business Week* (November 25, 1950), p. 26; and (January 6, 1951), p. 92.
46. Quotations are from *Variety* (November 16, 1949), p. 34; and *New York Times* (November 10, 1949).
47. Smith Interview, I.
48. On characteristics of entrepreneurs that hinder organizational development, see W. Gibb Dyer, Jr., *Cultural Change in Family Firms: Anticipating and Managing Business and Family Transitions* (San Francisco: Jossey-Bass, 1986), pp. 57–74. On the conditions for successful transitions from entrepreneurs to their successors, see John L. Ward, *Keeping the Family Business Healthy: How to Plan for Continuing Growth, Profitability, and Family Leadership* (San Francisco: Jossey-Bass, 1987), pp. 186–190. Ward identifies four key traits, all of which the Smiths demonstrated (p. 188): "a founder enthusiastic about passing on the business; a successor who can handle responsibility at a young age; trust between founder and successor; commitment to work things out together."
49. Smith Interview, I. On the challenges of the transition from the "new venture stage" to the "expansion stage" of corporate evolution, see Eric G. Flamholtz, *Growing Pains: How to Make the Transition from an Entrepreneurship to a Professionally Managed Firm* (San Francisco: Jossey-Bass, 1990), chapter 4; and for a more

abstract and theoretical overview, see Neil C. Churchill and Virginia L. Lewis, "The Five Stages of Small Business Growth," *Harvard Business Review* 61 (May–June 1983), pp. 31–32, 34.

50. Quotation from Edward E. Lane, interview with Bettye H. Pruitt and George D. Smith, June 7, 1988 (hereafter cited as Lane Interview).

51. On the arrangements with Drive-In Concession Company and others, see Emmanuel Kurland to First National Bank of Boston, March 24, 1950, in HGI corporate records. On the profitability of concessions: Cullman, "Double Feature—Movies and Moonlight," p. 72.

52. Smith Interview, I.

53. This glimpse of Mid-West Drive-In in 1950 is based on documents prepared in support of a loan application, including Emmanuel Kurland to First National Bank of Boston, March 24, 1950, and April 7, 1950, in HGI corporate records.

54. Kurland to Bank of Boston, April 7, 1950; and Jack H. Levin Associates, "A Study of Influences on Drive-In Theatres," p. 5.

55. Richard A. Smith, interview with Bettye H. Pruitt, July 22 and 28, 1993 (hereafter cited as Smith Interview, V). John Ward's analysis of patterns of successor development in family firms indicates that Phil Smith was indeed remarkable in delegating substantial responsibility to a son still in his mid-twenties: see Ward, *Keeping the Family Business Healthy*, table 15, p. 199.

56. The following description is based on Smith Interview, I; Marks Interview; Lane Interview; Spiess Interview; and interviews with Melvin Wintman, James Collins, Winifred Franklin, Doris Bamberg, and Ann Pave (see A Note on Sources).

57. Quoted in Downes, "Hamburg Palace on Commonwealth Ave."

58. This paragraph and the next are based on obituaries in *Boston Globe* (July 16, 1951) and *Variety* (July 19, 1961), and on Smith Interview, I and Marks Interview.

59. Marks Interview, Smith Interview, I.

60. Smith Interview, V. The consistency between Phil Smith's family life and business life fits the pattern identified by family firm analysts. Says John L. Ward, "well-managed businesses and healthy families . . . share many positive, constructive traits" (Ward, *Keeping the Family Business Healthy*, p. 55.). See also, Dyer, *Cultural Change in Family Firms*, pp. 35–37.

61. Levin Associates, *Study of Influences on Drive-In Theatres*, p. 14; and American Association of State Highway Officials, *Policy on Drive-In Theaters*, p. 2.

Chapter 2

1. Melvin R. Wintman, interview with Bettye H. Pruitt and George D. Smith, March 10, 1988 (hereafter cited as Wintman Interview). The idea of the generational shift of theater owners from showmen to businessmen is developed in Gary R. Edgerton, *American Film Exhibition and an Analysis of the Motion Picture Industry's Market Structure, 1963–1980* (New York: Garland, 1983), pp. 132–141.

2. Quoted in *Forbes* 101 (April 15, 1968), p. 70. Theater statistics from Hugo Uyterhoeven, "General Cinema Corporation," Harvard Business School Case #9-377-084, Boston, 1976, p. 25.

3. On the shopping-center phenomenon and details about Highland Park Village, see Kenneth T. Jackson, *Crabgrass Frontier: The Suburbanization of the United States* (New York: Oxford University Press, 1985), pp. 257–259. On J. C. Nichols's original shopping center, see *Business Week* (November 11, 1939), p. 24 and (November 1, 1947), p. 6.

4. *Business Week* (March 4, 1950), pp. 67–68.

5. "Markets in the Meadows," *Architectural Forum* 90 (March 1949): 115, 117–118; and "Trust Rides Shopping Center Boom," *Business Week* (July 22, 1950), pp. 80–84.

6. "Markets in the Meadows," p. 116; *Business Week* (November 25, 1950), p. 26; and Richard A. Smith, interview with Bettye H. Pruitt and George D. Smith, June 21, 1988 (hereafter cited as Smith Interview, I).

7. John C. Perham, "Shopping Centers: They Are Losing Some of Their Merchandising Magic," *Barron's* 35 (August 15, 1955): 22. The summer theater episode was remembered by James Collins, who managed the Cinema during those summers: James Collins, interview with Bettye H. Pruitt, June 23, 1988 (hereafter cited as Collins Interview).

8. Joseph Downes, "Hamburg Palace on Commonwealth Ave Will Be Duplicated Across the United States," *Boston Sunday Post* (September 30, 1956).

9. Smith Interview, I. See also, "Agreement: Mid-West Drive-In Theatres, Inc. with Philip Smith and Richard Smith," January 2, 1947, p. 5, in the files of Harcourt General, Inc. (hereafter cited as HGI corporate records.)

10. On contributions of drive-ins to total revenues, General Drive-In Corporation, Securities and Exchange Commission Registration No. 2-16523 (Washington, D.C., 1960) (hereafter cited as General Drive-In, SEC Registration), p. 8.

11. Howard Spiess, interview with George D. Smith, December 29, 1988 (hereafter cited as Spiess Interview). Theater statistics from *Boxoffice Magazine,* in Uyterhoeven, "General Cinema Corporation," exhibit 4, p. 25. A reference to the drive-in theater circuit as the " 'bread and butter' division" is in the General Drive-In Annual Report for 1961, p. 2.

12. Information on CinemaScope and George Stevens quote from Leslie Halliwell, *Halliwell's Filmgoer's Companion* (New York: Charles Scribner, 1988), p. 144.

13. Spiess Interview. For a description of an early drive-in CinemaScope installation in Salt Lake City, judged to be the first in the nation, see Jack Goodman, "A 'Robe' as Big as All Outdoors," *New York Times* (April 4, 1954).

14. Collins Interview.

15. General Drive-In, SEC Registration, p. 9.

16. Spiess Interview; Collins Interview.

17. "Smith Management Way," unpublished operations manual (1952), HGI corporate records, p. 49; and Collins Interview.

18. Collins Interview.

19. General Drive-In SEC Registration, p. 4.

20. Richard A. Smith, interview with Bettye H. Pruitt and George D. Smith, March 16, 1989 (hereafter cited as Smith Interview, II). It should be noted that the Smiths' motivation for going public fits none of the eight most common reasons identified in the literature on family firms ("to increase personal wealth, to diversify, to obtain equity capital for expansion, to attract and motivate employees, to avoid IRS valuation of company assets, to satisfy investment bankers, to 'professionalize' management, to sell out"). By the same token, they would not be bothered by the negative consequences commonly associated with that step— internal conflict, a focus on short-term results, unwanted scrutiny or interference from outside stakeholders, loss of control, or (at least in the short run) threat of takeover. See W. Gibb Dyer, Jr., *Cultural Change in Family Firms: Anticipating* *and Managing Business and Family Transitions* (San Francisco: Jossey-Bass, 1986), chapter 6, especially pp. 96–101.

21. Smith Interview, I.

22. Edgerton, *American Film Exhibition,* table 4, p. 28; U.S. Department of Commerce, Bureau of the Census, *Historical Statistics of the United States, Colonial Times to 1970,* Part I (Washington D.C., 1975), Series H878 and H884. Phil Smith commented on the opportunity provided by the mediocrity of television programming in General Drive-In's Annual Report for 1960.

23. See Malcolm S. Salter and Wolf A. Weinhold, *Diversification through Acquisition: Strategies for Creating Economic Value* (New York: The Free Press, 1979), pp. 173–174. In the parlance of the 1970s' most widely touted analytical technique, the growth/share matrix of The Boston Consulting Group, the theater business was rapidly becoming a "cash cow" (a market leader in a profitable but low-growth industry) that needed to be balanced with a "question mark" business (a developing company in a high-growth industry) that would absorb cash in the short run but eventually become a "star" (with a dominant position in a high-growth industry) and ultimately a cash producer. See D. F. Abell and J. S. Hammond, *Strategic Market Planning: Problems and Analytical Approaches* (Englewood Cliffs, N.J.: Prentice-Hall, 1979); G. S. Day, "Diagnosing the Product Portfolio," *Journal of Marketing* (April 1977), pp. 29–38; and Michael E. Porter, *Competitive Strategy: Techniques for Analyzing Industries and Competitors* (New York: The Free Press, 1980), appendix A. For theory and evidence that sophisticated investors tend to reward such a strategy, see Joel M. Stern, *Analytical Methods in Financial Planning,* 3rd ed. (New York: Chase Manhattan Bank, 1977), pp. 7–8.

24. General Drive-In Annual Report for 1960, p. 3.

25. Edward E. Lane, interview with Bettye H. Pruitt and George D. Smith, June 7, 1988 (hereafter cited as Lane Interview); Wintman Interview.

26. General Drive-In Annual Report for 1960, p. 7; Lane Interview.

27. General Drive-In, SEC Registration, p. 3.

28. Richard A. Smith, interview with Bettye H. Pruitt, July 22 and 28, 1993 (hereafter cited as Smith Interview, V).

29. Ibid. On the pattern of crisis more typically resulting from the unexpected death of a founder, see Dyer, *Cultural Change in Family Firms,* pp. 42–51. Dyer makes clear that most small firms experience crises of succession in such circumstances because, unlike Phil Smith, "most founders," having "strong needs for power and control," foster corporate cultures that lack the ability to function effectively without them. Ibid., pp. 69–74.

30. Smith Interview, II; and Smith Interview, V.

31. Smith Interview, V.

32. Uyterhoeven, "General Cinema Corporation," p. 16; Smith Interview, II.

33. The analysis of industries presented here is primarily Dick Smith's (Smith Interviews I, II, and V); but the framework and language employed in this presentation are derived from Porter, *Competitive Strategy,* chapter 1.

34. Howard Spiess graciously pulled together the documentation making possible this description of the evolution of theater management in the 1960s.

35. Lane Interview; and Morris Englander, interview with George D. Smith, April 27, 1989 (hereafter cited as Englander Interview).

36. For Smith's view of the bowling experience as "a healthy one for the management group," see Uyterhoeven, "General Cinema Corporation," p. 16.

37. Spiess Interview.

38. Ibid. This and the following two paragraphs also draw on Lane Interview, Smith Interview, V, Englander Interview, and interviews with Herbert Hurwitz, J. Atwood Ives, James McKenney, and William Zellen (see A Note on Sources for full citations).

39. The comparison between Smith and other theater owners is developed by *Forbes* magazine ("But Where Are the Profits," *Forbes* 108 [July 1, 1971], 37–39): "Smith muddied his shoes negotiating General's first 100 shopping center leases." It is impossible to draw a detailed portrait of the culture of the management group in this period. However, based on the attributes of Dick Smith's leadership style described in this paragraph, it most closely resembles what Dyer calls "the laissez-faire culture" found in some family firms. Such cultures are paternalistic in the sense that relationships are hierarchical and family leaders retain ultimate authority in defining the company's mission and setting its direction; but they are also characterized by high levels of trust in nonfamily employees and willingness to delegate to subordinates substantial authority in determining the specifics of how corporate goals are to be achieved. See Dyer, *Cultural Change in Family Firms*, pp. 24–29.

40. General Drive-In, Annual Report for 1962, pp. 1–2.

41. Englander Interview. On the strategies of others, see Edgerton, *American Film Exhibition*, pp. 38–39.

42. General Drive-In Corporation, Annual Report for 1961, p. 2; Spiess Interview.

43. Hollis Alpert, "Something New in Movie Communication," *Saturday Review* (June 9, 1962), p. 54, gives credit for the first twin to Don Rugoff, whose two-story twin theater opened in New York City in June 1962. Other theater owners who had by that time announced plans to build twins or remodel existing structures into twins were Walter Reade in New York and Joseph Levine and Ben Sack, both in Boston.

44. Alpert, "Something New in Movie Communication"; and General Drive-In, Annual Report for 1962, p. 2.

45. "General Cinema: King of the Flicks," *Business Week* (May 20, 1972), 31–32; Spiess Interview. Durwood also staked a claim as the the originator of both the twin theater and the concept of locating multiple screens around common projection and concession facilities. However, he did not open his first twin until 1963, and then it was by his own account "almost by accident," because a shopping-center developer offered him a space with "two side-by-side bays." For the claims and quotation of Durwood, see "Show Business: Quads, Sixplexes and Up," *Newsweek* (September 8, 1969), p. 71; and Edgerton, *American Film Exhibition*, p. 63, n. 85.

46. "General Cinema: King of the Flicks," p. 31; Edgerton, *American Film Exhibition*, p. 34. The analysis of industry structure presented in this section relies heavily on Edgerton.

47. Percentages calculated from Edgerton, *American Film Exhibition*, table 3, p. 23, and table 4, p. 28.

48. Quoted from General Cinema's 1978 federal 10-K form by Edgerton, *American Film Exhibition*, p. 107.

49. Ibid., pp. 54–55.

50. "But Where Are the Profits?" pp. 38–39; and Edgerton, *American Film Exhibition*, pp. 69–70.

51. The situation of General Cinema in the 1960s and 1970s fits the pattern characterized by Dyer as the "latent family firm," in which there is no visible connection of family members other than that of the one person running the business (Dyer, *Cultural Change in Family Firms,* p. xv). It is also Dyer who cites distrust or disagreement over how the assets of the company should be used (for example, dividends versus reinvestment) as the most common cause of conflict in family-owned businesses (ibid., pp. 87–88).

52. Edgerton, *American Film Exhibition,* pp. 35–37; Wometco Corporation, annual reports.

53. The comparison with Wometco provides a good case in point. Wometco was also a family company, organized by two brothers-in-law in 1925. Much like the Smiths, they began with indoor theaters, then went into drive-ins and shopping-center theaters and took the company public in 1959. At that time, they had already diversified into soft drink bottling, confections, vending machines, and television. With that mix of businesses, Wometco started larger and grew somewhat faster than General Cinema up to 1968. Yet by 1973, Wometco's revenues were little more than half of General Cinema's, and it was a relatively minor player in every industry in which it operated. See Wometco Enterprises, annual reports; and, for the position of Wometco in the theater industry in the 1970s, see Edgerton, *American Film Exhibition,* appendix table 15, pp. 201–221.

Chapter 3

1. Donald Kendall is quoted in *Miami Herald,* February 26, 1966, p. E-1. This edition of the *Herald* included a special advertising section, devoted entirely to the opening of the new plant.

2. John W. Bliss, interview with Bettye H. Pruitt, February 24, 1989 (hereafter cited as Bliss Interview).

3. Data on sales trends are from "Review of Product and Packaging Trends," *Beverage Industry* (March 24, 1972), p. 34. See also, "Contract Canners: A Major Threat to Your Business," *Bottling Industry* (February 4, 1964), p. 38.

4. Edward E. Lane, interview with Bettye H. Pruitt and George D. Smith, June 7, 1988 (hereafter cited as Lane Interview). American Beverage's annual report for 1967 noted that during the period 1963–1967, "our sales have almost doubled and earnings have more than quadrupled without any change in our marketing areas." In 1966 the company had net income before taxes of $1.5 million on sales of $16.6 million. See American Beverage Corporation Annual Report for 1967 in the records of Harcourt General, Inc. (hereafter cited as HGI corporate records).

5. General Cinema Annual Reports for 1961–1966. Leases are reported under "Commitments and Contingencies," as "aggregate minimum annual amount of rentals in effect on October 31."

6. That was the determination of General Cinema management in the mid-1960s according to Hugo Uyterhoeven, "General Cinema Corporation," Harvard Business School Case #9-337-084, Boston, 1976, p. 18.

7. Quoted in "Royal Little Looks at Conglomerates," *Dun's Review* 91 (May 1968): 27. According to *Fortune* in 1966, typical "growth companies" were those that had a "big technological lock, like Xerox," or those "latched onto the population explosion, like Coca-Cola"—or those that were successful conglomerates. See *The Conglomerate Commotion,* by the editors of *Fortune* (New York: Viking, 1970), p. 29. Textron and Litton were the fastest growing billion-dollar companies in 1966.

8. The significance of the separation of ownership and management in public corporations has been a theme of business literature since the 1930s, but has taken on far greater importance and urgency as the business community and its observers have attempted to evaluate the nearly continuous wave of mergers and acquisitions that began with the conglomerate movement of the 1960s. The distinction drawn here between owner-managers and professional managers is well grounded in both theoretical and empirical studies. See Catherine M. Daily and Marc J. Dollinger, "An Empirical Examination of Ownership Structure in Family and Professionally Managed Firms," *Family Business Review* 5, no. 2 (Summer 1992): 117–136, especially pp. 120–121, which provides a helpful review of the literature on this subject.

9. On the possible vending machine acquisition, see Uyterhoeven, "General Cinema Corporation," p. 18. The standard definition of a true conglomerate strategy has three elements. Within a five-year period an "Acquisitive Conglomerate" firm will have (1) grown in earnings per share at an annual rate of 10 percent or better; (2) made at least five acquisitions, three into new unrelated areas of business; and (3) financed its acquisitions largely through the issue of new equity shares. See Richard P. Rumelt, *Strategy, Structure, and Economic Performance,* reissue (Boston: Harvard Business School Press, 1986), p. 24.

10. Michael Lubatkin, "Merger Strategies and Stockholder Value," *Strategic Management Journal* 8 (1987): 48 suggests a refinement of the definition of conglomerate strategy to distinguish between conglomerate *diversification* strategy and conglomerate *acquisition* strategy, the latter being "a single act of diversification into unrelated areas followed by a series of moves intended to fortify the firm's competitive position in its newly selected business direction." Lubatkin's analysis of over a thousand mergers supports his contention that this distinction helps to account for superior performance such as that demonstrated by General Cinema. Performance measures relative to the *Fortune* 500 are from General Cinema Corporation, *Presentation to the New York Society of Security Analysts,* October 6, 1977, in HGI corporate records. Richard Rumelt's work provided, in 1974, the first systematic evaluation of the performance of highly diversified firms. In Rumelt's system of firm types, General Cinema falls somewhere between Acquisitive Conglomerate and Unrelated Passive ("active in unrelated areas [but not experiencing] particularly high growth rates or price earnings ratios [or engaging] in ambitious acquisition programs"). Its performance exceeded the norms for both types of firms. See Rumelt, *Strategy, Structure, and Economic Performance,* pp. 24, 90–92, 151–152, and a more recent work that draws similar conclusions about the performance of such firms, "Diversification Strategy and Profitability," *Strategic Management Journal* 3 (1982): 359–369.

11. In Rumelt's terminology (*Strategy, Structure, and Economic Performance,* pp. 38–40, 71), General Cinema's structure was "functional with subsidiaries," a form used by very few unrelated business firms. Within Alfred Chandler's analytical framework, the company in this period was still very much an "entrepreneurial enterprise." See Alfred D. Chandler, Jr., *The Visible Hand: The Managerial Revolution in American Business* (Cambridge, Mass.: Harvard University Press, 1977), pp. 9, 237–238, 413–415.

12. Richard A. Smith, interview with Bettye H. Pruitt and George D. Smith, March 16, 1989 (hereafter cited as Smith Interview, II).

13. Reportedly, at one time there were as many as 8,000 soft drink bottlers in the United States; in 1947 there were 5,200. See "General Cinema Projects Bright

New Image in Soft Drink Field," *Barron's* 49 (October 20, 1969): 35; and J. C. Louis and Harvey Z. Yazijian, *The Cola Wars* (New York: Everest House, 1980), p. 334.

14. Louis and Yazijian, *Cola Wars,* p. 338; and *Miami Herald* (February 26, 1965), p. E-8.

15. The Houston Pepsi franchise was later sold, but the company retained its bottling facility in Houston and marketed Golden Age products exclusively in that area.

16. In 1987 Darsky's achievements were recognized by his induction into the Beverage World Hall of Fame. See "The Sixth Annual Beverage World Hall of Fame Awards Presentation," pamphlet (November 2, 1987), copy in HGI company records.

17. Quoted in Terry Turner, "Biography in Brief . . . Julius Darsky" (January 23, 1955) in HGI corporate records.

18. *Miami Herald,* February 26, 1966, p. E-7.

19. Herbert G. Paige [letter of resignation] to Directors of American Beverage Corporation (January 25, 1967), in American Beverage Corporation, Board of Directors Meeting Minutes, HGI corporate records.

20. Smith Interview, II.

21. See "Soft Drinks: A Touch of Glamour," *Fortune* (July 1, 1966), pp. 160, 162; "Contract Canners: A Major Threat to Your Business"; and "Review of Product and Packaging Trends." Even as the soft drink industry continued its growth into the 1970s, observers continued to predict that the trend could not continue. See for example: "The Public's Crush on Private Labels," *Time* (October 4, 1971), p. 79; "Paradise Lost?" *Forbes* 111 (February 1, 1973), pp. 41–42; and Eric Aiken, "It's the Real Thing: Soft Drink Producers Face an Extended Stretch of Slower Growth," *Barron's* 53 (November 19, 1973): 3, 17–19.

22. In 1967 Coca-Cola's share of the total cola market was estimated to be 56 percent, Pepsi-Cola's 24 percent. Taken together, Coca-Cola products controlled 39 percent of the total soft drink market, those of Pepsi-Cola 18 percent. (Figures are from tables published in *Beverage Industry* [Copyright: Beverage Industry and John C. Maxwell, Jr., Oppenheimer & Co., June 16, 1972], photocopies in HGI corporate records.)

23. Financial data from American Beverage Company and GCC Annual Report for 1967.

24. Smith Interview, II.

25. Ibid.; Gilbert W. Butler, president Butler Capital Corporation, interview with Bettye H. Pruitt and George D. Smith, August 9, 1989.

26. Smith Interview, II; General Cinema Annual Report for 1968; and J. Atwood Ives, interview with Bettye H. Pruitt and George D. Smith, November 23, 1988 (hereafter cited as Ives Interview, II). Ives noted that instead of providing the normal 40 to 50 percent warrant coverage on the subordinated debt, Smith was able to induce the lender to take only 10 percent.

27. Based on A. C. Nielson Company data in GCC corporate records. In total sales—that is, including syrup sold to soda fountains, restaurants, and so forth— Pepsi-Cola held only 14 percent of the national market, based on data published in *Beverage Industry*.

28. Details on the acquisitions of 1968–1969 may be found in GCC Annual Report for 1968. At this time the company was the second largest Pepsi bottler in the United States. Other companies that were beginning to put together substantial soft drink divisions at this time were Wometco and RKO General, both of which had diversified holdings very similar to General Cinema's. Wometco bought into Coca-Cola, RKO General into Pepsi, Dr Pepper, and 7-Up. See Louis and Yazijian, *Cola Wars,* pp. 337–338.

29. Uyterhoeven, "General Cinema Corporation," p. 12.

30. Smith Interview, II.

31. Quoted in Uyterhoeven, "General Cinema Corporation," p. 11.

32. The "guerrilla warfare" quotation is from Bert J. Einloth III, interview with Bettye H. Pruitt, January 10, 1989.

33. Quotation from Robert T. Shircliff, interview with Bettye H. Pruitt, October 26, 1988.

34. Richard A. Smith to All Beverage Plant and Division Managers, February 2, 1970, in HGI corporate records.

35. Julius Darsky to Richard Smith, March 2, 1970, in HGI corporate records.

36. William Zellen to Herbert Paige, July 8, 1970; and Richard A. Smith to Herbert Paige, November 5, 1970, in HGI corporate records.

37. Richard A. Smith, "Beverage Operations Committee," August 13, 1970, in HGI corporate records.

38. Edward E. Lane to Beverage Operations Committee, September 2, 1970; Brian E. Veasy to Beverage Operations Committee, September 18, 1970; and Veasy, "Minutes of BOC Meeting #2," October 15, 1970, in HGI corporate records.

39. Quotation from Herbert Paige to American Beverage Managers, February 16, 1971; on Atlanta, see Nate Feldman to Harold Echols, September 28, 1970; on American Beverage division's model five-year plans, Paige to Brian Veasy, September 10, 1971, in HGI corporate records. Miami is held up as "an efficient and well-managed operation" in E. B. Veasy to Richard Smith, May 28, 1970. See also Herbert Paige to Marketing Committee, October 1970; Miles Dean to Bill Zellen, June 25, 1971; and Zellen to E. E. Lane, February 23, 1972, in HGI corporate records.

40. Dean to Zellen, June 25, 1971, in HGI corporate records; Shircliff Interview. See also Herbert Paige to Jack Kerin, February 3, 1971); Paige to Richard Smith, November 29, 1971; Paige to Brian Veasy, January 28, 1972; Zellen to Lane, June 21, 1972, in HGI corporate records.

41. Quoted in Uyterhoeven, "General Cinema Corporation," p. 12.

42. See "Beverage Operations Committee, Minutes of Meeting #10." The "third leg" quotation is from Uyterhoeven, "General Cinema Corporation," p. 18.

43. Alexander M. Tanger, interview with Bettye H. Pruitt, April 18, 1989 (hereafter cited as Tanger Interview).

44. Alexander M. Tanger to Richard A. Smith, June 24, 1969, draft in GCC corporate records; Tanger Interview.

45. *General Cinema Corporation Security Analysts Meeting,* New York City, May 2, 1973, n.p., in HGI corporate records. Regarding such justifications of diversification, see Malcolm S. Salter and Wolf A. Weinhold, "Diversification via Acquisition: Creating Value," *Harvard Business Review* 56 (July–August 1978): 176. Salter and Weinhold note, "Of the synergies usually identified to justify an acquisition, financial synergies are often unnoted while operating synergies are widely trumpeted. Yet our experience has been that the benefits most commonly achieved are those in the financial area."

46. Richard A. Smith, "Outline of Film Financing Proposal," January 4, 1972, in HGI corporate records.

47. Uyterhoeven, "General Cinema Corporation," p. 30.

48. "General Cinema: King of the Flicks," *Business Week* (May 20, 1972), p. 32.
49. "Levitz: the Hot Name in 'Instant' Furniture," *Business Week* (December 4, 1971), p. 90. See also, "Levit(z)ation," *Forbes* 109 (February 1, 1972): 16–17; and "Levitz Furniture Warehouses May Revolutionize the Whole Industry," *Advertising Age* 43 (February 7, 1972): 16.
50. Lane Interview.
51. Herbert J. Hurwitz, interview with George D. Smith, August 4, 1988 (hereafter cited as Hurwitz Interview); HGI corporate records.
52. Helpful insights into this business venture were provided by Herbert Hurwitz (Hurwitz Interview); and Hugo Uyterhoeven, teaching notes to "General Cinema Corporation."
53. The problems of this industry may be traced in stories on Levitz in *Business Week:* "Levitz Redecorates Its Image" (August 8, 1977), p. 59; "Levitz: When a Manager Veers from the Owners' Original Plan" (September 1, 1980); and "Levitz Furniture: Sitting Pretty as It Waits for the Recovery" (February 7, 1983), p. 76.
54. Quoted in Uyterhoeven, "General Cinema Corporation," p. 19.
55. General Cinema Annual Report for 1973, p. 4.
56. Eric G. Flamholtz, *Growing Pains: How to Make the Transition from an Entrepreneurship to a Professionally Managed Firm* (San Francisco: Jossey-Bass, 1990), pp. 35–48, provides a useful summary of the differences between entrepreneurial and professional management stages of corporate evolution and the relationships to firm size, as measured by revenues. Most companies, he indicates, move to professional management at the level of about $100 million.

Chapter 4

1. Quoted in Nate Feldman to Herbert Paige, October 5, 1971, in the records of Harcourt General, Inc. (hereafter cited as HGI corporate records). The specific reference is to Westinghouse, which acquired a number of 7-Up franchises around 1970. James Somerall is quoted in "The Big Push at Pepsi," *Dun's Review* 91 (February 1968): 36. See also J. C. Louis and Harvey Z. Yazijian, *The Cola Wars* (New York: Everest House, 1980), p. 338, noting conglomerates "new at the soft drink game," that "turned to their professional managers and their balance sheets, forgetting that soft drinks are a service industry and the small bottler whom they have just acquired is a tried and true expert in the special techniques of merchandising his products."
2. Michael E. Porter, *Competitive Advantage: Creating and Sustaining Superior Performance* (New York: The Free Press, 1985), pp. 1–2. The "inherent profitability" of the industry in which a company competes and "the determinants of relative competitive position within [it]," Porter argues, are the "two central questions [that] underlie the choice of competitive strategy. . . . Neither question by itself is sufficient to guide the choice. . . ."
3. Quoted in Hugo Uyterhoeven, "General Cinema Corporation," Harvard Business School Case #9-377-084, Boston, 1976, p. 12. On the choice of Paige, see also Beverage Operations Committee, "Minutes of Meeting #10," September 14–15, 1972, in HGI corporate records.
4. General Cinema Beverage Executive Committee, "Minutes of Meeting #2," January 30, 1973, in HGI corporate records.

5. See General Cinema, Annual Report for 1972, p. 5; and Beverage Executive Committee, "Minutes of Meeting #2."

6. Text of Herbert G. Paige speech (1972), in HGI corporate records.

7. Lawrence Gilligan, Miami plant controller, GCC Beverages, Inc., interview with Bettye H. Pruitt, February 1, 1989 (hereafter cited as Gilligan Interview).

8. Edward E. Jenkins, interview with Bettye H. Pruitt, January 31, 1989; and Mark Sobell, "Minutes of the First Annual GCC Management Meeting," March 11, 1974, in HGI corporate records.

9. Herbert Paige, Speech to First Annual Management Meeting, March 11, 1974, in HGI corporate records. Total volume of soft drink sales in General Cinema's franchise areas grew by 3 percent in 1972 and by 5 percent in 1973, versus growth of 6 and 7 percent in the nation as a whole in those years. GCC's growth in case sales of Pepsi-Cola products was below the national rate for Pepsi in 1973, and its share of the cola market in its areas was down by almost 2 percent, while nationally Pepsi's market share had grown slightly. See Mark Sobell to Herbert Paige, November 20, 1973; and Sobell, "1974 Beverage Division General Cinema Corporation Marketing Plan," n.d., in HGI corporate records.

10. Paige, Speech to First Annual Management Meeting.

11. Sobell, "1974 Marketing Plan."

12. Minutes of Corporate Division Review Meeting, December 2–3, 1976, in HGI corporate records.

13. These differences in line managers' receptivity to operations, financial, and marketing staff functions are clearly articulated in Minutes of the Third Annual Management Meeting, December 8–10, 1975, in HGI corporate records.

14. Uyterhoeven, "General Cinema Corporation," p. 15.

15. Herbert Paige, Speech to Annual Management Meeting, December 8, 1975, in HGI corporate records.

16. Paige, Speech to First Annual Management Meeting.

17. John W. Bliss, interview with Bettye H. Pruitt, February 24, 1989 (hereafter cited as Bliss Interview).

18. Paige, Speech to Annual Management Meeting, December 8, 1975.

19. Price data are from Martin Romm, "General Cinema Corporation," First Boston Research Report (August 29, 1977), p. 6. See also, Herbert Paige to Board of Directors, November 9, 1973, in HGI corporate records; Bliss Interview; and Louis and Yazijian, *Cola Wars,* pp. 307–308.

20. Bliss Interview.

21. General Cinema's volume of sales fell only 1.3 percent in 1975, versus Pepsi Metro, which lost 9 percent in sales volume between January and October 15. In 1974, the year price increases went into effect, sales volume rose only 2.8 percent, but net profit rose 53 percent. Paige estimated that the increase would have been 25 percent without a favorable sugar contract. In the same year, the division's rank among the twelve largest multifranchise bottlers on net income as percentage of sales rose from eleventh to fifth. See Herbert Paige, Speech to Annual Management Meeting, December 11, 1974, and Speech to Marketing Planning Meetings, October 1974, in HGI corporate records.

22. "Hard Trading in Soft Drinks," *Forbes* (December 15, 1977), p. 35; and "A Thirst to Acquire the Soft Drink Bottlers," *Business Week* (October 24, 1977), pp. 39–40. *Business Week* quoted one industry executive as saying: "Soft drinks are practically a staple of American life. Having an exclusive franchise to sell them is almost like owning an unregulated utility."

23. "Hard Trading in Soft Drinks," p. 36.

24. See Louis W. Stern, Oriye Agodo, and Fuat A. Firat, "Territorial Restrictions in Distribution: A Case Analysis," *Journal of Marketing* 40 (April 1976): 69–75; "Industry Urges House Passage of HR: 6684," *Beverage Industry* 65 (August 13, 1976): 4–5; Patricia Raber, "Territorial Franchises: Nine-Year Battle Pays Off," *Beverage Industry* 69 (August 1, 1980): 1, 5; and Raber, "Franchise Case Review Highlights Legal Confab," *Beverage Industry* 70 (January 30, 1981): 26.

25. For example, in 1978 George Haas, by then a leading deal maker in the industry, advised midwestern bottlers: "Every bottler should take a careful look at his business and determine the direction he wants to take it. Do you want to grow by acquisition? Or do you want to sell out as close to the peak as is possible?" See, George Haas, "The FTC and Acquisition Trends," *Beverage World* 97 (June 1978): 48.

26. "Thirst to Acquire the Soft Drink Bottlers," p. 40.

27. "Hard Trading in Soft Drinks," p. 36.

28. The quotations are paraphrases of Smith's remarks in Minutes of Corporate Division Review Committee Meeting, September 8–9, 1976, and March 9–10, 1977, in HGI corporate records. See also, "Dr Pepper: Pitted Against the Soft-Drink Giants," *Business Week* (October 6, 1975), p. 70.

29. See "GCC Beverage Division Overview," in Corporate Division Review Committee Minutes, December 2–3, 1976; Corporate Division Review Meeting Minutes, March 9–10, 1977; and John P. Koss, vice president of operations, General Cinema Beverages, Inc., interview with Bettye H. Pruitt, February 21, 1989 (hereafter cited as Koss Interview).

30. Sobell, 1974 Marketing Plan. The estimate for 1975 volume, based on market share, was calculated from figures in *Beverage World* 97 (April 1978): 18. See also Lane Stewart, "Sunkist's Rapid Ripening," *Beverage World* 98 (May 1979): 28–31, in which orange sodas were estimated to be a billion-dollar industry, with 7.5 percent of the total market. The largest sellers, Orange Crush and Coke's Fanta Orange, together were only 2 percent of the total soft drink market, and neither had national distribution.

31. Koss Interview.

32. "Sunkist's Rapid Ripening," p. 29.

33. "Hard Trading in Soft Drinks," p. 36; and H. Paige to GCC Directors, August 8, 1973, in HGI corporate records.

34. Koss Interview.

35. See "Crown Cork and SEC Settle Payments Suit," *The Wall Street Journal* (September 3, 1981). Also, Samuel Frankenheim to File, October 29, 1979; and Herbert Paige, memo to plants, January 1972, in HGI corporate records.

36. "General Policy—Purchasing," *Manual of Instructions* (January 1, 1973), p. A6; Herbert Paige to William Zellen, November 9, 1972, in HGI corporate records.

37. William D. Zellen, interview with Bettye H. Pruitt, March 29, 1988 (hereafter cited as Zellen Interview); and J. Atwood Ives, interview with Bettye H. Pruitt and George D. Smith, October 14, 1988 (hereafter cited as Ives Interview, I).

38. "Crown Cork and SEC Settle Payments Suit."

39. This account of the Paige affair is based on J. Atwood Ives interview with Bettye H. Pruitt and George D. Smith, November 23, 1988; Richard A. Smith, interview with Bettye H. Pruitt and George D. Smith, March 16, 1989 (hereafter cited as Smith Interview, II); Zellen Interview; and published accounts of the case.

40. D. Wheeler to B. Zitofsky, July 24, 1979, in HGI corporate records; "Former General Cinema Official Settles with SEC," *Boston Globe* (June 15, 1982); and "The Soda-Pop Sultan Takes a Fall," *Miami Herald* (October 7, 1984).

41. Koss Interview; Robert J. Tarr, Jr., interview with Bettye H. Pruitt and George D. Smith, April 26, 1988.

42. See "Soft Drinks: Are the Bubbles About to Burst?" *Financial World* 148 (June 1, 1979): 56.

43. Smith Interview, II.

44. Quoted in Ives Interview, I.

Chapter 5

1. The works of Alfred Chandler are the authoritative sources for long-term perspective on this phenomenon in American business. See, in particular, Alfred D. Chandler, Jr., *The Visible Hand: The Managerial Revolution in American Business* (Cambridge, Mass.: Harvard University Press, 1977). There is also an illuminating literature on the subject, aimed at helping contemporary entrepreneurs guide their companies through the transitions required by each stage of corporate evolution, including the following: Eric G. Flamholtz, *Growing Pains: How to Make the Transition from an Entrepreneurship to a Professionally Managed Firm* (San Francisco: Jossey-Bass, 1990); John L. Ward, *Keeping the Family Business Healthy: How to Plan for Continuing Growth, Profitability, and Family Leadership* (San Francisco: Jossey-Bass, 1987); W. Gibb Dyer, Jr., *Cultural Change in Family Firms: Anticipating and Managing Business and Family Transitions* (San Francisco: Jossey-Bass, 1986); and Neil C. Churchill and Virginia L. Lewis, "The Five Stages of Small Business Growth," *Harvard Business Review* 61 (May–June 1983), pp. 30–50. According to Flamholtz's research, the transition to professional top management usually occurs, and should occur, at some point between $10 million and $100 million in revenues (*Growing Pains*, pp. 40–41, 48). Advises Ward: "These forces [driving the movement through stages of corporate evolution] are unavoidable. No business owner, no matter how successful, is beyond their influence" (*Keeping the Family Business Healthy*, p. 22).

2. In 1973 Smith spoke to analysts of what he took to be the defining characteristics of "a true blue-chip growth company": "(a) managment in depth, (b) innovative marketing, (c) aggressive financial management, (d) willingness to drop losing operations or products and adapt to change, (e) consistency and legitimacy in reporting and accounting, (f) pricing flexibility, (g) ability to thrive in a competitive environment, (h) ability to increase earnings in up years and down years for the economy as a whole, (i) internal growth, regardless of the acquisition market, (j) limited exposure to government regulation." *General Cinema Corporation Security Analysts Meeting* (May 2, 1973), n.p., in the records of Harcourt General, Inc. (hereafter cited as HGI corporate records).

3. On the importance of the "revolution in management science" in the 1960s, especially in companies pursuing a strategy of growth through diversification, see Neil H. Jacoby, "The Conglomerate Corporation," *The Center Magazine* (July 1969), reprinted in Alfred D. Chandler, Jr., and Richard S. Tedlow, *The Coming of*

Managerial Capitalism: A Casebook on the History of American Economic Institutions (Homewood, Ill.: Richard D. Irwin, 1985), pp. 745–750. In 1991, 25 percent of the CEOs of the *Business Week* 1000 corporations had backgrounds in finance or accounting, 7 percent in law ("The Corporate Elite," *Business Week* [November 25, 1991], p. 180).

4. This interpretation relies on, but bends somewhat, Alfred Chandler's terminology of entrepreneurial and managerial enterprises. To Chandler, these two firm types were distinguished fundamentally by the unity or separation of ownership and control but also by the lack of professionalized management skills and techniques in the entrepreneurial enterprise. (See, for example, *Scale and Scope,* p. 238.) Certainly there are many examples of owner-managed firms today that undermine Chandler's assumptions. On the other hand, as indicated by the growing body of literature advising entrepreneurs on when and how to make the transition to professional management, there are many potential pitfalls in the process, and selling the company or stepping (or being forced) into a titular role are not uncommon alternatives to retaining managerial control. (See Flamholtz, *Growing Pains,* chapter 14.)

5. Technically speaking, General Cinema's structure was "functional with subsidiaries," a not uncommon transitional form for companies diversifying by acquisition. The characteristics that define such a structure, as described by Richard Rumelt, include "the lack of a true multidivisional type of headquarters office," the fact that division managers are "organizationally on a par with functional managers in the major area," and that "the central office must be active in day to day management of the major area and cannot gain a detached view of the firm as a whole." See, Richard P. Rumelt, *Strategy, Structure, and Economic Performance,* reissue (Boston: Harvard Business School Press, 1986), p. 38.

6. Richard A. Smith, interview with Bettye H. Pruitt, July 22 and 28, 1993 (hereafter cited as Smith Interview, V).

7. For the job description and qualifications, see Richard A. Smith, memo, June 13, 1974, in HGI corporate records.

8. J. Atwood Ives, interview with Bettye H. Pruitt and George D. Smith, October 14, 1988 (hereafter cited as Ives Interview, I).

9. Transcript of General Cinema Corporation Stockholders' Meeting of July 30, 1970, in HGI corporate records.

10. Minutes of Board of Directors' Meeting, November 15, 1974; and General Cinema proxy statements, March 6, 1973 and March 14, 1974, in HGI corporate records.

11. Ives Interview, I.

12. Ibid. The literature on stages of corporate evolution makes clear that the clash of cultures experienced by Ives reflected characteristic differences between proprietary and professional approaches to management issues. See Dyer, *Cultural Change in Family Firms,* pp. 32–34 and chapter 6; and Flamholtz, *Growing Pains,* pp. 43–46 and chapter 12.

13. The characterization of the company developed in the preceding paragraphs draws on interviews with Ives, Herbert Hurwitz, Edward Lane, William Zellen, and James McKenney (see A Note on Sources).

14. The list of Ives's responsibilities is from Smith, memo, June 13, 1974.

15. Chandler, *Strategy and Structure,* pp. 309–312. On the role of the financial staff, see pp. 287–288, 291: "The development of increasingly accurate and precise information for the use of the senior executives in planning, coordinating,

and appraising the activities of an enterprise as a whole was a major achievement of the American organization builders."

16. On the movement toward emphasis on strategic thinking and the broad impact of Chandler's work, see Thomas K. McCraw, "The Intellectual Odyssey of Alfred D. Chandler, Jr.," in McCraw, ed., *The Essential Alfred Chandler: Essays Toward a Historical Theory of Big Business* (Boston: Harvard Business School Press, 1988), pp. 13–14; and Frank F. Gilmore, "The Changing Nature of Policy Formulation," in *Business Policy: Teaching and Research,* ed. Bernard Taylor and Keith MacMillan (New York: John Wiley, 1973), pp. 33–35, 43–45. Peter Drucker's *The Practice of Management,* published in 1954 (New York: Harper & Row), emphasized the importance of strategic thinking, and at Harvard Business School in the same period, the professors in charge of the important Business Policy course began to reorient their teaching case material away from operational issues, relevant to the work of functional specialists, and toward more general questions faced by the top managers responsible for the enterprise as a whole.

17. See Norman Berg, "Corporate Role in Diversified Companies: A Working Paper," in Taylor and MacMillan, eds., *Business Policy: Teaching and Research,* pp. 307, 325, 345–346. In the decade after 1962, no fewer than eleven Harvard Business School doctoral dissertations were devoted to the study of diversified firms, and a body of related case material was developed for an MBA seminar, "Management Problems of Highly Diversified Corporations." See also, Bruce R. Scott's preface to the first edition of Richard P. Rumelt, *Strategy, Structure, and Economic Performance* (Boston: Harvard Business School, Division of Research, 1974), pp. v–vii. On the public statements of corporate executives, see also Dan Carroll, "What Future for Conglomerates?" *Harvard Business Review* 47 (May–June 1969), pp. 4–12 and 167–168.

18. Berg, "Corporate Role in Diversified Companies," pp. 309, 320–321, 325. Berg labeled the more traditional multidivisional form "diversified major." See also Jacoby, "The Conglomerate Corporation," p. 750.

19. Chandler, *The Visible Hand,* pp. 481–482.

20. Quoted in Norman Berg, "Strategic Planning in Conglomerate Companies," *Harvard Business Review* 45 (May–June 1965), pp. 85, 87. Berg deals extensively with this issue in a later work, *General Management: An Analytical Approach* (Homewood Ill.: Richard D. Irwin, 1984), chapter 14.

21. Smith is quoted in Hugo Uyterhoeven, "General Cinema Corporation," Harvard Business School Case #9-377-084, Boston, 1976, p. 21.

22. "General Cinema Corporation Organization Structure," June 17, 1976, HGI corporate records.

23. Minutes of Corporate Strategic Planning Committee for October 5, 1977, in HGI corporate records.

24. That interactive evolution of strategy and structure closely fits Berg's conceptualization of how the corporate role tends to be defined in diversified firms: "Even more so than in the single-business company, corporate strategy and the approach to the implementation of that strategy via organization structure and management processes are highly interdependent and are influenced by the role that the corporate office chooses to define for itself. The role chosen both stems from and helps to define the overall strategy or business mission of the corporation." Berg, *General Management,* p. 180.

25. Minutes of Corporate Strategic Planning Committee meeting, April 11, 1978, in HGI corporate records.

26. Ibid.

27. Minutes of Corporate Strategic Planning Committee for February 9, 1977 and October 13, 1977, in HGI corporate records.

28. Alexander M. Tanger, interview with Bettye H. Pruitt, April 18, 1989 (hereafter cited as Tanger Interview).

29. Minutes for Corporate Strategic Planning Committee meeting, October 13, 1977 and May 24, 1978, and H. Paige to J. A. Ives, November 14, 1977, in HGI corporate records.

30. Minutes of Corporate Strategic Planning Committee of April 11, 1978 and May 24, 1978, in HGI corporate records.

31. Beverage Management Board, minutes for August 29, 1978; CDR minutes for November 8, 1977; and quotation from Robert J. Tarr, Jr., interview with Bettye H. Pruitt and George D. Smith, April 26, 1989 (hereafter cited as Tarr Interview).

32. Quotation from Tarr Interview.

33. Gary R. Edgerton, *American Film Exhibition and an Analysis of the Motion Picture Industry's Market Structure, 1963–1980* (New York: Garland, 1983), p. 70; and Suzanne M. Donahue, *American Film Distribution: The Changing Marketplace* (Ann Arbor: University of Michigan Press, 1987), p. 130.

34. "General Cinema Attacks Distributors' Sales Methods," *Variety* (October 1, 1975), p. 3; Donahue, *American Film Distribution*, p. 32; and Edgerton, *American Film Exhibition*, p. 47.

35. Donahue, *American Film Distribution*, pp. 121–122; Edgerton, *American Film Exhibition*, pp. 78–80.

36. "General Cinema Attacks Distributors Sales Methods," p. 80. *Variety* pointed out that General Cinema was one of the theater chains accused by some distributors of being slow on payment of rentals. Interviewed by the reporter, Melvin Wintman vigorously denied that charge.

37. Donahue, *American Film Distribution*, pp. 125–126; General Cinema, Corporate Strategic Planning Committee, minutes for October 13, 1977; and GCC Theatres, Inc., minutes of 1977 Annual Meeting for Division Managers, Film Buyers, and Home Office Staff, October 17–21, 1977, in HGI corporate records (hereafter cited as 1977 Annual Meeting minutes).

38. Smith Interview, V; "GCC Trust Suit vs. Buena Vista to Test Per Capita Payoff Clause," *Variety* (August 30, 1978), p. 3; and Melvin R. Wintman, interview with Bettye H. Pruitt and George D. Smith, March 10, 1988 (hereafter cited as Wintman Interview).

39. The other two cases on splitting were in Virginia and Wisconsin. The government lost the first but won the second, shortly after the decision against General Cinema. For the decision on film product splitting, see General Cinema Corporation vs. Buena Vista Distribution Co., 532 Federal Supplement 1244 (1982). See also "BV Counters GCC Ire over Per Capita Clause with Product Split Suit," *Independent Film Journal* (December 1978), p. 7; and Samuel Frankenheim, interview with Bettye H. Pruitt and George D. Smith, March 17, 1989 (hereafter cited as Frankenheim Interview).

40. "Worst enemy" quotation from 1977 Annual Meeting minutes; "carnival effect," from Morris K. Englander interview with George D. Smith, April 27, 1989 (hereafter cited as Englander Interview). In 1978, American Multi-Cinema, GCC Theatres, and Loew's Theaters were the leaders by far in multiplexing among large chains. They were 98 percent, 82 percent, and 81 percent "multiplexed," respectively. However, 91 percent of General Cinema's multiple-screen theaters were twins and triples, whereas Durwood of American Multi-Cinema had built almost nothing smaller than a four-screen theater since 1969. For Durwood's strategy, see "Quads, Sixplexes, and Up," *Newsweek* (September 8, 1969), p. 71; and Jay M. Shapiro, interview with George D. Smith, March 17, 1989 (hereafter cited as Shapiro Interview).

41. Based on General Cinema Annual Reports, 1968–1979. William Zellen commented on shrinking profit margins in 1977 Annual Meeting minutes.

42. Howard W. Spiess, interview with George D. Smith, December 29, 1988 (hereafter cited as Spiess Interview); and Stanley Werthman, interview with George D. Smith, April 27, 1989 (hereafter cited as Werthman Interview).

43. D. Barry Reardon, interview with Bettye H. Pruitt, December 20, 1988 (hereafter cited as Reardon Interview). Sam Seletsky died in 1970. His position as head film buyer was filled by three different individuals over the next four years, and then by Barry Reardon, who was hired from Paramount and stayed with General Cinema from 1975 until 1979. Though he came from the outside, Reardon quickly became enmeshed in conflicts that Seletsky would have found completely familiar.

44. William D. Zellen, interview with Bettye H. Pruitt, March 29, 1988 (hereafter cited as Zellen Interview); Reardon Interview; and GCC Theatres, Inc., "Tables of Organization," October 1977, in HGI corporate records.

45. Spiess Interview; Zellen Interview; Reardon Interview; Shapiro Interview; Robert E. Painter, interview with George D. Smith, March 24, 1989 (hereafter cited as Painter Interview); and A. Anthony Trauber, interview with George D. Smith, November 16, 1989 (hereafter cited as Trauber Interview).

46. Cost-cutting measures are outlined in 1977 Annual Meeting minutes; morale problems reviewed in D. R. Knapp, Minutes of Theatre Division Staff Meeting of July 6, 1977, in HGI corporate records.

47. General Cinema Annual Reports for 1979–1984; GCC Theatres, Inc., Operations Department, activity reports for March 7, 1978 and August 9, 1978; and "Chain of 650 Bans Smoking," *Variety* (December 15, 1976), p. 5. Such measures to expand concession sales were common in the industry. Edgerton cites a 1978 study indicating that 60 percent of the profits in movie exhibition were made on concessions, while only 1.5 percent came from admissions (Edgerton, *American Film Exhibition*, p. 85).

48. Remarks by Richard A. Smith, General Cinema Corporation Presentation to the New York Society of Security Analysts, September 18, 1975, p. 7, in HGI corporate records.

49. "Entrepreneurs: Top Grade," *Time* (October 4, 1971), p. 80.

50. Quoted in Leslie Halliwell, *Halliwell's Filmgoer's Companion* (New York: Charles Scribner, 1988), p. 301; and "Entrepreneurs: Top Grade," p. 80.

51. "General Cinema Talks with New York Security Analysts," September 15, 1976, n.p., in HGI corporate records.

52. Other major chains involved in film production were United Artists Theatres, National General Theatres, and Plitt Theatres. Movies they brought to the screen included *Sunburn, Aloha, Bobby and Rose, Lifeguard, Bucktown,* and *Viva Knieval.* See Edgerton, *American Film Exhibition*, pp. 72–74.

53. Problems in the relationship with Grade are detailed in CSP Committee minutes for March 30, 1977. Grade said of the movies made jointly with GCC Films: "None of them was really a hit. But I'm not a philanthropist. I will make considerable money from those five films." See "Lew Grade to Hollywood Press: 'Still Fond of Those Bostonians,'" *Variety* (October 19, 1977), p. 3.

54. Smith is quoted in "On 730 Theatres, 75 New, GCC's Smith Mr. Sanguine as to Exhibition Future," *Variety* (October 12, 1977), p. 6; and in CSP Committee meeting minutes for April 11, 1978, in HGI corporate records.

55. "GCC's Smith Mr. Sanguine."

56. Richard A. Smith, interview with Bettye H. Pruitt and George D. Smith, January 12, 1990. For a detailed account of the Begelman affair, see the bestseller by David McClintick, *Indecent Exposure: A True Story of Hollywood and Wall Street* (New York: Dell, 1982), which describes Smith's negotiations with Columbia and his attitude toward the Begelman affair.

57. "General Cinema Explores Lifting Stake in Concern," *The Wall Street Journal* (January 3, 1979), p. 3; Frank Segers, "End General Cinema's Columbia 'Buy-In,'" *Variety* (January 10, 1979), p. 7; and J. Atwood Ives, interview with Bettye H. Pruitt and George D. Smith, November 23, 1988.

58. Segers, "End General Cinema's Columbia 'Buy-In.'"

59. On potential conflicts between Columbia and General Cinema, see Segers, "End General Cinema's Columbia 'Buy-In.'" Wall Street analysts were mystified by General Cinema's move; see "General Cinema Explores Lifting Stake in Concern," *The Wall Street Journal* (January 3, 1979), p. 3.

60. Tom Patterson, president of National Independent Theatre Exhibitors, quoted in Edgerton, *American Film Exhibition*, p. 74.

61. Smith is quoted in *Variety* (November 5, 1980), p. 36; Herbert J. Hurwitz, interview with George D. Smith, August 4, 1988 (hereafter cited as Hurwitz Interview).

62. Hurwitz Interview. Edward E. Lane, interview with Bettye H. Pruitt and George D. Smith, June 7, 1988.

63. Tanger Interview. General Cinema's 1975 Annual Report in fact announced its determination to withdraw "eventually" from the field, causing trouble with the Federal Communications Commission, which frowned on the purchase of broadcasting franchises for investment purposes. This was a problem in particular because litigation over the proposed format change at Chicago's WEFM was still pending. (It would be settled in General Cinema's favor in 1977, after five years of controversy.) In response, the company reaffirmed its commitment to operating its remaining broadcast properties "profitably in the public interest and in accordance with sound business policy," and it did so until 1986. "General Cinema Talks with New York Security Analysts"; and General Cinema Annual Report for 1975 and 1976.

64. Tanger Interview.

65. Smith Interview, V. For Smith the road not taken would be clearly marked by his longtime competitor, Sumner Redstone, who in 1987 parlayed his ownership of National Amusements, Inc. (owner of Showcase Cinemas) into Viacom International, one of the most successful cable companies of the 1980s and on its way to becoming a "world-class entertainment company" such as Smith described in 1993.

66. Criticism was voiced in both academic and popular business literature. See, for example, Robert H. Hayes and William J. Abernathy, "Managing Our Way to Economic Decline," *Harvard Business Review* 58 (July–August 1980), pp. 70–71 and Exhibit VI, p. 75; "The Penalties of Short-term Corporate Strategies," *Business Week* (June 30, 1980), pp. 70–72; and Steve Lohr, writing in the *New*

York Times Magazine (January 4, 1981), pp. 14ff. The literature on entrepreneurship and stages of corporate evolution also conveys this criticism in warnings to owner-managers of the trade-offs that come with professionalization. See, for example, Dyer, *Cultural Change in Family Firms,* pp. 99–100.

67. Notes from 1989 presentation by The Boston Consulting Group, n.d., in HGI corporate records; and Richard A. Smith, interview with Bettye Pruitt and George D. Smith, January 12, 1990.

68. Berg, "Strategic Planning in Conglomerate Companies," speaks to these issues at length. In a later work, Berg comments most perceptively on the human dimension of the tensions arising from allocation of resources in diversified firms: "It is all well and good to decide as the result of portfolio analysis that a given division is a dog, but how would you like to be the division manager of an operation so categorized?" Berg also warns that such a categorization can become, given the investment decisions that flow from it, something of a "self-fulfilling prophecy." Though neither theaters nor bottling were classified as "dogs" at General Cinema, the fundamental truths that Berg points out are pertinent. (*General Management,* p. 178.) One of the great values in viewing an issue like diversification strategy through the window of one company's history is the light it sheds on such concerns, which rarely appear in large-scale analyses or theoretical discussions.

Chapter 6

1. See Kenneth M. Davidson, *MegaMergers: Corporate America's Billion-Dollar Takeovers* (Cambridge, Mass.: Ballinger, 1985), chapter 11, "Acquisition Fever"; Malcolm S. Salter and Wolf Weinhold, *Diversification through Acquisition: Strategies for Creating Economic Value* (New York: The Free Press, 1979), pp. 16–17; and Alfred Rappaport, *Creating Shareholder Value: The New Standard for Business Performance* (New York: The Free Press, 1986), pp. 198–200. Useful overviews in the popular business press include "Deal Mania," *Business Week* (November 24, 1986), pp. 74–96; and Judith H. Dobrzynski, "A New Strain of Merger Mania," *Business Week* (March 21, 1988), pp. 122–126.

2. See, for example, "Dick Smith's Midas Touch at General Cinema," *Business Week* (October 22, 1984), p. 71; and John Paul Newport, Jr., "The New Show at Neiman-Marcus," *Fortune* 116 (April 27, 1987): 103.

3. Quoted in Newport, "The New Show at Neiman Marcus," pp. 104, 106; "Dick Smith's Midas Touch at General Cinema," p. 70. (Speech notes provided by Richard Smith.)

4. Smith's welcoming remark to the 1988 stockholders' meeting is quoted in William M. Bulkeley, "General Cinema's Core Businesses Run into Trouble," *The Wall Street Journal* (April 28, 1988), p. 6.

5. J. Atwood Ives, interview with Bettye H. Pruitt and George D. Smith, November 23, 1988 (hereafter cited as Ives Interview, II). This discussion of acquisition strategy and the origins of the investment-with-involvement idea also draws on discussions with Hugo Uyterhoeven, who was involved at the time as a member of General Cinema's board.

6. Salter and Weinhold analyzed Heublein's acquisitions in *Diversification through Acquisition,* p. 138.

7. Robert J. Cole, "9.7% Share of Heublein Acquired," *New York Times* (February 4, 1982), p. D16; and Richard A. Smith, interview with Bettye H. Pruitt and George D. Smith, January 12, 1990 (hereafter cited as Smith Interview, III).

8. Quoted in Sonny Kleinfield, *Staying at the Top: The Life of a CEO* (New York: New American Library, 1986), p. 69.

9. Smith Interview, III; discussion with Hugo Uyterhoeven.

10. General Cinema had earlier stated an intention to acquire as much as 25 percent of Heublein's stock. See *The Wall Street Journal* (April 27, 1982), p. F42, and (June 2, 1982), p. F20; *Boston Globe* (May 29, 1982), p. 17; and "General Cinema's Value," *Business Week* (May 10, 1982).

11. Smith Interview, III; Ives Interview, II. For comments on General Cinema's intentions, see Gene G. Marcial, "General Cinema's Value," *The Wall Street Journal* (May 10, 1982); and *The Wall Street Journal* (April 16, 1982), p. E8. The Heublein lawsuit was dismissed by the district court on a motion for summary judgment filed by General Cinema, a decision that was upheld on appeal: General Cinema Annual Report for 1983, p. 36.

12. As Salter and Weinhold pointed out (*Diversification through Acquisition,* p. 175), adaptation to General Cinema's management style would involve acceptance of "intensive planning and financial controls." Few of the men running major U.S. corporations in the 1980s could have been expected to submit willingly to that kind of discipline from another CEO.

13. See General Cinema Corporation Presentation to New York Security Analysts, November 4, 1982, in Harcourt General, Inc., corporate records (hereafter cited as HGI corporate records), pp. 15–16; and General Cinema Annual Report for 1983, p. 40.

14. For a comment on the downside of this transaction, see Nick Gilbert, "Dick Smith's Parking Lot," *Financial World* 156 (March 24, 1987): 120; and "General Cinema's Sweeter Deal," ibid. (July 28, 1987): 14.

15. General Cinema Corporation, Presentation by Richard A. Smith, President and Chairman, to the New York Society of Security Analysts, October 24, 1983, in HGI corporate records, pp. 6–7.

16. Hugo Uyterhoeven, "General Cinema Corporation," Harvard Business School Case #9-377-084, Boston, 1976, p. 20. On the importance of the new structure, Smith stated in 1983, "We . . . have the financial strength and flexibility to continue our search for major new business opportunities, and perhaps most important of all, we have a management structure to direct both the existing operating divisions and the strategic planning and execution of acquisitions needed for General Cinema's future growth," General Cinema Corporation, Presentation . . . to the New York Society of Security Analysts (1983), p. 7.

17. Smith Interview, III. See also the announcement of the OOC's creation in General Cinema Annual Report for 1983, p. 7.

18. Samuel Frankenheim, interview with Bettye H. Pruitt and George D. Smith, March 17, 1989 (hereafter cited as Frankenheim Interview).

19. Frankenheim Interview. On Skadden, Arps, see Davidson, *MegaMergers,* pp. 20–21.

20. Robert J. Tarr, Jr., interview with Bettye H. Pruitt and George D. Smith, April 26, 1989 (hereafter cited as Tarr Interview, I).

21. A. A. Trauber to J. P. Koss, November 19, 1981, HGI corporate records. See also Lily Chu, "General Cinema: Post Completion Reviews," Harvard Business School Case #9-186-184 (Boston, 1986).

22. J. Atwood Ives, interview with Bettye H. Pruitt and George D. Smith, October 14, 1988 (hereafter cited as Ives Interview, I); and quotation of Ives in John Jay, "Chewing into Cadbury," *The Sunday Times* (London) (June 5, 1988), section D.

23. These stories based on Ives Interview, II and Lane Interview and Hurwitz Interview (see A Note on Sources).

24. Smith Interview, III; Ives Interview, II. It should be noted that some General Cinema executives were critical of Smith for not being optimistic enough. Newport ("The New Show at Neiman Marcus," p. 106) cites the opinions of "former employees" that "Smith's lack of entrepreneurial daring contributed to the failures" of General Cinema's ventures into bowling, furniture retailing, and film financing and prompted the company to dismantle its communications division.

25. Smith Interview, III.

26. Ives Interview, II; Tarr Interview, I.

27. Tarr Interview, I.

28. Ibid. Details of the deal as it was announced can be found in Wendy Fox, "General Cinema Gets Carter Hawley Shares," *Boston Globe* (April 17, 1984), p. 59; and William M. Bulkeley, "Savvy 'Knight' Hopes to Profit Aiding Carter," *New York Times* (April 18, 1984), p. 33.

29. Ives Interview, II.

30. Comparative financial data were provided by Fox, "General Cinema Gets Carter Hawley Shares." On Hawley's record at Bergdorf Goodman, see Teri Agins, "A Tale of Two Retailers: Bergdorf Rose, Bonwit Fell," *New York Times* (June 26, 1989), p. B1. For Hawley's image in the business press, see, for example, "Fashioning a Comeback? Carter Hawley Hale Seems Poised for a Recovery," *Barron's* 63 (March 14, 1983): 24, 28–30; and Roger Neal, "Phil Hawley's Last Chance," *Forbes* (January 28, 1985), pp. 44–45. *Barron's* quoted one of the few Wall Street analysts with a positive view of the company's prospects in 1983 as saying, "CHH is attractive to the extent that nobody is expecting anything out of it."

31. Neal, "Phil Hawley's Last Chance," p. 45. It should be noted that Hawley always made a convincing case that he was doing the right things to improve CHH's performance. In addition to the sources cited in note 30, see, for example, Bill Saporito, "Makeover for a Plain-Jane Retailer," *Fortune* 117 (April 11, 1988): 68–71; and Claudia H. Deutsch, "Neiman Marcus Minds the Store," *New York Times* (September 4, 1988). The most detailed attack on Hawley can be found in Benjamin J. Stein, "A Saga of Shareholder Neglect," *Barron's* 67 (May 4, 1987): 8–9, 70–75, which might be contrasted to Stein's very positive article on General Cinema in *Barron's* the following year ("Family Values, Wall Street Style"). Stein served briefly as a consultant to a law firm representing plaintiffs in a class-action suit against CHH (see Martha Groves, "Flap Over Article," *Los Angeles Times* [May 10, 1987], p. IV-7). Other strongly negative articles on the CHH–General Cinema deal include Robert Metz, "Shareholders Lose in Carter Hawley Scramble," *Boston Globe* (July 24, 1984); "Carter Hawley's White Knight May Be an Invading Army," *Business Week* (April 30, 1984), p. 46; and Gene G. Marcial, "Carter Hawley: How Shareholders Missed the Boat," ibid. (December 3, 1984), p. 151.

32. As *Business Week* quoted one stockbroker: "The dividend is greater than the interest cost. GCC is making 3% on someone else's money." ("Dick Smith's Midas Touch," p. 74.)

33. Details on the deal in the preceding two paragraphs are from Ives Interview,

II; Fox, "General Cinema Gets Carter Hawley Shares;" "Dick Smith's Midas Touch;" and Jolie Solomon and Roy J. Harris, Jr., "Offer for Carter Hawley Is Changed to Require Only Majority Acceptance," *The Wall Street Journal* (December 2, 1986), p. 5.

34. The strategy for analyzing Walden Book is outlined in a "Walden Book" file in HGI corporate records. See also: "K mart Gets Waldenbooks," *Boston Globe* (July 24, 1984); and "Carter Hawley Kills Takeover," ibid. (July 27, 1984), p. 47.

35. Quotation from Ives Interview, II.

36. "Dick Smith's Midas Touch," p. 74. In that article, *Business Week* cited as evidence that General Cinema had looked at and turned down "such tender morsels as Entenmann's, Wm. Underwood, and Wometco Enterprises." See also, "General Cinema a Frustrated Shopper," and Bruce A. Mohl, "An Acquisitive General Cinema," *Boston Globe* (March 15, 1980). It should also be noted that Smith granted only rare interviews and gained a reputation as "shy" and even "reclusive." See, for example, Wendy Fox, "Varied Cast in Carter Hawley Struggle," *Boston Globe* (May 6, 1984), p. 94; Rita Kozelka, "Good Show: General Cinema's Deft Touch Is Just the Ticket," *Barron's* 69 (April 17, 1989): 18; and Jay, "Chewing into Cadbury."

37. Quoted in Gilbert, "Dick Smith's Parking Lot," p. 120. Practically every article written about General Cinema offers a version of this opinion. The cost-conscious approach also received high marks among academic observers and consultants. Alfred Rappaport, the guru of shareholder value, wrote in 1986: "Only a limited supply of acquisition candidates is available at the price that enables the acquirer to earn an acceptable economic return on investment. A well-conceived evaluation program that minimizes the risk of buying an economically unattractive company or paying too much for an attractive one is particularly important in today's seller's market." Rappaport, *Creating Shareholder Value: The New Standard for Business Performance* (New York: The Free Press, 1986), p. 200. While the main focus of academic research in the 1980s focused on the comparative value of related versus unrelated acquisitions (following Richard P. Rumelt's seminal study, *Strategy, Structure, and Economic Performance,* reissue [Boston: Harvard Business School Press, 1986]), empirical data pointed to the conclusion that in any type of acquisition competitive bidding would cause all the potential increase in value to go to the stockholders of the target company (Harbir Singh and Cynthia A. Montgomery, "Corporate Acquisition Strategies and Economic Performance," *Strategic Management Journal* 8 [July–August 1987]: 385). Similarly, a report by McKinsey & Co. on mergers concluded between 1972 and 1983 indicated that most were failures, especially "large unrelated acquisitions." A major cause for failure, McKinsey concluded, was that the premiums paid in such deals averaged 58 percent, as opposed to 26 percent for related acquisitions of comparable size: "These success rates are consistent with the theory that it is extraordinarily difficult to compensate for very high acquisition premiums" (quoted in "Diversification Blues," *Mergers and Acquisitions* 21 [May–June 1987]: 13–14).

38. Ives Interview, II; and General Cinema meetings with New York Security Analysts for years 1975–1978, in GCC corporate records. On changing trends in financial analysis, see Joel M. Stern, *Analytical Methods in Financial Planning,* 3d edition (New York: Chase Manhattan Bank, 1977), pp. 5, 7–8; Rappaport, *Creating Shareholder Value,* pp. 2–6; and "Shareholder Value: The Alchemy of the 80s," a special edition of *Planning Review* 16 (January–February 1988): 4–9. On the value creation potential of General Cinema's cash flow characteristic and use of leverage, see Salter and Weinhold, *Diversification through Acquisition*, pp. 172–174.

39. See General Cinema Annual Report for 1986, p. 39; and for commentary on the deal, Charles Stein, "General Cinema Will Sell Sunkist," *Boston Globe* (October 10, 1984), p. 73; and "Dick Smith's Midas Touch," p. 74. This discussion also draws on a conversation with General Cinema director Hugo Uyterhoeven.

40. Quotation from Deutsch, "Neiman Marcus Minds the Store." General Cinema Annual Reports for 1983–1986. For comments by Tanger and criticism by unnamed "former employees," see Bruce A. Mohl, "General Cinema Sells Station WHUE," *Boston Globe* (June 1, 1984), p. 34; and Newport, "The New Show at Neiman Marcus," p. 106.

41. On the attractiveness of free cash flow to corporate raiders, see Leslie Pittel, "Cherchez la Cash," *Forbes* 135 (June 3, 1985): 234–236.

42. The takeover-prevention intent of these changes was dutifully clarified in General Cinema's Proxy Statement, January 30, 1978, in HGI corporate records.

43. A suit filed by one General Cinema stockholder resulted in a settlement in which the by-laws were amended to ensure that a majority of the board and its key committees would be independent directors, that the stockholders could nominate candidates for the board, and that the special voting rights of Class B stock would be triggered by an outside party gaining 20, rather than just 15, percent of General Cinema stock. See General Cinema Corporation Proxy Statement, February 6, 1985, pp. 16–18. See also, General Cinema Annual Report for 1984, p. 43.

44. Hugo Uyterhoeven, interview with Bettye H. Pruitt and George D. Smith, October 6, 1988; Nelson J. Darling, interview with Bettye H. Pruitt, April 25, 1989.

45. Quoted in Ives Interview, III. The only two institutional investors that did not endorse the measure were British groups irrevocably opposed to any alteration of the one-share–one-vote principle. On the issues of super stock and the relationship between takeovers and corporate performance, related specifically to General Cinema, see Stein, "Family Values, Wall Street Style." See also, Harold M. Williams, "It's Time for a Takeover Moratorium," *Fortune* 112 (July 22, 1985): 133–134; and Steven Pearlstein, "The Corpocracy's Last Gasp," and Robert A. Mamis, "Sour Grapes," *INC.* 9 (October, 1987): 31–33.

46. Smith Interview, III.

47. Ibid. See also his comments in Jay, "Chewing into Cadbury."

48. By spring 1988, General Cinema's Cadbury holdings had appreciated 74 percent; see William L. Bulkeley, "General Cinema's Core Businesses Run into Trouble," *The Wall Street Journal* (April 28, 1988), p. 6.

49. See General Cinema Corporation Presentation to New York Security Analysts, October 28, 1987, in GCC corporate records; and for subsequent price fluctuations of General Cinema stock, Bulkeley, "General Cinema's Core Businesses Run into Trouble;" Stein, "Family Values, Wall Street Style," p. 8; and Kevin G. Salwen, "General Cinema, Its Own Outlook Strong, Offers a Bargain Bolstered by Built-In Assets," *The Wall Street Journal* (December 30, 1989).

50. See Neal, "Phil Hawley's Last Chance," pp. 44–45. In addition, statements about stock price fluctuations and operating performance for 1985–1986 are based on analyst's reports issued by Morgan, Olmstead, Kennedy & Gardner (which rated CHH stock a "buy"): David V. Jackson, "Carter Hawley Hale, Inc.," October 9, 1985 and May 20, 1986.

51. For their view of the business from public statements and as demonstrated by actions taken once GCC started running it: Claudia L. Deutsch, "Neiman Marcus Minds the Store," *New York Times* (September 4, 1988); and Lawrence Ingrassia and Roy J. Harris, Jr., "General Cinema to Expand into Retailing through Stake in Carter Hawley Spinoff," ibid. (December 10, 1986), p. 10.

52. Unfortunately, he could not do so without taking on a heavy burden of debt that would seriously hinder the restructured company's progress. CHH faced a tough slog through a hostile economic environment in the late 1980s, and by 1991—the year Hawley was due to retire—would end up in bankruptcy. On Hawley's view of the restructuring and his strategy for improving CHH performance, see Deutsch, "Neiman Marcus Minds the Store"; Ingrassia and Harris, "General Cinema to Expand into Retailing"; Bill Saporito, "Makeover for a Plain-Jane Retailer," *Fortune* 117 (April 11, 1988): pp. 68–71; and Jackson, "Carter Hawley Hale, Inc." On the tough climate in retailing, see Leslie Wayne, "Rewriting the Rules of Retailing," *New York Times* (October 15, 1989), pp. C1, 6.

53. See, Roy J. Harris, Jr., and David Stipp, "Carter Hawley Blocks Takeover Attempt with Plan to Spin Off Its Specialty Stores," *The Wall Street Journal* (December 9, 1986), p. 7.

54. See General Cinema Corporation Annual Report for 1987, pp. 16–17.

55. Robert J. Tarr, Jr., interview with Bettye H. Pruitt, May 1, 1992 (hereafter cited as Tarr Interview, II). See also General Cinema Annual Report for 1987 and Neiman Marcus Group annual reports for 1987–1989 for details on the expansion and remodeling of the chain.

56. Also like theaters, the department stores, once built or remodeled, could be maintained at the same level for many years with only minor expenditures, freeing up depreciation to contribute to cash flow.

57. See Saporito, "Makeover for a Plain-Jane Retailer," p. 69; Deutsch, "Neiman Marcus Minds the Store"; Bulkeley, "General Cinema's Core Businesses Run into Trouble"; and Salwen, "General Cinema, Its Own Outlook Strong, Offers a Bargain Bolstered by Built-In Assets."

58. On the Arthur D. Little report, see "Theatre Business in 1985: Smaller, But Not Obsolete," *Variety* (August 10, 1977), pp. 3, 30; and comments by Richard Smith in General Cinema Corporation Presentation to New York Society of Security Analysts, October 10, 1977, in HGI corporate records, pp. 9–10. On the theater building boom and its relation to film production, including comments by General Cinema spokespersons, see "Movie Screens Are Popping Up All Over," *Business Week* (May 14, 1984), pp. 76–77; "Big Bucks for the Big Screens," *Newsweek* (May 28, 1984), p. 63; and Peter Hall, "Life in the Old Movie Theater," *Financial World* 154 (March 20–April 2, 1985): 49.

59. This paragraph and the two following are based on interviews with Paul R. Del Rossi, Morris K. Englander, Robert E. Painter, Jay M. Shapiro, Howard W. Spiess, James C. Tharp, and Stanley Werthman (see A Note on Sources).

60. Howard W. Spiess, interview with George D. Smith, December 29, 1988 (hereafter cited as Spiess Interview).

61. For theater rankings by size, 1987–1990, see *Variety* 338 (January 31, 1990), p. 20. Average number of screens for new theaters in the years 1976–1986 are reported in General Cinema Annual Report for 1986, p. 18. The trend through the 1980s was toward larger multiplexes, with the average close to seven screens per unit in 1986.

62. General Cinema Corporation Annual Report for 1984, p. 11. Smith's views on the subject are quoted in "Movie Screens Are Popping Up All Over," p. 76.

63. General Cinema Corporation Presentation to New York Security Analysts, October 29, 1986, pp. 3–4; and "Super Video: 1986 Objectives," pp. 4–5, in HGI corporate records.

64. "Super Video: 1986 Business Objectives," p. 12; "Super Video Business Discussion," Corporate Division Review Presentation for May–June 1986, in HGI corporate records; General Cinema Corporation Presentation to New York Security Analysts, October 28, 1987, pp. 9–10; and General Cinema Annual Report for 1988, p. 39.

65. Presentation by General Cinema Corporation to the New York Society of Security Analysts, October 24, 1985, in GCC corporate records, p. 6. Attendance figures from "Movie Screens Are Popping Up All Over," p. 76; and Brian Bremner, "Coming Soon to a Theater Near You: Recession," *Business Week* (December 3, 1990), p. 127.

66. Disney created the Disney Channel; Paramount, Warner Brothers, and MCA joined with American Express and Viacom International as joint owners of Showtime and Movie Channel; Columbia joined with CBS and HBO in a joint venture to produce films for HBO, the leading cable movie channel. Reported in "How TV Is Revolutionizing Hollywood," *Business Week* (February 21, 1983), pp. 79–81, 84, 89. On the reintegration of the industry, see Stratford P. Sherman, "Back to the Future," *Fortune* 110 (January 20, 1986): 91–94; and Standard & Poor's *Industry Survey* (March 14, 1991), p. 35.

67. General Cinema, Annual Reports for 1985–1990. For the growth of rival theater chains, see "U.S. & Canada Theater Circuits Ranked by Size," *Variety* (January 31, 1990), p. 20.

68. Morris K. Englander, interview with George D. Smith, April 26, 1989. General Cinema's competitive problems were highlighted by the fact that the most dynamic theater chain in the late 1980s was Carmike Cinemas, a company that shunned big cities for locations in which it would be the only theater. See Chuck Hawkins, "The Movie Mogul Who Thinks Small," *Business Week* (June 2, 1990), p. 37; and Kathryn Harris, "Squeezing the Customers," *Forbes* 141 (July 23, 1990): 40. On the situation of the theater division in 1989, see General Cinema Corporation Presentation to Security Analysts, New York City, November 2, 1989, pp. 6–9, in HGI corporate records.

69. General Cinema Annual Report for 1990; Bremner, "Coming Soon to a Theater Near You: Recession"; and Harris, "Squeezing the Customers."

70. Paul E. Mullins, "The Home Market: Who Leads?" *Beverage Industry* 70 (January 16, 1981): 1. See also, Bob Lederer, "The View from Wall Street," *Beverage World* 99 (January 1981): 38, 42.

71. See Nancy Giges, "Clash of the Cola Titans Keeps Prices Low: Coke," *Advertising Age* (August 25, 1986), p. 25. The figures cited were provided by Coke in court papers filed in support of its effort to acquire Dr Pepper. According to that source, the portion of Pepsi products sold at promotional prices rose from 47 percent in 1980 to 55 percent in 1985. See also, Caroline H. Davenport, "Upside Pop: The Soft-Drink Bottlers Are Flourishing," *Barron's* 62 (January 11, 1983): 9.

72. In 1984 General Cinema's net profit margin was 10.6 percent versus the medians for the five largest bottlers of 6.2 percent and for the industry as a whole of 6 percent. See "Beverages: Yardsticks of Management Performance," *Forbes* 135 (January 14, 1985): 78. Virtually all of the beverage division personnel interviewed expressed frustration with the corporate priorities of the late 1980s.

73. "Beverages: Yardsticks of Management Performance," p. 78.

74. D. R. York to N. R. Wirtz, February 11, 1986; and E. L. Dressler to N. R. Wirtz, July 11, 1983, in GCC corporate records. See also, Davenport, "Upside Pop," p. 24, on MEI and other beverage companies growing through acquisitions, including Beverage Management, which went into bottled water, and Allegheny Beverage, which more than doubled its size in 1981 by acquiring a food service and vending company larger than itself. See also "Beverages: Yardsticks of Management Performance," p. 79.

75. Norman Berg's work on corporate-divisional relationships in diversified firms clearly suggests that such conflicts of interest, and the pain that they can engender, are an unavoidable fact of life in companies of this type. See "Strategic Planning in Conglomerate Companies," *Harvard Business Review* 45 (May–June 1965), pp. 85–87; and *General Management: An Analytical Approach* (Homewood, Ill.: Richard D. Irwin, 1984), chapter 14.

76. See Hugh S. Zurkuhlen and Owh Kian Ong, "U.S. Soft Drink Bottling Industry Outlook—Sparkling Profits Ahead," Salomon Brothers, Inc., Stock Research Report (November 30, 1987).

77. On CCE franchise areas in 1986, see Zurkuhlen and Ong, "Sparkling Profits Ahead," p. 5. On the detrimental effects of CCE's strategy of "commodity-like pricing," see "Coca-Cola Enterprises," a Donaldson, Lufkin and Jenrette Company Analysis (March 27, 1989); and Robert McGough, "The New Coca-Cola: No More Mr. Nice Guy," *Financial World* 158 (July 25, 1989): 30–34.

78. Monci Jo Williams, "Soft Drink Wars: The Next Battle," *Fortune* 111 (June 24, 1985): 70–72; and Thomas Moore, "He Put the Kick Back into Coke," *Fortune* 111 (October 26, 1987): 47–56.

79. Presentation by General Cinema to the New York Society of Security Analysts, October 24, 1985.

80. "F87 Strategic Focus," and "Value Added Pricing Summary," 1986 CDR presentations; and M. A. Fitzsimmons to Marketing Coordinators, January 22, 1987, in HGI corporate records. On PepsiCo's position, "General Cinema Plans a Premium Soft-Drink Line," *The Wall Street Journal* (November 18, 1985), p. 17.

81. Einloth Interview. On the problems created for both Coca-Cola and Pepsi by the resistance of multifranchise bottlers to new products, see Williams, "Soft Drink Wars: The Next Battle," pp. 71–72. See also Barker, "Pop in Soft Drinks," (*Barron's,* October 1985, p. 28), which quotes Pepsi's Roger Enrico as follows: "Growth in this industry is in our own hands, and as long as we can innovate, we can drive consumption."

82. Quotations in this paragraph and the next from Richard A. Smith, interview with Bettye H. Pruitt, March 13, 1992 (hereafter cited as Smith Interview, IV); and Tarr Interview, II.

83. Smith Interview, IV.

84. Smith Interview, III.

85. Smith's approach in this period fits the model of "philosophical orientation" described by John Ward as one that promotes the "family enterprise." Says Ward, "This philosophy holds that any decision must provide for *both* the satisfaction of the family and the economic health of the business." See John L. Ward, *Keeping*

the Family Business Healthy: How to Plan for Continuing Growth, Profitability, and Family Leadership (San Francisco: Jossey-Bass, 1987), pp. 143–145.
86. Smith Interview, IV.

Chapter 7

1. See "General Cinema 1990 First Quarter Report," General Cinema Corporate (March 1990), p. 28. In January 1992 General Cinema paid a fine of $950,000 to settle charges brought by the Federal Trade Commission that stemmed largely from that indecision. The FTC claimed that the company's initial purchase of Cadbury shares violated the requirement to file a statement of intent before purchasing more than $15 million in the stock of another company. General Cinema had resisted the charges on the grounds that the original intent had been solely to make an investment, but ultimately the company chose to avoid litigation by settling. See "General Cinema to Pay Fine," *New York Times* (January 9, 1992).
2. Richard A Smith, interview with Bettye H. Pruitt, March 13, 1992 (hereafter cited as Smith Interview, IV).
3. J. Atwood Ives, interview with Bettye H. Pruitt and George D. Smith, January 2, 1990 (hereafter cited as Ives Interview, III).
4. Smith Interview, IV.
5. Ibid.
6. Michael E. Porter (*Competitive Advantage: Creating and Sustaining Superior Performance* [New York: The Free Press, 1985], pp. 323–324) identifies "generic skills" in management as a class of "intangible interrelationships" that can form the basis for competitive advantage in diversified firms: "Often intangible interrelationships are manifested in a firm's use of the same generic strategy in a number of business units, reflecting management's skills in executing a particular strategy."
7. Ives Interview, III.
8. Smith Interview, IV.
9. During 1990, the official acquisition criteria began to include the notion that the greatest opportunity for General Cinema existed where not only marketing and distribution but also "future synergistic acquisitions" were the "keys to success." Compare General Cinema Corporation Annual Reports for 1989 and 1990.
10. Cash flow is defined as earnings from continuing operations before income tax and interest expense, plus depreciation. Maxwell's offer was only seven times HBJ's 1987 cash flow. See Harcourt Brace Jovanovich, Inc. and General Cinema Corporation, "Joint Proxy Statement/Prospectus" for Special Meeting of Shareholders to be Held on November 23, 1991 (October 25, 1991) (hereafter cited as HBJ/GCC Joint Proxy Statement), pp. 22, 32–33; Harcourt Brace Jovanovich, Annual Report for 1989, pp. 40–42; Stuart Weiss, "The Next Chapter," *Financial World* 158 (June 13, 1989): 30–31; and "First Boston," *Pensions and Investment Age* 16 (January 25, 1988): 69–70.
11. On HBJ's problems in 1989, see Leslie Wayne, "Can Harcourt Brace Survive Its Debt?" *New York Times* (April 15, 1990), pp. III-1, 6.
12. The original acquisition price of Sea World in 1976 taken from a report in *New York Times* (November 6, 1976), p. 27.
13. See ibid. (December 21, 1989), p. IV-4, 5; Wayne, "Can Harcourt Brace Survive Its Debt?" p. 6; Antonio N. Fins, "The Father-Son Saga at Harcourt Brace," *Business Week* (February 11, 1991), p. 29 (in which one publishing analyst

is quoted as saying, "God, What a mess he inherited"); and James C. Hyatt, "Jovanovich Quits Family Firm Post for Textbook Job," *The Wall Street Journal* (April 8, 1992), p. B2.

14. Quotations from Fins, "Father-Son Saga," p. 29; and Peter Jovanovich, interview with Bettye H. Pruitt, May 5, 1992 (hereafter cited as Jovanovich Interview).

15. William Reid, interview with Bettye H. Pruitt, May 7, 1992 (hereafter cited as Reid Interview).

16. Hugo Uyterhoeven, "Harcourt Brace Jovanovich," Harvard Business School Case #N9-392-045, Boston, 1992, pp. 4–5. This case presents much of the analysis and some of the presentation materials prepared for General Cinema by its consultants.

17. Quotations from Uyterhoeven, "Harcourt Brace Jovanovich," pp. 11–12.

18. Ibid., pp. 5–7, 27.

19. Richard A. Smith, interview with Bettye H. Pruitt, July 22 and 28, 1993 (hereafter cited as Smith Interview, V).

20. Lane would look back on that moment as one of the finest in his long career at General Cinema. Edward E. Lane, interview with Bettye H. Pruitt and George D. Smith, June 7, 1988.

21. For a discussion of prepackaged bankruptcy written about the time it was being proposed for HBJ, see Richard D. Hylton, "Business and the Law—Prepackaging a Bankruptcy," *New York Times* (November 26, 1990), p. IV-2.

22. For the specific terms of the merger and option agreements, see GCC/HBJ Joint Proxy Statement, pp. 44, 63–74.

23. Smith Interview, IV.

24. Reid Interview.

25. On Black and other vulture funds, see David Carey, "Bankruptcy Buzzards," *Financial World* (January 22, 1991): 60–61; Phyllis Berman and Roula Khalaf, "We're Doing Just Fine," *Forbes* 147 (March 18, 1991): 48–49, 52; and Beth Selby, "The Black Prince of Wall Street," *Institutional Investor* (August 1991), pp. 15–16, from which the greenmail quote is taken.

26. Caesar Sweitzer and Greg Meredith, interview with Bettye H. Pruitt, May 7, 1992 (hereafter cited as Sweitzer-Meredith Interview). On the shifts in financial markets, see *New York Times* (January 6, 1991), p. III-1 and (April 1, 1991), p. IV-1.

27. The roles of Apollo and Kemper came through in various accounts of the deal. See for example, Selby, "Black Prince of Wall Street," p. 15; Daniel Pearl and Joseph Pereira, "General Cinema Withdraws Its Offer of $1.1 Billion for Harcourt's Bonds," *The Wall Street Journal* (April 27, 1991); and Richard W. Stevenson, "Harcourt Offer Is Withdrawn," *New York Times* (April 27, 1991).

28. Smith Interview, IV.

29. Sweitzer-Meredith Interview. According to the *The Wall Street Journal* (Pearl and Pereira, "General Cinema Withdraws Its Offer"), Leon Black raised his stake in HBJ bonds in that Friday's trading.

30. Smith Interview, IV.

31. Bondholder committee member J. E. Merkin, of Ariel Capital Group, is quoted in Pearl and Pereira, "General Cinema Withdraws Its Offer"; Sweitzer-Meredith Interview.

32. Smith Interview, IV. HBJ average stock prices from GCC/HBJ Joint Proxy Statement, p. 19.

33. Smith Interview, IV.

34. Sweitzer-Meredith Interview. CPO's and their role in the negotiation process are discussed in GCC/HBJ Joint Proxy Statement, pp. 46–47.
35. Sweitzer-Meredith Interview.
36. Ibid.; and GCC/HBJ Joint Proxy Statement, p. 47.
37. Reid Interview; and William M. Bulkeley and Daniel Pearl, "General Cinema Extends Offer for Bonds of Harcourt, Threatens to End Its Bid," *The Wall Street Journal* (October 15, 1991).
38. Jovanovich Interview.
39. Ibid.

Chapter 8

1. Robert J. Tarr, Jr., interview with Bettye H. Pruitt, May 1, 1992 (hereafter cited as Tarr Interview, II).
2. Because the acquisition of HBJ was accounted for as a pooling of interests, General Cinema's financial statements for 1991 present consolidated results as if the merger had been in effect for the entire year. See General Cinema Annual Report for 1991, p. 21.
3. See General Cinema Corporation, "First Quarter Report and Annual Meeting Review, 1992," in GCC corporate records, pp. 16–32.
4. Jeffrey Evans of Standard & Poor's, quoted in Christopher Donnelley, "Harcourt Gets Fresh Start in General Cinema Takeover," *Investment Dealers' Digest* (December 23, 1991), p. 32.
5. Tarr Interview, II; and General Cinema Corporation, "First Quarter Report and Annual Meeting Review, 1992," p. 16.
6. Robert A. Smith, interview with Bettye H. Pruitt, May 1, 1992.
7. Tarr Interview, II.
8. Ibid.
9. Quotations in this paragraph and the next are ibid.
10. Quotation from "Presentation by General Cinema Corporation to the New York Society of Security Analysts," October 24, 1985, p. 12 in the records of Harcourt General, Inc. (hereafter cited as HGI corporate records).
11. Samuel Frankenheim, interview with Bettye H. Pruitt, April 28, 1992.
12. Richard A. Smith, interview with Bettye H. Pruitt and George D. Smith, January 12, 1990 (hereafter cited as Smith Interview, III).
13. Caesar Sweitzer, and Greg Meredith, interview with Bettye H. Pruitt, May 7, 1992.
14. As Peter Jovanovich remarked, "If HBJ hadn't been in so much trouble . . . I don't know that I would ever have been recognized as deserving a position." That was true, he argued, even though his family did not own a controlling interest in HBJ, and even though he had risen on his own in a competing firm and then for five years run HBJ's most profitable division. Peter Jovanovich, interview with Bettye H. Pruitt, May 5, 1992.
15. Tarr Interview, II.
16. Ibid.
17. Ibid. Tarr's employment contract is detailed in General Cinema Corporation, Proxy Statement for Annual Meeting of Stockholders, March 13, 1992, in Harcourt General Inc. corporate records, pp. 10–12.
18. Tarr Interview, II; Richard A. Smith, interview with Bettye H. Pruitt, March 13, 1992 (hereafter cited as Smith Interview, IV). The distinctions drawn by

Smith between family managers and professionals closely follow the literature on this subject. See Catherine M. Daily and Marc J. Dollinger, "An Empirical Examination of Ownership Structure in Family and Professionally Managed Firms," *Family Business Review* 5 (Summer 1992): 120–121.

19. Smith Interview, III.

20. Information on General Cinema Foundation giving was supplied by Kay Kilpatrick, Contributions Administrator and Director, Matching Gifts, Harcourt General, Inc., and Margaret H. Morton, Grants Management Associates.

21. The overview of 1992 in this and the following two paragraphs is based on General Cinema Corporation, Annual Report for 1992, and Harcourt General, Inc., Third Quarter Report, 1993.

22. Tarr Interview, II. On the reasoning behind the conglomerate discount, see Michael E. Porter, *Competitive Advantage: Creating and Sustaining Superior Performance* (New York: The Free Press, 1985), pp. 317–320. For a sample of the early 1990s perspective, see Porter, "Capital Disadvantage: America's Failing Capital Investment System," *Harvard Business Review* 70 (September–October 1992), pp. 65–82. Also compare Alfred Chandler's relatively neutral discussion of conglomerates in *The Visible Hand* (Cambridge, Mass.: Harvard University Press), published in 1977, to that in *Scale and Scope* (Cambridge, Mass.: Harvard University Press) which appeared in 1990.

23. Norman A. Berg (*General Management: An Analytical Approach* [Homewood, Ill.: Richard D. Irwin, 1984], p. 166) provides this important insight: "Just as there are always examples of spectacularly successful stock market investments, there are also examples of specific acquisitions which did, in fact, turn out to be undervalued at the time. Such individual examples should not obscure the low probability that skills at picking winners exist with enough predictability to provide a competitive advantage over time for an operating company with regard to their diversification strategy."

24. Anyone familiar with the stories of Horatio Alger will recognize these central elements of the paradigmatic American success story.

25. Quotation from Michael C. Jensen, "Eclipse of the Public Corporation," *Harvard Business Review* 67 (September–October 1989), p. 61; see also Chandler, *Scale and Scope*, pp. 621–627. Jensen focuses on the positive changes made through leveraged buyouts, which have created "new organizations . . . that are corporate in form but have no public shareholders and are not listed or traded on organized exchanges." For a helpful long-term overview of these developments, see George David Smith and Richard Sylla, *The Transformation of American Capitalism: An Essay on the History of American Capital Markets* (Cambridge, Mass.: Blackwell, 1993). Michael Porter ("Capital Disadvantage," pp. 74–75) presents an alternative model in the case of Cummins Engine, whose mangement in 1990 put together a 40 percent control block including shares owned by the founding family, employees, and two major customers, illustrating "how a creative management team can structure a 'privately owned, publicly traded' American company, approximating some of the advantages of the Japanese and German systems." The link between diversification and poor performance is central to the critique of corporate management, beginning with the seminal essay by Robert Hayes and William Abernathy, "Managing Our Way to Economic Decline," *Harvard Business Review* 58 (July–August 1980), pp. 67–77.

26. Richard A. Smith, interview with Bettye H. Pruitt, July 22 and 28, 1993.

A NOTE ON SOURCES

The research for this history has drawn on published and unpublished corporate documents of Harcourt General, Inc., and its current and past subsidiaries, as well as relevant external sources generally available in the business and business history literature. In addition, the research has involved extensive oral history interviewing. Following is a list of interviewees, with date of interview and corporate title as of that date.

Name	Date	Title
Doris Johnson Bamberg	December 20, 1988	Former Secretary to Phillip Smith
John W. Bliss	February 24, 1989	Former Senior Vice President of Operations, General Cinema Beverages, Inc.
Gilbert W. Butler	August 9, 1989	President, Butler Capital Corporation
William Caldwell	February 1, 1989	Marketing Service Manager, General Cinema Beverages, Inc., Miami Plant
James Collins	June 23, 1988	Former Regional Vice President, General Cinema Theatres, Inc.
Nelson J. Darling, Jr.	April 25, 1989	Director, General Cinema Corporation
Julius Darsky	July 20, 1988	Former President, American Beverage Division, and Director, General Cinema Corporation
Thomas Dennard	February 1, 1989	Miami Plant Manager, General Cinema Beverages, Inc.
Bert J. Einloth III	January 10, 1989	President, General Cinema Beverages, Inc., Vice President, General Cinema Corporation
Morris K. Englander	April 27, 1989	Former Vice President, Real Estate, GCC Theatres, Inc.

Name	*Date*	*Title*
Samuel Frankenheim	March 17, 1989	Senior Vice President and General Counsel, General Cinema Corporation
	April 28, 1992	Partner, Ropes & Gray
Winifred Franklin	March 30, 1988	Former Assistant to Richard A. Smith
Lawrence Gilligan	February 1, 1989	Controller, Miami Plant, General Cinema Beverages, Inc.
George C. Haas, Jr.	February 6, 1989	Former Beverage Industry Consultant to General Cinema Corporation
Herbert J. Hurwitz	August 4, 1988	Former Senior Vice President and Director, General Cinema Corporation
J. Atwood Ives	October 14, 1988; November 23, 1988; January 2, 1990; and November 14, 1991	Vice Chairman of the Board and Chief Financial Officer, General Cinema Corporation
Edward E. Jenkins	January 31, 1989	Group Vice President, General Cinema Beverages, Inc.
Peter Jovanovich	May 5, 1992	Former President and Chief Executive Officer, Harcourt Brace Jovanovich
Kay Kilpatrick	May 21, 1992	Assistant to Richard A. Smith and Contributions Administrator and Director, Matching Gifts, General Cinema Corporation
Brian J. Knez	May 1, 1992	Vice President, General Cinema Corporation
John P. Koss	February 21, 1989	Vice President, Operations, General Cinema Beverages, Inc.

Name	Date	Title
Edward E. Lane	June 7, 1988	Former Financial Vice President and Director, General Cinema Corporation
Nancy L. Marks	January 17, 1989	Stockholder, General Cinema Corporation
James McKenney	September 16, 1988	Professor of Business Administration, Harvard Business School, and Former Management Consultant to General Cinema Corporation
Marilyn Miletich	February 1, 1989	Senior Staff Accountant, Miami Plant, General Cinema Beverages, Inc.
James C. Moodey	January 17, 1990	Vice President and Treasurer, General Cinema Corporation
Robert E. Painter	March 24, 1989	Senior Vice President, Operations, General Cinema Theatres, Inc.
Ann Pave	January 16, 1989	Former Bookkeeper, Smith Management Company
D. Barry Reardon	December 20, 1988	Former Vice President, Film Marketing, General Cinema Theatres, Inc.
William R. Reid	May 7, 1992	Managing Director, First Boston Corporation
Gary Schirripa	February 24, 1989	Group Vice President, General Cinema Beverages, Inc.
Jay M. Shapiro	March 17, 1989	Senior Vice President, Development, General Cinema Theatres, Inc.
Robert T. Shircliff	October 26, 1988	Former President, Pepsi-Cola Allied Beverage Division and Director, General Cinema Corporation

Name	Date	Title
Richard A. Smith	June 21, 1988; March 16, 1989; January 12, 1990; March 13, 1992	Chairman and CEO, General Cinema Corporation
	July 22–28, 1993	Chairman, Harcourt General, Inc.
Robert A. Smith	April 26, 1989	Vice President, Corporate Development and Director, General Cinema Corporation
	May 1, 1992	Group Vice President and Director, General Cinema Corporation
Howard W. Spiess	December 29, 1988 and February 16, 1989	Former Vice President, Operations, General Cinema Theatres, Inc.
Sidney Stoneman	May 4, 1988	Director, General Cinema Corporation
Caesar Sweitzer, with Greg Meredith	May 7, 1992	Managing Director, Salomon Brothers
Alexander M. Tanger	April 18, 1989	Former President, Communications Group, General Cinema Corporation
Robert J. Tarr, Jr.	April 26, 1989	President and Chief Operating Officer, General Cinema Corporation
	May 1, 1992	President and Chief Executive Officer, General Cinema Corporation
James C. Tharp	March 23, 1989	Senior Vice President, Film and Marketing, General Cinema Theatres, Inc.
William Townsend, Sr.	February 1, 1989	Syrup Blender, Miami Plant, General Cinema Beverages, Inc.
A. Anthony Trauber	November 16, 1989	Vice President, Controller, General Cinema Corporation

Name	Date	Title
Hugo Uyterhoeven	October 6, 1988	Timken Professor of Business Administration, Harvard Business School, and Director, General Cinema Corporation
Stanley Werthman	April 27, 1989	Former Vice President, Concessions, General Cinema Theatres, Inc.
Melvin R. Wintman	March 10, 1988	Former President, General Cinema Theatres, Inc. and Executive Vice President and Director, General Cinema Corporation
William D. Zellen	March 29, 1988	Former Senior Vice President, Finance, General Cinema Theatres, Inc.

INDEX